The Hot "Cold War"

The Hot "Cold War"

The USSR in Southern Africa

VLADIMIR SHUBIN

PLUTO PRESS
www.plutobooks.com

UNIVERSITY OF KWAZULU-NATAL PRESS

First published 2008 by Pluto Press
345 Archway Road, London N6 5AA
www.plutobooks.com

Published in 2008 in South Africa by
University of KwaZulu-Natal Press
Private Bag X01, Scottsville 3209
South Africa
e-mail: books@ukzn.ac.za
www.ukznpress.co.za

British Library Cataloguing in Publication Data
A catalogue record for this book is available from the British Library

ISBN   978 0 7453 2473 9   (hardback)
ISBN   978 0 7453 2472 2   (Pluto Press paperback)
ISBN   978 1 86914 155 4   (University of KwaZulu-Natal Press paperback)

Library of Congress Cataloging in Publication Data applied for

This book is printed on paper suitable for recycling and made from fully managed and
sustained forest sources. Logging, pulping and manufacturing processes are expected
to conform to the environmental standards of the country of origin. The paper may
contain up to 70% post consumer waste.

10   9   8   7   6   5   4   3   2   1

Designed and produced for Pluto Press by
Chase Publishing Services Ltd, Fortescue, Sidmouth, EX10 9QG, England
Typeset from disk by Stanford DTP Services, Northampton
Printed and bound by CPI Group (UK) Ltd, Croydon, CR0 4YY

*In memory of Colonel Igor Ivanovich Uvarov,
one of the unsung Soviet heroes.*

Contents

LIST OF PLATES

"Treason is knowing how to write, and not writing."
Jose Craveirinha, Mozambican poet.

List of Abbreviations

AACRLS	Archives of Anti-colonial Resistance and Liberation Struggle (Namibia)
AAPSO	Afro-Asian People's Solidarity Organisation
ANC	African National Congress (South Africa)
ANC	African National Council (Zimbabwe)
APC	armoured personnel carrier
APN	Agentstvo pechati Novosti (Press-Agency Novosti)
CAMCO	Cuban-American Military Council
CANU	Caprivi National Union
CC	Central Committee
CIA	Central Intelligence Agency (USA)
CMEA (or COMECON)	Council of Mutual Economic Assistance
CONCP	Conference of the Nationalist Organisations of the Portuguese Colonies
COREMO	Mozambique Revolutionary Committee
CPSU	Communist Party of the Soviet Union
CWIHP	Cold War International History Project
DRC	Democratic Republic of Congo
FAPLA	People's Armed Forces for Liberation of Angola
FCO	Foreign and Commonwealth Office (UK)
FLS	Frontline States
FNLA	National Front for Liberation of Angola
FPLM	People's Forces for the Liberation of Mozambique
FRELIMO	Front for the Liberation of Mozambique
FRETILIN	Revolutionary Front for an Independent East Timor
FRG	Federal Republic of Germany
FROLIZI	Front for Liberation of Zimbabwe
GDR	German Democratic Republic
GIU	Glavnoe inzhenernoe upravlenie (Main Engineering Department of the GKES)
GKES	Gosudarstvennyi komitet po elonimicheskim svyazyam s zarubezhnymi stranami (State Committee for Economic Ties with Foreign Countries)

GRAE   Revolutionary Government of Angola in Exile
GRU   Glavnoe razvedyvatelnoe upravlenie (Department
                of Military Intelligence of the General Staff)
GUK   Glavmoe upravlenie kadrov (Department of
                Personnel, USSR Ministry of Defence)
GVS   Glavnyi voennyi sovetnik (Chief Military
                Adviser)
IDASA   Institute for a Democratic Alternative for South
                Africa
JMC   Joint Military Command (Zimbabwe)
KGB   Komitet gosudarsvennoi bezopasnosti
                (Committee of State Security of the USSR)
Komsomol   Young Communist League (USSR)
MAC   Anti-colonial Movement
MANU   Mozambican African National Union
MCW   military-combat work
MDA   Democratic Movement of Angola
MFA   Ministry of Foreign Affairs
MFA   Movement of the Armed Forces (Portugal)
MK   Umkhonto we Sizwe (South Africa)
MPLA   Popular Movement for the Liberation of Angola
MVT   Ministerstvo vneshnei torgovli (Ministry of
                Foreign Trade)
NAM   Non-Aligned Movement
NATO   North Atlantic Treaty Organization
NDP   National Democratic Party (Zimbabwe)
NGO   non-governmental organisation
OAU   Organisation of African Unity
ODA   People's Defence Organisation
OKABON   Otdelnaya krasnoznamyonnaya aviatsionnaya
                brigada osobogo naznacheniya (Independent Red
                Banner Special Purpose Air Brigade)
PAC   Panafricanist Congress of Azania (South Africa)
PAIGC   African Party for Independence of Guinea and
                Cape Verde
PCP   Portuguese Communist Party
PFZ   Patriotic Front of Zimbabwe
PF-ZAPU   Patriot Front – Zimbabwe African People's Union
PGU   Pervoe glavnoe upravlenie (First Main
                Department of the KGB)
PIDE   International and State Defence Police (Portugal)

PLAN	People's Liberation Army of Namibia
PRA	People's Republic of Angola
PRC	People's Republic of Congo
RENAMO	Mozambican National Resistance
RPG	rocket-propelled grenade launcher
RSAMH	Russian State Archive of Modern History
RSF	Rhodesian Security Forces
SAAF	South African Air Force
SACP	South African Communist Party
SADET	South African Democracy Education Trust
SADF	South African Defence Force
SANDF	South African National Defence Force
SARF	State Archive of the Russian Federation
SIDA	Swedish International Development Agency
SVR	Sluzhba vneshnei razvedki (Foreign Intelligence Service, Russia)
SWAPO	South-West Africa People's Organisation (Namibia)
SWATF	South-West African Territorial Force
TANU	Tanganyika African National Union
TASS	Telegrafnoe agentstvo Sovetskogo Soyuza (Telegraph Agency of the Soviet Union)
TRC	Truth and Reconciliation Commission
UDENAMO	Democratic National Union of Mozambique
UDI	Unilateral Declaration of Independence
UN	United Nations
UNITA	Union for Total Liberation of Angola
UNTA	National Union of Angolan Workers
UNTAG	United Nations Transitional Assistance Group
UPA	Union of Peoples of Angola
USA	United States of America
USSR	Union of Soviet Socialist Republics
VDV	Vozdushno-desantnye voiska (airborne troops)
VTA	Voenno-transportnaya aviatsiya (Military Transport Aviation)
YCL	Young Communist League
ZANLA	Zimbabwe African National Liberation Army
ZANU	Zimbabwe African National Union
ZANU-PF	Zimbabwe African National Union–Patriotic Front
ZAPU	Zimbabwe African People's Union

Preface

This book is devoted to the events in Southern Africa in the three decades (1960–90) that in world history are commonly regarded as the years of the "Cold War". However, just as in many other parts of the globe, the wars that were waged in the region were not cold, but rather hot. This led me to decide on this particular title for the book.

I am sure that a comprehensive history of the events in the region; that is, the history of the liberation struggle and defence of the sovereignty of independent African states, can and should be written by Africans themselves. Fortunately, at long last some serious steps have been taken in this respect in recent years. The South African Democracy Education Trust (SADET) and Archives of the Anti-colonial Resistance and Liberation Struggle (AACRLS) in Namibia have been particularly active in this respect. On a regional level the matter is being tackled in a project initiated by the Southern African Development Community under the patronage of Brigadier Hashim Mbita, former Executive Secretary of the Organisation of African Unity's Liberation Committee.

The theme of the "Cold War" – the confrontation of the USSR and the USA, the two so-called superpowers, has been examined (and exploited) by academics for many years. Moreover, in recent years its scope has been broadened to include the world "periphery".[1] However, I believe that too often Moscow's involvement in Southern Africa, especially the role of the Soviet military, is covered inadequately or even distorted, and in this book I hope to set the record straight.

To do this I did my best to use primary sources. These include documents from Russian official and informal archives and also documents of the African National Congress and South African Communist Party in South African archives. The problem has been that most of the relevant materials, at least so far as the Russian archives are concerned, are still classified. The 30-year law on declassification seems to exist only on paper so I have tried to contact participants in the events in question, both from the USSR/Russia and the Southern African countries. Naturally, in addition to this, I have used the notes, handwritten and sometimes hardly legible, that I accumulated during the years of the liberation struggle, as well as my memory, as fragile as it may be. Thus I should apologise in advance for any errors that may result from this somewhat imperfect process.

I regard this book as an academic one, but my association with Southern Africa, which began over four decades ago, inevitably makes it somewhat personal. I went to Africa – to Egypt – for the first time in April 1960, while still a student of the Moscow State Institute of International Relations. My life thus became connected with Africa at an early stage. Soon after my first mission to Egypt and after getting my MA in International Relations and Oriental Studies, I was conscripted and had to serve the next seven years as an officer of the USSR Armed Forces. My involvement with the liberation movements in Southern Africa began in January 1967, when, as a crewmember of a Soviet Air Force transport plane, I arrived in Dar es Salaam to bring Mozambican freedom fighters to the USSR for military training.

Later, having left the Soviet Armed Forces and joined the staff of the Soviet Afro-Asian Solidarity Committee in March 1969, I became deeply involved in political and practical support of the liberation movements in Southern Africa, especially as the Committee's secretary from 1972 to 1979. Then, after three years of full-time doctoral studies, I came into the field again, this time as a desk officer of the African Section of the Communist Party of the Soviet Union (CPSU) International Department. I headed this section (renamed into a group) from January 1989.

Lastly, I have to express my gratitude to all the people who in one way or another have made the publication of this book possible, especially: Jan Burgess, editor of the *Review of African Political Economy* who prompted my contact with Pluto Press; Roger van Zwanenberg, chairman of Pluto, above of all for his patience, and his colleagues Robert Webb, Ray Addicott and Tracey Day who formed the editorial team, and Barbara Bradley for turning my Russo-English into a proper language.

Introduction

Despite the distance between Russia and Southern Africa, the first time Russia interfered militarily, albeit indirectly, in the affairs of that region was over a century ago, when about 200 Russian volunteers, among them officers, joined the Boers in their fight against British Imperial forces.

Why were the Russian authorities and the Russian public in general so interested in the developments many thousands of miles away? It would be accurate to say that an obvious reason was human sympathy for the "weaker side", typical of the Russian mentality. Nevertheless, the "love of the Boers" was also undoubtedly prompted by a strong aversion to Great Britain. The war in South Africa started when Russian-British rivalry, especially in Central Asia, had turned their relationship far from amiable.

Sixty years later history repeated itself in a rather different context: 1960 became known as "Africa Year". It witnessed the independence of 16 countries on the continent. I spent most of that year and half of 1961 in an African country, Egypt, and returned to Moscow on 10 July 1961. A couple of days later I found myself in a two-storey structure adjacent to a huge grey building with the star on all sides of its tower on the Gogolevsky Boulevard. At that time the big building housed several departments of the Soviet General Staff, and the small one was used by its administrative services, including an accounting section of the Desyatka – the jargon name for the Tenth Main Department of the USSR Armed Forces General Staff, which was responsible for Soviet military co-operation with foreign countries.

Standing at the division between clients and accountants, I saw next to me a stout handsome major general in his late 30s, rather young by Soviet standards. It was none other than Victor Kulikov, who 15 years later became Marshal of the Soviet Union, Chief of General Staff and a little later Commander-in-Chief of the Warsaw Pact United Armed Forces. What really drew my attention was a ticket in his hand, issued by Ghana Airways.[1] For me it was further proof that Desyatka was active not only in Northern Africa (that I knew well from my own experience), but in Sub-Saharan Africa as well.

In truth this became clear to me even earlier, in late August 1960, when ten Soviet Ilyushin-14 transport planes with Congolese insignia landed in Athens and then Cairo on their way to the Congo. They were going there to help Patrice Lumumba to move his troops to Katanga, which was controlled by separatist Moise Tshombe. It was the murder of Lumumba in connivance with the Central Intelligence Agency (CIA) and Belgian intelligence service, the betrayal of the head of a lawful government by the UN command in Congo and the UN's misuse of the Ghanaian troops sent there that brought Ghana's leader, Kwame Nkrumah, closer to Moscow and prompted him to invite Soviet military advisers.

Not only Congo, but also most of the southern part of the African continent became a battlefield again. The first shots were fired by the forces of liberation on 4 February 1961, when an abortive attempt to storm prisons in Luanda took place. It was followed by the "use of violence" by the African National Congress (ANC) in South Africa, Front for the Liberation of Mozambique (FRELIMO) in Mozambique, South-West Africa People's Organisation (SWAPO) in Namibia and Zimbabwe African People's Union (ZAPU) and Zimbabwe African National Union (ZANU) in Zimbabwe.

So Russia/the USSR once more had to determine its attitude to the war in Southern Africa. Once again, resembling the days of the Anglo-Boer War, it began rendering its political support and military assistance to the side that in its opinion was fighting for a just cause. In fact, Moscow provided assistance to the anti-colonial struggle in different parts of the world during the entire "Soviet period" of Russian history. Supporting "the struggle of people for national liberation and social progress" was confirmed as one of the aims of Soviet foreign policy in the 1977 USSR Constitution.[2] It was the USSR that at the UN General Assembly session in 1960 proposed to adopt the Declaration on Granting Independence to Colonial Countries and Peoples.

The second evident reason for Soviet involvement also seems to be similar to the "old days": rivalry with another powerful country. This time it was not the British but the USA, Moscow's "Cold War" adversary. Indeed there is a tendency, particularly characteristic of Western academics and politicians, to look at the armed conflicts in Southern Africa (and particularly in Angola) primarily through the distorting prism of superpowers' rivalry during the "Cold War".

Of course the state of USSR–USA relations did play a role in Moscow's decision-making on Southern Africa (just as the Russian-

British confrontation did during the Anglo-Boer War). However, the Soviets did not assist liberation movements and African Frontline States only because of the "Cold War". To put it in the language of the day: such actions were regarded as part of the world "anti-imperialist struggle", which was waged by the "socialist community", "the national liberation movements", and the "working class of the capitalist countries". So the Moscow–Washington confrontation was definitely not the only reason for the USSR's involvement in Southern Africa.

In reality the "Cold War" was not part of our political vocabulary; in fact the term was used in a strictly negative sense. It was considered to be the creation of "war mongers" and "imperialist propaganda". For us the global struggle was not a battle between the two "superpowers" assisted by their "satellites" and "proxies", but a united fight of the world's progressive forces against imperialism. Petr Yevsyukov, who for 15 years was the main conduit between Moscow and the liberation movements in the Portuguese colonies – the Popular Movement for the Liberation of Angola (MPLA), FRELIMO and the African Party for Independence of Guinea and Cape Verde (PAIGC) – writes in his memoirs: "The October [1917] Revolution, and then the victory of the anti-fascist coalition in World War Two, decisively influenced the balance of forces in the world in favour of progress, struggle for national liberation, especially in Africa and Asia. The 'Cold War' did not stop this process ... Assistance to nationalists from socialist countries, first and foremost the Soviet Union, was a natural reply to their appeal for such help."[3]

Although the tendency to see the events in Africa from the 1950s to the 1980s through the prism of the "Cold War" was very strong, in confidential documents Western leaders admitted that the issue was much more complicated. For example, in 1962 President John F. Kennedy told the Portuguese Minister of Foreign Affairs, Alberto Franco Nogueira: "It is evident from what happened to former French, Belgian and British territories in Africa that these pressures stemmed from the basic desires of the populations and were not due to any external agency."[4]

* * *

This book does not claim to be a comprehensive coverage and analysis of the developments in Southern Africa during the "Cold War", nor does it consider the theoretical issues of international relations at the time. Moreover, I am not trying to argue with numerous books and articles that have been published on the subject. I do disagree on a few occasions in this book, but only if I have found gross inaccuracies or controversies.

I am afraid that this narrative has to be uneven, perhaps even patchy. It depends to a great extent on the availability (or rather non-availability) of archive material, success (or failure) in my search for witness-participants, preservation of my personal notes and the state of my memory. When the relevant archives are finally opened, future researchers will most probably criticise me for my mistakes, but, it is to be hoped, not for my errors of judgement. In any case I am convinced that we should not wait for this "manna" to become available, but rather try to write the history as fully and as truthfully as we can under the circumstances.

Part One

Angola

1
Armed Struggle Begins

When describing the Soviet attitude towards the liberation struggle in Angola and its actions in this respect, we have to rely largely, although not uncritically, on witness-participants, owing to the lack of accessible documents. Yevsyukov recalls in his memoirs:

The term inter-party ties within a framework of my duties meant everything, starting with knowledge and responsibility for all proposals for all-round assistance, including financial ones, made to the CC [Central Committee]. I had to start, so to speak, from scratch, from accumulation of information, knowledge. There were quite enough sources: current information from our embassies, their annual reports, information from the KGB [Committee of State Security of the USSR], GRU [Department of Military Intelligence] of the General Staff, TASS [Telegraph Agency of the Soviet Union], APN [Press-Agency Novosti], correspondents of Soviet newspapers and magazines, material from foreign information agencies and the foreign press. After some time I became the person best informed about the Portuguese colonies.[1]

Some contacts between the Soviets and the MPLA leaders were established even earlier. Mario de Andrade took part in the First Conference of Writers of Asian and African countries in Tashkent, the capital of Soviet Uzbekistan, held in 1958. There was also an exchange of letters between him and Ivan Potekhin, chairman of the newly established Soviet Association of Friendship with African Countries, who was a founding director of the Africa Institute in Moscow. In particular, de Andrade, writing on behalf of the Anti-colonial Movement (MAC) – whose members were from Angola, Guinea-Bissau and Mozambique – requested Soviet scholarships for African students, but Potekhin's response hardly satisfied him: "... unfortunately I have to delay my reply to this question because at this time our association does not yet have a capacity to invite young African cadres to study in the Soviet Union".[2] Anyhow, relations with anti-colonial movements, including the provision of scholarships, soon became a domain of another non-governmental organisation (NGO) – the Soviet Afro-Asian Solidarity Committee.

The first reference to the situation in Angola and other Portuguese colonies in the Committee's archives is contained in the letter of 4 November 1959 sent by Lucio Lara on behalf of the MAC from Frankfurt to the Secretariat of the Afro-Asian People's Solidarity Council (later, "Organisation", AAPSO) in Cairo. Lara suggested organising an international campaign of protest against Lisbon's repressions. The Committee supported the idea and was ready to act through its representative in Cairo, provided that consent from the Soviet Ministry of Foreign Affairs was received.[3] It was obtained, and 3 August, the date of the massacre in Guinea-Bissau in 1959, was chosen.

Mario de Andrade came to Moscow again in August 1960 to take part in the International Congress of Oriental Studies, then as guest of the Soviet Writers' Union. During his meetings at the Solidarity Committee, Africa Institute and other bodies he, in particular, spoke about the MPLA's contradictions with the Union of the Peoples of Angola (UPA, headed by Holden Roberto), calling it "rather a racist organisation and due to its ties with the USA, a reactionary one".[4] As for practical matters, his only request was for "political literature in foreign languages".[5]

Yevsyukov continues: "The International Department knew about the existence of the MPLA from various sources, mainly from press publications, although Portugal was thoroughly hiding the information on the events in Luanda."[6] According to him the first representatives of the MPLA – Mario de Andrade, who was its president while Agostinho Neto, elected its honorary president in 1960, was in prison and then under police supervision; and Viriato da Cruz, general secretary – came to Moscow "in the second half of 1961", that is, several months after the beginning of the armed struggle on 4 February 1961.[7] "They both made a good impression as serious people who knew the situation and were candid in their accounts and judgments and 'an important decision to begin multi-sided assistance to the organisation' was taken."[8]

The archive documents confirm that the MPLA leaders came to the USSR on 22 July 1961 at the invitation of the Solidarity Committee. At the meeting in the CPSU headquarters with Nuretdin Muhitdinov, member of the Presidium (Politburo) and secretary of the Central Committee, they raised a number of important issues, such as financial assistance, the provision of arms and the training of party cadres in the Soviet Union in various fields.[9]

Soon US$25,000 were allocated to the MPLA from a so-called "International Trade Union Fund for assistance to left workers' organisations, attached to the Romanian Council of Trade Unions".[10] It was established in 1950 on the initiative of the Soviet Communist Party to render material assistance to "foreign left parties, workers' and public [non-governmental] organisations, which are subjected to persecution and repression".[11]

There are many stories about "Kremlin gold", but although Moscow played a leading role in the distribution of allocations, originally only half of the contributions to this fund came from the USSR, with the remainder coming from China, Czechoslovakia, Romania, Poland, Hungary and the German Democratic Republic (GDR). Bulgaria joined later, in 1958. China withdrew in 1962 after the Sino-Soviet split. Initially the fund's board comprised representatives from the Soviet, Romanian and Polish parties, and the decision taken by the Politburo envisaged that "material assistance will be rendered according to unanimous decisions of the Board", whose members were to be appointed annually by the agreement of the contributing parties.[12] However, a paradox is that, unlike during "the time of Stalin", Moscow later became the sole distributor of the fund "according to an old verbal understanding".[13]

Moscow earlier expressed political support for the MPLA at the highest level. In reply to Mario de Andrade's message, Nikita Khrushchev declared: "The patriots of Angola can be sure that the sympathies of the peoples of the great Soviet Union are fully on their side."[14]

During his next visit to Moscow, a year later in July 1962, de Andrade was worried by the position of the Congolese government, which was creating various kinds of obstacles to MPLA activities, as well as by the attempts of the UPA to absorb the MPLA into the National Front for the Liberation of Angola (FNLA), which the UPA had created with the Democratic Party of Angola.[15] He said also that MPLA had sent a number of delegations to African countries to explain to them the situation following the creation of the "so-called GRAE", Holden Roberto's "government in exile", in April 1962.[16] De Andrade also had a meeting at the CPSU International Department[17] and most probably again raised the issue of financial support and co-operation in the military field.

Yevsyukov claims that after his escape from Portugal "with the help of Portuguese communists", Neto "immediately flew to Moscow. The negotiations with him ended quite successfully."[18] This is not very accurate; indeed, the Solidarity Committee immediately invited him via the Soviet embassy in Leopoldville (Kinshasa), and the visit was planned for January 1963, but he could not make it. So Neto apologised to a Soviet diplomat in New York, where he attended a meeting as a petitioner to the UN Committee, and expressed the hope that he could come in late February or early March.[19]

The Soviet attitude to the anti-colonial struggle in Angola was opposite to the Western support, be it overt or covert, of Lisbon. Though the Washington administration under John F. Kennedy initially portrayed itself as champion of Africa's liberation, in reality its attitude to developments in the Portuguese colonies was primarily determined by strategic considerations. This can easily be seen from a document by the Foreign Office describing a meeting in 1961 between British and US officials: "The [British] Secretary of State drew attention to the great importance of the Portuguese islands off Africa for Western air communications, and Mr Nitze[20] confirmed that the Pentagon was very much alive to these considerations."[21]

Co-operation between Portugal and the leading Western countries took place both on bilateral terms and within the North Atlantic Treaty Organization's (NATO's) structures. It included the exchange of intelligence information, which was sometimes rather implausible. Thus in August 1961 Portuguese Minister of Foreign Affairs Franco Nogueira informed the US embassy that according to Portuguese Army sources, "The main base of the Soviet explosive supplies for sabotage purposes in the east African countries is located in Yemen." He claimed that from there supplies were shipped to the Comoros and finally to Tanganyika and Mozambique.[22] Just imagine: a Soviet base in Yemen ruled by a feudal emir, another one in the French-controlled Comoros and finally supplies being delivered to non-existing (in 1961) rebels in East Africa!

However, soon after the first visits of MPLA leaders to Moscow the situation in this organisation began to worry the Soviets. "Reports began coming in about differences which arose between A. Neto from one side and M. de Andrade and V. da Cruz on the other", writes "Camarada Pedro" (Yevsyukov). "The aggravation of relations between them resulted in the sidelining of M. de Andrade from leadership. Meanwhile V. da Cruz, having cut off relations with Neto, left for China ... The break-up of relations between these people caused a rather negative reaction among MPLA members and was beyond our understanding."[23] According to Yevsyukov, when the post of general secretary was abolished, Neto "in fact remained the single leader of the movement".[24]

Yet again, this is not the precise story: da Cruz was dismissed from his position before Neto took over from Andrade. Besides, Yevsyukov reduced the cause of the conflict to personal quarrels. However, it seems that, at least as far as da Cruz was concerned, the differences were political. He insisted on the need for the MPLA to come into a rival movement, the FNLA, so that "scores of well-trained soldiers of the MPLA" would teach "the use of arms to thousands of Angolan peasants".[25] The influence of "Mao Zedong thought" is quite evident here, and it is hardly accidental that later da Cruz was welcomed in China and got a permanent position there at the Afro-Asian Journalists' Association, which soon became Beijing's propaganda tool in a sharpening Sino-Soviet conflict. He died there in 1973.

2
Zigzags of History

The detailed history of Soviet relations with the Angolan liberation movements and of the military involvement in that country, just as in Africa as a whole, still has to be written. Practically all information on Soviet assistance to freedom fighters, even of a purely humanitarian nature, had for many years been withheld from the public in the USSR and abroad. It was only after almost ten years, in 1970, in an interview with *Pravda*, that the head of the Soviet delegation to the International Conference of Support to the People of Portuguese Colonies, held in Rome, Professor Vassily Solodovnikov, for the first time clearly stated that Moscow was supplying "arms, means of transport and communications, clothes and other goods needed for a successful struggle" to the liberation movements and that "military and civilian specialists are being trained in the USSR".[1]

This conference, attended by 171 national and international organisations, was a great success. Nevertheless, preparing for it was a rather difficult matter. The Italian authorities were not happy at all to have it held in Rome; after all, Portugal was a fellow member of NATO and some details of preparations for the conference deserve description.

To begin with, when a preparatory meeting took place in the Italian capital in March, the Soviet representatives, including myself, could not attend, because visas were only issued to them on the very day of the gathering. However, if the Soviet delegates were to be refused visas, Moscow was not ready to render financial assistance to the conference.

So a decision was taken at the CPSU International Department to send Yevsyukov to Rome in a roundabout way, via Cairo, where a mobilisation committee in support of the anti-colonial struggle had been established at the AAPSO headquarters. However, on the second day of his stay in Cairo a Soviet consul rushed into his hotel room to inform him that cholera had been detected in Egypt and that to avoid getting stuck "Camarada Pedro" had to fly to Rome immediately.

The consul was efficient enough to get him a visa just ten minutes before take-off (a bottle of Stolichnaya vodka presented to his Italian colleague apparently helped), but on his flight to Rome Yevsyukov was worried whether the Soviet embassy in Italy would be informed about the time of his arrival. It was not, but when he finally reached its office, he found a message from Moscow there: the Italian embassy kindly requested Mr Yevsyukov not to deal with political matters while in Rome.

However, as Yevsyukov writes in his memoirs, "... being already in Rome I could not act otherwise but carry out my mission, especially since, strictly speaking, it was not of a political nature".[2] Indeed, his main task was to receive a guarantee that the Soviets would get visas to take part in the conference. He managed to get a "word of honour" from Lucio Luzzatto, Vice-President of the Italian National Assembly (a leftist Socialist and a leading organiser of the conference) that at worst the Soviets would get visas right at the airport upon arrival.

The worst did not happen; the representatives received visas on time and really enjoyed the conference. Moscow's assistance to its organisers was substantial: we provided air tickets to dozens of delegations and made a financial contribution, though it took a long time for me to cash a cheque for about US$8,000 in an Italian bank.

Apart from drawing the attention of broad international circles to the struggle against Portuguese colonialism, it resulted in the first ever papal audience for Agostinho Neto; Amilcar Cabral, PAIGC General Secretary; and Marcelino dos Santos, FRELIMO Vice-President in the Vatican. Yevsyukov rightly calls it "a shattering blow to Portuguese colonialism, to the policy of the Portuguese branch of the Catholic church",[3] which supported the colonial war: it signified the recognition of the legitimacy of the liberation struggle waged by the MPLA, the PAIGC and FRELIMO.

The conference was especially important for the mobilisation of various political forces in Western Europe to support the liberation movements. For example, Agostinho Neto was invited to Sweden by the Social Democratic Party immediately afterwards, though it took nine more months to take a positive decision on "educational and medical supplies – vehicles were later included – directly to the MPLA" by the Swedish International Development Agency.[4]

These developments, however, were not at the expense of the traditional contact with Moscow and its allies. A very clear statement on that matter was made in Rome by Amilcar Cabral: "We will receive assistance from everybody. We are not anticommunists. Who wants to help us can help, but don't put any conditions. Don't think we shall leave our old friends for the sake of new ones."[5]

The liberation struggle in Angola was hampered by the existence of liberation movements, rival to the MPLA. The FNLA, headed by Holden Roberto, was formed in 1962; its predecessor, the UPA, began armed action in Northern Angola in March 1961. Then, Jonas Savimbi, former general secretary of the FNLA, founded the Union for Total Liberation of Angola (UNITA), which carried out limited operations in the south-eastern part of the country. Of these organisations only the MPLA took part in preparing for the conference and was present in Rome. However, at one of the sessions a young man tried to come to the platform, shouting pro-UNITA slogans, but was promptly pushed out of the hall.

That was my first "acquaintance" with UNITA. It could have taken place earlier, if not with the organisation (it was founded in 1966), at least with the tendency, personified by Jonas Savimbi, who, after his resignation from the FNLA, visited Moscow in 1964 as a guest of the Soviet Afro-Asian Solidarity Committee, but I only joined this body later, in March 1969. Taking into account the role played by Savimbi in the tragic history of Angola, this visit deserves more attention.

Savimbi's biographers write that he had a meeting with "Soviet leaders", and according to Fred Bridgland his interlocutors in "Eastern Europe" "... were only interested in recruiting new members for the MPLA".[6] At a time when "sensitive" archive documents are still sealed, it is very difficult to clear up all the circumstances of his visit. As in many other cases we have to rely on reminiscences, but witness-participants often differ in their judgements, though Savimbi definitely did not meet a Soviet leader. Oleg Nazhestkin[7], a KGB officer who was dealing with Angola in the early 1960s as third secretary of the Soviet embassy in Leopoldville, writes:

When Savimbi began criticising Roberto with an obvious intention of placing himself at head the UPA, our [KGB] officers intensified their work with him to try to 'tear him off' Roberto. A trip by Savimbi to Moscow was organised, where he was received by the First Deputy Head of the International Department of the CPSU Central Committee (CC), R.A. Ulyanovsky.[8] However, Savimbi was too ambitious: he did not accept the Soviet proposals of uniting all patriotic forces in Angola as a condition of rendering effective support to the Angolan liberation movement by the USSR.[9]

Nazhestkin's last point is hardly accurate: by that time Moscow had already been providing assistance to the MPLA for several years. Besides, Yevsyukov describes the visit in a different way: "During the meeting at the Soviet Afro-Asian Solidarity Committee[10] [and not at the CPSU headquarters, although Ulyanovsky might have taken part in the meeting] Jonas Savimbi tried to make us believe that he was ready to co-operate with A. Neto, that they knew each other well in their youth, but the latter resolutely rejects all proposals on interaction and combining the efforts of MPLA and UNITA in the struggle against colonisers."[11] He continues: "However, the question of reconciliation between A. Neto and J. Savimbi was not facing us. This would be beyond our capacity."[12] Yet in another document Yevsyukov names Savimbi among "agents of imperialism" "unmasked" as a result of "time-consuming discussions" at the committee.[13]

Soviet assistance to the MPLA was really versatile. "Camarada Pedro" recalls a fascinating incident. In urgent cases the leadership of the liberation movements, who knew his *nom de guerre* – "Pedro Dias" – and the number of his post office box, could send him a letter by ordinary international mail. Once, a letter came from Agostinho Neto, who complained about the shortage of cartridges for Soviet-made Tokarev pistols and asked for them to be sent urgently. "To confirm his request and to avoid a mistake he enclosed a cartridge in the envelope. This was probably the only case in the history of the postal service."[14]

According to available (or, rather, accessible) archive material, financial assistance to the MPLA increased steadily: from US$25,000 in 1961 to US$145,000 in 1966 and US$220,000 in 1973.[15] A lot of civilian goods – foodstuffs, clothes, etc. – were supplied as well. The MPLA members who were operating in Cabinda or lived in Congo-Brazzaville expected a ship to bring supplies to Pointe-Noir, just as later those on the eastern front or in Zambia expected one to come to Dar es Salaam. However, this reliance on assistance from the Soviet Union and other friendly countries had a negative effect too: it produced a culture of "non-production", in particular because the bulk of the MPLA members were from the urban population and not exactly fond of farming.[16]

Assistance to the MPLA in Angola, as well as to other liberation movements, was co-ordinated by the CPSU CC through its International Department, while several government bodies were also involved in it. An important step was a trip by a group of Soviet officials to Tanzania, Zambia, Congo (Brazzaville) and Guinea (Conakry) in early

1967 at the decision of the Central Committee. Yevsyukov writes: "... an urgent necessity arose to evaluate the state and prospects of this [anti-colonial] war, to try to study the situation on the spot, if not inside these countries [Angola, Mozambique and Guinea-Bissau], then at least from the territory of the neighbouring states" to help the CPSU CC "to determine the line on our co-operation and policy in the region".[17]

The members of the group were Petr Manchkha, Head of the International Department's African Section; Yevsyukov; Gennady Fomin, Head of one of the African Departments of the Soviet MFA; and Vadim Kirpichenko, his counterpart in the KGB, future lieutenant general and First Deputy Head of the PGU (First Main Department) – Soviet political intelligence. The trip resulted in "the Politburo's decision on our future policy towards African countries, in particular, on our all-round support to the militant nationalists in the Portuguese colonies".[18]

Yevsyukov's story is supported by the memoirs of Kirpichenko, who describes how, apart from discussions with the leaders of the movements and of adjacent independent African states – Tanzania, Zambia, Congo, and Guinea – the group looked for other sources of information as well. He gives interesting detail. When the group was in Congo, its members met a Soviet doctor who worked in the MPLA military hospital in Dolisie, next to the Angolan border. He told them that wounded militants were coming there regularly, implying that some action did take place. The doctor also told them that "commanders and commissars worked well in the units and the military discipline was not bad".[19]

It should be underlined that although the move towards Marxism by the leaders of the liberation movement was welcomed in Moscow, it was not regarded as a precondition for Soviet assistance. I recall how Professor Ulyanovsky said to us, members of the Soviet delegation to the above-mentioned conference in Rome: "We don't request ideological loyalty from the liberation movements."

Let us look now at the most crucial periods of Soviet-Angolan relations. Unfortunately, as was mentioned above, we have to rely primarily on "oral history" and written memoirs, which have begun to appear in Russia during the last decade.

In particular, the Angolan part of the memoirs written by Karen Brutents, former Deputy Head of the CPSU International Department, who was a member of the Soviet delegation to the MPLA Congress in December 1977 (he later became Gorbachev's adviser in the

Presidency) is of interest. He believes that Angola became "one of the key points of the USSR and USA rivalry in the 'third world'. In the context of its irrational logic Angola occupied a place completely disproportional to its significance and the confrontation there (just as the events in the Horn of Africa) noticeably influenced Soviet-American relations as a whole, the destinies of the détente."[20]

Brutents continues:

Our support to the MPLA was dictated not so much by ideological, as [others] often think, but rather by pragmatic considerations: it was the only national movement ... which waged a real struggle against colonisers. The relative role of the ideological linkage is testified to by the fact that at a particular time the CPSU CC Politburo even took a decision to recognise the MPLA's competitor, the FNLA headed by H. Roberto, who was later proved to be connected with the CIA. Only bureaucratic delays and especially protests by some African leaders and the Portuguese left prevented its realisation.[21]

However, "Camarada Pedro" tells a rather "tragicomical" story that hardly confirms that this was a well-thought-out "pragmatic" decision.[22] Nikita Khrushchev, then both the CPSU First Secretary and Soviet Prime Minister, heard about the formation of the GRAE while on holiday in the Crimea and got angry that the USSR had not yet recognised the new government.

This "government", though it was recognised by a number of African countries, was a failure. This is well illustrated by "an assessment of the present situation in Angola and a forecast of the likely trend of developments", sent from the British Consulate in Luanda to the embassy in Lisbon and the Foreign and Commonwealth Office in London:

Holden Roberto's "provisional government in exile" is regarded here [by the Portuguese authorities in Angola] as rather a poor joke, as well as it may seem unless other nations start recognising it. News of the struggle between the UPA and MPLA has been greeted with satisfaction; but while it is clearly to the interest of the Portuguese that the Kilkenny cats should waste their energy fighting each other it would be awkward if the conflict were to result in the demise of the one and the unchallenged supremacy of the other. The Minister of Overseas Territories himself seems to fear that the weakening of UPA might bring MPLA to the top. I have no evidence of any intention to negotiate with either side.[23]

However, bypassing the CPSU International Department (the body which dealt with the MPLA and the liberation struggle in Angola in its various aspects) the Soviet governmental decision was urgently taken. Moreover, it happened while MPLA leader Agostinho Neto was visiting Moscow and the Deputy Head of the Department, Dmitry Shevlyagin, was instructed to tell Neto "in a suitable form" about the recognition at the very last moment (the official information was to be published the next day). According to Yevsyukov, an eyewitness, "the discussion ... went in a way, pleasant for the MPLA leader, all his requests were met". It was coming to an end when Shevlyagin informed him that the Soviet government was studying the question of possible recognition of Holden Roberto's government. "I translated Shevlyagin's statement word for word", Yevsyukov writes. Shevlyagin's statement "sounded ... like a death sentence for A. Neto, who did not expect such an end to the meeting. Shevlyagin's final words, alleviating the blow, were meaningless."[24]

Yevsyukov who accompanied Neto, continues: "On the way to the hotel I was feverishly thinking how to save the situation. I knew well who Holden Roberto was and understood even better that we had made a mistake, betraying our friends ... The only man who could correct the situation and save the MPLA was Alvaro Cunhal, General Secretary of the Portuguese Communist Party."[25] Fortunately, Cunhal happened to be in Moscow as well and Yevsyukov suggested Neto call him immediately and ask him to interfere. "Camarada Pedro" who, by the way, spoke perfect Portuguese, went up to Cunhal's room and briefly explained the situation to him.

Cunhal, a hero of the anti-fascist struggle in Portugal, enjoyed high prestige in the USSR. So, "the next day and on the following days no information on our recognition of the [Roberto's] government appeared in *Pravda* and it couldn't appear". On the contrary, *Pravda* published an article written by Yevsyukov's immediate superior, Veniamin Midtsev, and its content was so contrasting that the US embassy even phoned the Soviet Ministry of Foreign Affairs to find out who its author was.[26]

But perhaps Khrushchev should not be blamed too much. Having visited Leopoldville, a special mission of the newly-founded Organisation of African Unity (OAU) Liberation Committee, comprising representatives of Algeria, Congo-Leopoldville, Guinea, Senegal, Nigeria and Uganda, unanimously recommended that all African or external aid to Angolan liberation fighters be channelled through the FNLA exclusively and that all independent African states accord diplomatic recognition to the GRAE. This choice was largely caused by da Cruz's defection; he and a small group of his supporters demanded to "withdraw all authority" from the movement's steering committee, to constitute a new leadership of the MPLA and to join the FNLA.[27]

Such a recommendation allowed Roberto to launch a diplomatic offensive. Dmitry Dolidze, then General Secretary of the Soviet Solidarity Committee, met Holden Roberto at his request in Nairobi, on 17 December 1963, during celebrations of the independence of Kenya. Alexander Arkadaksky, an official of the CPSU African Section, was present at the discussion as well.[28] Roberto was interested in the recognition of his organisation by the AAPSO. He claimed that he was not against union with the MPLA, but only if the latter agreed to unite under the leadership of UPA (this term was still used), which allegedly controlled 75 per cent of the Angolan territory.[29] Underlining the recognition of his organisation and his government by the OAU Liberation Committee and twelve African states, including Algeria, he even accused Neto of being "an agent of Portuguese colonisers who was let out of prison with the intention to use him to split the national liberation struggle in Angola".[30]

Roberto was planning to visit China and when he was asked whether he wanted to make a stopover in Moscow, the FNLA leader expressed his readiness "to come to the USSR to establish ties with the Soviet Solidarity Committee at any time", provided he was given a ticket: "I am a poor man and don't have money to pay for the fare."[31] Dolidze stated that Roberto was "nervous, guarded, mistrustful"; nevertheless, apparently influenced by the position taken by the Africans, in particular by his Kenyan hosts, he proposed maintaining contact with Roberto and even inviting him to the USSR as a guest of the Solidarity Committee.[32]

Roberto's "overture" did not bring any results, but the problems in the MPLA's relations with Moscow were not over. They deteriorated when Neto signed an agreement with Roberto on 12 December 1972 on the creation of the joint body, having agreed to the second role in its leadership, the Supreme Council of Revolution. This step, according to Yevsyukov, "completely disoriented MPLA members and supporters, as well as us".[33] Indeed, in contrast to the earlier period, the FNLA had by that time become weaker both inside and outside Angola. In 1965 the OAU retreated from its previous position and its Liberation Committee began to distribute its assistance (as limited as it was) to MPLA as well, and then in 1971 the OAU "formally withdrew" the recognition it extended to GRAE in 1963.[34]

However, it would be wrong to say that the Soviets had not been informed about a forthcoming agreement between the MPLA and FNLA. The "reconciliation" between Neto and Roberto was announced in Brazzaville on 9 June 1972 under the auspices of Presidents Marien Ngouabi and Mobutu. Soon after, in late August 1972, a delegation of the Soviet Afro-Asian Solidarity Committee visited Congo-Brazzaville. The fact that the delegation included "Camarada Pedro" shows that its mission was connected more strongly with the situation in Angola than with the "host country". Quite significantly, during their discussions with the Soviets the Congolese officials spoke about their support to the liberation struggle in Angola, but did not make much difference between the MPLA and FNLA/GRAE. It looked as if they wished to get rid of the danger caused by the MPLA's presence and stop the use of Congolese territory for attacks against the Portuguese in Cabinda.

The delegation felt that the idea of unity between the two organisations – the MPLA and FNLA – took a concrete form, though these two sides had different interests. In principle Neto and Roberto, as well as their "hosts", Ngouabi and Mobutu, had already come to an agreement, yet "nobody knew" what form the unity would take – a front, joint headquarters or a co-ordination council. Mobutu insisted in particular that the MPLA headquarters should move to Kinshasa, otherwise he would not allow the movement to use the territory of Zaire. The Soviet delegation also noticed a rise in disagreements within the MPLA, as some prominent members, such as former President Mario de Andrade, were distancing themselves from its leadership.[35]

Pascoal Luvualu, then a member of the MPLA leadership and head of the trade union organisation UNTA[36], visited the USSR in late September 1972. At a meeting at the Solidarity Committee he underlined that the expected "merger of actions" of the two movements should not "change the attitude to the MPLA and material, moral and political support to it".[37] He insisted that friends of the MPLA should not recognise the FNLA even after the expected agreement, because though "Holden Roberto represents nothing",[38] the MPLA leadership was evidently concerned that he would try to receive assistance from the "fraternal [to MPLA] countries".[39]

At that period MPLA delegations were sent to a number of friendly countries. Their mission was rather difficult, if at all possible: according to Luvualu, while talking about the alliance with the FNLA, the leadership of his organisation nevertheless sought "to prepare the recognition of the MPLA as the only representative of the fighting people of Angola".[40]

When Alexander Dzassokhov,[41] who led the discussion from the Soviet side, asked Luvualu, whether the Soviets should continue trying to isolate Holden Roberto and criticise him, as had been done at the January 1969 international conference on Southern Africa in Khartoum, or consent to a compromise "to assist your efforts", Luvualu insisted that "the friends should not go for a compromise, Holden has lost the confidence not only of the people, but even of his entourage." The continuation of Moscow's attitude to him would "force him to make concessions". Luvualu explained that an alliance with Roberto was Mobutu's condition for the MPLA's presence in Zaire. Rather optimistically Luvualu expressed the hope that the "MPLA would be in the centre of the alliance".[42]

Dzassokhov assured Luvualu that the Soviets would "orient themselves according to the MPLA's actions". Underlining that every organisation should itself determine its attitude in the international arena, in particular to social democrats and China, he nevertheless mentioned that at the AAPSO conference in Cairo in January 1972, the MPLA had distributed "thousands" of booklets about Neto's visit to China "as if the MPLA lives only by ties with Beijing". Luvualu's reply was hardly acceptable: "This was done because information on ties with other countries had not yet been prepared."

For several years another sensitive point in discussions between MPLA and Soviet representatives was the persistent delay in convening the organisation's (first ever!) congress. It may look strange to some readers, but it was Moscow ("totalitarian", "authoritarian", whatever you name it), which pushed this matter, while Neto and his supporters were not in a hurry, probably as they were not sure about its possible outcomes. According to Luvualu, a relevant commission continued its work and a congress would be convened "as soon as it becomes possible".[43]

Later, at the celebrations of the 50th anniversary of the Soviet Union on 22 December 1972, the MPLA was represented by Floribert "Spartacus" Monimambo, then a member of its top body, the Political and Military Coordinating Committee. At the discussions with the Soviets he underlined that the MPLA, in spite of the agreement with the FNLA signed on 12 December, remained the leader of the national liberation movement in Angola. He tried to convince us that the MPLA had managed to stop the Portuguese offensive on the "Eastern Front", which was primarily of a "psychological nature" and resulted in many refugees fleeing from Angola to neighbouring Zambia and Zaire.[44]

It looks as if he played down the negative effects of this offensive. Not only refugees, but also a significant number of MPLA armed units had to retreat to Zambia.[45] In any case Monimambo knew very well the problems that faced the movement, and described them to us. For instance, bringing supplies into Angola was a tremendous task: trucks could only go 100 kilometres inside, and it took two or three weeks to bring supplies to the areas of operation on foot.[46] He also underlined that Portugal had intensified its propaganda, was trying to bribe local African chiefs, distributing leaflets portraying the hardships of the people and the life in "luxury" of the MPLA leaders. While MPLA radio was in a position to broadcast for only 15 minutes from Brazzaville and 20 minutes from Lusaka (moreover, not at the best time), Portuguese propaganda continued 24 hours a day.[47]

Monimambo informed us that the MPLA congress was planned for 1973 and spoke about the *reajustamento* (reorganisation) campaign within MPLA. This campaign began on Neto's initiative soon after a group of MPLA high military commanders, including future Chief of Staff of the Angolan Armed Forces "Xietu" (Joao Luis Neto), returned from studying in China. It was launched in conditions of growing differences within MPLA as a reaction to the complicated situation that arose after the Portuguese counter-offensive. Having been influenced by their studies in China, these commanders advanced a slogan that everything possible should come from the people, that the movement should learn from the people, should listen to them, and that everybody should go to the front (and not stay in Lusaka).[48] That campaign resulted in the demotion of a number of leading figures in the MPLA.

Though Monimambo did not openly object to the MPLA's alliance with the FNLA, he emphasised a number of negative consequences: the "resurrection" of Holden Roberto, a possibility of subversive activities against the MPLA in future in Zaire, even elimination of its leaders, a gap for the penetration of enemy agents. Among the positive aspects he mentioned the prospect of the resumption of supplies to the First Region, north-east of Luanda, where MPLA fighters had been isolated for years, and prospects of guerrilla action in cities. The aim was "not a merger, but a unity" and the MPLA would "preserve its face".[49]

In describing the new united body, the Supreme Council of the Angolan Revolution (its headquarters were supposed to be in

Kinshasa), Monimambo tried to prove to us that although Holden Roberto had become its president and Agostinho Neto his deputy, decisions would be taken by the two of them together. He also expected that MPLA would in reality play the decisive role in the united military command. The MPLA leadership called on the socialist and "revolutionary democratic" countries to recognise the new front officially but to maintain close contact with the MPLA.[50]

Finally, Neto led the MPLA delegation to Moscow in late January 1973 and tried to convince his Soviet interlocutors that the agreement with the FNLA meant "a new stage for the movement", which should present the MPLA with the opportunity to reach "vital centres of the country"; that even if Holden Roberto became the president of the new united front, Neto as vice-president would control the secretariat, supplies and military affairs, and that his organisation would "continue to exist as MPLA but in alliance with the FNLA". Trying to show that he was fully satisfied with this arrangement, Neto even said that it had been difficult to convince Roberto "to stand at the head" of the new alliance.[51] Like his colleagues earlier, Neto insisted that for the time being the USSR should maintain its (rather negative) attitude to the FNLA until the MPLA expressed "another opinion".

When analysing the situation in Angola, Neto spoke about the manoeuvres of Lisbon, such as the creation of "states (*estados*)" instead of "overseas provinces" and elections to the "Legislative Assembly" in Angola. He regarded "Angolan capitalists" (settlers) as even more reactionary than Lisbon, and underlined the rise of separatist moods among "500 thousand colonists" that were attracted by the example of the Rhodesian Unilateral Declaration of Independence (UDI).

Neto also spoke about the danger of the infiltration of Portuguese agents into MPLA ranks and the "strange behaviour" of some elements who were trying to use "tribalism and regionalism", apparently hinting at growing tension within his organisation.[52]

At the same time he claimed that inside Angola the MPLA had more forces than Holden Roberto; moreover, according to him, Roberto's position in the FNLA itself was not secure: a rebellion against him had recently been suppressed by Zairean troops, who killed 47 people. Besides, Neto hoped that the MPLA would be able to work actively among a million Angolan refugees in Zaire. He said that many Zaireans welcomed the fact that the MPLA could be in Zaire. Furthermore, he believed that Mobutu ("a little Napoleon") needed the MPLA in Zaire for his own prestige.

Neto also informed us that proposals about the alliance had been discussed in MPLA ranks from June to December 1972 and insisted that the decision taken had been a "collective" one. Its consequences were discussed as well: "some are worried, and the others are optimistic".[53] Neto thought that "there was no need to convene an MPLA congress" under the circumstances, "though the Soviet diplomats are always enquiring when it will take place".[54]

The discussion on practical issues uncovered a number of problems, especially some concerning Angolan students in the USSR. Lucio Lara, who accompanied Neto, in particular expressed his concern about the behaviour of some students who were violating discipline by marrying Soviets[55] or leaving the USSR without the leadership's permission. He even insisted that the Angolan students should not receive graduation certificates; instead these should be sent to the MPLA headquarters.

In spite of Neto's assurances, the confusion caused by an alliance with an "arch-enemy" who had become a superior to the MPLA president aggravated differences within the MPLA's ranks to a great extent. Two so-called "revolts" within MPLA ranks against Neto's leadership took place – the *"Revolta do Leste"* (Eastern Revolt), led by Daniel Chipenda, who was based in Zambia, and the *"Revolta Activa"* (Active Revolt), led by Joaquim Pinto de Andrade and his brother Mario Pinto de Andrade in Congo-Brazzaville. Chipenda's *revolta* was brewing in 1971–72,[56] and finally, in July 1973 he and his supporters issued a statement criticising Neto.[57] They accused Neto of "presidentialism" and called for the convening of the MPLA congress. They also strongly opposed the agreement with FNLA. The *Revolta Activa* followed on 11 May 1974.[58]

Zambia became an important rear base for the MPLA on a par with Congo-Brazzaville when in May 1966 the movement launched the armed struggle in the eastern part of Angola, in the Third Region (districts of Moxico and Cuando-Cubango), followed by the Fourth Region (districts of Lunda and Malange). Initially the MPLA's offensive on the Eastern Front caught the Portuguese unaware and guerrilla units advanced a long distance inside the country. They almost reached Luena. Another column was directed to Malange, but it suffered a defeat. MPLA units also operated in the district of Bie, where they confronted UNITA. In this period Cabinda (the Second Region) was regarded mostly as a school for training cadres to be sent to other fronts, though some raids continued there as well.[59]

From the threshold of the 1970s Daniel Chipenda became the MPLA top commander on the Eastern Front. According to Paulo Jorge, incumbent MPLA CC secretary and former Minister of Foreign Affairs, Chipenda "was a person who on MPLA's behalf was in contact with various organisations, including international support organisations and the embassies"[60] (in Lusaka). It was indeed so; thus he was our main interlocutor from the MPLA when we, members of the Soviet Solidarity Committee's delegation, visited Lusaka in August 1969. We had rather fruitful discussions, which prompted the adoption of a special decision by the CPSU CC to admit wounded fighters from the MPLA and other liberation movements to the USSR for treatment at military hospitals, in addition to "quotas for rest and treatment", provided to the MPLA by the CPSU.[61]

These discussions also resulted in a visit of Soviet journalists and cameramen being arranged to the liberated areas of Angola. A year later, on 12 July 1970, a team of Soviet journalists and cameramen crossed the Zambian-Angolan border with a group of MPLA fighters. It included in particular Oleg Ignatyev of *Pravda* and Anatoly Nikanorov of *Izvestia*, the two leading Soviet dailies. After completing the mission, before boarding an Aeroflot plane in Dar es Salaam, they gave a press conference and Agostinho Neto, who had just returned from the Rome conference and a follow-up visit to a number of European countries, was the first speaker there.[62]

In particular, Neto said:

The Soviet journalists have visited one of the liberated zones in Angola ... We shall be glad if they tell the world the truth about our struggle and our hardships. Let the Soviet people, whose sympathy and support we have felt all these years, daily and hourly, learn about it; let the peoples of those countries, whose governments do not acknowledge our movement – and are, moreover, helping the Portuguese colonialists with weapons – learn about it. I mean, in the first place, the states of the NATO bloc, and especially Britain, who had decided to sell arms to the South Africa Republic.[63] What does this mean as far as we are concerned? This means that the weapons bearing "Made in England"[64] death mark will cross South Africa as transit goods and make their way to the Portuguese butchers, causing the death of thousands more people in our country.[65]

The report of the Soviet team was really impressive: they were brave enough to film the Portuguese garrison from a distance of 300 metres and witness an attack of an MPLA unit on Cayanda fort.[66] Later they did their best to fulfil Neto's request: a series of articles was published and a documentary film, *By Guerrilla Trails of Angola*, was produced.

The theme of contradictions within the MPLA and Moscow's attitude to them were touched upon in Nazhestkin's articles. In particular, he wrote: "…it was difficult to understand why many officials from the Old Square [that is from the CPSU headquarters] tried with enviable persistence to portray Chipenda as a 'consistent unswerving revolutionary' …".[67]

Indeed, Yevsyukov in his memoirs does not conceal his sympathy for Chipenda: "Daniel Chipenda in those times when I knew him was a member of MPLA leadership, dealing with military matters. A forthright and frank man, he did not hide his critical attitude to some decisions of Neto, concerning the armed struggle against the Portuguese."[68] This assessment was drastically different from the opinion expressed by Neto in 1975: "Imperialism tried to split our movement and used Chipenda for this purpose. This man is corrupt, and if we were to enquire in the PIDE [Portuguese secret police] archives we will find out his connections with the PIDE in the years when he was a student."[69]

In any case, it is not accurate to speak about "many officials from the Old Square" – the whole "chain of command" dealing with Angola, from a desk officer to the Central Committee Secretary, consisted of just four or five people. More justified, however, is Nazhestkin's observation about "a personal dislike" of Neto by some CC officials who "regarded him as an inconvenient figure".[70]

Indeed, Neto was often an "inconvenient" interlocutor; his sincere adherence to Marxism-Leninism (though initially hardly overt)[71] went along with a strongly independent mind. I heard, for example, that once, at an appointment with Boris Ponomarev, the CPSU International Secretary, whom Neto had met several times earlier, the MPLA leader asked aloud who was the man he was talking to. In this way Neto wanted to express his dissatisfaction that he was not received at a higher level, by Leonid Brezhnev.

According to Yevsyukov, Neto's colleagues used to criticise him in private. One of them was Reverend Domingos da Silva, who was vice-president of the MPLA.

The post of vice-president was a purely nominal one, and he did not hide it. He was needed in the Directory Committee just as a representative of the clergy … The Reverend spoke with me many times tête-à-tête, and I had no reason not to trust this respected old man. He knew A. Neto from childhood and spoke of him in an uncomplimentary way, as of a man of vanity, an imperious man.[72]

Moreover, according to da Silva, it was Neto's pride that "caused animosity between tribes … and led to civil war",[73] but such an opinion cannot be justified.

The author's Angolan interlocutors underlined that Neto always behaved very independently of Moscow and, allegedly, Soviet representatives, especially those from "special services", did not like it. He preferred to receive assistance from Yugoslavia, led by Tito, which he regarded as independent as well as Marxist-Leninist. He was striving for ideals of socialism, but did not tolerate any pressure, any foreign interference.[74]

In any case, the position of the "Old Square" was adopted not just on the basis of the knowledge and opinions of its individual officials, but taking into account a huge volume of information coming from a range of sources along different channels. In particular, a sceptical attitude to the MPLA president's decision to form an alliance with the FNLA was typical not only of the functionaries of the International Department, but of many Soviet officials dealing with Angolan affairs, be it in Moscow or in Africa.

The following is one telling example. Victor Kulikov, mentioned earlier, then Chief of the Soviet General Staff, on 21 December 1973 sent a memorandum (*zapiska*) to the CPSU CC under the title, "On the situation in the national liberation movement in Angola", in which he wrote about "termination of the combat actions in Angola" in view of a split in the MPLA, putting the blame for it on Neto. He was accused of "ignoring the national question [ethnic problems] in the formation of leading bodies, underestimation of political and educational work and one-man methods of leadership", which resulted in "sharp aggravation of inter-tribal contradictions and a spilt in the party". The letter spoke about repression of Neto's opponents, dismissal of Chipenda and rebellion of MPLA fighters in major camps in Zambia. In particular, it accused Neto of trying to break rebels' will to resist by a "hunger blockade", "using the fact that all the assistance to MPLA was still at his disposal". The memorandum claimed that the strength of the MPLA combat units was reduced from 5,000 to 3,000 and that the Portuguese were able "to transfer part of their punitive forces from Angola to Guinea-Bissau."

It criticised Neto's agreement with the FNLA, which "profited only Holden's organisation" and "so far gave nothing to the MPLA". The

Chief of the Soviet General Staff also claimed: "Neto has always treated with suspicion the cadres who completed their training in the USSR and could render him necessary assistance, perceiving them as promoters of Soviet influence."[75] (This was in drastic contrast to the group of commanders who studied in China in 1971–72, after Neto's visit to Beijing.)

Kulikov suggested instructing the Soviet ambassadors in Zambia and Congo-Brazzaville to express the concern of the Soviets to Neto and Chipenda, and draw their attention to the need for urgent steps to overcome the crisis and to resume the liberation struggle as well as "to remind [them] that the assistance provided by the Soviet Union to the MPLA depends on the state of this struggle". Moreover, the letter envisaged to "study the expedience of establishing contacts" with the FNLA, provided the decision to invite Mobutu to the USSR was taken and the "prospects of a joint struggle of the MPLA and FNLA" were discussed with him.[76]

Kulikov's opinion, albeit in a slightly weaker form, was supported by Ulyanovsky, whose proposals were approved on 10 January 1974 by the CPSU CC Secretariat.[77] In particular, the Soviet ambassador in Lusaka was instructed to meet both Neto and Chipenda and to call on them "to restore the unity of the party and thus not to allow the Portuguese colonisers and their agents to finally subvert the Angolan national liberation movement".[78]

This archive document shows that John Marcum in his acclaimed book *The Angolan Revolution* was wrong at least in the timing of the events. He writes: "Because of the MPLA's growing disarray, the Soviet Union reportedly withdrew support from Agostinho Neto during 1972 and 1973 … After a period of support for Neto's volatile rival for power, Daniel Chipenda, however, the Russians apparently abandoned Chipenda and invited Neto to Moscow in early 1973 ….".[79] In reality, however, the archive document in question confirms that a more negative attitude to Neto developed in 1973, after his agreement with Roberto, especially towards the end of that year.

Moreover, in spite of the crisis, MPLA cadres, both civilian and military, continued their studies in the USSR. In December 1972, six MPLA fighters, including future general, ambassador and now Minister Roberto Leal Ramos Monteiro "Ngongo", came to the training centre in Perevalnoye in the Crimea for a ten-month course in artillery, in particular Grad (Hail) rocket launchers. Another group (*escadra*) of about 30–40 men studied there as infantry commanders. Then two more *escadras* of infantrymen came, as well as a group of

artillerymen, who completed their studies in Perevalnoye around
the new year of 1974. Parallel to this, a group of Angolans studied
in Moscow at a higher level.[80]

The story of "Ngongo" and his comrades vividly demonstrates the
difficulties the MPLA were facing at that time. They were supposed
to return to Africa in October 1973, but their departure was delayed
for about a month because of the *Revolta do Leste*.[81] The Eastern Front
was practically divided into two: the northern area was controlled by
pro-Neto forces (just like the MPLA office in Lusaka), and Chipenda
controlled the southern part.[82] His actions were facilitated by the
fact that fighters from local tribes were sometimes suspicious of the
northerners; the Portuguese propaganda claimed that they, as a rule
better-educated, were colonising the locals.

Of six artillery specialists who studied in the group of "Ngongo",
one stayed on in the USSR, because he was admitted to hospital as a
TB patient, and five managed to reach Lusaka, overcoming a lot of
difficulties. They were actually detained in Tanzania,[83] but managed
to escape from the camp, having changed clothes with the help of
"Xietu". Of these five, four (except "Ngongo") were originally from
the southern section of the Eastern Front and returned only to die
there. One was poisoned; others were probably killed in action.[84]

Paulo Jorge says that when the "Eastern Revolt' took place, assistance
to the MPLA was suspended "for a while in order to understand what
had happened ... even the Soviet Union suspended their assistance.
We had to explain the situation to them".[85]

Apparently this suspension did happen, but only for several
months in 1974, after the failure of all Soviet efforts to reconcile the
two "factions", and not earlier. As for assistance, in 1973 it remained
versatile. Supplies, such as foodstuffs, continued as well. However,
the Angolans were not always satisfied with the arms they received;
thus the MPLA, as distinct from PAIGC and FRELIMO, did not receive
Strela (Arrow) anti-aircraft rocket launchers, and they suspected this
to be "a part of the strategy to put pressure on Neto".[86]

As mentioned earlier, in 1973 MPLA was allocated US$220,000 in
cash apart from assistance in kind. Although the archive document
does not specify whether this money was transferred to Neto
personally, this was most probably the case.[87]

Nazhestkin refers to a copy of the message from the Soviet
ambassador to Zambia, Dmitry Belokolos, kept in the archive
of the SVR (Foreign Intelligence Service), the PGU's successor. In

compliance with an instruction from Moscow he informed Neto about the "suspension of assistance to MPLA until the question of restoration of the unity of the MPLA leadership with Chipenda's group is resolved".[88] He did not date this message, but the CC's decision of 10 January 1974 was more cautious; the ambassador had to inform Neto and Chipenda that "... the requests for military and other material assistance for 1973 have been complied with. The equipment for the MPLA has been delivered to the PRC [Congo-Brazzaville] and Tanzania. However, the continuing disagreements in the MPLA hamper the provision of assistance to the party by the Soviet organisations."[89]

Nevertheless, neither Moscow's advice nor its leverage was fruitful. Yevsyukov writes:

In our opinion, the achievement of agreement between A. Neto and D. Chipenda was necessary and possible. The decision was taken to send a group of Soviet comrades from the International Department of the CC CPSU and GRU to Zambia. All our efforts to reconcile these two men for the sake of the common cause had not produced a positive result. I became convinced that the differences were rooted in the personal ambitions of the two and not in their concern for the fate of the struggle.[90]

In practice, however, Yevsyukov was hardly impartial. In April 1974, just ten days before the Portuguese revolution, he and I travelled to Oxford to take part in the Easter Conference of the European solidarity groups that supported the anti-colonial struggle. On the very first day we met a Russian-speaking young Angolan who greeted "Camarada Pedro". "Who is he?" I asked Yevsyukov. "Pedro van Dunem or 'Loy', a graduate of the MEI [famous Moscow Energy Institute]", he replied and added: "A good guy, but you see, he is *netovets* [Neto's supporter]."[91]

It looks as if the growing negative attitude to Neto finally prevailed. Judging by Nazhestkin's words, in 1974 initially a part of the allocation was handed over to Neto, but then "... an instruction came to our *rezedentura* [KGB station] in Lusaka to suspend the transfer of the rest of [financial] assistance for 1974 [to Neto] and to pass it to Chipenda ...".[92]

Nevertheless, whatever criticism of Neto that "Camarada Pedro" and other Soviet officials had, they never made it public: on the contrary, a booklet in English praising and quoting Neto was published in early 1974 and Yevsyukov, its co-author, signed and presented it to me on 5 April 1974.[93] Even during this period Soviet organisations maintained contact with the Neto-led MPLA. Thus, on 12 June 1974 Pascoal Luvualu sent a reply to a letter from the Solidarity Committee, saying, in particular: "We are convinced that the Soviet people, as in the past, will not spare efforts and will be always on our side ... ."[94]

3
From the Portuguese Revolution to Angola's Independence

By the time of the April 1974 Portuguese revolution, which opened the prospects for Angola's rapid transition to independence, Moscow's relations with its old friend – the MPLA – were at the lowest ebb ever and it took the USSR leadership some months to make a final choice and to resume supporting Neto and his followers. James Ciment claims in his book on the wars in Angola and Mozambique: "... the situation in the capital and countryside rapidly deteriorated during the summer and autumn of 1974. With the left increasingly ascendant in Lisbon and Luanda, officials began turning a blind eye to Soviet shipments of small arms to MPLA. Thus, when whites again rioted in November, they were met by African self-defence committees, nominally controlled by MPLA and armed with AK-47."[1] However, Ciment does not refer to any source and in any case this is rather far from reality: for several months after the Portuguese revolution, officials in Moscow were still hesitant to make a choice between Neto and Chipenda.

The most critical moment was a so-called "Congress of MPLA" convened in Zambia in August 1974. The inverted commas are relevant here because this gathering was organised not so much by the Angolans as by their "host countries" – Zambia, Congo-Brazzaville, Zaire and Tanzania. In fact the ratio of Neto's supporters and those of the two "rebellions" had been determined by the foreign presidents and it was not in favour of the MPLA president.

After rather futile discussions Neto and his supporters took a brave decision – they left the venue on 22 August[2] and a month later convened their own inter-regional conference of MPLA militants in Moxico province inside Angola.[3] There Neto was confirmed as the top leader and the MPLA Politburo was formed. Meanwhile, those who remained at the congress elected Chipenda to the highest post in the MPLA and, as I heard, a report on the event from Lusaka was even broadcast by Radio Moscow.

Oleg Nazhestkin, mentioned above, claims that Soviet (political) intelligence "played a decisive role" in the change of Moscow's position in favour of Neto, and "in the second half of 1975 the assistance to the MPLA was resumed".[4] However, again, in reality the situation was more complicated.

First and foremost this "decisive role" was played by broad support for the MPLA after the April 1974 Portuguese revolution inside Angola, especially in Luanda, and for most Angolans this organisation was symbolised by Neto.

Information in favour of Neto was also coming from countries friendly to Moscow. Thus, in early May the MPLA delegation headed by Neto for the first time visited the GDR as guests of the ruling Socialist Unity Party of Germany and a bilateral agreement on co-operation was signed. According to Neto's German interlocutors, he was sceptical about the prospects of the MPLA's co-operation with the new government of Portugal, because he opposed the creation of the federation of Portugal and its colonies and insisted on the complete independence of Angola.[5] As for supplies, the MPLA limited its request to civilian goods and did not ask for arms.[6]

Relevant information also sometimes came from utterly unsolicited sources. In the last days of August 1974 an international NGO conference against colonialism and apartheid was convened by the UN and the OAU in Geneva, and on one of the days of its work I had a very interesting discussion with Lars-Gunnar Eriksson, a Swedish social democrat, who was then the director of the International University Exchange Fund, and his representative, who had just returned from Zambia, where he had monitored the procedures of the MPLA "congress". They did their best to convince me that Neto was the "most progressive African leader after Lumumba" and underlined: "Your comrade Vladimir in Lusaka is making a mistake."[7] Imagine, a Western social democrat was encouraging a Soviet communist to support an African Marxist! The minutes of my discussion with Eriksson, naturally, found their way to the CPSU International Department, but of course, this was not the only argument.

When Angolan students who took part in the "congress"[8] were about to return to the USSR, Agostinho Neto instructed them "to tell everything that happened" and they did describe to us all the details of the controversial developments in Zambia: how the "congress" had to be opened not by the leaders, but by MPLA young pioneers; how Zambian soldiers were stationed around the congress venue; how members of Chipenda's group were singing the praises of Mobutu;

how workers in Lobito sent a message to Kaunda, threatening to begin boycotting goods destined for Zambia ... .[9] Also important was the fact that the ruling Portuguese Movement of Armed Forces and the Portuguese Communist Party, then rather influential, refused to recognise Chipenda as the new MPLA leader.[10]

More information, approving of Neto, was coming from the Soviet embassies in Africa as well. The ambassador to Congo-Brazzaville, Yevgeny Afanasenko, played a very positive role.[11] Another ambassador, Sergey Slipchenko in Dar es Salaam, took a similar position.

By the end of 1974 the Soviet attitude was becoming much more positive. Although Chipenda had many supporters on the Eastern Front, especially from his ethnic group, the Ovimbundu, his claims for the top position in the movement failed dismally, as well as his attempts to establish his own office in Luanda. Under these circumstances he declared in February 1975 that he was joining the FNLA as a deputy to Roberto.[12] Apparently he regarded this step as the only chance to remain an important political figure, while for Roberto this new alliance provided an opportunity to proclaim the broad national character of his organisation.[13]

In December Moscow received an MPLA delegation headed by Henrique (Iko) Carreira (after the proclamation of independence he became the first Angolan Minister of Defence). Though the delegation was of a military nature (Pedro van Dunem, responsible for logistics in FAPLA, came as well) its members were regarded as guests of the CPSU and stayed in the famous (though modest) party hotel Oktyabrskaya in Plotnikov pereulok (Carpenter's Lane in translation), near Arbat, a famous Moscow street.

At a meeting with my comrades and me at the Solidarity Committee, Carreira spoke about the earlier wish of the "fraternal African countries" to "present the MPLA as an organisation, acceptable to Mobutu". For this purpose they tried to change its leadership: Zambia and Zaire supported Chipenda, while Congo-Brazzaville supported Mario Pinto de Andrade; even Tanzania for some period became hostile to Neto.[14] But the developments after 25 April "freed the political potential of the people" and "the friends of the MPLA" understood "the reality inside Angola". To those foreign countries that opposed the MPLA leadership, they could say: "You abroad want to destroy the organisation, which is an internal one."[15]

In Carreira's opinion, by that time the main line of division was between the FNLA, "supported by imperialists" and the MPLA, "supported by progressive forces". Among those "progressives" he singled out the Movement of the Armed Forces (MFA), which was in power in Portugal at that stage, and emphasised that the MPLA had entered into "a strategic and tactical alliance" with it.[16] However, the right-wing forces in Portugal were supporting the FNLA. "Though the Portuguese authorities in Angola are ready to render assistance to MPLA, we can't count on their military intervention on the side of the MPLA. The [Portuguese] army is tired."[17]

At that stage Mobutu "left the club" of African countries and relied on FNLA forces to seize power in Angola. Meanwhile, "talks about a split in the MPLA" stopped and Tanzania, Zambia and Mozambique (a transitional government headed by FRELIMO had already been formed there) supported the MPLA led by Neto.

Carreira called the situation "controversial" and spoke about a political hegemony of the MPLA in Angola but admitted its "weakness from the military point of view", at a time when the FNLA had a 10,000-strong army and was preparing to seize power by force. "The battles are waiting for us."[18] In his opinion the confrontation "between various groupings in Angola" was inevitable; it could find its expression "in political as well as in military ways". Under these circumstances the MPLA leadership decided to conclude an agreement with UNITA on joint military and political action with the aim "to make UNITA neutral and to prevent it from making an alliance with FNLA, which is a pro-imperialist organisation".[19]

Carreira expressed satisfaction that "comrades [in the USSR] understood the situation". "With their assistance we shall deliver a final blow to the forces of reaction." Speaking about a forthcoming (10 January) meeting of the three Angolan movements and Portugal in Alvor, he said he expected that it would result in the announcement of the date of independence ("The MPLA is not interested in delay, July would be fine") and the formation of a provisional (transitional) government, which, however, would not have full power.

On behalf of the Solidarity Committee I invited the MPLA to send its delegation, which preferably had to include members who had worked underground before April 1974, to the USSR and Carreira reciprocated with an invitation to the Committee's delegation to Luanda.[20]

Several "fact-finding" and (later) solidarity visits of the Soviets to Angola helped them better to understand the developments there as well. The first Soviet citizen who visited Luanda after the Portuguese revolution was Oleg Ignatyev, a veteran *Pravda* correspondent who had earlier several times visited liberated areas of the three Portuguese colonies where the armed struggle had been waged. He arrived there from Lisbon on 16 September 1974 for a short visit, returning on 24 September.[21] At that stage the MPLA did not yet have official representatives in Luanda, but he met, among others, a leader of the Democratic Movement of Angola (MDA), which had been established "for the purpose of disseminating and elucidating the aims and tasks of the MPLA". It was Antonio Cardoso, who before the revolution served 13 years in Salazar and Caetano's prisons and concentration camps.[22]

Then, at the beginning of January 1975, on the eve of the formation of the transitional government, a Soviet journalist, Igor Uvarov,[23] who for over four years had been working at the TASS office in Algeria, was sent to Angola and stayed there for about two months.[24]

Uvarov flew in from Lisbon by the TAP flight at night. The Angolan capital met him with a lack of electricity and sounds of small arms fire. A Soviet passport caused a great surprise at immigration control. He had well-hidden money in small, US$20 notes, but no taxi could be found. Fortunately at that very time the Portuguese High Commissioner, Admiral Alva Rosa Coutinho (he collaborated closely with the MPLA[25] and his replacement in January 1975 by Antonio Silva Cardoso was regarded as a victory for Holden Roberto), was leaving Angola and one of the people who took part in the ceremony gave the journalist a lift. That was one of the leaders of the Zairean opposition who was later kidnapped by Mobutu's thugs and shot.

It was this new-found friend who advised Uvarov to check into the Tivoli Hotel[26] and helped him to contact the MPLA leadership. So Uvarov paid a visit to Lucio Lara, who, having come to Luanda in November 1974, headed the MPLA machinery there in anticipation of Neto's arrival. Earlier, in December, Uvarov met Iko Carreira in Plotnikov pereulok and received from him a recommendation letter for Lara, but the MPLA leader just threw it into his table box.

What was behind this not particularly friendly action? Lara's scepticism about Moscow's role?[27] Or, as Uvarov thought, a more personal reason? The problem was that in December 1974 another journalist from TASS arrived in Luanda, but stayed there for only a few days. A car he had rented had been stolen and, to avoid trouble, he preferred to leave the country urgently. Nevertheless, according to Uvarov he "invented", so to speak, and published an interview with Lara. Uvarov thought that Lara had been informed about this and had therefore not welcomed another TASS correspondent.

Plate 1   Igor Uvarov in retirement at his dacha (country house).
Source: Uvarov family archive.

One detail demonstrates the complexity of the situation in Luanda in those days: there were a couple of correspondents from South Africa and thanks to one of them, of *Die Beeld*, Uvarov managed to be present at the ceremony of the launch of the transitional government on 31 January 1975.[28] The South African, who was going there with a member of the FNLA top leadership, simply pushed him into the car and only later disclosed that this was a Soviet journalist.

The transitional government was problematic from the very beginning, not only because it consisted of forces that had been rivals for many years, but because of foreign interference as well. Thus, nine days before its formation, on 22 January, the 40 Committee of the US National Security Council approved providing Holden Roberto with US$300,000 to enable him "to compete" with other movements in the transitional government.[29] Soon after, in February, Roberto's well-armed forces moved from Zaire into Angola and began attacking the MPLA in Luanda and Northern Angola.[30]

As for the USSR, in Uvarov's words, "Moscow by that time knew nothing properly about the situation in Angola. We knew about the regions the MPLA had divided the country into, but the situation in practice was quite different."[31] Anyhow, Uvarov began sending telex messages to TASS describing and analysing the situation. Soon he managed to reconnect with the MPLA, including the FAPLA Chief of Staff, "Xietu". A little later he was introduced to Neto, who entertained him in his villa with whisky and nuts, and was finally given the opportunity, once a week or so, to transmit more confidential messages (in addition to ordinary telexes) to the Soviet embassy in Brazzaville (and so to Moscow) via MPLA radio stations there and in Luanda.

To report personally on the situation, which was "awful", especially prior to the return of Agostinho Neto, in the absence of regular reliable flights to neighbouring countries he managed in late February to charter a small plane (in those days the cost was still reasonable, about US$800) and come to Brazzaville. After listening to his story Ambassador Afanasenko suggested recalling him to Moscow for debriefing.[32]

Meanwhile, Agostinho Neto was met by a triumphal reception in Luanda, where he returned on 4 February, on the 14th anniversary of the beginning of the uprising in Luanda. His return coincided with the visit of the delegation of the Soviet Solidarity Committee, headed by Alexander Dzassokhov, who had been invited by the MPLA. Sergey Vydrin, a Solidarity Committee official who accompanied him, recalls how they went to Luanda via Paris and Lisbon. When their plane reached Luanda, it could not land because "about 300,000 people had assembled there" to meet Agostinho Neto who at that very moment returned home after 15 years of exile.[33] So the Portuguese pilots had to land at a military airfield. Dzassokhov and Vydrin's luggage included "a heavy load of cinema and photo equipment, a gift for the Angolans", but it was lost in Lisbon and found "by a surprise coincidence" only on the day of their departure from Luanda, allegedly "having been brought from Rio de Janeiro".[34]

Neto gave instructions that the Soviets had to be accommodated in an excellent hotel on the seashore. But one evening armed people knocked at Dzassokhov's door. They were looking for the head of the Soviet delegation and said they wanted "to go to Moscow to study Marxism-Leninism". However, Dzassokhov told them that they were not a political delegation but had come to study the "specifics of agriculture" in Angola. "Maybe our agricultural equipment will be of use ... ." "We had a contact telephone number," Vydrin continues,

we immediately phoned our [MPLA] "liaison" and he quietly evacuated us at night from our fashionable hotel ... We were housed in one of the MPLA camps. We met Neto, other influential politicians and public figures. Nobody believed that it was supporters of Marxism who had got interested in us at the hotel, therefore, when our stay was over, Neto instructed his security service to accompany us in a civilian airline plane to Lisbon.[35]

One more detail: at a rally at the Luanda stadium attended by over 50,000 Angolans, one of the speakers was Moses Mabhida, executive member of the ANC and (though still covert in those days) of the South African Communist Party (SACP) Central Committee. Among others present were three Cubans, including the ambassador to Tanzania, and two Chinese journalists.[36]

If anybody in Moscow still had doubts about Neto's influence in the MPLA and in Angola as a whole, the eyewitness report by Dzassokhov's delegation removed them. In their discussions with the delegation, Neto, Lopo do Nascimento, future first Prime Minister of independent Angola, Iko Carreira and other leaders of the MPLA analysed the balance of forces. They explained that the FNLA had about 4,000 soldiers in the north as well as 2,000 in Luanda and it could bring more from Zaire with the assistance of Mobutu and Washington. UNITA, assisted by white settlers, had about 4,000, mostly in the southern provinces and around Nova Lisboa (now Huambo). Neto and his comrades proudly said that support for the MPLA proved to be even higher than they expected, and that 10,000 people volunteered to join its armed units. They feared that Zaire would launch an attack against Angola (and their fears were justified), but the high spirits of the MPLA leadership were well demonstrated by Lopo do Nascimento, when he compared the transitional government, formed after Alvor, with Kerensky's provisional government in Russia prior to the October 1917 revolution. Against the background of growing assistance to its political competitors (for example, Mobutu bought several hotels for the FNLA, and supplied it with ten Mercedes buses), the MPLA expected from its friends, in addition to political assistance, means of transport, radio communication and printing equipment (a printing shop had already been supplied by Sweden), loudspeakers, etc.[37]

The next quite important Soviet visitor to Angola was Navy Captain Alexey Dubenko[38] who came to Luanda in March under cover and stayed there for some months.

Moscow supported the Alvor agreement but against the background of growing assistance to the MPLA's rivals from Zaire, a number of Western countries, South Africa, and, for a certain period, from China, supplies to the MPLA had to continue. China, which established good relations with Zaire after Mobutu's visit to Beijing in January 1973, soon began supplying the FNLA with arms.[39] A month after the Portuguese revolution, on 29 May 1974, a group of 112 Chinese military advisers arrived in Zaire to train Roberto's troops. Furthermore, China published a press release on their arrival;[40] apparently it expected the FNLA to play a leading role in independent Angola and wanted to demonstrate its contribution to Roberto's future successes. Later, in July 1975, Deng Xiaoping, then Vice-Premier, and Ho Ying, Chinese Vice-Minister for Foreign Affairs, received an FNLA delegation in Beijing.[41] China's contact with UNITA intensified as well. In March 1975 Deng Xiaoping received another Angolan delegation, headed by UNITA's general secretary, Samuel Chiwala.[42]

The crisis in the MPLA affected its fighting capacity: some trained cadres remained with Chipenda, others had to do "civilian" duties after their return home. Urgent assistance in training was needed, and in March a large number of MPLA members left again for the USSR. They constituted a core of the future 9th Brigade (although 9th in number, it was practically the first regular unit of FAPLA); the upper echelon, 20–30 commanders, underwent a crash course of training in the famous Higher Officer courses, "Vystrel", in Solnechnogorsk near Moscow, and the bulk, up to 200 individuals (company commanders, armoured personnel carrier (APC) crews, etc.) in Perevalnoye, in the Crimea.[43] However, when they completed their course in late June, owing to the lack of trained cadres not all of them remained in the ranks of the 9th Brigade. Some were sent to the southern regions of Angola.

In the last days of April 1975 "Camarada Pedro" left for Luanda together with Gennady Yanaev,[44] then chairman of the Committee of Soviet Youth Organisations, and "Camarada Eduardo", Eduard

Kapsky, who was then an associate professor at the Institute of Social Sciences.[45] At the meeting in the Solidarity Committee prior to their departure for Luanda, Yevsyukov spoke sceptically about the prospects of the transitional government: the three movements had great ideological differences, their leaders felt animosity to each other, and besides there was no tradition of coalition governments in Africa. He was worried by the fact that the authorities of Congo-Brazzaville would not agree to the "massive support" of the MPLA, being afraid of possible retaliation from Zaire. He was also aware that the Cuban Deputy Chief of Staff had made a trip to some of the African countries.[46]

Yevsyukov believed that Holden Roberto was not in a position to achieve a majority at the upcoming general election and envisaged a further aggravation of the situation in a month or two, but it happened even earlier.

The delegation was invited to take part in the 1 May celebrations in Luanda, and the visit was regarded in Moscow as a demonstration of solidarity with the MPLA, but the situation in the Angolan capital was hardly conducive to public functions. Fighting broke out after an FNLA attack on the National Union of Angolan Workers' (UNTA) headquarters on 29 April was carried out to subvert the 1 May celebrations, planned by the trade union centre.[47] The delegation members and other passengers of the TAP plane (Portuguese Airlines was the only company flying to Luanda) could see neither the capital nor even the lights of the runway; the aircraft had to use its own searchlights.

Only one elderly Portuguese official was in the large hall of the airport. Astonished to find Russians among the passengers, he was nevertheless very helpful and managed to contact the MPLA headquarters.[48] Meanwhile, "there was no doubt that war was really waged in town; short bursts of sub-machine-gun fire were heard from all directions".[49]

Finally, after an hour, MPLA representatives picked up the delegation. It took a long time to bring the Soviets to town: at every crossroads, patrols stopped the car to check it and, as had been advised by the Angolans, the Soviets stated that they were businessmen.

At the destination it was recommended that they sleep on the ground floor: somebody was firing from time to time from the top floor of the opposite building. Then in the morning the delegation was transferred to a house in the outskirts of Luanda, in an area by and largely controlled by MPLA units.

The next day the delegation was invited to the MPLA headquarters for a meeting with Neto. Yevsyukov, who was often critical of Neto, on this occasion paid justice to him in his memoirs:

The discussion began in a small garden near the building, but soon bursts of sub-machine-gun fire were heard and bullets began whistling over us. A. Neto suggested continuing the discussion at the other side of the building. To my surprise externally he appeared quite in control of himself, I did not suspect that he could be so fearless.[50]

Yevsyukov continues: "… there was no political benefit from our visit".[51] This is hardly so, because the first-hand information was extremely valuable for Soviet policy-drafters and policy-makers in Moscow. After the return to Moscow the delegation presented a comprehensive, 15-page long report, which contained an analysis of the situation, conclusions and recommendations.[52] In addition its members had a comprehensive discussion at the International Department.

They had the chance to meet Agostinho Neto three times and also had discussions with Lucio Lara, Iko Carreira and other MPLA leaders.[53] In particular, Neto described the MPLA stand in the following way: "They all call us 'red' here; though our organisation is a movement composed of different social forces, we are on the same side of the barricades with socialist countries."[54]

Neto underlined the readiness of the MPLA leadership to co-operate with other nationalist organisations and to participate actively in the work of the coalition government and preparation for elections. More than once it took steps to broaden its contacts with UNITA, but while the FNLA intensified its armed provocation, UNITA was continually forming a closer alliance with it. So in his opinion the only way out for the MPLA was "armed action" based on its support from the people.[55]

The delegation made a very interesting forecast: "… representatives of various US information services in Luanda are keeping UNITA as a reserve, sizing Jonas Savimbi up, and a situation cannot be excluded when the USA will give up their support of the FNLA in favour of UNITA".[56] That is exactly what happened later. No less correct was a forecast that a leading Portuguese Communist Party (PCP) member gave to the delegation when it was in transit in Lisbon on the way back home: "The developments in Angola will finally result in dismembering the country into zones of influence of different nationalist groupings."[57]

The gravity of the situation was well understood: the MPLA was in a "state of defence". In fact, Neto confessed to the delegation that he did not expect the MPLA to win the (absolute?) majority at elections. Rostislav Ulyanovsky, who was present at the debriefing meeting together with Petr Manchkha, even asked the delegation's members whether the MPLA had a "system of underground organisations".[58]

Yanaev and his colleagues stated that the transitional government had been paralysed and the drafting of the constitution of the independent Angola was still at Chapter 1. They reported that Neto hoped to influence Portugal, using its desire to preserve its economic interests, which were threatened by the American expansion. However, Portugal "had no time for Angola"; it was too busy with its own problems. MPLA leaders criticised the leader of the Portuguese Socialist Party (future president) Mario Soares, who "spoke the same language as Roberto and Savimbi".[59]

Moscow at that stage was interested in establishing a liaison mission in Luanda or at least a permanent presence of Soviet correspondents. However, even MPLA representatives were not too enthusiastic; they complained that their organisation had already been accused of being "pro-communist".[60] Meanwhile the CIA reopened its station in Luanda in March[61] and, according to Neto, it "mobilised armed whites" to act as provocation.[62]

As Neto had said, the MPLA at that stage had about 6,000 fighters, concentrated mostly in Luanda and along the coast. Supplies for them came in a Yugoslav ship, the *Postoina*, which arrived in the port of Luanda in the last days of April, but it had to leave for Pointe-Noir on the Portuguese High Commissioner's order after Roberto protested.[63] At the first MPLA congress in 1977 Neto publicly confirmed this fact. Yet apparently at least some of the arms had been confiscated by the Portuguese authorities and kept at depots until Angola's independence.[64]

The delegation made a number of sound conclusions, such as: "An armed conflict between the revolutionary-democratic elements [read: MPLA] and the forces of reaction in Angola looks inevitable, especially after the departure of the Portuguese army. What will be its result, whether Angola will preserve its territorial integrity – all this will finally depend on the strengthening of the MPLA's positions ... ."[65]

One of its recommendations was "to sound through diplomatic channels the position of major African countries on the process of decolonisation in Angola to determine the possibility of broadening the front of MPLA supporters in Africa".[66] This was done; the messages to a number of African leaders (and to the PCP) were sent from the Soviet leadership.

The report, which was not classified, did not mention arms supply; it just recommended "meeting as far as possible the MPLA's requests for various material assistance".[67] However, according to Yevsyukov, the MPLA leadership and Neto in particular were apparently satisfied with the Soviet assistance; no new requests had been made to the delegation. Moreover, the movement did not even use the whole "quota" for military training in the USSR; it was organised mostly inside Angola. The supplies for the whole brigade (three battalions) had been brought to the Soviet ports by mid May but they could not go further than Pointe-Noir in Congo-Brazzaville and from there the hardware was expected to be brought by small ships to the Angolan ports or to be transported by small planes.[68]

At last, on 4 July 1975, Neto, who was in Brazzaville for talks with President Ngouabi, told Ambassador Afanasenko that the "PRC [People's Republic of Congo] allowed the MPLA to use its territory for the transport of arms, military equipment and other cargo supplied to the movement by the Soviet Union and other friendly countries ... In order to export supplies to Angola, they allotted the port and airfield at Pointe-Noire."[69]

Stockwell, in his book, quotes the words of a CIA desk officer: "The Soviets did not make the first move in Angola. Other people did. The Chinese and the United States."[70] He claims that the Soviet Union began "significant arms shipments" to the MPLA in March 1975 and then "in response to the Chinese and American programs" launched "a massive airlift", using An-12 and giant An-22 transport planes.[71] However, as was mentioned earlier, in mid May a lot of hardware was still in Soviet ports. This included "a large quantity of small arms, 82 mm mortars and some portable Grad-P".[72]

General "Ngongo" recalls that massive amounts of military supplies began coming into Pointe-Noir around August–September 1975. He returned from the USSR and was stationed near Quifangondo, but had to leave for Pointe-Noir to settle some confusion: inscriptions on the boxes were in Russian (he could at least read it) and he had to find fuses for mortar shells to send them to Benguela.[73]

In Washington, July 1975 was a month of decision-taking on Angola. According to the CIA memorandum "large supplies of arms to Roberto and Savimbi would not guarantee they could establish control of all Angola, but that assistance would permit them to achieve a military balance which would avoid a cheap Neto victory".[74] On 16 July the Africa Division of the CIA prepared a covert action plan for the Angolan operation. The matter was apparently regarded as quite urgent, as President Gerald Ford approved it the same day. On 27 July, US$8 million was added to the original sum of US$6 million.[75]

However, the decision to interfere in Angola on the side of the MPLA's rivals was not universally supported in the US establishment. For example, Tom Killoran, American Consul General in Luanda, regarded the MPLA as the best qualified to govern Angola and thought that its leaders sincerely wanted peaceful relations with Washington. It is hardly accidental that he was not even informed when the decision to fund the FNLA was taken in January 1975.[76]

Moreover, the CIA station chief in Luanda, Robert W. Hultslander, came to share his assessment:

... the MPLA was the best qualified movement to govern Angola ... Although many outwardly embraced Marxism, they were much closer to European radical socialism than to Soviet Marxist-Leninism ... Despite the uncontested communist background of many of the MPLA's leaders, they were more effective, better educated, better trained and better motivated. The rank and file also were better motivated (particularly the armed combatants, who fought harder and with more determination) ... Unfortunately, the CIA's association with the FNLA and UNITA tainted its analysis. As is frequently the case when intelligence collection and analysis are wedded to covert action programs, objectivity and truth become victims of political expediency. I believe this was the case in Angola. No one wanted to believe the Consulate's reporting, and Killoran's courageous and accurate analysis was ignored. He sacrificed his career in the State Department when he refused to bend his reporting to Kissinger's policy.[77]

In fact, even much earlier Washington expressed some hope of bringing the MPLA into the Western orbit. In July 1963 a State Department dispatch to the US embassy in Leopoldville said: "US policy is not, repeat, is not, to discourage MPLA (Neto–Andrade faction) move towards West and not to choose between these two [MPLA and UPA] movements."[78]

Hultslander's views on the FNLA and UNITA, expressed also in an interview with Piero Gleijeses, are telling as well:

I admit that I developed a bias against the FNLA and its leaders, which I never tried to hide. Its ties with Mobutu merely added to my assessment that this organization was led by corrupt, unprincipled men who represented the very worst of radical black African racism. My personal experience only served to reinforce my opinions. I was disgusted by the briefings I received in Kinshasa, and my meetings with FNLA leaders and contacts. As an aside, which underlines my assessment: our senior FNLA contact in Luanda tried (unsuccessfully) to use our sensitive facilities to transport stolen goods.

I had little direct contact with UNITA. My knowledge of this movement is rudimentary, and thus not worth your consideration. As you are aware, UNITA had little presence in Luanda, either politically or militarily, during the time I was there. I was deeply concerned, nevertheless, about UNITA's purported ties with South Africa, and the resulting political liability such carried. I was unaware at the time, of course, that the U.S. would eventually beg South Africa to directly intervene to pull its chestnuts out of the fire.[79]

This interview also shows that the CIA's knowledge of the Cuban role was rather limited: "I believe [Cubans] did not arrive in any numbers until after we departed ... Although we desperately wanted to find Cubans under every bush, during my tenure their presence was invisible, and undoubtedly limited to a few advisors."[80] However, by the day that US staff left Luanda, on 3 November 1975, the Cuban military mission, established in August, already consisted of several hundred persons.

In its policy towards Angola, apart from the desire to protect its economic and political interests, Washington was influenced by its obsession "to stop the advance of communism"; in particular, 1975 was the year of the final (and shameful) defeat of the US in Vietnam and the demise of the "pro-American" forces in Ethiopia.

Neto told Afanasenko in July 1975 that the MPLA had decided to request additional military and financial aid from Moscow and to send to Moscow an MPLA delegation, headed by Iko Carreira.[81] So in August the MPLA top military commander was back in Moscow, and by that time the situation had become much better for the MPLA. On 19 and 21 August my colleagues and I met Carreira again. He was accompanied by Pedro van Dunem and Costa da Andrade. One of the themes was practical assistance to the MPLA by the committee, which, in particular, sent five buses and ten jeeps to Pointe-Noir for the MPLA and was intending to donate to it radio-telephone equipment for intra-city communications and wireless stations with a range up to 1,000 kilometres. Besides, the MPLA needed fuel, foodstuffs and medicine,[82] apart from the needs of its armed forces, FAPLA, which were discussed in the International Department and government structures.

Carreira told us that the MPLA anticipated the developments. Though it expected massive armed clashes in September; these actually took place in July.[83] Speaking about the activities of the transitional government, he underlined that the FNLA had sabotaged it. For example, the Ministry of Agriculture, headed by its representative, moved 20,000 cattle out of the country. It also disrupted steps for the creation of a united army, drawn up in the Alvor agreements.

FNLA troops tried to advance towards Luanda to increase their presence in the capital, but failed and by the end of June they were concentrated in the two northern provinces. Roberto had to agree to negotiations, which took place in Nakuru, Kenya. According to the agreement reached there, each movement had to reduce its troops in Luanda to 500, and the MPLA, according to Carreira, "took steps to clear the capital from excessive FNLA troops" and succeeded in three to four days.[84] In response the FNLA proclaimed the beginning of war and its column of about 5,000 troops, eleven APCs and three Panhards tried to advance towards Luanda, but was stopped.[85]

The FNLA still had more troops than the MPLA[86], but its potential for mobilising new recruits was limited. The main concern of the MPLA leadership was a threat of intervention from Zaire and it tried to come to an agreement with UNITA to resist it jointly, but Savimbi hesitated. Carreira believed that UNITA would agree if it were to feel "the strength of the MPLA".[87]

The MPLA expected the international public to condemn "foreign interference in Angolan affairs". At the same time it was glad that ships from the GDR (bringing in particular ambulances and medication), Poland and Yugoslavia were calling at the port of Luanda and it saw no obstacle to Soviet ships doing this as well.

All in all, the MPLA's representatives were optimistic. They believed that, if provided with more material assistance, their organisation would be in a position to strengthen the blockage of routes for Zairean interventionist forces, seize the coastal areas controlled by the FNLA and then begin the liberation of the northern provinces.[88]

The attitude to UNITA was different. The MPLA representatives (they continued coming to Moscow on various occasions) informed the Soviets that it would be "difficult to proclaim independence without UNITA's participation".[89] Talks between the MPLA and UNITA took place in Portugal, but failed. Nevertheless, even after the beginning of hostilities, the MPLA did not want to "cut off all ties" with UNITA. Its leaders believed that the areas controlled by UNITA did not "constitute a military threat" – the underestimation of the menace from South Africa, just a month before its massive intervention, was obvious. Their attention was still concentrated on the threat from Zaire, though they spoke about the "South African Army's provocations" as well.[90]

South African troops moved from Namibia into Angolan territory on 8 August, ostensibly to protect the Calueke Dam on the Cunene River. By the end of the month they had reached Perreira de Eca, the capital of the Cunene province. In September the South Africans began to supply arms to UNITA and the FNLA and to train their forces at Rundu in Northern Namibia.[91] Soon South African instructors appeared with UNITA and FNLA units inside Angola.

The independence date was approaching, and the Portuguese authorities were in trouble about arrangements for the ceremony of transferring power. Here again a witness-participant provided a fascinating story. One day in October, Igor Uvarov was invited for a talk by the Portuguese High Commissioner, Lionel Cardoso,[92] who told him that Portugal, which had long ago, in Alvor, agreed on the date of Angola's independence, 11 November, was facing a problem: whom to transfer power in Angola to? He said that the day before the Portuguese authorities in Angola had informed the MPLA Politburo that they could not transfer power to this movement alone and would have to transfer it to "the Angolan people". Cardoso asked Uvarov to pass a message to Moscow, asking it to influence the MPLA so that the transfer of power would have "a joint nature". Reminding the Soviet correspondent that earlier the Portuguese troops had helped the MPLA to "chase FNLA and UNITA units away from Luanda", he even said that if their leaders came to Luanda for the ceremony of transfer of power, these organisations could be "beheaded".[93]

The most crucial moment in Soviet-Angolan relations, the moment of crucial decision-taking, was the eve of independence. As in many other cases, the Cold War historians are still arguing on who made the "first move" in Angola: Washington or Moscow? Georgy Kornienko, former Soviet First Deputy Minister of Foreign Affairs, writes in his memoirs: "In the Angolan episode of the 'Cold War', as in most of its episodes …, Washington said 'A', but in this case as well, Moscow did not refrain for a long time from saying 'B'."[94] He believes that with the worsening of Soviet-American relations, related to Angola in particular, the progress in the talks on strategic arms stopped and correspondingly Brezhnev's visit to the USA was postponed and then did not take place at all.[95]

However, I share the opinion of Ambassador Vladillen Vasev, former deputy head of the USSR mission in Washington and later head of the Southern African Department at the Soviet Ministry of Foreign Affairs, who believes that if it had not been Angola, the USA would have found another excuse for "cooling off" relations with Moscow.[96]

Furthermore, I am convinced that it would be a gross (and harmful) simplification to look at the developments in and around Angola just through the spectacles of the USA–USSR confrontation. The complexity of the situation concerning Angola can be seen from the fact that in July 1975 "pro-imperialist" Mobutu expelled the US ambassador from Zaire, arrested and even sentenced to death several alleged CIA agents, having accused Washington of preparing a coup against him,[97] while Kaunda, a "progressive" president of Zambia, soon practically sided with Pretoria in common support for UNITA. Zambian governmental propaganda played its role as well, though sometimes rather clumsily: I recall a picture of a maize field in its *Z* magazine, which insisted that this very maize grown by UNITA helped Zambia to overcome the effects of the drought![98]

When Moscow provided extensive training to MPLA personnel in the USSR and increased supplies of arms via Congo-Brazzaville, it had to take into account that, distinctly from the MPLA, Holden Roberto could fully rely on a neighbouring country, Zaire, which was his secure rear base for almost 15 years. Moreover, it was Zaire to which Beijing managed to send not only arms for the FNLA but instructors as well. Besides, UNITA was receiving support from China from its inception. As for Zambia, it continued supporting Chipenda but gradually switched to UNITA. Finally, South Africa, which occupied and ruled Namibia, was becoming an active player in the game against the MPLA as well.[99] MPLA representatives began to worry that Pretoria was supplying arms to UNITA, whose leaders were ready to begin a "tribal war".[100]

Moreover, it would be wrong to imagine that the Soviet Union was just a "monolithic" structure where a top-down approach prevailed. Yevsyukov recalled how Nikolay Podgorny, who received him in the Kremlin after his appointment to the post of the first Soviet ambassador to Mozambique, wanted to know his opinion on the Angolan issue. Should the Soviet Union render all the required support to the MPLA in spite of the expected negative reaction from Washington? Yevsyukov, though his attitude to Neto was hardly objective, did his best to encourage Podgorny to be firm on the issue of assistance to the MPLA.

Kornienko writes about the "sad consequences of the two approaches in the Soviet foreign policy – state and ideological – and the related institutional confusion".[101] According to him, when after the independence of Angola [rather, on the eve of it] "the civil war, provoked by the USA actions, began to flare up", the Soviet Ministry of Foreign Affairs (MFA), together with the Ministry of Defence and the KGB, prepared a proposal, approved "by and large" by the CPSU Politburo, to provide the MPLA with all kinds of political support and "certain material support", but not to get involved in the civil war in Angola "in the military sphere". However, just a few days later the CPSU International Department, headed by Ponomarev, having secured initially the signatures of Marshal Grechko (the Defence Minister) and the KGB chairman Yury Andropov, managed to get the support of Gromyko as well to meet the MPLA's requests for (still limited) arms supplies.[102]

Anatoly Dobrynin, who was the Soviet ambassador to the USA for almost 25 years, writes that the International Department played "a leading if not decisive role in the Soviet involvement in the Angolan adventure [sic] ... the Soviet Ministry of Foreign Affairs had nothing to do with our initial involvement and looked at it with some scepticism'.[103] The first sentence is perfectly correct, but all important political decisions on international affairs, even if pressed for by the International Department, had to be supported by the MFA, and, depending on the their nature, often by the KGB and Ministry of Defence as well.

In fact Kornienko's words confirm the existence of such a procedure. He did not specify when exactly these different decisions were taken. However, from reminiscences of Nazhestkin it becomes clear that they were taken before the designated date of independence. He recollects how Vladimir Kryuchkov, then the head of the PGU and a close associate of the KGB chairman Yury Andropov, "one day in October" [1975] instructed him to go to Luanda urgently.[104]

According to Nazhestkin, before his departure from Moscow the MFA and International Department's officials advised to him to "exert influence on Neto and encourage him to reconcile with Roberto and Savimbi and to restore a tripartite coalition".[105] But when he came to Brazzaville, more flexible instructions waited for him there – instead of "influencing" the MPLA leader he just had to voice his opinion on the possibility of such a coalition and ascertain the MPLA's attitude to it. Moreover, just some hours later he received another instruction signed "on a higher level". Nazhestkin's new task was to tell Neto about "the readiness of the Soviet government to recognise Angola as a sovereign state as soon as the MPLA leadership proclaims it [and], to establish diplomatic relations ... ."[106]

This narrative confirms Kornienko's words about the changes in the attitude of the top Soviet leadership. However, I believe the reality did not lie in "two approaches in the Soviet foreign policy", these changes reflected rapid changes in the situation in Angola, in particular when foreign intervention, especially that by South Africa, became evident.

Some people underline the fact that the mission to meet Agostinho Neto in Luanda was entrusted to a KGB officer and not to a diplomat.[107] I believe there were several good reasons for this. As was mentioned before, the Soviet Ministry of Foreign Affairs hardly dealt with the liberation movements. On a higher political level they were a "domain" of the CPSU International Department. Moreover, this mission required some personal rapport with Neto, but the official of the department who knew the MPLA president well, "Camarada Pedro", was not available; he was already packing, having been appointed the first Soviet ambassador to Mozambique. Besides, the mission to besiege Luanda was quite dangerous and an officer of the Committee of State Security was more suitable for it than a civilian.

Nazhestkin came to Luanda on 2 November via Brazzaville and met Neto that night. According to him Neto was moved by the news from Moscow, saying, "At last your people understood us. So, we shall co-operate and fight together."[108]

This reaction of Neto probably reflected some initial doubts he and his associates had about Moscow's position. In this respect, part of reminiscences of Boris Putilin, then first secretary of the Soviet Embassy, is revealing:

We were "barking" at each other with Lucio Lara in September 1975 right in the middle of a street in Brazzaville. He shouted: "You have divided the whole world with America and decided that Angola is not in the sphere of your influence. You don't help us the way you should ... .'"[109]

It is not clear what the basis for Lara's concern was, but several Western authors, such as Ciment, make a ridiculous claim that "at independence" of the Portuguese colonies Moscow and Washington made "geopolitical arrangements" that "placed Mozambique in the Soviet orbit and Angola in the Western one".[110]

Even later, when Putilin moved to Luanda, some Angolan partners would ask him: "Why don't you bring your wife here? – I can't do it without a CC decision. – No, you are afraid of the South Africans. As a matter of fact, you, Soviets, want to drop us."[111]

What is indisputable, however, is the fallacy of the idea, so popular among Western leaders, academics and mass media for many years, that Cubans acted in Angola as Soviet "proxies". Even many years later, when an interviewer asked Gerald Ford whether he saw "as a patron in the 1970s that there was war by proxy in Africa", the former US president replied: "Well certainly in this case, the Angolan case, you could say that the Soviet Union was taking advantage, and letting proxy forces carry out its military desires and objectives in the African continent."[112]

Nevertheless, the archive documents and oral sources prove that Havana's decision was its own. For example, Kornienko and his "boss", Andrey Gromyko, as well as Grechko and Andropov, found out about the Cuban movement of (combat) troops to Angola from a message by the Soviet ambassador to Guinea, who informed Moscow about the forthcoming technical landings of Cuban planes in Conakry.[113]

However, for historical truth to be told, it has to be added that Moscow did know earlier about the first stage of their involvement. I recall that Petr Manchkha, then the head of the African Section at the CPSU headquarters, informed SWAPO President Sam Nujoma about the imminent arrival of 500 Cuban instructors in Angola.[114]

In one of his articles Nazhestkin quotes "one of the reports of our intelligence on a conversation with Neto". The MPLA leader allegedly explained his approach to Cuba for assistance by "the cessation of the Soviet assistance at the beginning of 1975", which put the MPLA "on [the] verge of defeat".[115] It sounds rather strange, because before that, in the last days of 1974, Carreira expressed to my comrades and me his satisfaction with the discussion he had with Soviet party and military officials.

At that stage Havana's relations with Congo-Brazzaville improved greatly. At the request of President Ngouabi, Cuba sent instructors and a combat unit there to protect that country from possible Zairean invasion.[116] The Soviets were aware of the Cuban presence and activities there. According to Putilin he knew in particular that two Cuban pilots were flying a small plane between Angola and

Brazzaville, and that a Cuban ship under Somali flag was "shuttling" between Pointe-Noir and Angolan ports.[117] In his view, when bringing hardware from Cuba to Angola, such as two shiploads of T-55 tanks, the Cubans knew that it would be replaced by more modern arms from the Soviet Union.[118]

Odd Arne Westad writes: "In 1975, Fidel Castro initiated Cuban armed support for the MPLA without Moscow's agreement or knowledge, and thereby reduced the Soviet leaders' role for several crucial months to that of spectators to a war in which the Cubans and their Angolan allies gambled on prospective Soviet support to win."[119] He is right on the first point, but wrong on the second: instead of being "spectators", the Soviets were supplying the MPLA with arms and training its cadres during "several critical months" even before the Cuban involvement, and sent advisers and instructors to Luanda a few days after independence.

Soviet-trained personnel with Soviet-supplied arms took part, together with Cubans, in a decisive battle on the Northern Front on 10 November 1975 at Quifangondo, just 30 kilometres from Luanda city centre. Stockwell writes in his book that 122 mm Cuban rocket launchers fired on Zairean and FNLA troops in salvos of 20 missiles simultaneously and that CIA "observers", who were on a ridge to the north of the battlefield, estimated that 2,000 rockets poured like rain on the advancing "small army". [120]

This "army" had heavy guns – a strange combination of them – some Soviet-designed, received by Mobutu from North Korea and others Western-designed, brought by a South African ship to port Ambriz and manned by South African Defence Force (SADF) personnel. According to Stockwell, however, their range was half that of BM-21 Grad rocket launchers.[121] Besides, Soviet-made rocket launchers were stationed on trucks and could relocate quickly. Moreover, one of the North Korean guns exploded on the first shot, killing its Zairean crew, and the second misfired, injuring the crew.[122]

"Fear has big eyes", says a Russian proverb. Apparently this is true of the CIA "observers" as well, because General "Ngongo", who commanded the artillery of the FAPLA 9th Brigade, told me a quite different story right in Quifangondo, on the hill where his rocket launchers had been positioned.

On the previous evening the advancing FNLA/Zairean troops and mercenaries began firing at the Luanda refinery and the area of Grafanil, where arms depots were situated, using heavy guns placed on the northern side of the hills (one can hardly call them "a ridge"). Then, the next morning several French-made APCs, manned by white mercenaries, began moving towards Quifangondo, while Roberto and Mobutu's infantry concentrated in the palm forest or, rather, a grove a bit behind that.

The bridge over the Bengo River was blown up by the defenders and when the APCs approached it, they were hit by the fire of 76 mm Soviet-made anti-tank guns with joint Cuban and Angolan crews. Soviet-made recoilless B-10 guns were also used. Then the palm grove was covered by rockets from six portable Grad-P[123] of the 9th Brigade. Their position was to the south-east, on another hill, near the water reservoir supplying Luanda. The rocket launchers were behind the top of the hill, invisible to the enemy, but the observation post, where "Ngongo" and his chief of staff stayed, was on its northern side.

Initially their task was to silence the enemy's heavy artillery. They fired on its positions but without success (contrary to Stockwell's story, the range of those portable rocket launchers was shorter). Then, having received the order from the brigade's commander, "Ndozi" (David Moises), they hit the enemy's infantry in the grove with about 60 (not 2,000!) rockets, six at a time, and not 20 simultaneously. Then the 9th Brigade began its offensive. As for the BM-21, manned by Cubans, they were used later, near Caxito.[124] Besides, "Ngongo" believes that the number of 800 FAPLA soldiers and 200 pro-MPLA Katangans at Quifangondo, mentioned in Gleijeses's book,[125] is an exaggeration.[126]

This is not to say that FAPLA's offensive did not have its own problems. Thus "Ngongo" recalls that while the artillery units were well disciplined, infantrymen of the same 9th Brigade would sometimes leave the trenches for Luanda. Even later, advancing to Ambriz, his Grad artillerists once found the enemy in a position that was supposed to have been occupied by the brigade's infantry, and had to fire at FNLA forces point-blank.[127]

Heavy battles took place south of the capital as well. Cubans and FAPLA resisted the South African interventionist forces mingled with UNITA and FNLA (that is, former MPLA fighters, "sold out" by Chipenda to Holden Roberto).[128]

As for the Soviets, there were only four USSR citizens in Luanda on the eve of Angola's independence. Igor Uvarov was supposed to return to Luanda in July, but he got stuck in Brazzaville for three weeks, waiting for a chance to fly to the Angolan capital, that is, for a plane "connected with the MPLA" that from time to time flew there.[129] On 25 October Oleg Ignatyev followed him,[130] and before long two others with Soviet diplomatic passports: Alexey Dubenko, who earlier left Luanda, and Oleg Nazhestkin.[131]

Against the background of stories about "Soviet proxies", Uvarov's narrative about the first contact between Soviets and Cubans in Angola is really fascinating. At the request of Neto Uvarov went in an old Dakota (DC-3) plane to Henrique de Carvalho (now Saurimo) in the east of Angola. The Portuguese army had already left this region and it came under the MPLA's control. He was asked to see whether an airport there could be used for bringing in supplies. The runway was in a good condition, but all the navigation equipment had been taken out or destroyed. There Uvarov met two persons who asked the MPLA commander who the white man with him was. "A France-Press correspondent", the Angolan replied. But when Uvarov in his turn asked the commander who these two people were, he told the truth: "Cubans", and at Uvarov's request introduced him to them. These two Cubans' mission was to put the radio station in order, but as Uvarov found out when he was flying back to Luanda together with one of them, the Cuban had earlier spent about six months in Moscow, studying quite different subjects.

He told Uvarov that he was a member of a group of seven, an adviser and six instructors, who were training local cadres. All in all, by that time (it happened, most probably, in early September) about 80 Cubans were stationed in the Lobito and Mocamedes coastal cities controlled by the Portuguese who sympathised with the MPLA. Thus contacts were established, and before long, Cubans, in uniform and with Kalashnikovs in hands, called Uvarov at the hotel. Their commander was Raoul (Díaz Argüelles) who was later killed in action. Soon Uvarov met "Polo" (Leopoldo Cintra Frias), who had replaced Raoul as the head of the Cuban military mission.[132]

Then at the last moment two more Soviets arrived to take part in the ceremony of President Neto's inauguration. Moscow instructed Ambassador Afanasenko to fly in from Brazzaville as the head of the Soviet delegation. Putilin colourfully describes the incident:

I was with him, the poor fellow. We were coming to Luanda, and there was nobody at the airport. Our An-12, a military one but with Aeroflot insignia[133] landed, a ladder went down, but whom to turn to? I descended and then at some distance away saw a soldier with an American self-loading rifle, supported by a rope; he held his finger on the trigger and aimed at my belly. So pleasant!

We did not know who was commanding at the airport, but in any case I could not run to that person, he would open automatic fire and riddle me with bullets. I suspected he did not even speak Portuguese.

At that moment the commander of the guards at the airport, an Angolan who knew me personally, saved me. He ran for 150 metres shouting: "Boris!" This helped me.

Then we were guided to the hotel. The late Alexey Ivanovich Dubenko and Igor Uvarov were there.[134]

At 11 o'clock on 11 November the Soviets went to attend the inauguration ceremony in the municipal hall, followed by a rally in the square. Ambassador Afanasenko spoke first; he conveyed a message from the Soviet leadership, followed by representatives of Brazil, Nigeria and others.[135]

According to Putilin, another plane with dignitaries was supposed to come to Luanda for the independence celebration: a Romanian delegation headed by the Minister of Foreign Affairs and "a crowd of various ambassadors from Western countries", who allegedly expected that the FNLA would control the capital. However, when their plane was approaching Luanda, at midnight on 10 November, independence was proclaimed and happy Angolans began firing into the air. The pilots did not dare to land and went to Libreville.[136]

Meanwhile, a so-called People's Democratic Republic of Angola,[137] proclaimed by the FNLA and UNITA on 11 November in Nova Lisboa (Huambo), was not recognised by even a single country. It was dysfunctional from the very inception, and, moreover, armed clashes between UNITA and FAPLA forces began immediately in that area.

4
Second War of Liberation

It was only on 16 November that the first group of Soviet military instructors arrived in Luanda. One of its members was Andrey Tokarev, a 19-year-old student of the Military Institute of Foreign Languages. The group, headed by Captain Evgeny Lyashenko, left Moscow on 31 October by a regular Aeroflot flight and arrived in Brazzaville the next day. It had a specific technical and purely defensive mission – to train Angolans in the use of Strelas. They had been informed that Zaire, which supported the FNLA, had obtained Mirages from France and the MPLA leadership anticipated air raids on Luanda. In a week's time the group was transferred to Pointe-Noir and on 16 November it was joined there by a larger group of instructors headed by Colonel Vassily Trofimenko. On the same day, that is five days after the proclamation of Angola's independence, all these 40 Soviet military specialists, including five interpreters, arrived at Luanda by an An-12 military transport plane (of course again with Aeroflot markings).[1]

One of these officers recalls: "We had a feeling that we could be captured. We had been waiting for two hours [after landing]. The aircraft engines were on – we were ready to take off ... [Then] A man in foreign uniform came by car to the aircraft. He proved to be a comrade from GRU [probably Boris Putilin]. Even he only found out accidentally that we had arrived."[2]

This group included specialists in combat use of a variety of Soviet-made equipment and interpreters; some of whom were selected from the training centre in Perevalnoye. Apart from training Angolan personnel in the remote part of the Luanda Airport, they often had to go to the front line, especially "Comrade Yury", Colonel Yury Mitin, who was adviser to "Ngongo". As a rule Cubans accompanied them on these missions.[3] Besides, on 21 January 1976 some of them took part in the ceremony of the transfer of the first Soviet-made MiGs to FAPLA.[4]

In comparison, US personnel came to Angola much earlier, well before independence. A team of infantry instructors was sent to

Zaire, allegedly to train UNITA selected cadres, but the CIA station in Kinshasa hurried to redirect them to Ambriz and Silva Porto. CIA "paramilitary officers" were also training UNITA forces in Silva Porto, and the FNLA in Ambriz. A retired US Army colonel was hired on contract and sent to the FNLA command in Ambriz. Officers, acting inside Angola, were allowed to go around armed.[5]

The Soviet involvement in Angola produced many "unsung heroes". For example, the historians still have to find out (or, rather, recall) the name of the deputy commander of Air Transport Wing from the town of Ivanovo who, on the eve of Angola's independence, risked his life and the life of his crew to airlift two BM-21 rocket launchers urgently from Brazzaville to Pointe-Noir, where the runway was unfit for his heavy aircraft.

Putilin recalls that these rocket launchers were brought to Brazzaville from the USSR by giant An-22 Antei ("Antheus" in Russian). The need to strengthen MPLA troops in Luanda was obvious, and the Soviet embassy enquired from Moscow how they should be brought there. "We asked the Centre [read: Moscow] to bring them by air directly to Luanda. But our request was not granted, because until independence nothing for Neto was sent directly to Angola." The railway was suggested instead. Indeed, a narrow gauge railway connected Brazzaville and Pointe-Noir, but the size of the wagons was insufficient for these heavy arms and no funds had been allocated for this purpose either.

So although an An-22 weighs 130 tons and the runway in Pointe-Noir was fit for 90 tons only, this was the only way out, but high Congolese officials rejected the plan, since they were afraid the runway would be damaged. Putilin had to ask German Predvechnyi, who, as counsellor of the Soviet embassy, liaised with the Congolese ruling party, for help. Only President Ngouabi himself could give final approval and the Soviets found him at the cemetery: he was praying for his late mother (1 November was Mothers' Day in Brazzaville). The only precaution that was taken was two tanks placed near the end of the runway in case the plane went off it. Then on 2 or 3 November the rocket launchers were transported in 24 hours to Luanda by a Cuban ship. Quite timely, the embassy in Brazzaville received a cable message from *Desyatka* allowing the use of BM-21 in combat operations.[6]

The two rocket launchers were placed to the north of Luanda next to the battalion of the elite Special Forces of the Cuban Ministry of the Interior, urgently sent to Angola. Castro decided to dispatch combat troops there on 4 November.[7] The first batch from that battalion left Cuba on 7 November in two outdated Britannias and after a 48-hour flight reached Luanda in the evening of 9 November.[8] In Putilin's opinion this unit was hardly fit for regular warfare, because it was trained to operate as a small group of guerrillas, most likely in Latin America.[9] However, quite probably, by sending such a specialised unit the Cuban leadership was preparing for the worst: Castro told its personnel that if Luanda fell they would fight a guerrilla war as long as the MPLA fought.[10]

Meanwhile, Moscow began assisting in the transportation of Cuban combat units to Angola. According to Putilin, Soviet Il-62 passenger planes made 120 flights there. This co-operation between Cubans and Soviets sometimes took place in unanticipated ways. Putilin recalls:

Sixteen wounded Cubans were brought to Brazzaville in a small plane. So we initially placed them in a maternity hospital, which we had built as a gift [to Congo-Brazzaville]. A chief doctor and a surgeon were ours, Soviets. We invited them to Ambassador [Afanasenko] and told them: "Free a ward, the wounded are coming." – "How can that be?" "You have studied field surgery," we replied, "so – come on, treat them."

Wounded Cubans were thus brought and admitted. President Ngouabi's sister was having a baby at that time, so Ngouabi called in the Cuban ambassador

and shouted at him: "Who is president? You or I?" But then Ngouabi did assist them ... Francophone meetings took place there at some time, and near Brazzaville villas were built to accommodate presidents of former French colonies, so two villas were given to the wounded Cubans – out of sight. A Cuban doctor who specially came there treated them. But our doctors assisted him.[11]

The complexity of the situation in and around Angola at the end of 1975 is clear from the discussions between American and Chinese top leaders. Earlier, in June, an MPLA delegation visited China and was assured that Beijing would terminate all forms of military aid to all three Angolan movements until the granting of independence to Angola.[12] Indeed, the Chinese withdrew their instructors from FNLA camps. However, assistance to MPLA rivals continued, and Beijing and Washington were practically in one boat as far as the situation in Angola was concerned.

Gerald Ford, who was accompanied in particular by the Secretary of State, Henry Kissinger, and George Bush, then chief of the US

Liaison Office, met Mao Zedong on 2 December 1975 during his trip to China and the notes on their discussion are rather revealing. When Mao Zedong said "It seems to me that the MPLA will not be successful", Ford replied: "We certainly hope not."

Both sides were obsessed with the role of the Soviets:

Mao: "I am in favour of driving the Soviet Union out."
Ford: "If we both make a good effort, we can."

However, both Mao Zedong and Deng Xiaoping were worried by Pretoria's involvement.

Mao: "South Africa does not have a very good [sic] reputation."
Ford: "But they are fighting to keep the Soviet Union from expanding. And we think that's admirable ... ."

Deng was visibly worried: "You mean you admire South Africa?" So Ford had to retreat: "No. They have taken a strong stance against the Soviet Union. And they are doing that totally on their own, without any stimulation by the United States."[13]

The discussion continued with Deng Xiaoping on 3 December 1975. In particular, the Chinese vice-premier said: "We hope that through the work of the two sides we can both bring about a better situation there." However, he was once again worried by "the relatively [sic] complex problem", namely "the involvement of South Africa". In reply, Kissinger tried to appease him: "We are prepared to push South Africa out as soon as an alternative military force can be created."

According to Deng, neither Tanzania nor Zambia would allow Chinese weapons to pass to UNITA through their territories because of "the involvement of South Africa". "We are in no position to help [the anti-government forces] except in the north through Zaire." In reply, Kissinger promised to "talk to Kaunda", while Deng embarked on approaching Mozambique, though he "didn't expect great results".[14]

Deng was right in his doubts. On the contrary, Mozambique strongly supported the MPLA in the most crucial days. Sergio Vieira, a prominent leader of FRELIMO, writes:

We participated with our small air fleet [inherited] from the Portuguese Army (the Nord-Atlas, Dakota ...) in the supply of weapons and ammunition to Angola. We gave them financial support. We sent our BM-21 to protect Luanda; they were very relevant to crush the FNLA/Zaire/mercenaries' invasion from the north. With Tanzania we made a great effort to neutralise the Kaunda approach to UNITA. We sent Marcelino [dos Santos] to Luanda to participate in the Independence Day, with a letter recognising the independence the very moment it was proclaimed. And so many more things occurred in the diplomatic field. We created a Day of Solidarity that was based on the voluntary contribution of one day's salary to Angola.[15]

There was something like a "division of labour" in the American and Chinese efforts to defeat the Angolan government. The US president asked the Chinese: "Will you move in the north if we move in the south?" "But you should give greater help in the north too", replied Deng, encouraging Ford: "It is worth spending more money on that problem. Because it is a key position of strategic importance."[16]

Then the so-called Minister of Foreign Affairs of the Roberto-Savimbi "government", Wahall Neto, circulated a statement in Kinshasa on 14 December, calling China "a reliable comrade-in-arms of the FNLA-UNITA coalition in the struggle".[17]

Washington tried to put pressure on Moscow concerning the Angolan situation. When Kissinger met Brezhnev and Gromyko on 22 January 1976 he tried to put this issue on the table. However, Brezhnev replied: "Don't mention this word [Angola] to me. We have nothing to do with that country. I cannot talk about that country." Gromyko was less abrupt but equally firm; when Kissinger spoke about the Cubans' presence there the Soviet Minister of Foreign Affairs insisted: "We have nothing to do with that. We have given some equipment to the legitimate government – that's all ... We have sent no troops."[18]

On 1 February 1976, *Pravda*, the official organ of the Soviet Communist Party, wrote: "The whole world knows that the Soviet Union looks in Angola neither for economic, military nor other advantage. Not a single Soviet man is fighting with arms in hand on Angolan soil."[19] By and large this statement was correct, though later Moscow did acquire facilities for its aircraft and naval ships in Angola. Neither was the Soviet military supposed to take part in actual fighting, but in reality, as will be explained below, it did happen sometimes.

In January 1976 the first Angolan Minister of Foreign Affairs (and future president), Jose Eduardo dos Santos, visited Moscow twice. The first time he was in transit to Helsinki, where he took part in the session of the highest body of the World Peace Council together with Ambrosio Lukoki, member of the MPLA Central Committee, and Afonso van Dunem ("Mbinda"), who headed Neto's secretariat in the party. These two came to Moscow a little earlier and we had a chance to discuss the developments with them.

They regarded the conflict in Angola as part of the struggle between the forces of imperialism and progress, and underlined that hostilities there were not a civil war, but naked aggression. "American imperialism is our direct enemy", underlined the MPLA representatives. In particular they drew our attention to the "strange borders" of Angola, which contributed to the gravity of the situation prior to independence: about 2,200 kilometres with Mobutu's Zaire, pro-Savimbi Zambia, Pretoria-occupied Namibia. The only friendly border was with Congo-Brazzaville in Cabinda, isolated from the main part of the Angolan territory.

They could not hide the disappointment with the position of African states (the results of the OAU emergency summit in Addis Ababa from 10 to 13 January 1976 were not particularly encouraging: in spite of the proved facts of the South African and Zairean aggression, 22 delegations voted for recognition of the People's Republic of Angola (PRA), 22 voted against and two abstained). But they were at least satisfied that the USA had not managed to impose the idea of so-called "national unity" in Angola in Addis Ababa.[20]

The pressure from Washington was really severe. Murtala Muhammed, head of the Federal Military Government of Nigeria, said in his speech at the summit:

In the days before opening of this Session, we witnessed a flurry of diplomatic activities on the part of the United States. Not content with its clandestine support and outpouring of arms into Angola to create confusion and bloodshed, the United States President took upon himself to instruct African Heads of State and Government, by a circular letter, to insist on the withdrawal of Soviet and Cuban advisors from Angola as a precondition for the withdrawal of South African and other military adventurers. This constitutes a most intolerable presumption and a flagrant insult on the intelligence of African rulers.[21]

The Nigerian leader contrasted the policy of the USSR and that of the USA:

We are all aware of the heroic role which the Soviet Union and other Socialist countries have played in the struggle of the African people for liberation. The Soviet Union and other Socialist countries have been our traditional suppliers of arms to resist oppression, and to fight for national liberation and human dignity. On the other hand the United States which now sheds crocodile tears over

Angola has not only completely ignored the freedom fighters whom successive United States administrations branded as terrorists, she even openly supported morally and materially the fascist Portuguese Government. And we have no cause to doubt that the same successive American Administrations continue to support the apartheid regime of South Africa whom they see as the defender of Western interests on the African continent.[22]

Our discussion with Angolan comrades continued when they came to Moscow again together with dos Santos. Initially, on the way to Helsinki, he spent just a few hours at the Sheremetyevo airport and we, from the Solidarity Committee and the Soviet Peace Committee, took care of him. But on the way back (from Helsinki he proceeded to Stockholm) his visit was an official one; the flags of the Soviet Union and Angola were waving near the VIP entrance of the old Sheremetyevo terminal, and so many Soviet Ministry of Foreign Affairs officials surrounded dos Santos that even Petr Manchkha could not elbow himself in to shake hands with the Politburo member of the "fraternal party".[23]

Dos Santos's programme of discussions with the high Soviet government officials was intensive; nevertheless, he visited the Solidarity Committee's premises as well. Dos Santos called his mission to Moscow "extraordinary"; it was taking place while "the second liberation war" was waged in Angola against South African and Zairean troops who had invaded the country under cover of the FNLA and UNITA.[24] The Angolan Minister of Foreign Affairs correctly underlined to us that the USA and France were assisting these troops. Their first aim was to prevent the independence of Angola, but they failed. The second target was to divide the country: South Africa, whose troops occupied five provincial centres, wanted to establish its control in the south, "to ensure a new border to the north of the Benguela railway".[25] However the Angolan (and Cuban) troops launched a counter-offensive and had already advanced about 60 kilometres towards Nova Lisboa. "This offensive was made possible by material and technical aid from the USSR and assistance of Cuba in the training of our units and by combatants."[26] In the north of the country the situation was good; almost all the areas had been liberated.

In the political sphere the aim was "to establish the people's power", to create committees in villages and city blocks. At the same time he criticised the "positions of some leftist groups, some Maoist tendencies" that did not understand "the realities of revolution", though they had some influence in the Angolan mass media. He spoke also about acute economic problems, caused to a large extent by the departure of Portuguese specialists.

Dos Santos was satisfied with the success in the diplomatic sphere. By that time the PRA was recognised by 43 countries, including 23 in Africa, which was just one less than a majority of the OAU members. He was content with his visits to Finland and Sweden. In Helsinki he met the Prime Minister and the general secretary of the Social Democratic Party. Social Democrats and even centrists spoke about support for MPLA, but at the level of the government there were difficulties with the recognition of the PRA. "They have their own method of interpretation of international law", commented the Angolan minister.[27] Meanwhile, Finnish communists and youth put pressure on the government on the issue of recognition.

In Sweden dos Santos met the Minister of Foreign Affairs and the Minister for Development Cooperation and had discussions in the Swedish International Development Agency (SIDA) "in an atmosphere of mutual understanding". They were "watching the developments in Angola". We could feel that he was not happy with the delay of recognition by Stockholm as well (it happened only on 18 February), but he nevertheless underlined: "For us it is important that they support us and not the other side." Dos Santos hoped that the admission of Angola into the Organisation of African Unity would exert a great influence on the position of the Nordic countries.

In spite of the limitations, one should not underestimate the positive aspects of Swedish policy towards Angola. Thus, on 4 February, on the anniversary of the 1961 uprising, Olaf Palme published an article under a clear-cut title, "The war in Angola: Continuation of the liberation struggle", in a leading Swedish newspaper, *Dagens Nyheter*. In particular he wrote: "It is important to remember that the war waged in Angola is not between 'the Free World' and 'Communism' [and] that it must not in a prejudiced way be viewed on the basis of the clichés of the Cold War or from the perspective of the conflict between the super powers." However, in the same article he insisted that Stockholm was critical of "massive military support" to the MPLA from the Soviet Union.[28]

Among practical issues we discussed with the Angolan Minister of Foreign Affairs, special attention was paid to preparations for the Solidarity Conference scheduled in Luanda for the first days of February. Dos Santos called for broad participation, especially from the Western countries, "of more or less progressive people".[29] In his turn

Alexander Dzassokhov, who was to lead the Soviet delegation to the conference, expressed the hope that African political organisations, including some ruling parties, would take a more definite position than their governments.[30]

The conference, whose organisation was greatly facilitated by the Soviet and GDR Solidarity Committees, was a great success. Eighty-one delegations came from abroad.[31] The MPLA leadership called it "one of our greatest victories"; indeed, soon after it "the stream of recognition" became rapid – by 20 February 1976, 40 African countries had recognised the PRA, though the main reason for this was, of course, the successes on the battlefield.

For the Soviets in those days criticism of China by conference participants was of special importance. Its negative role was mentioned in a resolution and Neto himself mentioned in his speech that only one socialist country remained in the "unnatural alliance" (of Angola's enemies).[32]

The situation concerning the Soviet delegation to the conference was quite serious. Many years later Dzassokhov rather colourfully described his experience in Luanda:

The KGB *resident* [station chief] warned me about a possible attempt to abduct me and the head of the Cuban delegation. It was quite compatible with the logics of our rivals' behaviour ...

As soon as it became known that they were "hunting" for us, trying to eliminate or abduct us, neither at breakfast nor at lunch, or in the intervals between them, could I see any member of the Soviet delegation next to me, apart from Ivan Plakhin, a GRU general, and Vikenty Matveev, a political writer from *Izvestia* newspaper. All the other members of the delegation would no longer come close to me. They thought: who knows what may happen – they will abduct Dzassokhov and us in addition. But Plakhin Ivan, I believe, Fyodorovich [his patrimonial name was Fedotovich], was a man of such an open Russian soul, that he would never leave me alone. And he did it inconspicuously, without pathetic sentimentalism. Besides I got to know that he was one of the subordinates of Hadzhi Mamsurov[33] in military counter-intelligence.[34]

Later in the same month, February, Moscow welcomed the foreign guests of the CPSU 24th Congress. Among them was a delegation from the MPLA, which visited the Solidarity Committee, just as many others, but its composition requires special mention in this discussion. Naturally, the CPSU invitation was addressed to the top leadership of the MPLA. However, understandably, under the conditions of war, Neto could not come. Instead the delegation was headed by Alves Batista, a Politburo member and Minister of Internal Administration, better known as Nito Alves, who would soon play a tragic role in the history of his country and even affect Luanda's relations with Moscow.

Alves acted inside Angola during the liberation struggle and was practically unknown in Moscow before Angola's independence, but as a representative of the fighting Angola he received an exceptionally warm welcome. When we met him at the Solidarity Committee, Alves spoke in particular about a new law on "people's power", "opening the transitional period to the building of socialism",[35] about new structures to be formed at different levels. In his words, the MPLA was trying "to use the laws of dialectical and historical materialism" while establishing a socialist economy, which would include "maximum limitation of tendencies to develop a private sector".[36] He believed that with the establishment of the system of studying Marxism-Leninism, "step by step, in ten years' time tribalism will disappear in Angola". He ended his speech at the congress with the words "Long live world socialism!"[37]

Then, in May 1976, Lopo da Nascimento, the first Angolan Prime Minister and MPLA Politburo member, visited Moscow as head of a governmental delegation and signed a number of bilateral agreements. He was followed by the "party and government delegation" headed by Agostinho Neto who, on 8 October 1976, signed the Treaty of Friendship and Co-operation between the USSR and PRA, as well as the agreement on co-operation between the MPLA and the CPSU.

5
Troubles Again

In fact co-operation between the parties under the new conditions began even before the 1976 agreement. In July 1976 a group of Soviet party officials, which was headed by Valery Kharazov, Second Secretary of the Communist Party CC in the (then) Soviet republic of Lithuania, and included Petr Manchkha and Dr Boris Petruk from the International Department, came to Luanda as consultants.

Before their departure for Luanda, these officials met Boris Ponomarev. His expectations were rather high: "The party in Angola should be an initiator of Marxist-Leninist parties on the African continent." He called on the members of the group to acquaint themselves with "the history of the struggle, led by Neto".[1] Speaking about MPLA leaders, he praised Lopo do Nascimento, who impressed the Soviets during his visit to Moscow a month earlier as a "well-trained and clever man, not an extremist".

The Party should not be created in the same way as ours: the people are not ready, propaganda was conducted against communism, and this will strain relations with imperialist states. Brezhnev told them [probably to Lopo do Nascimento]: "Three main questions: strengthen the people's power from top to bottom ... create a party, make the masses feel the results of the new rule, put the economy right."[2]

Ponomarev instructed the group to help Angolans with advice, taking into account local conditions: "Advise, but do not impose. [Tell them] We came to assist but the decision is yours." He specifically warned them about the "moods of dependants": "We can't help everybody. We are assisting at the limit of our capacity."

During their stay in Angola, the group visited a number of provinces and met several top MPLA leaders. The nature of the discussions deserves our attention. In particular, on 12 July 1976 Lucio Lara, a member of the MPLA Politburo and Central Committee Secretary, had a long (three hours!) working lunch with the Soviet group. A broad range of issues was discussed. Lara stated that the formation of a "vanguard party" in Angola was an urgent necessity. He underlined that the idea was not to reorganise the MPLA into a party, but to create a party within the MPLA, and the latter would remain as a broad movement of people's masses.[3]

In his opinion this new party had to be a party of the working class, but, though Marxism-Leninism would be its ideological basis, it would be a mistake to call it communist. After years of fascist propaganda many Angolans looked at communism with prejudice and this prejudice could not be removed overnight. Because of family traditions and social prejudices many active and committed MPLA members would refrain from joining the new party if it was to be called communist. Besides, Angola was surrounded by countries where anti-communist propaganda was intensive: strong anti-communist moods existed in South Africa, Namibia and partly in Zambia. If a communist party was openly proclaimed in Angola, South Africa and Zaire could make an unholy alliance under the guise of needing to protect their borders from the threat of communism.

Lara thought that time was needed to sensitise the people on the need of a vanguard party, to ensure middle strata that the party would preserve all the best traditions and aims of the MPLA: "We should not offend those who support all the measures of the people's government but are not yet ready to join the party, including members of numerous religious groups. Catholicism is regarded by the indigenous population as a religion of colonisers, but members of various African churches and sects such as Tokoism participated actively in the liberation struggle."[4]

Speaking about the difficulties Angola was facing, Lara noted that although the country lacked specialists, the departure of the Portuguese was a positive phenomenon. Most of them shared the Fascist ideology and in any case would not be the MPLA's assistants in building socialism. "If they had not left, we would have to chase them away, and that would set the world public opinion and especially public opinion in Portugal against us."

As for the possible results of the group's work in Angola, Lara was somewhat cautious: together with Angolan comrades they could prepare some draft documents on the new party's programme or status, or "materials which would later prove useful for the preparation of such documents".[5]

The discussion with Lara continued on 6 August. This time he spoke realistically about the problems the MPLA faced: "We don't know our country well enough. We are not yet able to run it. We are very cautious to draw a line of our actions." Among the problems, he singled out regionalism and, in particular, the situation in Huambo, where during UNITA's rule the MPLA "lost many cadres". "The party should be a national entity and not the party of one or two regions."[6]

Nito Alves also met the delegation three months before he lost his ministerial post. There was nothing, or almost nothing, in his words to indicate the forthcoming troubles. In rather rigid categories he spoke about classes in Angola, "a danger of national chauvinism" and the advance "from revolutionary democracy to dictatorship of proletariat". Just as others, he was of the opinion that the MPLA could probably remain as a front and a party could be created within it. Even when he criticised the fact that "hundreds became 'militants' in 20 to 30 days and now posed as heads of departments" he referred to the "MPLA Politburo's opinion" on this issue.

Only one point in his talk sounded alarming: "We should neutralise petty bourgeoisie, not to strangle it, but to stop its way into the party leadership … One cannot make a revolution with PIDE agents in the leadership."[7]

The MPLA congress took place in December 1977. There, contrary to previous ideas, shared by the Soviet consultants, the MPLA itself was transformed into the "MPLA – Partido do Trabalho" (Labour Party), which meant that many former members of the movement lost their "political home".

However, some months before the congress the relations between Luanda and Moscow had faced a new test. On 27 May 1977 some forces within the MPLA, headed by Nito Alves, who had already been removed from high party and governmental posts, arranged an abortive *coup d'état* under leftist slogans. Most of his supporters were MPLA members who were inside the country or imprisoned during the liberation struggle, especially the youth, who had not acquired experience abroad.[8]

Unfortunately many in Angola and beyond believed that Nito Alves in his conduct enjoyed the support of Moscow, especially of the "Soviet special services".[9] For example, Ciment writes: "Alves also had the tacit backing of the Soviet Union … ."[10] Why did they think so? Perhaps there were several reasons for it. Alves positioned himself as a genuine socialist, a left-winger, defender of *poder popular* – "people's power". Moreover, in his document, distributed after his dismissal from the ruling bodies, he referred to his discussions with some of the Soviet officials. The fact that units of the 9th Brigade, mentioned above, were used by Alves as a strike force could also have contributed to such claims. Another reason was Alves's visit to Moscow.

However, I believe that the rumours of Soviet involvement in "Alves's coup" were deliberately spread by Western circles, as well as some forces within Angola, which questioned its "too close" links with Moscow and exploited earlier differences between Neto and Moscow to convince the MPLA leader of its hostile intentions. Several Western authors accused the Soviets of at least "denying intelligence to Neto".[11] However, while this claim is repeated from one book to another, I have never seen any reference to substantiate it.[12]

The only "hard proof" was the appearance of Nito Alves in a Soviet documentary film seen by Angolan and other African officers who studied in Moscow in the early 1980s. Some of them regarded this fact as a demonstration of Soviet support to Alves, but the reality was much simpler: filmmakers just knew nothing about the tragedy of 27 May!

I also heard various stories from Angolan academics and officials: some claim that a counsellor of the Soviet embassy urgently left Luanda after the coup had failed, in a single plane that departed from Luanda that day; others told me that two officials had left before the Angolans came "to ask them questions". It is difficult to establish facts 30 years later in the absence of accessible archive documents, but all I have found to date is that just one junior diplomat did leave Luanda with a clear mission: to accompany Soviet women and children evacuated from Angola.

Anyhow, when Neto came to Moscow on an official visit in August 1977, he surprised his Soviet interlocutors with a sudden statement. According to Karen Brutents, former deputy head of the International Department, at the beginning of the Angolan president's meeting with Leonid Brezhnev and other Soviet leaders,

after traditional common phrases Neto suddenly turned to the theme of recent military mutiny in Luanda and, ignoring diplomatic nuances, said: "Here I came, because such a thing – mutiny – happened, and I wanted to find from you personally, has Moscow taken part in a conspiracy against me or not? Because, as I have been informed, many of your people were involved."[13]

The situation was aggravated by the fact that Brezhnev, who had already been partly incapacitated, instead of (rightfully) rejecting such an accusation, just began to read a text prepared for him earlier about "the good situation" in the USSR and "the expected excellent harvest", so it looked as if the Soviet side was evading an answer and was therefore confirming Neto's doubts! Only later that day one of the Soviets pronounced an "addendum", rejecting such a supposition and confirming that Moscow had not moved aside from its support to Neto.[14]

In any case Moscow's relations with Luanda survived this tragic episode in the history of the MPLA and independent Angola, but the Soviets still suffered some "casualties". According to Brutents, "Angolans ... claimed that some of our advisers were involved in the intrigues of the Angolan military against Neto as a weak and hesitating man, etc. As a result the Soviet military representative in Luanda, N. Dubenko, was recalled."[15] To be exact, not only the "military" took part in Alves's coup; besides, Dubenko's name was Alexey, and it looks as if he became a scapegoat, although after his return to Moscow until his untimely death he continued his service in the Ministry of Defence, dealing with liberation movements.[16]

One more fact has been exploited by the enemies of Angolan-Soviet co-operation. This is the death of Agostinho Neto in Moscow on 10 September 1979. Slanderous statements followed from various quarters. Fred Bridgland, a well-known British journalist, whose familiarity with Western (and South African) intelligence sources is quite impressive (as distinct from, as we shall see later, his knowledge of Soviet policy and personas), writes, referring to the *Daily Telegraph*: "Western intelligence officials leaked their scepticism about the circumstances of Neto's death. They suggested that Neto was assassinated by a deliberate bungling of the operation so that a more pliable man, less likely to flirt with the West, could be installed in Luanda ... ."[17]

The truth, however, is that Neto's arrival in Moscow was a surprise even for those who were dealing with Africa in the International Department. Andrey Urnov recalls:

I still remember how all of us got flabbergasted, when he was brought to Moscow; for all of us in the International Department it was a complete surprise. Everybody understood he came to die. I am not at all sure that a Politburo decision to accept him for treatment had been taken. If such a decision was taken, it had been taken at the very top and at the last moment, after the fact.[18]

In any case it would have been worse if the Soviets refused to receive the severely ill Angolan president; they would surely have been accused of causing his death by withholding medical treatment.

6

"General Konstantin"

Soviet-Angolan co-operation was becoming increasingly all-inclusive, but in view of the situation in the country and in the region, its military aspect was the most important. The co-operation was mutually advantageous. Soviet naval ships could enter the port of Luanda. Moreover, the Angolan capital later became a venue of the headquarters of the 30th Operational Squadron of the Soviet Navy. In the late 1980s it consisted of eleven ships, three of which would remain in Luanda, and the rest were protecting fishing ships in the Atlantic Ocean.[1] In the opinion of General Valery Belyaev, who served in Angola at that time, "This squadron by the very fact of its presence was restraining the South African aggression against Angola. Besides, we had a powerful communication centre there which at any moment allowed us to contact any point on the globe, be it with Soviet embassies, consulates and contingents of the Soviet armed forces."[2] Soviet surface ships and submarines could refuel there and their crews could get rest.[3]

In addition, Tu-95RT reconnaissance aircraft of the Soviet Navy were allowed to land in Luanda. Flying from Severomorsk on the Kola Peninsula in the Soviet north to Havana, then to Luanda and back to Severomorsk, they "were giving a full 'picture' of the situation in the Atlantic".[4]

The involvement of the Soviet military in Angola is accompanied by many myths. In some Russian periodicals and on internet sites one can find stories by self-appointed "Spetsnaz [Special Forces] veterans", which are far from the truth. However, with the exception of the logistical unit, which supported naval reconnaissance aircraft and the headquarters of the navy squadron, there were no regular Soviet units in Angola. At some stage the dispatch of a communication battalion was envisaged, and it was already on the way to Luanda by sea, but for some reason or another it was turned back.[5]

The most important aspect of versatile military co-operation between Moscow and Luanda was of course Soviet assistance to FAPLA. The heroic actions of well-trained and well-equipped Cuban forces in Angola in late 1975 and early 1976 are comprehensively discussed, especially in Piero Gleijeses's excellent book. These events and the ones described below remain, quite correctly, a point of reference in the speeches of Cuban leaders. Much less is said about the Soviet role. Unfortunately it is the one least truthfully described in existing literature. Too often it has been grossly distorted; if initially many politicians and authors tried to portray Cubans as "Soviet proxies", a new tendency appeared after the "collapse" of the Soviet Union: downplaying the role of the Soviets and emphasising the differences between Havana and Moscow. It is now the right time to set the record straight.

Indeed, under pressure from Cuban forces and FAPLA, by the end of March 1976 South African troops had to withdraw from Angolan territory. The Zairean interventionist forces were defeated as well. However, this was not the end of the war, as many in Angola and abroad expected. After his visit to Angola in March 1977, Fidel Castro stated: "Things are going well in Angola. They achieved good progress in their first year of independence ... There are no grounds for dissatisfaction there." But at the same time he was concerned about developments in the Angolan armed forces: "The Defense Ministry is doing hardly anything to fight bandits in the north and south of the country. The bands are particularly active in the center of the country."[6]

Such a situation, aggravated by repeated attacks by the SADF from Namibian territory, created a need for increased assistance from Moscow. The Soviet *assessors* (advisers) in Angola carried out what used to be called "international duty", often in remote camps, in an unhealthy climate and under persistent threat from the Pretoria-led UNITA bands or the South African Army and Air Force. Initially they stayed in Angola on their own and only later were their families sometimes allowed to join them, depending on the venue where they stayed.

Many Western and South African authors who dared to describe the role of the Soviet military in Angola fell "victim" to their own ignorance or, possibly, too much reliance on faulty intelligence sources. They regularly mention "General Konstantin Shaganovitch" as a top Soviet commander in Angola. Fred Bridgland even took "General Shaganovitch's offensive" as the title for a whole section of his book describing military action in Angola. Moreover, "Konstantin Shaganovitch", according to Bridgland, was "a known chemical warfare expert", and this was used to substantiate the claim that the Angolan brigade that faced the SADF had "chemical weapons in its armoury".[7]

The same author also invented "Shaganovitch's subordinate 'Mikhail Petrov', first deputy in the Soviet Politburo in charge of counter-insurgency policy".[8] Perhaps Bridgland meant Army General (and future marshal) Vassily Petrov, Commander-in-Chief of the Soviet Ground Forces and later the First Deputy Minister of Defence. If so, Petrov was first and foremost "in charge of" regular warfare, and could by no means be described as junior to "Shaganovitch".[9]

"Mikhail Petrov" and "Konstantin Shaganovitch" are mentioned in one publication after another. A couple of "Sovietologists", Michael Radu and Arthur Klinghoffer, even claimed that after the "failure" of the Angola offensive against UNITA that "General Shagnovitch's career may have reached a premature end".[10] The same "experts" alleged that "Mikhail Petrov, the overall commander of the allied Cuban, South Yemeni and Ethiopian forces during the Ogaden campaign"[11] was appointed "second in command in Angola".[12]

"Shaganovitch" appears not only in a rather silly book by Riaan Labuschagne, who claims to be a successful spy for the racist Pretoria government,[13] and in a "masterpiece" of propaganda by Willem Steenkamp,[14] but even in an official presentation to the South African Truth and Reconciliation Commission by a group of former top commanders of the South African National Defence Force (SANDF) – Magnus Malan, Konstand Viljoen, Jannie Geldenhuys and Kat Liebenberg.[15]

The reality, however, is very far from these statements. With the growth in the number of instructors and advisers from the USSR, Major General Ilya Ponomarenko[16] was appointed as the head of the newly created Soviet military mission in early 1976. His (and his successors') official title was Chief Military Adviser – Adviser to the Minister of Defence. The next people to occupy this position were Lieutenant General Vassily Shakhnovich[17] (1978–80) and then Lieutenant General Georgy Petrovsky (1980–82).

For his excellent service during World War Two Petrovsky received the highest Soviet award – a Gold Star of Hero of the Soviet Union and before coming to Luanda he occupied the important post of Chief of Staff of the Transcaucasian Military District. But having left on holiday in 1982, he did not return to Angola, ostensibly for health reasons. So in May that year came a new GVS (*Glavnyi voennyi sovetnik* – Chief Military Adviser).

I hope I will not be accused of "great power chauvinism" if I say that in the Soviet Union there was a very popular and very unofficial series of jokes about "Radio Armenia" in the form of questions and answers. When I read stories about "Konstantin Shaganovitch" I recalled one of them – "Is it true that locksmith Abramian won 10,000 roubles in the state lottery?" a question comes. "True, quite true, however, it was not locksmith Abramian, but Academician Ambartsumian;[18] he has not won, but lost, not 10,000 roubles, but just ten, and not in the state lottery, but playing cards. Otherwise it is quite true ... ."

So, stories by Bridgland, Labuschagne, and others, are also "quite true"; however, General Konstantin's family name was not "Shaganovitch", but Kurochkin; he did not come to Luanda in December 1985, as Bridgland claims[19], but left in June of that year; he was not "a chemical warfare expert", but (prior to coming to Angola) had been for ten years First Deputy Commander of the famous Soviet VDV (*Vozdushno-desantnye voiska* – paratroopers).[20] Otherwise it is quite true ...

At the same time Bridgland (and his friends) grossly miscalculated the number of Soviet military personnel in Angola: "Intelligence agencies estimated that Shaganovitch had about 950 fellow Soviets in command and training posts in Angola",[21] while the man in charge of them, General Kurochkin, said that the strength of "the Soviet advisory apparatus" he had headed was "about 2,000 persons".[22]

Stephen Ellis, a British academic (and a former editor of the *African Confidential*) and his co-author, a renegade from the African National Congress (ANC) and SACP who used an ambitious (and deceiving) pen-name "Sechaba" (meaning "People") improved Bridgland's story: they claimed in their *Comrades against Apartheid* that "a Soviet General Konstantin Shaganovitch" supervised "in part" "the Angolan government offensive against the SADF-backed UNITA in September 1987".[23] Indeed, "General Konstantin" arrived in Angola that year for a short time at the head of a group of 17 Soviet officers, but only later, after the failure of that offensive, and his mission was somewhat in the nature of damage control.[24]

So it seems that Bridgland, Ellis, "Sechaba" and their followers performed a miracle: they managed to merge a deceased person, Vassily Shakhnovich, with the living Konstantin Kurochkin! All these "creators" of "Konstantin Shaganovitch" have one thing in common: none of them indicate a source of that "wonder". Yet it cannot be anything else but faulty intelligence supplied by Pretoria and/or its

Western partners. Faulty indeed, because Soviet documents captured by South Africans during their invasion into Angola in August 1981, shared by them with the US authorities and finally published as an addendum to the report by Senator Denton, chairperson of the "Sub-committee on Terrorism" contain a reference to "Chief Military Adviser in the People's Republic of Angola Lieutenant General V. Shakhnovich", dated April 1980.[25] Alas, the authors in question did not care about primary documents; they preferred to rely on their informants.

An "improved" version was published by a traitor, former Cuban Air Force Brigadier General Rafael del Pino, who fled to the USA. He wrote about "Army General Konstantinov".[26] So this time del Pino "promoted" Kurochkin to a four-star general and his first name became the basis for his family name. Taking into account that, like every other turncoat, del Pino is now serving his new masters, we can guess that US intelligence information on the Soviets in Angola was hardly better than that of the SADF.

It is worth noting that the "creators" of "Shaganovitch" tried to connect him with del Pino, claiming that they worked out plans of operation together. However, the name of this renegade is mentioned only once in Kurochkin's notes: del Pino as general inspector of the Cuban Air Force came to Luanda in September 1984 to investigate a very unfortunate incident: three MiG-23s were lost in one day. One crashed after an emergency landing at Luena airport and two others lost orientation and landed on an untarred runway. The planes could not take off from there and the Cubans destroyed them to avoid their capture by the enemy. "General Konstantin" was angry: he told del Pino that instead of destroying the aircraft without consulting anybody, Cubans at least could have detached precious equipment from the aircraft and evacuated it by helicopter.[27]

As for "Shaganovitch's" expertise in chemical weapons: on the contrary, as we shall see later, it was South African troops that used them in Angola.

"General Konstantin", no doubt, was the most outstanding Soviet officer in Angola. Kurochkin headed the Soviet military mission in Angola at a very crucial period. Thus, just three days after their first meeting, Minister of Defence Pedro Maria Tonha "Pedale" urgently called him and, having informed him about new aggressive acts by the South African Air Force and Army in Angola, requested to move the SKR (patrol ship) *Neukrotimyi* (meaning "Indomitable") of the Soviet Navy from Luanda to Mocamedes. Moscow granted this

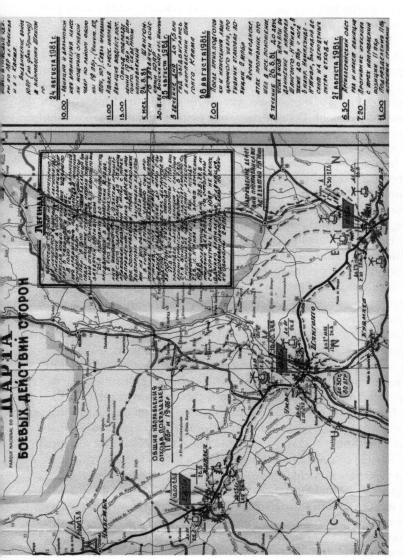

Plate 2 Map of combat actions, August 1981 (SADF "Operation Protea").

Source: Archive of the Union of Angola Veterans.

request without delay.[28] Similar action was taken later as well; for instance, in late July 1982 another Soviet naval ship, *Timoshenko*, (named after the famous Soviet marshal) was sent to the same port to strengthen its air defence.[29]

This state of affairs by itself makes the author consider "General Konstantin's" activities in detail. What is more, I had a chance to use a precious primary source: Kurochkin kindly proposed that I consult three notebooks, containing minutes or summaries of almost all the meetings he had in the three years of his service in Africa. They are especially valuable because they were written straight away, without any further "improvements", which unfortunately occur frequently in memoirs and "oral history".

Introducing Kurochkin to "Pedale" on 12 May 1982 and six days later to President dos Santos, Soviet Ambassador Vadim Loginov emphasised his rich combat experience acquired in Afghanistan.[30] The next day, after the first meeting with "Pedale", Kurochkin visited the Cuban military mission and had a comprehensive discussion with General Rohelio Asevedo Gonzales, its deputy head (the top commander, Raul Menendez Tomassevich, was in Cuba at that time), followed by "a small *brindis*" (party).[31]

Kurochkin met with Tomassevich a little later, and their discussion showed the similarity of views on the problems in FAPLA, such as a lack of "political educational work", a widening "abyss" between officers and men.[32] There was a certain "division of labour" between Cubans and Soviets: apart from their own combat units, Cubans took care of the forces destined to fight "bandits", that is, light infantry brigades[33] and units of the ODA (People's Defence Organisation) that is, militia, while the Soviets were attached to more regular forces.[34]

The degree of co-operation and mutual respect (at least at this stage) is evident from the fact than when Tomassevich expected a request from the Angolan command for a critical analysis of the situation, he wanted to co-ordinate his approach with that of Kurochkin.[35]

On 20 May Kurochkin was already moving: together with "Pedale", he visited the 2nd Military District (Cabinda) and the following week he went to the 5th District in South Angola.[36] In its centre in Lubango he met in particular the group of Soviet advisers and specialists working with SWAPO and discussed with its head, "Colonel Nikolay" (Kurushkin), "the future of SWAPO, its position in Angola and its interrelations with FAPLA".[37] Later he visited the Tobias Hanyeko Training Centre of the People's Liberation Army of Namibia (PLAN) and its regular brigade and was quite impressed. He liked "the high revolutionary spirit, organisation and discipline" there: "If FAPLA had five such brigades, the south of the country could be protected. For the present all this is absent in FAPLA brigades."[38]

Kurochkin's report to "Pedale" assessing the situation in the south set a model for their relationship. "General Konstantin" was forthright: a lot of armament, concentrated in the area, particularly in the 2nd Mechanised Infantry Brigade ("which will decide the fate of this area") in Cahama could not be used owing to a lack of personnel. Only 55 per cent of the prescribed number was available, and in reality infantry companies consisted only of 20–30 men. Here, however, morale was high enough.

Much worse was the situation in the 3rd Infantry Brigade, which had only ten to twelve men in each company and had not yet started engineering works after redeployment. Kurochkin also informed "Pedale" that the minister's earlier decision to deploy the 11th Infantry Brigade to Cuvelai had been carried out only in part. In reply, "Pedale" shared Kurochkin's concerns, and admitted that a number of his orders had not been executed on time.[39]

"General Konstantin" was glad to report to the minister that the supplies "of all kinds of equipment" from the USSR were carried out "strictly according to plan" and sometimes even ahead of schedule.[40] More problematic was the supply of "double-use" hardware, such as Ural and Gaz-66 trucks, to be acquired on less favourable conditions than arms and ammunition. The delegation, headed by "Pedale", signed a relevant agreement in Moscow in January 1982. The FAPLA command then asked to speed up the delivery and the equipment was brought to Soviet ports, but the Angolan authorities were not in a hurry to sign the appropriate contracts.[41] In fact, the automobiles for FAPLA were being acquired from eleven different countries![42]

During his first two months in Angola Kurochkin visited all military districts and got acquainted with practically all infantry and motorised brigades. On 6 July he had a chance to present both written and oral reports to President dos Santos. Just as with "Pedale", he did not beat about the bush. Apart from the issues discussed earlier with the Minister of Defence and Cubans, he mentioned the "theft of arms" – AKs, machine-guns, Strela-2M from the Military College in Huambo. "There is no proper discipline in this respect in the brigades either, there is a great leakage of arms [there] – as a result we are arming the enemy."[43]

Kurochkin emphasised: "An Angolan soldier is a good soldier. As for the officers, they need special attention. I am getting the impression that an abyss separates officers and soldiers. The higher an officer's post is, the deeper the abyss. When an officer reaches the level of a battalion or brigade commander and higher, he begins to consider soldiers a lower race." "They regard themselves as elite", commented dos Santos.[44]

"Such an officer allows himself to steal foodstuffs from soldiers", continued "General Konstantin". "He would be shot for such a crime in the USSR ... The prosecutors and military tribunals don't charge such people for their crimes [in Angola]", complained Kurochkin, though he made a reservation: "Not all officers are like that, there are good ones too."

Kurochkin suggested having monthly meetings and dos Santos agreed, "unless the need for an urgent meeting arises".[45]

Supplies, training and advice were not the limit of Soviet military assistance to Angola; an important aspect of it was sharing intelligence information. Thus, at the meeting with "Pedale" on 14 July 1982, when new South African aggression was expected, Kurochkin informed him about the composition, strength and expected character of operations of the South African forces deployed in Northern Namibia and the Angolan province of Cunene.[46]

The nature of relations between Soviets and Cubans in Angola is often distorted. Thus, del Pino claimed: "... all the military co-ordination with soviet assessors of FAPLA in Angola with Cuban troops were totally severed with the arrival of Army General Konstantinov [sic]. The problem, of course, was not Konstantinov, who was following instructions from the Soviet government."[47]

This is very far from the truth. The co-ordination, which began with Uvarov's visit to Henrique de Carvalho, continued for almost 15 years, even if in a number of cases the opinions of the two sides differed. When the Cuban Deputy Minister of Defence, General Abelardo Calome, and the Communist Party Central Committee secretary, Carlos Aldana, came to Angola in July 1982, they reviewed the situation comprehensively, together with Kurochkin and his assistants. All of them were united in their concern about the growing activity of UNITA and lack of practical action to counter it.

Calome gave such an example: "We pressed for the redeployment of four MiG-17s with four Angolan pilots and two Cuban instructors to Menonge to support operations against UNITA. The result is: the Angolan pilots are already [back] in Luanda. Angolan crews of Mi-8 helicopters are refusing to take part in combat action against UNITA."[48] He was especially worried that UNITA had penetrated even the territories that "historically always had been under the MPLA's control". In his opinion, while the Angolan leadership was worried by the situation, "a number of responsible officials" believed that as soon as the issue of Namibian independence had been settled, all difficulties for Angola would be over. However, in Calome's opinion, shared by Kurochkin at that stage, the danger from UNITA would grow.[49] "We can't imagine how to make FAPLA fight in such a short time", said the Cuban general.[50]

Both sides believed that the withdrawal of South African troops from Namibia would create serious problems for UNITA and in anticipation of this step it would intensify its actions. On the other hand, in Aldana's opinion such a withdrawal would cast doubt on the further presence of Cuban troops in Angola. It would be difficult to justify their presence there and "the question of their gradual withdrawal would be settled".[51]

Aldana was even more critical of the situation in Angola, if not arrogant: "It is not a secret to us that Angola exists only because the Cuban troops are here."[52] He suggested dealing with the question of contracts on supplies from the USSR on a trilateral basis. "We don't need to beat around the bush because we understand perfectly well that though we say that Cuban troops in Angola receive equipment and arms from FAPLA, we receive them from the Soviet Union, and its resources are not unlimited either", he correctly said, but still proposed to grant favourable terms to Angola, especially in contracts for helicopters.[53]

The Cuban representatives suggested holding a tripartite meeting of Cuba, the USSR and Angola at a high level to discuss the military and political situation in Angola. Kurochkin supported this idea, and it was agreed to convey a common opinion to the top leadership in Havana and Moscow.[54] Such meetings became regular events and were usually convened on a rotation basis in Havana, Moscow and Luanda.

When Cuban and Soviet representatives were invited to meet President dos Santos they had one more meeting to co-ordinate their positions. They expected positive results from a forthcoming meeting of the Angolan Supreme Council on Defence and Security. Aldana underlined that the situation in the country "will be considered by those people, who have not yet discredited themselves in this disorder, Lucio Lara, Lopo do Nascimento and others".[55]

At the meeting, held on 26 July, dos Santos's analysis of the situation was quite realistic. He attributed UNITA's successes to "relative supremacy in communication and better supplies ensured by South Africa, in particular the use of aircraft, including helicopters. The UNITA command achieved better control of its units than us." In his opinion UNITA used both guerrilla warfare tactics and, in the eastern part of Angola, regular and semi-regular units.[56] So the government forces had to change their tactics, to create mobile well-armed and well-trained units equipped with helicopters.

The meeting of the Supreme Council (and the preceding meeting of the MPLA Central Committee) also discussed the strategic issues and the majority came to the conclusion that in spite of the strengthening of UNITA, South Africa remained "the main enemy": it was trying to expand its economic, political and military influence over the whole of Southern Africa, using "traitors of people" – UNITA in Angola, RENAMO in Mozambique, the Lesotho Liberation Army, etc.[57]

Besides, the president described in detail Angola's talks with the USA on the implementation of the UN resolution on Namibia. He referred to the joint Angolan-Cuban statement of 4 February 1982,[58] which envisaged the possibility of the withdrawal of Cuban troops if Namibia became independent and Pretoria stopped open and covert aid to UNITA.

Both Kurochkin and Calome supported the idea of forming airborne ("landing assault") brigades and suggested that it could be done on the basis of two existing units to save time and resources. In this context Calome specifically expressed readiness to provide Cuban crews for helicopters, if the need should arise.[59]

However, some differences soon arose between the Soviet and Cuban military in Angola. General Tomassevich informed Kurochkin on 15 November 1982 that a special commission of the Cuban General Staff had completed its work in Angola and made recommendations, which concerned regular troops as well, which was the "domain" of the Soviets. Moreover, the Angolan side knew nothing about this work ("maybe, with the exception of Lucio Lara and 'Ndalu' [Antonio dos Santos Moises, newly appointed Chief of General Staff], but hardly so").[60]

"General Konstantin" was obviously offended by the lack of consultation with the Soviet mission – in his words, "such an action is at least incomprehensible with relations of mutual trust which exist between us" – and Tomassevich had to apologise.[61]

Apart from "ordinary" officers, in a number of cases Angolan top military commanders were sent to Moscow for military studies. Thus, having left his ministerial post, Iko Carreira went to the Soviet

General Staff Academy, where he completed a course in June 1982. Then, in September 1982 Colonel "Xietu"[62] headed a group of five Angolan commanders, sent to the famous Frunze Military Academy in Moscow.[63] However, most probably, as a former Chief of General Staff, he regarded this step as "honorary exile" and did not take his studies seriously enough. Later, General Konstantin had to report to the Angolan president that "Xietu" and some other officers had not passed the initial course in the academy and were using "all possible excuses", including MPLA meetings, to leave for Angola instead of studying. As a result they lagged behind in the programme.[64]

The type of relationship between Soviet advisers and the Angolan military is evident from the fact that they were present when top commanders made reports at the conference of FAPLA top personnel on 22–24 September 1982, but they were absent when these reports were discussed by the Angolans. "General Konstantin" was invited to make a presentation at the conference as well. He was followed by Iko Carreira, who specifically mentioned that "he heard nothing about steps to conduct armed struggle against South African regular units and UNITA bandit formations. Only the [Soviet] Chief Military Adviser spoke about it."[65]

After his return from Moscow, Carreira was appointed by President dos Santos to head a special commission on the reorganisation of FAPLA, which had to complete its work by December. The Soviets were requested to assist him.[66] But this work began rather slowly and besides, although the Angolan president asked Kurochkin's opinion on the final document, it took a long time to get it.[67] Then Carreira was appointed as Commander of the Air Force, but according to Kurochkin, he was hardly a successful one: "Iko Carreira agrees that there are faults, but takes no measures."[68] Indeed, the situation in the air force was often critical. For example, the cadets were starving in the Air School in Negaje and because of the poor health of eleven pilots of the new Su-22 fighter-bombers, only three could fly.[69]

Differences arose from time to time between Soviets and Angolans as well. One of the "stumbling blocks" was the question of payment for "grey" hardware, such as transport Mi-8 helicopters and trucks. By 1983 Angola had suspended these payments for two and half years; for two years payments had not been forthcoming even for the services of Soviet civilian pilots, though they were daily risking their lives. In fact, two civilian pilots of An-26 had by that time been captured by UNITA after an emergency landing and another plane crashed near Lubango. Meanwhile, Luanda made all payments to capitalist countries on time.[70]

When the representatives of the Soviet trade mission emphasised this fact at a meeting with "Pedale", the minister moved to politics: he spoke of the October 1917 revolution, which "illuminated the way to all people fighting for their independence and freedom, in particular, people of Africa", "great Lenin", "sincere and selfless assistance of the Soviet Union, which made revolution and the independence of Angola possible ...".[71]

It is hard to say to what degree such rhetoric helped him and his colleagues to get concessions from the USSR; it hardly affected the mood of Soviet trade representatives, but Moscow's political leadership was apparently more susceptible to such phrases. Unfortunately, even after the Angolan leadership had allocated financial resources specifically for paying for helicopters and transport aircraft, the central bank again delayed payment.[72]

Another discrepancy between the two sides emerged when in January 1983 newspapers in Lisbon reported that Angola had requested Portuguese military instructors to come to Angola to train commandos.[73] When Kurochkin raised this question with "Pedale", the minister explained that the instructors would be recruited from among Angolan citizens, who used to serve as commandos in the colonial army and, with the help of the left forces in Portugal, among Portuguese "progressive former officers".[74]

However, soon the Angolans admitted, though confidentially, that, apart from this, the Portuguese authorities had agreed to train up to 40 Angolan instructor-commandos in Portugal, but tried to convince "General Konstantin" that this "temporary measure" did not mean the replacement of Soviet and Cuban advisers, and the training of one or two commando battalions, at the utmost a brigade, would not prevent the formation of assault brigades, agreed upon earlier.[75] However, the Soviets were worried. "The Soviet side in no way is imposing its opinion, but there is a definite sense first to get acquainted with training of such units in the USSR", suggested Kurochkin to dos Santos on 16 February 1983.[76] Such acquaintance did take place, but the Angolans did not change their minds, even when the Soviets divulged to them that some of the Portuguese instructors had allegedly undergone earlier training in the USA and had been connected with certain American agencies.[77]

Several commando battalions were formed, but, according to Kurochkin, they were "very badly trained"; their individual training was good, but their performance as platoons, companies and battalions was very poor, and their discipline was very low.[78]

In fact the training of commando units by Portuguese instructors, recruited by "red admiral" Rosa Coutinho, began earlier when Iko Carreira was still Minister of Defence. When in early 1983 he was appointed as Commander of the Air Force, he again resumed the formation of special units, air force police.[79]

From time to time discussions between Angolan, Cuban and Soviet representatives touched upon rather "sensitive" issues. Thus, on 12 February 1983, General Tomassevich informed Kurochkin that the Chief of Staff, General "Ndalu", had divulged to him the decision of the leadership "to eliminate Savimbi physically inside or outside Angola". The head of the Cuban mission, having discussed the matter with his superiors, expressed the opinion of the Cuban side that this was "a purely internal matter of Angola". "General Konstantin" was on the same wavelength: "This question is not a subject for discussion; this is an internal matter of Angola."[80]

A high level of co-operation and mutual understanding between the Soviets and Cubans is evident from the fact that in February 1983, at the request of dos Santos, joint recommendations on the struggle against UNITA were worked out and presented to the Angolan president.[81] Then Soviets and Cubans jointly participated in drafting the plan of a major operation, approved by dos Santos as Commander-in-Chief.[82]

The concentration of all units that were designated to take part in the operation, in their initial positions, was ordered by 1 July 1983 in anticipation of the order by Minister "Pedale" to begin Phase 1 of the operation.[83] After its completion, Phase 2 was to begin in the province of Cuando Cubango, closer to the Namibian border. The mood was quite optimistic, which was reflected in particular by the Cuban leadership's intention to cut its contingent in Angola by 3,000 or even as many as 5,000 soldiers at the expense of logistical and other supplementary units.[84]

However, the beginning of the operation (as happened several times earlier and later) was delayed. On 18 July Kurochkin expressed concern about this to the Chief of Staff, with whom he had a very good rapport. "Ndalu" assured him that they would start in three days' time.[85] However, even a week later it started in only one direction.[86]

When Kurochkin raised the same issue on 19 July with "Polo", who had come again to Angola, replacing Tomassevich, the Cuban

Plate 3   Generals Kurochkin and "Polo", Luanda, 1984.

Source: Archive of the Union of Angola Veterans.

commander hinted at political reasons for such a delay. According to information at his disposal, talks were taking place between Angola and the USA, as well as South Africa, on the issue of Namibia and the withdrawal of the Cuban troops from Angola. A plan for such a withdrawal was allegedly drafted by the Angolan Minister of the Interior, Manuel Alexandre Rodrigues "Kitu", but the Cubans found out that its authors were actually Americans.[87]

After a short visit to Sumbe on 1 August 1983 Kurochkin met "Ndalu" the next day and described the situation in that area

Plate 4   Soviet Ambassador Vadim Loginov, Kurochkin, Angola Defence Minister "Pedale", "Polo", Angola, circa 1984.

Source: Archive of the Union of Angola Veterans.

(the 7th Military District) as "difficult": there was a lack of small arms, transport and communication, as well as uniforms. Even communication between the District Command and the General Staff was "practically absent". He advised "Ndalu" to visit Sumbe and to attach Soviet advisers to the district.[88]

On the same day General Konstantin described the situation in Sumbe to "Polo", but other developments overshadowed it. While the Angolan offensive was delayed, UNITA and Pretoria outstripped the Angolan command. "Polo" informed Kurochkin about "the most difficult situation" in Moxico province, which he had just visited. UNITA became increasingly active; 139 enemy radio posts were detected there. He even decided to ask permission from Havana to withdraw Cuban advisers (about 350 persons) from that area. This proposal worried Kurochkin, who believed that in this case the whole province, including its capital, Luena, would be lost (there were Soviet advisers with their families there as well). Kurochkin insisted that, under the circumstances, "not weakening, but increasing our support" was required. The Angolan command was transferring an infantry brigade to Luena and it would be advantageous to deploy a Cuban infantry or tank battalion there.[89] Indeed, "Polo" soon reconsidered his position and decided to deploy two battalions there.[90]

Nevertheless, the situation in Moxico continued to deteriorate. Having brought to the region heavy arms from South African-occupied Namibia and concentrated several thousand troops there,[91] by 2 August UNITA troops reached the airfield of Cangamba. Ninety-two Cuban servicemen were surrounded in the area, together with about 800 Angolan troops.[92] They successfully defended the town and on 9 August UNITA was forced to withdraw. Then, as had happened more than once, Pretoria came to help its "clients" by bombing the town.[93] In this situation the top Cuban command in Havana decided to change operational plans and to begin a new operation on 8 August, having sent more servicemen to Angola, namely a battalion of special paratroopers. The operation was to continue for a month and "Polo" had to inform the Angolan president that this would be the last operation in the area with the participation of Cubans.[94]

Kurochkin did not oppose the Cuban plan but expressed a number of reservations and comments. In particular, he thought that preparations for the operation should be better and it should therefore begin later, and that the brigades, stationed in Southern Angola, should not be redeployed to the north as the Cubans suggested.

Kurochkin also objected to the involvement of the SWAPO brigade in fighting UNITA. The issue of involving PLAN units was raised more than once. Initially the Soviets were quite reluctant to support this idea: "The use of the SWAPO units in fighting UNITA should not be a rule, though in some cases they may be pulled in operations to acquire combat experience."[95] "General Konstantin" was unyielding again: "This is the future of the Namibian Army and we have no moral right to use SWAPO in the struggle against UNITA. [More so, because] The border with Namibia is closed by South African troops and SWAPO practically doesn't receive any reinforcement."[96]

One of the issues that "Polo" discussed with Kurochkin was participation of the Soviet advisers and specialists in combat action of FAPLA brigades. Kurochkin explained that five or six Soviets were available in each brigade; their participation in combat action was "categorically prohibited", but they would willingly take part in preparing for the operation.[97]

However, this "categorical prohibition" was hardly always observed. Moreover, "General Konstantin" himself insisted that if an Angolan unit carried out a raid, Soviet *assessors*, attached to it, had to go as well. Later, in 1987, such an approach was endorsed by Moscow: by order of the Minister of Defence Soviet specialists had to be included directly in FAPLA battle formations, and not at the command posts as before.[98]

At the first stage of their involvement, because of lack of time and information, they used to have at best only a basic knowledge of Angola, but in due course a system of crash training was created. Having come from their units to *Desyatka* they would spend a week in training: eight hours of lectures a day and "self-preparation" in the evenings. Colonel Vadim Sagachko, who served in Angola in 1988–91, recalls:

It covered all relevant matters: the history and geography of the country, national peculiarities, operational situation, information on combat action, structure and arms of FAPLA and those of the enemy, that is, the SADF and armed formations of UNITA. The lecturers were officers from *Desyatka* itself, as well as from medical, logistical, intelligence and other structures.

Before their departure for Angola they were warned that their participation in combat action was "not excluded" and they should take care of their lives, be cautious and not "butt in" into wrong places. Moreover, several lectures were given by officers who had earlier served in Angola, some of whom had been wounded.[99]

In some cases, the line between advising and commanding was rather thin. Several months after his arrival in Angola Sagachko, who served as an adviser to the commander of the 10th Brigade, which protected a 53-kilometre section of the vital road between Menongo and Cuito Caunavale, was called to Luanda. He reported to Lieutenant General Petr Gusev, the GVS, how the defence of the road was organised and what enemy forces the brigade was facing.

The general was not satisfied:

Why are you loafing instead of eliminating the enemy? Why is there a UNITA base at a distance of 40 km from you? I order you to destroy it.
   – Comrade General, all forces and means of the brigade are dispersed over a distance of 50 kilometres, and I cannot expose the road.
   – You can borrow a tank company from the Cubans, put the infantry on tanks and destroy the enemy base by a powerful strike.
   – But the brigade commander will not act without an order from the Front HQ. To carry this out the Angolan Minister of Defence should give an order to the front commander, which should give one to my brigade commander. Comrade General, it is you who are an adviser of the minister. Give him an order to destroy this base.

- What are you saying, how can I give an order to the Minister of Defence of a foreign country?
- Comrade General, how can I give an order to the brigade commander of a foreign country?"

After this dialogue Sagachko was ordered to return to his brigade and not to appear in Luanda again.[100]

However, to return to the situation around Cangamba in 1983: it remained critical for several weeks. According to the Angolan top command, UNITA forces, about 4,500-strong, were supported by white mercenaries and South African helicopters. Moreover, they informed "General Konstantin" that South African Air Force planes had bombed Cangamba and carried out reconnaissance flights over Luena.[101]

As for Angolan forces in the area, they were under the command of Lieutenant Colonel "Ngongo", then the Deputy Chief of General Staff.[102] He was joined for a short time in Luena by "Polo" and Soviet Major General Valentin Gromov, who was "Ndalu's" adviser.[103] "Ngongo" recalls that the situation was so complicated that "Ndalu" called him at 02:00, and two hours later they, together with "Polo", went to Luena by An-26. In "Ngongo's" opinion, when UNITA troops began their offensive towards Cangamba, they showed that they wanted to take power in Angola; they wanted to advance to Luanda from there. By that time UNITA had formed so-called "strategic fronts", and South Africa provided them with artillery support.[104]

The activities of Angolan troops were directed from Luena. There were many casualties, but the ratio of FAPLA to UNITA losses was 1–10.[105] Moscow did its best to assist, thus 10,000 AKS, 1,000 light machine-guns, 400 Kalashnikov machine-guns and ammunition were urgently brought to Angola by giant An-22 planes, and more by sea.[106] Dozens of Mi-8 and some Mi-25 helicopters were arriving to be assembled in Luanda and immediately put into action. A vital contribution to the success on the battlefield was made by MiG-21s, which were "storming" UNITA positions, and even An-26 transport planes were used as bombers. Transportation of personnel and goods was performed by five An-12s with Soviet crews. Two more planes were sent in late August from the USSR to transport goods for FAPLA free of charge and another three for the Cubans.[107]

Kurochkin believed that it was the right time to take the initiative and to destroy the remnants of UNITA in the area, but the Cuban command changed their mind and decided to postpone the operation for 1984. Finally he had to agree with this postponement.[108]

During these difficult days UNITA forces numbering about 1,500 troops attacked the city of Sumbe (formerly Novo-Redondo), the capital of South Kwanza province, where hundreds of foreign *cooperantos* (civilian specialists), including Soviets, worked. However, they were rebuffed by 230 Cuban civilians, including 43 women, who only had small arms, and about the same number of Angolans, also mostly civilians.[109]

All in all, in spite of differences which arose from time to time, co-operation between the Soviet and Cuban commanders in Angola was very productive. At that period it was decided that arms and equipment would be sent to the Cuban troops in Angola directly from the USSR, and that they would also receive foodstuffs directly from the same source.[110] When a special high-level delegation headed by Jorge Risquet had a meeting with Kurochkin on 17 August 1983 in the midst of the rebuffing of the UNITA offensive, there was full agreement of views on "the assessment of the military and political situation in the PRA, the joint plan of combat actions for the rest of 1983 and for 1984".[111] But the Cubans were adamant, they said (though "in a diplomatic way"): "If the supplies [from the USSR] are not increased, the Cuban troops would have to leave Angola." They were going to raise with Moscow the question of sending more air defence hardware, a squadron of An-12s and even MiG-23s with (initially) Soviet crews.[112]A day earlier "Polo" was even more straightforward: "If socialism is needed in Africa, something has to be done, if it is not wanted, we shall leave. We shall not make it without your assistance. Angolans don't have anything and can't do anything."[113]

Apparently it was not so easy for the Cubans to deal with Kurochkin, a straightforward, resolute and experienced commander, but no doubt he won their respect. When General Carlos Fernandez Gondon, head of Military Counter-intelligence, came from Havana in late September 1983 with a commission, composed of more than 50 officers, he told "General Konstantin" that one of his tasks was to organise the work of the Cuban military mission in such a way that it would be compulsory to solve the matters between the Cuban and Soviet sides before discussing them with the Angolans. Furthermore, Gondon thanked Kurochkin on behalf of Raul Castro for his close co-operation with the command and General "Polo" in particular and invited him to Havana on behalf of the Cuban leadership.[114]

With the intensification of the South African Air Force (SAAF) flights over Angolan territory, the task of defending Luanda became urgent as well. By the end of 1983 a unit of Pechora anti-aircraft missiles was to arrive for this purpose and meanwhile this mission was performed by "Admiral Nakhimov", a "big anti-submarine ship", that is, a frigate according to the Western classification.[115]

The situation in Angola worried the Soviet leadership, both military and political. Kurochkin was in regular contact with Marshal Nikolay Ogarkov, Chief of General Staff, and Marshal Dmitry Ustinov, the Minister of Defence. On 20 August 1983, during the most difficult period, a special message of support from the Soviet leader, Yury Andropov, was delivered to dos Santos. It was brought to him by the chargé d'affaires, Yury Lipatov, and Kurochkin. The Angolan president expressed his thanks for "the feeling of solidarity" and voiced the intention to send a high-level delegation to Moscow to explain the new requests for assistance. He admitted that Angola had big debts to the USSR, but named the defence of the Angolan revolution as the main task. "As to other questions, including payments of debts, they will be solved later; Angola has great potential." He informed the Soviet representatives that Angola rejected the US proposal to discuss the schedule of the Cuban troops' withdrawal. "We are convinced that they have no desire to solve the problem of Namibia as well as other problems of Southern Africa. Until we find that they have a good will in this question, we shall refrain from other talks."[116] So if the intensification of UNITA's operation was intended to put pressure on the Angolan government, the effect was just the opposite.

The counter-offensive against the so-called "2nd strategic front" of UNITA in the centre of the country became imperative, and for this purpose all resources had to be mobilised. Thus, Kurochkin soon had to agree to deploy two SWAPO battalions in the operation towards Andulo, as well as an ANC battalion near Kibashe.[117] On 24 August he had a comprehensive discussion on this matter with Sam Nujoma. The SWAPO president informed him that PLAN units had been moved from Lubango to Malange at the request of dos Santos: "SWAPO is an internationalist and it wishes to help to defend the revolutionary gains in Angola. We want to take part in routing the enemy, not to be a retaining force, but to defeat it. For this we must be let into the plan of the operation", said Nujoma. He also asked to send SWAPO units to the area near Calulu where Namibian refugee camps were located. In reply Kurochkin had to say that the plan should be adopted soon and that most probably the Angolan minister and

Chief of Staff would inform Nujoma about it.[118] Nujoma's request was taken into account: while two battalions were involved in the counter-offensive, the third one was stationed near the refugee camp (or, rather, settlement) to defend it from UNITA's attacks.[119]

The complexity of relations between Cubans and Angolans is evident from "Polo's" request to Kurochkin not to give a single RPG-7 or a single anti-tank mine to FAPLA, because they were falling into the enemy's hands and being used in ambushes and the mining of roads.[120] On his part, "Pedale" was not happy with the conduct of the Cuban aviation. According to him, it performed combat sorties only in the operational areas of Cuban forces, but did not support Angolan troops, though both MiGs and helicopters were available.[121] Nevertheless, at that time, around September 1983, joint infantry Angolan-Cuban units were formed,[122] followed by a joint helicopter regiment.[123] Thus "Polo" and the top command in Havana agreed to incorporate 136 Cuban "advisers" in the ineffective Angolan 3rd Brigade. However, they were to be organised as a separate battalion[124] and therefore could hardly be called "advisers". Moreover, in response to the proposal of the Cubans, supported by the Soviets, a joint command post was created, housed in the Angolan president's residence and directly subordinate to him.[125]

Together with the troops of the Angolan 4th Military District and ANC fighters, the PLAN brigade was the most successful in the offensive. General Gromov, who visited the area of operation, reported to "Pedale" on 19 September that the brigade, 1,126-strong, was "ready to carry out any mission assigned".[126]

Joint involvement in strengthening the Angolan Army usually produced a real camaraderie between the Soviet *assessors* and Angolan commanders, though it often took time. Thus initially "General Konstantin" was not entirely happy with "Ngongo's" actions in Malange, blaming him for scattering means and forces there.[127] He even complained once about "Ngongo's" behaviour: the Angolan commander reduced twofold the number of new officers to be sent to 13th and 18th Airborne Assault Brigades (their formation was Kurochkin's favourite project), and "arrogantly" refused to give any explanation for this decision, since he was not "subordinate to the Soviet Chief Adviser".[128] But after some months of joint work Kurochkin changed his opinion entirely: he suggested "Pedale" and dos Santos create a new post of First Deputy Minister for "Ndalu" and make "Ngongo" Chief of General Staff. "However, the President commented it would not be easy to appoint 'Ngongo' to this post." "The 'Old Guard' does not have a strong desire to admit new members."[129]

A major operation with participation of Cuban troops was planned for early October in central Angola, but its start was postponed several times, and it began on 15 October.[130] It was regarded as highly important: in his message to the Cuban mission command Fidel Castro ordered it to gain a victory at any cost.[131] The operation was quite successful, both its first stage and the second, which began on 1 November.[132] A great role was played by the air force, which performed 1,004 combat sorties and 160 reconnaissance flights.[133]

This success made it possible to think about the next major operation intended to destroy "the first strategic front" of UNITA in Moxico and Cuando Cubango in 1984.[134] Meanwhile, another operation, named "27th Anniversary of the MPLA" and aimed at destroying "the remnants of the 2nd strategic front of UNITA" was to begin on 10 December, but again delays occurred, though "General Konstantin", as distinct from "Polo", insisted that it should start on time to forestall the enemy.[135]

Finally, the operation started, but some days earlier, on 6 December, Pretoria had launched Operation Safari, intensifying its intervention in South Angola. Most probably it had two aims: to lower pressure on UNITA and simultaneously to get more concessions from the Angolan government at the bilateral talks, which resumed with the USA as "mediator". Bombing of FAPLA positions was followed by attacks on the ground. According to Kurochkin's report to dos Santos, Pretoria concentrated up to ten battalions there, including three battalions "from Namibia" (from the so-called South-West African Territorial Force – SWATF) and two from UNITA, but the Angolan brigades were (initially) effectively repelling enemy attacks.[136] These actions vindicated Kurochkin's earlier reluctance to transfer units from South Angola. However, South Africans managed to occupy Cuvelai and to defeat the Angolan 11th Brigade there.[137]

The developments in this region again brought about some differences between Kurochkin and "Polo" The Cuban commander suggested withdrawing three Angolan brigades to the north, where air cover could be provided. However, "General Konstantin" thought that it would be wrong to leave well-equipped positions and that these brigades were powerful enough to rebuff even a numerically stronger enemy.[138]

Undeniably the resistance offered by the Angolan troops in late 1983 and early 1984 to new South African aggression was much stronger than before. General Konstand Viljoen, then the Chief of the SADF, called this response "unexpectedly fierce".[139]

"Pedale" supported Kurochkin's approach; in his own words, he could not understand the strategy of the Cuban command aimed at bringing all the forces back to the second echelon of defence.[140] However, this very strategy was confirmed in Fidel Castro's message to dos Santos, divulged by "Polo" to Kurochkin on 7 January 1984. Castro regarded the withdrawal of the Angolan brigades close to the area of deployment of Cuban forces (Jamba-Matala-Lubango) as the only way out. Besides, Fidel claimed that the airplanes based in Lubango could not operate over Cahama, Mulondo, Cuvelai (that is, over the area of fighting) because of too long distances and the superior nature of the South African Air Force.[141]

That message was a response to dos Santos's request for the opinion of Havana and Moscow on the situation. The Soviet reply was quite different: "By no means should the brigades of the 5th Military District be withdrawn ... By no means should the territories up to Mocademes-Lubango-Menonge line be given up to the South Africans, because it is fraught with political consequences."[142] On the contrary, Moscow recommended strengthening these brigades by creating two or three tactical groups, preferably with Cuban tank and motorised infantry battalions for each group. Besides, Moscow was of the opinion that friendly aviation could be involved in air combat over Cahama and Mulondo. "Pedale" supported this view.[143]

Kurochkin, referring to the request of the commander of the military district and "all the fighters of the 53rd Brigade", suggested cancelling the order of its retreat. "Pedale" replied that it had already been cancelled, though reserve positions had to be prepared.[144]

This retreat was advised by "Polo" after the brigade had been bombed; four soldiers were killed and six wounded. Kurochkin was furious: "'Polo' is interfering in matters that are not his concern when he gives advices on the retreat of the 53rd Brigade without co-ordinating with me."[145] (Indeed, this was a violation of the rule, established by Havana itself!) "The question of the withdrawal of the brigades of the 5th Military District to the North is outside the competence of the [Soviet] Chief Military Adviser and the Commander of the Cuban Military Mission. It must be settled at governmental level", he told the General Avila Truhilho, Chief of Staff of the Cuban Mission, on 9 January 1984.[146]

The Cubans were not happy either. As Kurochkin stated much later in an interview: "Cubans poached on me ... ."[147] In his discussions with the author, "General Konstantin" was very candid, though he used more polite words:

My relations with Cubans were complicated initially and, through their seniors in Havana they even expressed [to Moscow] their displeasure with my activities. Then a serious commission headed by Army General Valentin Varennikov, First Deputy Chief of the [Soviet] General Staff arrived. This commission [it consisted of 11 persons who arrived on 13 January 1984 and spent several weeks in Angola] visited all military districts, got acquainted with the work of our specialists and came to the conclusion that I was right.[148]

It was during that visit that I met both Varennikov and Kurochkin for the first time, though the purpose of our trip to Angola was very far from the Cuban-Soviet differences. It will be discussed later.

Varennikov and his team's mission to Angola is described in detail in his memoirs.[149] According to him initially, when the CPSU Politburo discussed Fidel's proposal on withdrawal of troops to the north, it was suggested that the proposal be accepted, but Varennikov nevertheless had to go and make a study of the situation on the spot. Having visited the forward areas, he found that the local Angolan command, just like "General Konstantin", opposed this idea. So he had to look for a way out – not to aggravate relations with the Cuban top leadership but at the same time not to make wrong decisions. He did find it: at the meeting with the Angolan and Cuban command, to the surprise of those present, he spoke in support of "Fidel's wise idea"[150] but transformed it into a proposal to create several echelons of defence between the front line and the area of deployment of Cuban forces. Such a "face-saving" suggestion satisfied everybody, including the Cubans. According to Varennikov Jorge Risquet told him: "I knew that everything, as always, would end happily. The Soviet comrades can find a way out even where there is none."[151]

After that Fidel Castro himself invited Kurochkin to Cuba. "The Chief of [Soviet] General Staff and in fact the Minister [of Defence], Marshal Ustinov, personally confirmed the expediency of such a trip. I spent a lot of time in Cuba [from 7 to 14 February 1984]; the Cubans warmly welcomed me. Fidel himself met me and I had a detailed discussion with Raul."[152] Raul Castro received Kurochkin at his villa [the general used the Russian word *dacha*] and later even sent him ice cream and cheese several times. "He had a good cheese-making shop there."

Kurochkin believes the Cuban command in Angola misinterpreted his position and his conduct in their reports to Havana, but during his stay in Cuba the situation was made clear and Fidel himself told "General Konstantin" that he had received wrong information.[153]

In Kurochkin's view the problem was that the Cubans were not eager to fight. They were in Angola, but they were avoiding participation in combat, and he felt it was necessary to compel them to be more active in the interest of the cause. However, Fidel explained the reason for such an attitude to him: "In your country the losses may be unnoticeable, but in our small country the human losses become known and have a great effect, therefore we are really trying to avoid losses in Angola."[154]

At his meeting with Kurochkin Castro underlined that the problems of Angola at that time were political rather than military. He was worried: "Angola began negotiating with the USA and South Africa behind our backs." He referred to his letter to dos Santos in which the Cuban leader stressed that as soon as Pretoria began withdrawing its

Plate 5   Fidel Castro and General Kurochkin, Havana, 1984.

Source: Archive of the Union of Angola Veterans.

troops from Namibia, Havana would immediately draw up a schedule of the withdrawal of the Cuban troops. In Fidel's opinion the moment was not the most suitable for talks:

Our forces are growing and the talks could be started in more appropriate conditions. It would be much more advantageous to conduct negotiations in a year or a year and a half's time: we would have MiG-23s, *Kvadrats* [anti-aircraft missile installations] and a much stronger air defence. The talks should have been interrupted as soon as South Africa attacked Cuvelai, just as Angola did after the attack on Cangamba … We dispatched a thousand more men to Angola … we applied for urgent additional supplies of arms, tanks and MiG-23s from the Soviet Union, we dispatched some arms from Cuba. And after all this the PRA government decided to negotiate … What do they want? To make peace with South Africa and to leave us to conduct a struggle against UNITA?

In this case the nature of our mission in the PRA is changing. It will not be justified, because our current presence enjoys sympathy, but with the departure of South Africa from Namibia our struggle against UNITA will subvert the prestige of Cuba. This will be interference in domestic affairs, and we are not colonisers … If South Africa leaves Namibia, we would be obliged to leave Angola within a year.[155]

Castro was rather bitter and very candid: "This is not 1975. We shall save Angola, defeat UNITA. But can we be sure that the history of Egypt, Somalia, and Mozambique would not be repeated? … We can win a war, and after that the Western countries will come, give $2 billion or $3 billion and bribe Angola."[156]

Raul Castro added even more bitter (and hardly justified) words: "They have already sold out SWAPO and the ANC, and now they are trading our troops."[157] Indeed, the rumours that Luanda had discussed the future of the Cuban contingent without Havana's participation were the most painful for Fidel and Raul. However, at the bilateral summit the next month Angolans insisted that no such discussions had taken place.[158] Nevertheless, some months later Chester Crocker, who headed African affairs in the State Department during Reagan's administration, at a meeting with the Angolans, again insisted on a "linkage" between Namibian independence and Cuban withdrawal.[159]

Fidel suggested that Kurochkin have a rest for some days in Varadero and Marshal Ogarkov gave Kurochkin his consent for this. It looks as if the Cuban leadership was quite satisfied with the discussions. Fidel invited him to have a rest in Cuba again, and even received him some years later, when Kurochkin visited Cuba as the first Deputy Head of the GUK (the Main Department of Personnel of the Soviet Armed Forces) although, of course, it was beyond protocol.[160]

On 14 February 1984 the final meeting took place with Raul (Fidel had to leave for Moscow to attend Yury Andropov's funeral). It is clear from Raul's words that the Cubans anticipated an earlier settlement in Namibia: "The maximum [in fighting UNITA] should be done this year, because next year we'll have to leave." However, Jorge Risquet, who also took part in the meeting, added: "If the negotiations fail, the situation may become complicated. It would be good if the Soviet combat ships could come to the area of Mocamedes more often".[161]

Apart from Fidel and Raoul, Kurochkin met other top Cuban commanders in Havana. Thus General Ulysses Rosales del Toro, Chief of the FAR General Staff, asserted that Cuba had saved Angola "from mortal danger" at least three times: in 1975 and 1976; during Nito Alves's mutiny ("fortunately no blood was shed", he claimed) and when the victory at Cangamba destroyed UNITA's strategic plan to split the country. He stated Havana's "principled position": the struggle against UNITA should be waged by Angolans themselves, while Cubans were to prevent the enemy's penetration through the Mocamedes–Menongo line. However, they assumed an "additional obligation" to help in fighting "the counter-revolutionary groupings" and involved about 7,000 men in doing this.[162]

After the visit the Cuban mission's attitude to Kurochkin changed and "Polo" lent a more attentive ear to his words. However, apart from goodwill, as "General Konstantin" admitted, he had particular leverage in dealing with the Cubans (and Angolans for that matter): most of the transport planes in Angola and their crews were Soviets (including, by March 1984, a dozen An-12s).[163] They were directly subordinate to him, and the supplies of both Cuban and Angolan troops depended on them to a large extent.[164]

Soon after Kurochkin's return to Luanda he and "Polo" had a meeting with "Pedale", who informed them about talks with the USA and Pretoria. From his words it was clear that a month-long cease-fire suggested by South Africa and its promise to withdraw troops from the Angolan territory would be at the expense of SWAPO: "They [Pretoria] think about getting rid of Namibia. SWAPO should be very flexible to achieve liberation ... South Africa suggested that SWAPO conduct talks with the [puppet] government inside Namibia. If SWAPO misses this opportunity now, it will face a lot of difficulties later."

"Pedale" also claimed that the question of the Cubans' withdrawal had not been discussed.[165] Then, on 21 February 1984, the Angolans informed the Soviets and Cubans about the agreement reached at the talks in Lusaka. It included a ban on the presence of SWAPO and the Cubans in the area in Southern Angola to be evacuated by the South Africans. A Joint Angolan-South African commission had to be formed to monitor the SADF's withdrawal, but according to "Pedale", the Angolans rejected Pretoria's proposal to monitor the movements of SWAPO jointly as well.[166]

However, less than a week later the Angolan Minister of Defence complained to Kurochkin that SWAPO was violating the agreement by sending several groups with the mission to penetrate into Namibia. Angola asked SWAPO "to retreat a bit from the positions occupied", but in "Pedale's" words, "they do not always inform us and sometimes deliberately give wrong information".[167]

The relations between SWAPO and Luanda continued deteriorating. SWAPO continued transferring its forces, even by truck, into the "prohibited" area. Some skirmishes took place and "Pedale" was worried that the situation could develop into hostilities between FAPLA and PLAN.[168]

However, the Cuban leadership's approach was quite different. Thus Fidel called joint monitoring of SWAPO units by Angolan and South African patrols "impermissible and incredible".[169] To influence the developments, the Cuban leadership invited dos Santos to visit Havana. His visit took place during 17–20 March 1984 and all the most important problems – Angola's negotiations with South Africa and USA, the struggle against UNITA, bilateral co-operation – were discussed.[170] By that time the Cuban leadership had taken a decision to withdraw its troops from Angola in 18 months after the South African withdrawal from Namibia, although it did not divulge this to dos Santos.[171] All in all, the talks with dos Santos, where mutual respect and goodwill were expressed, were assessed as sincere. The Cuban leaders were convinced that the Angolan president was honest and frank.[172]

It is worth mentioning that when dos Santos met the Soviet ambassador, Vadim Loginov, and Kurochkin on 26 March, his assessment of the talks in Havana was practically identical to that of the Cubans.[173] (An interesting detail: he explained to Fidel that among the reasons for talks with the USA and South Africa was a wish to avoid "the complete isolation of Angola by the countries of Southern Africa and Lusophone countries".[174])

The differences between the Soviets and Cubans in Angola remained. "Polo" once even told Kurochkin that he had "made anti-Cuban attacks" at the joint meeting with "Pedale", when the Soviet general suggested returning heavy armament to infantry brigades.[175] Moreover, though initially both sides agreed to begin a major operation in Moxico and Cuando Cubango during the dry season in August 1984, and this position was endorsed by dos Santos,[176] the Cuban command soon changed their minds. This change was prompted by UNITA's attack on Kibala, not far from Luanda.[177] It should be underlined that the Angolan command supported Kurochkin on this issue: "This operation must strike the enemy in its heart, break its management", said "Ndalu". At the same time he suggested decreasing the depth of the operation and ensuring the supplies of troops. He recalled "a sad story" when the FAPLA troops occupied settlements in these provinces and then "died there from lack of food and water".[178]

The Cubans' approach was mostly political: their decision to take part in the operation or not was dependent on the results of talks with "Kitu", the head of the Angolan team at the meetings with Americans and South Africans, who was in Havana at that time.

Anyhow, the operation in Moxico and Cuando Cubango started but soon the attention of the Angolan command and its advisers was drawn to the area of the capital: UNITA attacked several settlements and installations around it. Kurochkin believed that the enemy began an "unprepared offensive" towards Luanda exactly to stop the FAPLA operation and therefore suggested continuing it. "Pedale" decided to continue the first stage of the operation, which developed quite successfully. However, "Polo" had "an opposite opinion"; in particular he refused to involve Cuban pilots of MiG-23s in bombing UNITA's stronghold in Jamba, close to the Namibian border, referring to "a limited range" of this type of aircraft.[179]

One of the problems which constantly worried Kurochkin during his stay in Angola was weak friendly intelligence and especially the leakage of information to the enemy. Once he plainly said to dos Santos: "UNITA knows all operational plans."[180]

Talks with "Kitu" in Havana resulted in drafting a joint Angolan-Cuban platform for negotiations with South Africa and USA. No less important was the fact that the Cubans (as a rule headed by Risquet) now had a chance to take part in the negotiations,[181] initially "behind the curtain" and later in front of it.

In spite of the agreements, which had been reached more than once, in particular during "General Konstantin's" visit to Havana about the need to form a common Soviet-Cuban position, the differences continued. At the meeting with the Angolan president and military leaders on 29 September 1984, Kurochkin stated that combat action in the 6th Military District (that is, in the south-eastern part of Angola) had acquired "a classical character": UNITA was attacking in battalions, armed with Chinese-made submachine-guns, both its offensive and counter-offensive were supported by artillery. He believed that the last two weeks of the dry season should be used for a further FAPLA offensive.

"Polo's" position was quite the opposite: "The war in Angola is not classical. It has a guerrilla character." Such a contradiction was noticed well by the Angolan President: "Here we see two different concepts of the conduct of war." He admitted that UNITA had "found out the plan of operation", withdrawn its forces from the area under attack and entered the areas of oil and diamond production and coffee plantations. In his opinion the defence of economic projects became a priority, especially of the Benguela railway. So dos Santos took a decision to cease the operation.[182] Thus "Polo" won this time, though at the next meeting with Kurochkin he underlined that it was "the President's own decision".[183]

In spite of defeats by FAPLA, Savimbi boasted at the UNITA congress that by 20 December 1984 he would be in Luanda with 7,000 of his troops,[184] but he failed. Meanwhile, the tripartite Soviet-Angolan-Cuban consultations, which had become an annual event, were held in Moscow in January 1985, resulting in the decision "to strengthen the defence capacity, independence and territorial integrity of Angola".[185]

This decision was fully justified because Pretoria continued its operations in Angolan territory even after a temporary withdrawal of its units from Southern Angola. *Time* magazine wrote on 10 June 1985: "Embarrassment piled on embarrassment for the South African government last week after the ambush of a nine-man commando unit by Angolan troops ... ." South Africa was supposed to have withdrawn the last of its soldiers from Angola in April 1985, but the captured leader of the commando squad, Captain Wynand du Toit, during a press conference in Luanda admitted that his unit had been sent into Angola to blow up the Malongo oil refinery, jointly owned by American Gulf Oil Corporation and the Angolan state-owned oil concern, Sonangol.[186]

General Kurochkin left Angola in June 1985. At the farewell ceremony "Pedale" strongly expressed the attitude of Angolan comrades-in-arms to him: "Words are not enough to describe all the qualities which our friend and comrade General Konstantin possesses ... His assistance was invaluable to us ... ."[187]

Indeed, Kurochkin regularly met the Angolan president (and Commander-in-Chief) and at these meetings as well as at the conferences with top Angolan and Cuban commanders "General Konstantin" was always sincere in the assessment of the situation. The Angolan president appreciated such an approach. "The President likes you sincerely, he likes the fact that you reveal the true state of affairs in FAPLA without any embellishment", dos Santos's assistant once said.[188] Time and again Kurochkin's reports were more precise and truthful than information received by the Angolan top leaders through "regular" channels.

In appreciation of his service the President of Angola sent him a rather unusual gift, a Mercedes car. Kurochkin said later in an interview: "However, the [Soviet] Defence Minister strongly 'recommended' declining the offer. 'Perestroika' had begun in the country. So I haven't succeeded in driving the gift."[189]

7
Cuito Cuanavale and After

Kurochkin himself recommended his successor, Lieutenant General Leonid Kuzmenko, who was his colleague: before coming to Angola Kuzmenko was Deputy Commander of the VDV for combat training.[1] But to match "General Konstantin" was not easy for anybody. Two years later, in 1987 a new GVS came, Lieutenant General Petr Gusev, Deputy Commander of the Carpathian Military District in Western Ukraine. However the VDV people were there as well, the most prominent of them being Lieutenant General Valery Belyaev who, from 1988 to 1991, was the adviser to the Chief of General Staff and for some time Acting GVS. [2]

A major offensive against UNITA's 1st Strategic Front, so important in Kurochkin's opinion, was launched later, in mid 1985, after he had already left Angola. This operation, named "MPLA Second Congress", was planned in two directions: towards Cazombo in the eastern part of Angola and in the south-east. It resulted in the liberation of Cazombo but its main goal was a different one, namely Mavinga, and the troops were secretly concentrated in that direction.[3]

UNITA, supported by Pretoria, tried to keep Cazombo under its control and offered stiff resistance, and part of the forces, destined for the advance to Mavinga, had to be transferred there. Nevertheless, when FAPLA was already approaching Cazombo, an offensive towards Mavinga began as well. UNITA was taken aback and in September 1975 South Africa had to move its troops there. FAPLA's actions were hampered by long routes of supply and sandy terrain: to travel 100 kilometres, vehicles (which often got stuck) required up to 200 litres of fuel. Air support was complicated as well: South African forces acquired radar to detect aircraft, especially helicopters, at low altitudes. As a result, FAPLA's offensive was rebuffed with a massive loss of arms and equipment.[4]

It is worth noting that on 20 September 1985 – the same day the South African Minister of Defence, Magnus Malan, admitted that his forces had intervened in support of UNITA – Savimbi, at a press conference in his "capital", Jamba, near the Namibian border, claimed that his troops were acting alone.[5] In previous years regular SADF units operated in the Cunene province, not very far from the Namibian border, but in 1985 they penetrated much deeper.[6]

However, South African special units, as a rule posing as UNITA, were active in other regions as well. When they damaged two Soviet vessels and sank a Cuban vessel in the Angolan port on 5 June 1986, Moscow's reaction was stern: "South Africa is responsible for an act of terrorism in the port of Namibe in Angola. Actions of this kind cannot go unpunished."[7]

The next offensive against UNITA's stronghold began in 1987. Meanwhile, Washington's support for UNITA (and therefore, in practice, for Pretoria's troops) was increasing. In July 1985 the US Congress repealed the Clark Amendment, which had banned aid to UNITA.[8] If Savimbi's earlier visits to the USA were informal, in January 1986 Ronald Reagan received UNITA's leader in the White House, saying: "We want to be very helpful to Dr Savimbi and what he is trying to do."[9]

A new offensive culminated in the "battle of Cuito Cuanavale". Though much has been written about FAPLA's advance, South African interference and counter-offensive, Cuban reinforcements and fierce fighting near this town, this battle and its effect on further developments in the region remain points of controversy.[10] In the opinion of Chester Crocker, the decisive positive shift in the process of negotiation on a political settlement took place before the major battle started. For his part, a former top SADF commander claimed in his memoirs that his forces had no intention whatsoever of taking Cuito Cuanavale.[11] Fidel Castro, on the other hand, declared that it was a turning point: "From now on the history of Africa will have to be written before and after Cuito Cuanavale."[12]

General "Ngongo" believes that South Africa was especially interested in the airfield of Cuito Cuanavale. Having captured it and transferred its aviation there, South Africa, using UNITA forces in the central part of Angola (some strong UNITA units were not far from Luanda) would create a direct threat to the MPLA government.[13]

Further research is needed, and to begin with extracts are offered from the diary of a Soviet veteran, Igor Zhdarkin, who had been serving at Cuito Cuanavale for several months in 1987 and 1988:

10 October 1987

... On 1 October *assessors* of the 21st and 25th brigade returned from the operation on the river Lomba. There ... a misfortune happened. They were

Plate 6   Soviet *"assessors"* at Cuito Cuanavale, 1987.
Source: Archive of the Union of Angola Veterans.

'covered' by a shell from a high-velocity gun of South Africans. As a result Oleg Snitko, an interpreter, suffered a lost arm and a broken leg. He died in 36 hours. Others were unlucky as well: four were wounded and shell-shocked ... .[14]

27 November 1987
Today is hardly different from the previous days. [Our brigade is] under fire, the neighbouring brigades were under fire too.

There is dead silence on Angola on the Soviet radio ...

The enemy continued firing at Cuito. At 18:00 a salvo was launched at it by [rocket launchers] Kentrons ... I could not get through [by radio] to Cuito for a long time. Finally they informed us that shells had exploded right on the [Soviet military] mission territory. They haven't yet informed us about the results.

28 November 1987
All night and morning there was a tiring, exhausting silence: not a single shot, no sound of an engine, nothing.

Because of it we couldn't get sleep for a long time. Besides, we were worried about what happened in Cuito.

At 6.00 we found out that Colonel A. Gorb had been killed, an aged man, very quiet, kind and polite ... Everybody respectfully called him "Dyadko" ["Uncle" in Ukrainian]. He has spent over a year in Angola.[15]

Nevertheless, in spite of the fact that contrary to the 1899–1902 period the Russians/Soviets and Boers were on the opposite sides of the front line in Angola, perhaps it would not be too wrong to characterise their relationship as a kind of "love–hate". The same veteran, who probably was too kind to Boers, says:

South Africans are remarkable gentlemen ... I believe firing on our camp was not envisaged in their plans.

Why? Because before 11 March 1988 [a day when severe fighting at Cuito Cuanavale took place] they sent us an ultimatum: "Soviets, leave Cuito Cuanavale, we don't want to touch you."

The leaflets were in English ... The Angolans brought those leaflets to us: "Here it is written in English, we don't understand ..."

We informed Luanda about it. The order came from Luanda: 'You, over there, take care of your security. Don't leave the Angolan brigade, but take care of your security ...'.[16]

However, some actions of the SADF could hardly be regarded as "gentlemanly behaviour":

29 October 1987
At 14.00 we received awful news, At 13.10 the enemy fired on a nearby 59th Brigade by chemical shells with poisonous substance. As a result many persons got poisoned, four are unconscious, and the Brigade Commander is bleeding when coughing. The Soviet advisers in this brigade were affected as well. The wind blew to their side, and all of them are complaining about headaches (very severe) and nausea.

This news made us very worried; the thing is that we don't even have the most obsolete gas masks.[17]

The failure of FAPLA's offensive and further developments proved once more the existence of differences between Moscow and Havana, especially between their military commanders towards the military strategy in Angola, but, just as in the cases discussed above, they were differences between comrades-in-arms, and not between rivals.

These relations were rather different from those between Pretoria and UNITA. If one is to believe Savimbi, he had to pay South Africa for bombing and shelling "FAPLA junkets around Lomba": "At the end of the fighting they handed us a bill. It was huge and we asked our friends [the USA?] to pay."[18]

Moreover, I believe, Soviet-Cuban differences are exaggerated nowadays, after the political changes in our part of the world. Speaking in 2005, on the occasion of the 30th anniversary of the Cuban Military Mission in Angola, Fidel Castro quite correctly said: "Angola's post-victory [in early 1976] prospects without the political and logistic support of the USSR were non-existent." However, he also stated: "the Soviets, worried about possible US reaction, were putting strong pressure on us to make a rapid withdrawal. After raising strong objections, we were obliged to accede, at least partially, to the Soviet demands."[19]

Fidel continued:

This is not the right time to discuss the differing strategic and tactical conceptions of the Cubans and the Soviets.

We trained tens of thousands of Angolan soldiers and acted as advisers in the instruction and combat operations of Angolan troops. The Soviets advised the military high command and provided ample supplies of weaponry to the Angolan armed forces.[20] Actions based on the advice given at the top level caused us quite a few headaches. Nonetheless, great respect and strong feelings of solidarity and understanding always prevailed between the Cuban and Soviet military.[21]

The last sentence is quite correct, but the previous ones deserve some comment. As can be seen from the text above, the Soviets' role was not limited to advising "the military high command" and supplying weapons. They also trained thousands of Angolans, both in the training establishments and in the field, serving just as the Cubans as "advisers in the instruction and combat operations of Angolan troops". On the other hand, Cubans constituted an important element of the Joint Command Post and took part in the most important discussions with the Angolan leadership.

In his speech Fidel paid special attention to the fighting at Cuito Cuanavale and further developments:

Desperate calls were received from the Angolan government appealing to the Cuban troops for support in fending off presumed disaster; it was unquestionably the biggest threat from a military operation in which we, as on other occasions, had no responsibility whatever.

Titanic efforts by the Cuban political and military high command, despite the serious threat of hostilities that hung over us as well, resulted in assembling the forces needed to deliver a decisive blow against the South African forces ...

This time, Cuban troops in Angola numbered 55,000.

So while in Cuito Cuanavale the South African troops were bled, to the south-west 40,000 Cuban and 30,000 Angolan troops [and PLAN as well], supported by some 600 tanks, hundreds of pieces of artillery, 1,000 anti-aircraft weapons and the daring MiG-23 units that secured air supremacy advanced towards the Namibian border, ready literally to sweep up the South African forces deployed along that main route.[22]

The resounding victories in Cuito Cuanavale, especially the devastating advance by the powerful Cuban contingent in south-west Angola, spelled the end of foreign aggression.[23]

This time the SADF involvement was so wide in scale that it was impossible to hide it. Contrary to the events of 1975–76, Pretoria began stressing it. On 11 November 1987 this fact was admitted by General Jannie Geldenhuys, Chief of the SADF, and moreover, the next day Magnus Malan, Minister of Defence, declared that otherwise UNITA would suffer a defeat. Savimbi was visibly irritated, and claimed that the South African troops and air force did not take part in operations. However, apparently Pretoria, which suffered heavy pressure from the anti-apartheid forces at home and abroad, wanted to demonstrate its success, and, in spite of the statement by UNITA's leader, it publicised a visit paid to the occupied areas of Angola by President Botha, his Foreign Minister Pik Botha, and two more ministers, future contenders for the post of the National Party leader, de Klerk and du Plessis, who allegedly went there to congratulate the troops on their "victory".

Let us try to evaluate these developments. Indeed, when the Soviets advised the top Angolan command to carry out an offensive operation in the south-east, towards Mavinga and Jamba, they probably under-estimated the threat of massive involvement of the SADF. But this very involvement, an overt intervention by Pretoria, as distinct from 1975, gave the Cubans the "moral right" to cross for the first time in many years the Mocamedes-Lubango-Menonge line and to begin advancing to the Namibian border.

Ten years later, in 1998, Fidel Castro criticised the conduct of the Soviets: "The advisers ... thought they were waging the Battle of Berlin, with Marshal Zhukov in command, thousands of tanks and 40,000 cannons. They did not understand, nor could they understand the problems of the Third World, the setting of the struggle and the type of war that must be waged in that setting."[24]

With all due respect I have to say that this assessment is not fair. The Soviets advisers could and did understand "the problems of the Third World", the Soviet military were involved in one way or another in dozens of conflicts there, and in particular (unfortunately) they had to acquire very rich experience in counter-guerrilla warfare in Afghanistan.

As for tanks and cannons, finally the Cubans, according to another statement by Fidel, themselves concentrated under his overall command 1,000 tanks, 1,600 anti-aircraft weapons and artillery pieces, and 1,000 armoured vehicles in Southern Angola; and on 10 March, while the South Africans remained bogged down in Cuito Cuanavale, with the support of aviation they began advancing towards the Namibian border.[25] This offensive carried out by many thousands of Cuban, Angolan and SWAPO troops was exactly a regular warfare operation!

Jorge Risquet writes:

Given the nuclear détente agreements that were to be signed between Gorbachev and Reagan in the very near future, the act of sending 20,000 more men to Angola may seem contradictory. But the situation demanded it. We decided to inform them [the Soviets] of it as a foregone fact. In early December, the Chief of the General Staff, Division General Ulises Rosales del Toro, made the announcement in Moscow to Marshal Akhromienev [Akhromeev]. For my part, since I was participating as a representative of the Communist Party of Cuba at the Congress of the French Communist Party, where we know that the Soviet delegation was headed by the second in command, Igor Ligachov [Yegor Ligachev], I was made responsible for officially informing the Communist Party of the Soviet Union. In the end, after asking several questions, Ligachov said to me, "You people don't consult, you inform," slapping my leg as an affectionate gesture meant to soften his criticism.[26]

Ligachev was, no doubt, right. To consult does not mean to be subordinate, and consulting each other is a must for genuine allies. In any case it would be naive to think that by the time of the meeting in Paris, two weeks after Risquet informed the Angolan leadership about the reinforcement of the Cuban forces the Soviets would not yet know about it.

However, more important is the fact that these actions were not received negatively in Moscow, at least among those who were directly dealing with Southern Africa. Adamishin, then the Deputy head of the Ministry of Foreign Affairs, which was traditionally more "cautious" than the CPSU International Department, notes that at his meeting with Chester Crocker in Lisbon in May 1988 that the US representative was worried by the Cubans' advance towards the Namibian border. Crocker was interested in urgently stopping this "dangerous game". However, Moscow's interests were different: "not to hamper it, even help it in every possible way, but to see to it that it does not get out of control".[27]

Risquet further writes: "It was more obvious than ever [by May 1988] that the military situation has compelled the South Africans to accept a solution that would prevent the liberation of Namibia from being achieved through war ... ." [28] Adamishin virtually confirms this view: "We had a secret understanding with the Cubans that they would not cross the border with Namibia. But – it was also agreed upon – there was no reason to declare it publicly."[29]

Richard Bloomfield, a former American diplomat, in his by and large sober assessment of the situation in Angola (a rather rare case among Western academics) wrote in 1988, before the conclusion of the talks on the political settlement in South-Western Africa: "It is ironic that if the US-brokered settlement comes into effect, it will be in large measure due to the fighting ability of the very Cuban forces that the United States insisted for so long were the chief obstacle to such an agreement and to a decision by the Soviet Union that Angola was not such a strategic prize after all."[30] His is right in the first case, but hardly in the second one; thus the archive documents show that on 7 February 1989 the Soviet Politburo discussed "additional measures" needed "not to allow the weakening of the defence capability of Angola as Cuban troops withdraw from the country".[31]

Let us try to sum up. Did the "Cold War" affect the developments in Angola? No doubt. Much later, in 1995, Jose Eduardo dos Santos said: "The Cold War superpowers who once used our differences in their proxy battles are now trying to forget their old differences. But they must not forget old obligations. We look on them now as partners."[32] However, I believe that the history of the civil war and foreign intervention in Angola cannot be regarded as "proxy battles". True, close relations between Luanda and Moscow were of concern for Washington and its allies. Yet I would rather support an earlier statement Iko Carreira made in May 1976: "We have to understand that our opting for socialism has brought us into confrontation with imperialism, and imperialism is going to use every possible means of fighting us, from sabotage to the supplying of small armed groups [later big ones] to try to create instability amongst our people."[33]

The debacle of South Africa and UNITA at Cuito Cuanavale and the advance of Cuban, Angolan and SWAPO forces towards the Namibian border created a favourable atmosphere for the completion of talks on the so-called Angolan-Namibian settlement on conditions acceptable to Luanda and Havana and for the signing in December 1988 of the New York agreements. The Soviet contribution to their success was made mostly by Ambassador Vladillen Vasev and, at a later stage, by Deputy Minister of Foreign Affairs Anatoly Adamishin, whose published memoirs, *The White Sun of Angola* – a rejoinder to his American counterpart Chester Crocker's *High Noon in Southern Africa: Making Peace in a Rough Neighbourhood*[34] – was published in Moscow in 2001.

According to Adamishin, Washington's "programme-maximum" at the talks included not only the withdrawal of South Africans and Cubans from Angola, and the independence of Namibia, but "an additional prize" as well, that is "bringing Savimbi to power or at least power-sharing". However, the USA finally had to "lower the stakes". "To us it was easier in a certain sense. We always proceeded from the point that what is suitable for our friends will be suitable for us as well. We'll not ask for anything beyond it ... And we didn't ask ... ."[35]

Although Adamishin is critical of some aspects of Soviet conduct in Southern Africa, nevertheless he rightly writes:

If we hadn't come to the assistance to the MPLA, 7,000 miles from our borders [in 1975], who would have benefited from it? Little doubt, it would be South Africa ... What would be further developments in the region, if the racist South Africa had grabbed Angola in addition to Namibia? How many more years would its domination by force over the region continue? For how many more years would apartheid survive?

And 13 years later, in 1988 ... South Africa would not have left Angola of its own will, had it not faced the dilemma: to wage a large-scale war against the Cubans, to declare total mobilisation, to risk a lot of whites' blood or to settle for a compromise ...

It is clear that the Cuban factor was not the only one; the [Pretoria] government had all the time to look back at the situation in the country [South Africa]. But the Cuban military pressure brought about equilibrium on the battlefield, which was a certain forerunner of the talks to follow. However, the Cuban role became efficient owing to our support, including first of all, supplies of arms.[36]

In February 1986, at the 26th Congress of the CPSU, Mikhail Gorbachev emphasised the need for regional conflicts to be settled politically. Later many academics and politicians presented that step as something entirely new in Soviet policy. However, the Soviet Union had been involved in a search for political solutions in many military conflicts during the previous decades, inter alia in Korea, Vietnam, South Asia and the Middle East. In fact the talks about ending the war in Korea began in Stalin's days, in 1951! The main difference was that Gorbachev's statement was powerfully enunciated and was followed by lively diplomatic activity.

In fact the Angolan-Cuban Joint Declaration issued in Luanda and Havana on 4 February 1982, some years before the Gorbachev era, said:

If the selfless struggle of SWAPO, the only legitimate representative of the Namibian people, and the demands of the international community managed to achieve the true solution of the problem of Namibia, based on strict fulfilment of UN Security Council Resolution 435/78, and led to a truly independent government and the total withdrawal of the South African occupation troops to the other side of the Orange River, which would considerably diminish the threat of aggression against Angola, the Angolan and Cuban governments would study reinitiating of the implementation of the plan for the gradual withdrawal of Cuban forces, in a time period agreed upon by the two governments.[37]

Many people, especially in Africa, expected that the New York agreements and impending independence of Namibia would facilitate a political settlement in Angola as well. In June 1989 Mobutu managed to convene a meeting in Gbadolite, his ancestral home, which became the de facto capital of Zaire. There, in the presence of 18 African heads of state, dos Santos and Savimbi shook hands. However, either Mobutu actually misinformed them about the essence of the deal or Savimbi quickly changed his mind and withdrew his concessions, but hostilities continued until the peace agreement signed in Bicesse, Portugal, almost two years later, on 31 May 1991, which officially prevented the MPLA government and UNITA from acquiring weapons.

A discussion of the developments that led to Bicesse is beyond the scope of this work. However, one point should be emphasised: apart from the geopolitical changes and reforms within the Angolan political system, the peace process was facilitated by successful action of FAPLA against Savimbi's forces. In February 1990, when Cuban troops had already left Southern Angola, government forces carried "Operation Zebra" and finally fulfilled their task by capturing Mavinga.

In his second book of memoirs Brutents writes: "... if not for the Cubans, we practically would not prevent handing over Angola to Savimbi" (as a result of the 1988 agrement).[38] It depends who he means by "we". If he meant Eduard Shevardnadze and his collaborators, this is quite probable. In fact Gorbachev's Minister of Foreign Affairs on the threshold of 1990s was in a hurry to trade the interests of the USSR and its friends for the fictitious benefits of co-operation with the West and even with Pretoria. It was Shevardnadze who, in August 1990, gave his approval for a visit to the USSR by a delegation headed by Kent Durr, South African Minister of Trade, Industry and Commerce, which constituted a very serious breach of the boycott policy. It was Shevardnadze who, in December 1990, just a few weeks before his disgraceful resignation, met Savimbi in Washington first and foremost to please his American partners. To the best of my knowledge he took this decision single-handedly as well, without a preliminary discussion in Moscow.

Vladimir Kazimirov, Soviet ambassador to Luanda and then Head of the African Department in the MFA, writes that after that meeting,

vacillations nearly appeared in Moscow – whom to orient ourselves to? Our embassy [in Luanda] defended orientation towards dos Santos in defiance of the fashion of those days and in spite of various "democrats". Shevardnadze's assistants and even our press began showering praise on Savimbi, pointing to his intellect, sense of humour, etc. It reminded us how the Americans praised him, underlining in our discussions that he was quoting Rousseau in French, Mao Zedong in Chinese, etc. However, the champions of democracy could not but see that, in addition to Savimbi's cult, witchcraft, corporal punishment and other "democratic" pearls of the Middle Ages were flourishing in UNITA.[39]

Indeed, *Isvestia*'s correspondent reported from Washington:

The first meeting in history of the UNITA leader and a Soviet leader of such a high level took place in an atmosphere that both sides described as 'successful', and in addition to it Shevardnadze called the meeting warm and quite friendly. Jonas Savimbi, a young witty man, who knows well the developments in the Soviet Union and advances a programme, essentially, in the spirit of our *perestroika*, to all appearances did not make a bad impression on his wise and experienced interlocutor.[40]

Kazimirov concludes:

The end of Jonas Savimbi is well-known now[41], but somehow we don't hear from the other side of the ocean [nor from former Soviet journalists, I would add] repentance expressed to the people of Angola who for a quarter of a century had been bearing the full brunt of a destructive war due to the fanaticism of the UNITA leader, for so long accommodated by the USA and on their advice by other governments.[42]

Brutents continues: "In essence, they [New York agreements] meant our departure from Southern and Central Africa."[43] Hardly so: Moscow's military assistance to Luanda continued for at least two and half years, albeit in diminishing volume.

The "departure" began later, when even before the Bicesse accord Shevardnadze and US Secretary of State James Baker announced that the USSR and USA were prepared to suspend arms shipments after a cease-fire between the government forces and UNITA.[44] The implementation of this step dramatically changed the position of the Soviet military in Angola.

General Belyaev said later in the interview:

As a whole, it is difficult for me speak for the leadership and to assess it [this step]. We are military people and we were carrying out an order. Of course it was painful to see how our work of many years was collapsing. We already had a good knowledge of Angola, beginning from the theatre of operation and up to local ethnic specifics ... As for the Angolans, they did not accuse us of betrayal.[45]

Moscow's co-operation with Luanda in the military field stopped, only to be resumed, this time from the government of Russia, when, on the one hand, Savimbi's refusal to honour his obligations became evident, and, on the other hand, when in the mid 1990s Russia's foreign policy became motivated more by its national interest and not by a desire to please the West at the expense of old friends in other parts of the world.

Efforts to stop the war in Angola in the 1990s were made by various sides: the UN, the African states, and the *troika* of Russia, the USA and Portugal, formed after the agreement in Bicesse. But the military equilibrium did not help to solve the problem and, in the opinion of General "Ngongo", which I share, a political agreement between the government in Luanda and the armed opposition was finally reached after UNITA had lost the war and its leader was no more.[46]

Part Two

Mozambique

8
Moscow and FRELIMO

Just as in the case of the MPLA, the first contact of the Soviet Union with the Mozambique liberation movement was connected with ... poetry. Like Mario de Andrade, Marcelino dos Santos, who was in exile in Western Europe, took part in the Afro-Asian Writers' Conference in Tashkent in October 1958.[1] Describing further development of Moscow's relations with the liberation Movement of Mozambique we have to turn again to "Camarada Pedro"'s reminiscences.

According to Yevsyukov, the first information on organisations of Mozambican nationalists, though very limited began reaching Moscow in the very early 1960s. The foreign press published some reports on the Mozambican African National Union (MANU) and the Democratic National Union of Mozambique (UDENAMO), but they were not sufficient for an assessment of the situation and of the nature of these organisations.

As he recalls, one of the first Mozambicans who came to Moscow was Adelino Gwambe, General Secretary of UDENAMO. His host was the Solidarity Committee, but as "an interested person" Yevsyukov was present at all the meetings with him.[2]

In the letter to the CPSU Central Committee the Solidarity Committee's leadership emphasised: "... till present time we do not have any ties and contacts with representatives of the national liberation movement of Mozambique".[3] Taking to account that UDENAMO was the only Mozambican organisation represented at the conference of the nationalist organisations of Portuguese colonies in Casablanca in April 1961, it suggested satisfying Adelino Gwambe's request and receiving him in Moscow in June–July 1961.[4]

Having received consent from the CPSU headquarters, the Solidarity Committee sent a cable to Gwambe via the headquarters of the Tanganyika African National Union (TANU), inviting him to Moscow at a time convenient for him.[5] This visit took place in September 1961, and in the letter to the Committee, written during his stay in Moscow and signed by him and Marcelino dos Santos,

Gwambe requested support in several fields, including "immediate financial assistance" and organisation of military training.[6]

Yevsyukov writes very critically about Gwambe:

This man left a strange impression because of his extremes and limited worldview. It was not difficult to see through him. He came to the Soviet Union from the USA and not with empty hands. In spite of all his attempts to present himself as a genuine and single representative of Mozambican freedom fighters it was absolutely clear that we face a petty political adventurer, whose main aim was to misinform us and to receive more money.[7]

An interpreter who accompanied Gwambe described to Yevsyukov how in the first day of his stay in Moscow Gwambe refused to eat, he was only drinking *kefir* (a Russian version of yogurt). He explained it by the fact that his comrades in struggle were suffering from hunger and hardship and he could not eat because of solidarity with them. But by the end of the day he was hungry enough to eat his supper with a great appetite and never recalled his "hungry comrades" again.

Visiting the Armoury Museum in the Kremlin, Gwambe was impressed by old armours, hauberks, swords and maces. He asked the interpreter whether the Soviet Army has those weapons. When the interpreter, who apparently had a good sense of humour, gave a positive answer, Gwambe acclaimed: "It would be good to arm all our fighters with these weapons!" "Camarada Pedro" concludes: "UDENAMO General Secretary's visit to Moscow gave nothing to us to understand the national liberation movement in Mozambique. His inadequacy was quite evident."[8]

Nevertheless, Moscow agreed to assist UDENAMO, and as archive documents show, US$3,000 were allocated to this organization from the "International Fund" in 1961.[9]

Dr Eduardo Mondlane produced a much better impression on the Soviets. According to Yevsyukov, he came to Moscow several months after Gwambe, on his way from the USA to Dar es Salaam.[10] The Soviets already heard of him as of a serious person, an academic, UN official. During the meetings at the Solidarity Committee he described his immediate plans: after arrival in Dar es Salaam he wanted to unite nationalist organisations and to begin the active struggle for independence. At the same time he was not in a hurry to begin armed actions, he correctly understood that they should be properly prepared. In Yevsyukov's opinion, Mondlane's words were well founded, he knew the situation in his country well and his ideas were fully supported by the Soviets.[11]

Step by step, Mondlane's plans were carried out. On 25 June 1962 the Front for Liberation of Mozambique (FRELIMO) was founded, Mondlane was elected its President and Reverend Uria Simango Vice-President. Soon the post of Secretary for Foreign Affairs was taken by Marcelino dos Santos, known earlier to the Soviets as General Secretary of the Conference of the Nationalist Organisations of the Portuguese Colonies (CONCP), a successor of MAC. In this capacity he sent in a letter to the Solidarity Committee earlier, in January 1962, requesting "an annual subvention of ten thousand sterling pounds",[12] and the request was partly met, thus in 1965 that organisation received US$8,400.[13]

Yevsyukov writes: "The election of Mondlane was not a surprise for us. The prestige of this man was unconditional."[14] Under his leadership FRELIMO worked actively both on the international arena and among the population of Mozambique, while former leaders of MANU and UDENAMO mostly left the Front. In Yevsyukov's opinion Mondlane was a committed man, who was becoming a "convinced champion of the radical policy" and therefore became "the main threat for hostile forces".[15]

However, judging by the archive documents, initially the situation was more complicated. Gwambe and three other UDENAMO representatives were in Moscow in July 1962, soon after the formation of FRELIMO as delegates of the World Congress for Universal Disarmament and Peace. At the meeting with the Solidarity Committee, Gwambe, who had not received a leading post in the new organisation, severely criticised Mondlane.[16] Several former members of UDENAMO were also complaining to the Soviet Embassy in Dar es Salaam: "the leadership of FRELIMO had been captured by pro-American elements and all activities of FRELIMO are directed by the United States Embassy in Dar es Salaam".[17] They even claimed to have ousted Mondlane and Simango from their posts,[18] but finally an internal struggle in FRELIMO was won by its president.

Naturally, the Soviets tried to assess the situation and asked the opinion of their African friends. In particular, during a founding conference of the OAU in late May 1963 in Addis Ababa, Mario de Andrade told Latyp Maksudov, a Soviet representative in AAPSO: "Mondlane is an honest man, however he is not a politician, but a missionary ... Mondlane doesn't hamper [Marcelino] dos Santos's work, and here a lot can be done. Dos Santos is working, therefore FRELIMO exists and acts."[19]

Dos Santos himself was rather candid. He told Maksudov:

Everybody knows and we know that FRELIMO President Eduardo Mondlane is an American, but now there is no [other] man in Mozambique, who could lead the struggle and around whom the forces, struggling for independence could unite... Mondlane up to now is the only man – educated, who has connections and influence abroad. After all, he is [black] Mozambican, and not a white or mulatto, as I am. One should not forget also, that Mondlane is able to get money. True, they say, he is getting it from the USA government, but this money goes to the struggle ... We decided from the very beginning to let Mondlane be at the head of the movement, and we shall work inside the movement and guide it. Later [if needed] it would be possible to replace Mondlane.[20]

Earlier, on 17 May at the meeting at Dar es Salaam with a Soviet diplomat, Mondlane described the situation in Mozambique and international activities of his organisation. It looks like he was rather optimistic, thus in his words FRELIMO ("allegedly", as a diplomat put it in his report) "established contacts with liberation armed forces acting on the territory of Mozambique".[21] According to Mondlane, FRELIMO was "for contacts both with the West and with the East on the issue of Mozambique liberation" and maintained the policy of "Panafrican neutralism in the Cold War".[22]

Nevertheless, the embassy remained somewhat sceptical for a long time. In a paper on "The Situation in the NLM of Mozambique",[23] drafted on 24 September 1963 and signed by Vyacheslav Ustinov, its Counsellor,[24] it referred to claims of Mondlane's rivals and stated: "It is difficult to say to what degree all these accusations are correct. However, on the basis of discussions and personal observations an impression is formed that Mondlane is connected with the Americans and gets financial assistance from America."[25]

In spite of positive assessments of Mondlane by Oscar Kambona, then a Tanzanian minister and first head of the OAU Liberation Committee, who called him "a sincere and honest man, able to lead the liberation movement in Mozambique",[26] as well as by the ANC and SACP leading members, the embassy was still hesitant: it had an impression that "the creation of FRELIMO did not bring a noticeable benefit to the National Liberation Movement of Mozambique".[27]

The report continued: "FRELIMO President Mondlane due to his contacts with Americans and insufficient organisational experience turned out to be an unpopular figure. In spite of tentative attempts in the recent period by him and other FRELIMO leaders to move to the left, it is improbable, that FRELIMO, at least in the nearest period, will become a fighting organization".[28]

The Embassy concluded: "Mondlane forwarded a request to go to the USSR several times. We believe that it is not expedient to receive him alone. However, it would be desirable to invite him with a delegation of Mozambicans (for example, with Vice-President Simango, International Secretary Dos Santos) on an occasion of some festivities or a conference."[29]

As for practical assistance, the first request to receive FRELIMO cadres for military training in the USSR and to supply war materials was forwarded early, when newly appointed General Secretary of FRELIMO David Mabunda visited Moscow in summer 1962,[30] but no action was apparently taken due to a complicated situation in FRELIMO: Mabunda, who opposed Mondlane, was soon removed from his post.

Then, in a letter to the Solidarity Committee of 15 November 1963, Marcelino dos Santos (he signed it as Acting President, apparently in the absence of Mondlane and Simango) requested to receive 30 persons for military training, to provide financial and material assistance for refugees and propaganda, as well as medical treatment for FRELIMO members. FRELIMO leadership also wanted to send a delegation headed by Mondlane to Moscow.[31]

This time the embassy was receptive; it suggested inviting a three-man delegation and providing 10–15 places for training.[32]

According to Yevsyukov, soon after the armed struggle had been launched in September 1964 Mondlane came to Moscow to discuss assistance in material supplies, especially arms, as well as in training. He was accompanied by Alberto Chipande, future Minister of Defence of independent Mozambique. Mondlane introduced him as a man who made the first shot in the liberation struggle. FRELIMO's requests were met by the Soviets.[33]

It is worth mentioning that a restrained attitude to Mondlane was expressed by the Cubans as well. After his visit to a number of African countries, including Mozambique in 1977, Fidel Castro told the leaders of the GDR: "There used to be differences between us and the FRELIMO, going back to the times when FRELIMO was in Tanzania and Che Guevara had spoken to Mondlane there. At the time Mondlane did not agree with Che and said so publicly. Thereafter news articles against Mondlane were published in Cuba."[34]

While co-operation of FRELIMO with Moscow began developing, parallel to it, and perhaps at a higher rate, it developed with Beijing.

Apart from China's active involvement in Africa in the early 1960s, the "Tanzanian factor" apparently was important as well: relations of this host country with China were dynamic. From 1965, Chinese instructors were involved in training FRELIMO fighters in Tanzania. However, I also heard from my predecessor in the Solidarity Committee, Valery Zhikharev, who accompanied the FRELIMO leader during his visits to the USSR, that Mondlane spoke increasingly critically of the Chinese policy;[35] probably it was hard for him as an intellectual to reconcile himself with the excesses of the "Great Proletarian Cultural Revolution".

FRELIMO was lucky to have Tanzania as its solid rear base. "Camarada Pedro" writes:

I remember especially well very resolute and reasonable attitude of Tanzanian president Julius Nyerere to the problems of war for independence in Mozambique. Julius Nyerere was a clever and far-sighted statesman and, I think, simply a good man. Sometimes we asked him for advice and his replies were always business-like and sincere.[36]

However, these relations were not always rosy. Arkady Glukhov, who was a Counsellor of the Soviet Embassy for "inter-party ties", recalls that one day he met Mondlane on the beach, and when they had swum far into the Indian Ocean, far from anybody's ears, the FRELIMO president complained to him that of ten crates of Soviet arms, destined for his movement, the Tanzanians delivered only eight. He asked the embassy to inform Moscow but not to exaggerate the incident, because otherwise this channel of supplies could be closed.[37]

Initially Eduardo Mondlane was rather optimistic about the progress of the struggle for independence. Oleg Shcherbak, then a young diplomat in the Soviet embassy in Tanzania (and later an ambassador) recalls how soon after the armed actions began in September 1964 the President of FRELIMO told him that they would meet in Lourenco-Marques in a year and half.[38] However, the struggle became protracted and cost many lives, including the life of Mondlane.

Unfortunately I never met Mondlane – he was killed on 3 February 1969, a month before I joined the Solidarity Committee. The terrorists tried to cover their trail and, moreover, to put FRELIMO at odds with Moscow: the explosive device was hidden in a book on economics by a Russian prominent social democrat, Georgy Plekhanov, published in Moscow.

The murder of Mondlane opened up contradictions within FRELIMO. Some problems, however, were noticeable even before. When Bahadur Abdurazzakov, a Soviet representative in the AAPSO Secretariat, attended the 2nd FRELIMO congress in the Niassa province in 1968, he noticed the absence of delegates from Cabo-Delgado: a local provincial leader, Lazaro Nkavandame, defected from the organisation.

After Mondlane's death, at the FRELIMO Central Committee meeting in April 1969, Reverend Uria Simango, Mondlane's deputy, was not confirmed FRELIMO president, but became just a head of the triumvirate, comprised of him, Marcelino dos Santos and Samora Machel, the Front's top military commander.

In this capacity Simango, accompanied by Joachim Chissano and Candido Mondlane, visited Moscow in July–August 1969 as a guest of the Solidarity Committee. He was, of course, welcome, though the Soviets would have preferred to have discussions with Machel, who was regarded as the strongest leader in FRELIMO. Alas, Machel decided to lead a similar delegation to Beijing.

The FRELIMO delegation had fruitful discussions in the CPSU International Department, with the Soviet military, at the Solidarity Committee and other NGOs. In particular, it invited a team of the Soviet officers and journalists inside Mozambique. (This idea was realised, but some years later.)[39]

An informal meeting with Simango and Chissano, over a bottle of Stolichnaya in the Leningradskaya hotel, also took place, although on a personal level (is it because I have never been baptised?) I felt closer to the latter and not to the Reverend.

However, soon the crisis broke out. Simango distributed a paper titled "A Gloomy Situation in FRELIMO", and in October 1969 was expelled. Dos Santos visited Moscow in early March 1970 and informed us that the crisis was over.[40]

During the crisis Simango's supporters tried to appeal to Moscow; one of them visited the Soviet Embassy and told its officials about close relations of FRELIMO leaders with Washington. He claimed that after Mondlane's death an American diplomat visited its Headquarters to find out who would receive the US$100,000 annual allocation, destined for the late FRELIMO president.

However, Moscow fully supported the new leadership of FRELIMO. It was elected at the Central Committee meeting, which took place in the FRELIMO camp near the Tanzanian-Mozambican border on

9–14 May 1970; Samora Machel became its president and Marcelino dos Santos its vice-president.[41]

No doubt, Samora Machel was an extraordinary figure. Yevsyukov claims that he knew "the peculiarities of Machel's nature and the motives of his actions" well enough to paint a picture of this "national hero and a simple man": "He was a talented man ... a person of natural gifts, but he was lacking education, possessed, say, by Eduardo Mondlane ... He was resolute and capable of infecting people with his enthusiasm; he knew the crowd and knew how to influence it. He could speak to simple people and surprised experienced diplomats and politicians by his mind."[42]

"Camarada Pedro" recalls how during the march of the Soviet team with guerrillas in the liberated areas of Mozambique in 1973,[43] General Ivan Plakhin who was at its head, trying to please Machel, said "You are walking well, this is the way I imagine a President." Machel objected: "No, there will be an educated President in independent Mozambique." However, Yevsyukov suspected that Machel did think about the presidency: "In any case he [earlier] resolutely moved to the post of FRELIMO President."[44]

One of the issues we discussed with Marcelo dos Santos and later with Armando Guebuza, who represented FRELIMO at the celebration of Vladimir Lenin's centenary, was the preparation of the Rome conference, considered in a chapter on Angola. Moreover, Guebuza presented a profound analysis of the situation inside Mozambique. In particular he explained the difficulties FRELIMO initially faced in the eastern part of the Niassa province where the Portuguese applied indirect rule and tribal chiefs enjoyed absolute power. Quite a different situation was in the province of Tete where FRELIMO launched the armed struggle in March 1968. There the population was facing colonial authorities daily, especially those Mozambicans who worked in mines or on plantations.[45]

In the years of the armed anti-colonial struggle the relations between Moscow and FRELIMO developed steadily, though rather slowly, and it looks like their scope did not entirely satisfy the Mozambicans.

However, with the development of the armed struggle the Soviets increasingly appreciated FRELIMO's successes, Moscow's representatives saw it with their own eyes. Apart from a group of officers (and "Camarada Pedro") mentioned above, *Pravda* correspondent Oleg Ignatyev visited the liberated areas of Mozambique even earlier, in 1971. Large-scale training for FRELIMO fighters was organised in

Perevalnoe and other places in spite of many difficulties, especially due to inadequate level of education.

I myself visited Tropical Africa for the first time in January 1967 with a crew of an An-10 plane from the OKABON, the famous Independent Red Banner Special Purpose Air Brigade, with a mission to bring FRELIMO members for military training to Simferopol, and I will never forget how, on the long journey to the USSR, some FRELIMO cadres were reading big-lettered ABC books in Portuguese. Many of them were wearing just T-shirts, but even in the southern part of the Soviet Union where the Crimea is, January is a cold month. So when we landed, the bus, heated inside, was brought right up to the ladder and Africans were ordered to rush into it. Fortunately, the situation was soon corrected: a decision was taken to provide some funding to "equip" recruits from the African liberation movements, that is, to buy some clothes for them before their departure for training.

The leadership of FRELIMO was satisfied with a good quality of military training, but noted that the Soviets "wanted to show that they had fulfilled the quotas" and would not admit that some students failed.[46] A similar situation arose in the "Party school", that is, in the Institute of Social Sciences, when Mozambicans received political training. "By definition all those who were coming out were good."[47]

Quite a good level of training of Mozambicans before and after independence was achieved also in the Soviet universities, though allegedly sometimes, in particular at the Lumumba University in Moscow, "political considerations and the wish to please overcame the scientific assessment", and even persons with inadequate school training could receive degrees.[48] A peculiar feature of the attitude of the FRELIMO's leadership towards students was its efforts to keep them informed with the situation at home. Therefore the Soviets were requested to arrange trips of two or three students every year to Dar es Salaam.[49]

Financial assistance was provided to FRELIMO as well, though its degree raises questions about the degree of closeness between Moscow and the organisation. Thus there is no reference to FRELIMO in the accessible lists of financial allocations in 1960s, and in 1973 FRELIMO received just US$85,000, much less than the MPLA and PAIGC in tiny Guinea-Bissau.[50]

Moreover, Sergio Vieira, a prominent leader of FRELIMO in the years of armed struggle and later a Minister of Security, believes that the Soviet material assistance to the liberation struggle in

Mozambique was not always adequate as far as modern arms were concerned. They were coming in "small quantities – one battalion maximum" a year, with a lack of ammunition for previously delivered weapons.[51] Mozambicans were also sensitive that for a decade their host in Moscow was the Solidarity Committee and not the CPSU Central Committee or the top military establishment.

Meanwhile, the needs of FRELIMO units were growing, especially after the beginning of the Portuguese offensive in June 1970. It was given a pompous name – the "Gordian Knot", but this did not help them finish off FRELIMO units. On the contrary, the offensive was rebuffed with heavy losses for colonial troops.[52]

In 1971, FRELIMO fighters crossed the Zambezi River, and in July 1972, armed operations began in the province of Manica i Safala, which was regarded as an economic centre of the country. Joachim Chissano, who represented FRELIMO at the 50th anniversary of the USSR in December 1972, was very candid in analysing the situation inside Mozambique. He stated: "The enemy knows that he can't win a military victory." He mentioned the rise of the anti-war movement in Portugal, the low morale of the colonial troops, successes of the information campaign[53] waged by FRELIMO and the opposition forces in Portugal. He spoke about a growing mood in favour of a unilateral independence among the Portuguese settlers in Mozambique. Some of them were critical of the lack of protection from the Portuguese troops and stood for a white government but with a mostly African-manned army. They claimed that they were not against the independence of Mozambique, but against "the communist FRELIMO": "The Portuguese authorities will leave, and the African army will remain."[54] However, in Chissano's opinion such a plan could work only if Pretoria fully supported it.

He underlined that before launching a new front in Monica i Safala "the USSR and other socialist countries had rendered FRELIMO big assistance in arms and other equipment". He noted that modern arms were coming to FRELIMO "primarily from the USSR".[55]

However, Vieira counterpoises Moscow's stand with that of Beijing whose officers worked with FRELIMO in Tanzania since 1965 and recalls a night-long (from 21:00 till 5:00) discussion between the FRELIMO delegation headed by Machel, and Chinese Premier Chou Enlai in September 1971. According to Vieira, that same day Mozambicans were informed that a shipload of 10,000 tonnes of weapons and ammunition was leaving Shanghai for Dar es Salaam.

These supplies helped FRELIMO to rebuff the Portuguese offensive and then to launch a general offensive in 1972.[56]

In Vieira's opinion such a state of affairs reflected the fact that the "CPSU and USSR considered Africa quite a secondary issue".[57] The situation improved when Machel visited Moscow for the first time in 1970, and especially after his meeting with Victor Kulikov the Chief of the General Staff; new supplies included RPG-7s, Grads, recoilless BM 10 guns and Strela 2M, as well as more lorries, fuel, uniforms, boots, food and increased financial allocations.[58]

Why did the Soviets exercise a certain restraint for a long time? Was it because Samora Machel was regarded as being too close to Beijing? Or was it because of his critical approach to Moscow, at least at that stage?

Machel's reserved attitude to the Soviet Union was evident from his discussion with the ANC delegation headed by Oliver Tambo in 1974. He warned South Africans to be vigilant toward the Communist Party in their country because of its connection with Moscow. Though admitting "the decisive importance of Soviet aid to Mozambique", FRELIMO's leader "stated that the USSR and the CPSU were not genuine friends of the African people, were racist and were interested in dominating Africa".[59]

Such a statement shows a definite bias, and was quite probably influenced by Machel's close relations with Beijing at that period. These relations were strengthened when he visited China in February 1975 and was received virtually as a head of state.[60] The Chinese leadership even provided a special plane to bring him from Dar es Salaam to Beijing, and Mozambicans, always "protocol-minded", highly appreciated this fact. However, apart from protocol matters, Beijing's political stand perhaps was closer to Machel's thoughts. Yevsuykov believes that Machel's characteristic feature was "leftist extremism"; more than once he spoke about "commitment and respect to J.V. Stalin". Later, during his trip to the Soviet Republic of Georgia at the head of the Mozambican official delegation, at his request he was provided with Stalin's portrait.[61]

Besides, relations between China and FRELIMO reflected close co-operation between Beijing and Tanzania in that period: "... if the FRELIMO has done better in respect of Chinese aid, this is thanks to the influence in Peking [Beijing] of Tanzanian government", wrote an Indian researcher.[62]

9
Transitional Period

As distinct from the situation in Angola, by the time of the Portuguese revolution FRELIMO's leading role in the liberation struggle was undisputed. Earlier attempts to "resurrect" UDENAMO failed, just like efforts, initially supported by Zambia, to create an alternative to FRELIMO – the Mozambique Revolutionary Committee (COREMO).

Soviet supplies of sophisticated weapons played a role in bringing the Portuguese armed forces to the brink of collapse. In particular Strelas, which from 1973 had been used effectively in Guinea-Bissau, played an important role in Mozambique as well, as it put an end to the enemy's air supremacy: "Rhodesia stopped its air raids and the Portuguese [aircraft] were more or less grounded. Grad-P also was important."[1]

However, Machel's encounters with the Soviets in the period that followed April 1974 hardly satisfied him. Sergio Vieira recalls the discussion between Machel and the Soviet delegation in August 1974. At that time Moscow and FRELIMO's leaders disagreed on the assessment of the situation. The Soviets called for talks on the peaceful settlement, but the Mozambicans, in spite of the fact that the Portuguese government included progressive army officers, socialists and communists, continued the armed struggle. However, the conflict was caused not so much by the essence of differences as by their form. According to Vieira, the head of the Soviet delegation, a member of the CPSU Central Committee, instead of asking the FRELIMO leadership for their assessment of the situation, began the meeting by reading a message from Moscow, but refused to pass a written text to them.[2]

FRELIMO leaders were going to inform the Soviets about the progress of their negotiations with Lisbon. At the earlier meeting in Lusaka in June 1974, Mario Soares, Minister of Foreign Affairs and leader of the Socialist Party, conveyed Lisbon's position ("That was 100 per cent Spinola's position", comments Vieira), which insisted on a cease-fire while the issue of decolonisation was the last to be discussed.

The Mozambicans, on the contrary, were adamant that a ceasefire could be achieved easily if the goals of the liberation struggle were attained. Therefore they called for the recognition of the right to total independence, transfer of power to FRELIMO as the sole and legitimate representative of the Mozambican people and fixing the date of independence. They agreed to continue the talks only after the completion of negotiations on Guinea-Bissau.[3] It was clear that in that country the Portuguese would be obliged to surrender power to PAIGC and the FRELIMO leadership was going to use that as a precedent.

FRELIMO's approach at the meeting was supported by Otelo da Carvalho, who represented the Movement of the Armed Forces (MFA). Soon the new Portuguese government, headed by Vasco Goncalves, recognised the right for self-determination, and at confidential meetings with the MFA FRELIMO reached an agreement that was confirmed during another meeting in Dar es Salaam attended, apart from the military, by Soares and another civilian minister, Almeida Santos. It was decided to meet openly and officially in Lusaka and to sign an agreement.

So, according to Vieira, the Soviets "gave a lecture on the need for peace and said that we were jeopardising the democratic process in Portugal". Machel was visibly disappointed. He changed his mind and in short told them he believed that the delegation had come to congratulate FRELIMO on the successes of the struggle that even contributed to the fall of fascism, to say that "the continuation of the armed struggle was necessary to force the Portuguese right wing to accept peace and independence for the colonies" and "to tell [us] that the sacrifices of the Soviet people in supporting us had borne results".[4]

However, Andrey Urnov of the International Department recalls another version of the events: when Samora met the delegation he told them that FRELIMO fighters would "kill your friends", that is, the Portuguese.[5]

In any case it would be wrong to think that the Soviets' being in favour of a cease-fire meant the cessation of Soviet support to FRELIMO. What is more, at exactly the same time, in August 1974, a further Soviet military team entered Mozambique together with its fighters. It was headed by Colonel (later Major General) Fyodor Fedorenko and included two more officers of the "Northern Training

Centre". Their mission was to study the situation on the spot, and, having spent some days in Dar es Salaam, they flew to Mtwara, then moved to the main FRELIMO camp in Nachingweia and finally went by Land-Rover to Ruvuma River. They crossed it by canoe, accompanied by a team of 115 FRELIMO fighters headed by Sebastiao Mabote, the future Mozambican Chief of General Staff.[6]

They went into the territory that FRELIMO called "the liberated areas". Portuguese garrisons were still there in certain places and the group walked using trails from one guerrilla base to another, avoiding the enemy. The Soviets highly appreciated the organisation of these bases, which were tidy, with proper logistical and medical facilities. Apart from combatants they met local peasants, and some of them would walk for several hours to meet the team. Inside Mozambique they met Alberto Chipande. Once they visited a Portuguese stronghold, which had just been taken over by FRELIMO after mortar fire and an attack. They had a chance to see the enemy installations, such as a dugout with six layers.

The way back to the Tanzanian border was even harder; on the last day the team covered about 80 kilometres. They crossed the tributaries of the Ruvumo one by one on pirogues. In the Tanzanian capital they had a comprehensive discussion with Joachim Chissano and met Samora Machel. Around 25 August 1974 they left for Moscow.[7]

FRELIMO succeeded in their demands for a leading role for their organisation in the Transitional Government, which was headed by Chissano. Yet the situation in Mozambique remained very tense. On 7 September 1974, the day the agreement between FRELIMO and Portugal was signed in Lusaka, white settlers tried to prevent the installation of the Transitional Government by force, but failed. Then Uria Simango, who supported the coup, and his colleagues "went to Smith to ask him to invade Mozambique. He was willing, but needed the green light from Vorster."[8] But "Vorster refused to receive the delegation and made a public statement saying that he wanted good relations with Mozambique, he would not interfere and, besides, he wanted peace and stability in the region." At that time he "was involved in a so-called détente exercise with Kaunda and had made the commitment to respect the will of Mozambique (FRELIMO)". South African interference would mean putting an end to the détente. Besides, for Pretoria to attack Mozambique would mean "to confront Portugal, when the Portuguese government was very popular in the entire West ... Spínola was still the Head of State."[9]

This stance of Vorster was reciprocated by FRELIMO. On 18 September 1974, immediately after the installation of the Transitional Government in Mozambique, Chissano stated that FRELIMO did not want to start a new war and did not pretend to be a reformer of South African policy: "This job belongs to the people of South Africa."[10]

We were glad to meet Chissano in Lourenco Marques when we came there on the last day of April 1975 as a delegation of the Soviet Solidarity Committee. It was headed by Malik Fasylov, Minister of Foreign Affairs of Kazakhstan, and among the members was Andrey Urnov from the CPSU International Department. ("Camarada Pedro" could not come, because he was due in Angola at the same time.) But reaching the capital of Mozambique was not easy. After a long journey via Aden and Nairobi (we had to wait for a delayed Air India flight in Aden for several hours) we reached Dar es Salaam and there received confirmation that the FRELIMO-led Transitional Government was ready to receive us.

On 30 April we travelled to Lourenco Marques from Dar es Salaam by an East African Airways plane, which had to land at the Malawian airport of Blantyre. All transit passengers were requested to proceed to the air terminal and there a young police or immigration officer almost jumped in excitement when, after approaching various passengers, he finally saw Soviet passports. Most probably the Malawian authorities were informed in advance about our trip and his task was to "detect" us.

It took several hours to settle the dispute. The Malawian authorities insisted that we illegally arrived in Malawi and should be deported to Dar es Salaam by the next flight; they even took our luggage off the plane. A local representative of the airlines, a white man, probably from Rhodesia, declined to help and even accused us of violating the Warsaw Convention of 1929. But we flatly refused to stay in Malawi, and our position was supported by the Norwegian captain of the aircraft, who refused to leave without us and, as we heard later, even phoned the Minister of Foreign Affairs of the country to let us go. Our luggage was put aboard again, and the captain apologised for the delay "due to immigration problems". However, when we landed in Lourenco Marques we found that one of the film cameras we were bringing to FRELIMO was missing.

It was clear that Pretoria was shocked by the developments in Mozambique even though it tried to put on a brave face. When I switched on Radio South Africa on 1 May 1975, there were three main news items: "the communists captured Saigon", a top-ranking delegation came from Moscow to Lourenco Marques, and a South African sportswoman was refused the right to participate in a competition somewhere in Latin America. Switching over to the local Mozambican radio brought a further surprise: the "Internationale" in Russian!

On that day I went to a rally at one of the factories together with Luis Bernardo Honvana, a famous Mozambican writer and intellectual, who at that stage was secretary to the Prime Minister. He was driving a Volkswagen, having put a Kalashnikov next to him.

The FRELIMO leadership in Mozambique, in particular Joachim Chissano and Armando Guebuza, Minister of Home Affairs and National Political Commissar, warmly welcomed the Soviet delegation. A trip to five provinces was organised. We visited eleven towns and spoke on more than 30 occasions at various rallies and meetings. Unfortunately we could not land near the base in one of the FRELIMO strongholds in old liberated areas in Niassa. The pilot of the small plane of the EMAC Company chartered by FRELIMO made several attempts in three different places, but according to him what could be called runways were too uneven and too short.

Our short stay in Vila Cabral (now Lichinga) was particularly interesting. The administration there was still headed by the Portuguese Acting Governor and his compatriots were fascinated to meet the Soviets, though they hardly understood the role Moscow was playing in the world and its intentions. "Are you going to do in Portugal the same you are doing in Mozambique?" one of them asked us.

More pleasant was a visit to the villa of a Soviet graduate where we stayed. After getting a degree in agriculture, he spent several years in the bush as a FRELIMO fighter. He showed us pictures of himself and his Soviet wife on their wedding day, and asked us to take her a letter, after checking his Russian. It was still very good, though one phrase made us smile: "*My zahvatili Mozambique*" ("We conquered Mozambique"). Naturally we had a "standard" Russian "hundred grams" of vodka (that would be two doubles in the West) and our new Mozambican friend was repeatedly saying "*Kak v Soyuze, kak v Soyuze*" ("Like in the [Soviet] Union, like in the Union") ... .[11]

We met many other Mozambicans who had studied in the USSR, mostly in military training centres, from Floriano Umberto, a district commissar of FRELIMO in Muruppa[12] to Chissano and Guebuza, who asked us to convey greetings not only to the Soviet leadership but also especially to "Camarada Pedro".

Joachim Chissano received the delegation on the day after our arrival. He described in detail the situation in Mozambique in the transitional period. He was satisfied with the beginning of practical co-operation between the USSR and Mozambique, in particular with the visit of a group of Soviet economists some weeks earlier.[13]

The discussion with Armando Guebuza began when he was flying with us in the same plane from the capital to Nampula, and continued later in this office. He asked the Soviet Solidarity Committee, which "has been helping FRELIMO for so many years", "to find new forms of rendering possible assistance". In particular, FRELIMO wanted cadres to be trained both inside the country and in the Soviet Union. As to material assistance, his main emphasis was also on the solution of social problems, including health.[14]

After our return to Moscow we did our best to meet all the requests of the FRELIMO leaders. In particular, in addition to the governmental channel, 500,000 roubles were allocated from the Soviet Peace Fund to purchase a variety of equipment – from typewriters and stationery to metal beds for boarding schools. It was a substantial sum in those days (all these goods were extremely inexpensive in the USSR), although less than half what I initially suggested.

Mozambican comrades were worried by the incident in Blantyre and since we had to go back to Dar es Salaam by the same route, they took appropriate measures. When we were leaving, Guebuza, hugging me, said "Don't worry about Blantyre." Indeed, this time all the passengers were "kindly requested to remain aboard" and the same lieutenant, walking along the passage, pretended that he did not know us.

We came back from Mozambique in a very cheerful mood. We could see that most of the country was intact, because the guerrilla war took place mostly in the remote northern provinces. The victory of the liberation movement in Mozambique opened new prospects for its friends in neighbouring countries. "Three more years for Zimbabwe and ten for South Africa", I said to my colleagues. Certainly, I was extremely optimistic, but not too far out: the former became independent after less than five years, and in 15 years' time the ANC was unbanned and began talks with the government on the eradication of apartheid. However, could anybody imagine that after a decade Mozambique would be in disarray due to the actions of RENAMO, organised by the Rhodesian intelligence in 1976 and then "adopted" by Pretoria?

In late May 1975, Moscow established a liaison mission in Mozambique accredited to the Transitional Government. It was headed by Arkady Glukhov, who from 1968 to 1973 worked in the Soviet embassy in Dar es Salaam as a counsellor responsible for "inter-party ties", including contact with the leadership of FRELIMO, then based in the Tanzanian capital. Just like Yevsyukov he knew well and respected Eduardo Mondlane and Joachim Chissano who, after the death of Mondlane, became the main link man with Moscow while Samora Machel spent most of his time "in the zone of combat action".[15]

10
Independent Mozambique: Machel's Death

Yevsyukov was a member of the Soviet "party-governmental delegation" (in such cases the word "party" was put before "government"!), headed by Deputy Minister of Foreign Affairs Leonid Ilyichev,[1] which took part in the independence celebration in Mozambique in June 1975.[2] The efficiency he displayed during this mission and especially the visible respect he enjoyed from the Mozambican leadership and from President Machel personally, apparently helped him to "win the race" for the post of ambassador in the newly independent country, though many at the top of the Ministry of Foreign Affairs were not happy with the appointment of party officials to ambassadorial positions, preferring their own "career diplomats".[3]

Yevsyukov came to Maputo[4] in November 1975 and the fact that he was well known to the leadership of FRELIMO, that he even shared with some of them, including President Machel, the hardships of the march in the days of the guerrilla struggle, helped him in his ambassadorial work. "In any case it was much easier to receive the approval of my African friends [than that of Moscow]", writes Yevsyukov, although he adds: "But, frankly speaking, for me personally there were no big or insurmountable difficulties to get the approval of the leadership in Moscow", since during his work in the International Department he had established good business relations with many heads and officials of the Soviet ministries and other bodies.[5]

However, even in such favourable circumstances it was not easy to meet the requests and wishes of the Mozambican leadership. Thus Samora Machel wanted to make his first overseas visit as president to the USSR. He even delayed his trips to other countries, but he and his people did not know and could not imagine how difficult it was for "Camarada Pedro" to convince Moscow of the expediency of the visit and to ensure at least a short meeting of Machel with Brezhnev. Yevsyukov makes a very interesting observation: "Leonid

Ilyich [Brezhnev] was already a sick person and it looks as if he was not much interested in the problems of Africa. In these matters he wholly trusted Minister A.A. Gromyko, whose thoughts were obviously not pro-African."[6]

After the visit, which took place in May 1976, "it seemed to everybody (and in the highest degree to our Mozambican friends) that all possibilities for future all-round development of Soviet-Mozambican relations were open".[7] However, "further developments proved our economic malfunction or, rather inability and even unwillingness" to use unfolding opportunities, such as the utilisation of Mozambique's natural resources for mutual benefit. Yevsyukov is critical of the Soviet "state machinery" for requesting endless concordances, requests for more feasibility studies, more calculations and proofs. [8]

In his assessment of bilateral economic relations Sergio Vieira virtually concurs with "Camarada Pedro". In his opinion they were "essentially good" in the years of Brezhnev (he underlined Soviet supplies of oil to Mozambique on favourable conditions), but "the very complicated bureaucratic system of the Ministry of Foreign Trade"[9] caused many problems.

Yet another reason for the lack of success was more important – the "evolving civil war" in Mozambique.[10] Indeed, some activities of RENAMO, guided, or rather commanded, by Pretoria, were specifically directed against joint Soviet-Mozambican projects. The most tragic consequences in this respect were brought about by the attack on 20 August 1983 on the mining township of Morrua, north of Zambezi, where a group of Soviet geologists was stationed. Two of them were killed by bandits on the spot, and of 24 who were kidnapped, two died in RENAMO's "custody', five managed to escape and 15 were released, sick and exhausted, most of them only after six months.[11] Unfortunately, however, all attempts to find out what happened to Yury Gavrilov and Victor Istomin, whom bandits separated from the main group, failed. The only message Moscow received from Pretoria after confidential contacts had been established was rather ambiguous: the South African authorities believed they were no more.

In Yevsyukov's opinion, the leadership of Mozambique, and Machel in particular, made mistakes as well. Machel's "leftist extremism", mentioned above, found expression in his attitude to those Portuguese who were ready to co-operate with FRELIMO and regarded Mozambique as their motherland, but had to leave the country owing to rigid conditions put on their stay and their citizenship. Their departure caused a decline in the Mozambican economy.[12]

Yevsyukov concludes: "To understand and assess the life and activities of S. Machel one needs to know the facts of his controversial life and the features of his character well: on the one hand, he was gifted by nature and on the other he lacked education and tried to compensate for it by imitating the strongmen of this world ... ."[13] Yevsyukov rightly says: "... many of his actions, which looked unjustified at a first glance, should be assessed in the context of war and the passions of the time in which he was born and grew as a politician and statesman ... milksops don't make national liberation revolutions".[14]

The visit of Nikolay Podgorny, Chairman of the Presidium of the USSR Supreme Council (that body was informally called "a collective president"), in March 1977 was supposed to be the next milestone in the development of Mozambique's relations with the Soviet Union. As Yevsyukov recalls, Mozambicans "prepared for this visit in a very responsible way and absolutely thoroughly".[15]

Podgorny and his delegation[16] were impressed by the "atmosphere of high morale, friendship and sincerity". "I recall", Yevsyukov continues, "a mass rally in the centre of the city [Maputo], where a large crowd was singing the '*Internationale*'."[17]

This was not a surprise, because a month earlier FRELIMO at its 3rd congress reorganised itself into a "Marxist-Leninist party". I want to emphasise that the choice in favour of socialism was made by the Mozambicans themselves, and not imposed by Moscow even if, according to Vieira, they were influenced by the words of Marshal Grechko, who, on the eve of his death, at the meeting with Chipande and his delegation in Moscow in April 1976, suggested making their intentions known. "He told us it was time we stated our true colours, as everybody knew that we were building our country under the principles of socialism ... We discussed that a lot. That discussion contributed to the decisions we took later on the [FRELIMO] 3rd congress."[18]

When, at the celebration of independence, Machel called the socialist countries "natural allies" of Mozambique, these words did not originate in Moscow. Moreover, Yevsyukov writes that these very words worried "bureaucrats" from the Soviet MFA. On 31 March 1977 Machel and Podgorny signed the Treaty of Friendship and Co-operation. To draft it together with the Mozambicans, a few Soviet diplomats came to Maputo about a week earlier, but either they were instructed so strictly or incorrigible bureaucracy was established in their genes, but all the reasonable proposals of the Mozambicans made them feverishly search in a file with samples [of treaties] and if they did not see a precedent they categorically rejected an initiative ... The views on one point remained incompatible. Idiocy from our side was evident. The [Mozambican] friends suggested writing about the Soviet Union as a *natural ally.* Even my guarantee that this word would not cause objections did not help.

Only when Deputy Minister Ilyichev took part in the final discussion were these words retained in the text.[19]

Other bilateral agreements were concluded as well. However, one of the envisaged documents remained a draft: "... the Mozambican side turned out not to be ready to sign a document on co-operation in the military sphere",[20] though the delegation included Sergey Sokolov, First Deputy Minister (and later Minister) of Defence. Sergio Vieira explains the reason for this. The draft, proposed by Moscow, foresaw the right of Soviet naval ships to call in Mozambican ports. However, the Mozambicans wanted guarantees from Moscow against probable action of Pretoria in response, and, not having received these, refrained from signing.[21]

Unfortunately, the positive effect of Podgorny's visit was lost after his dismissal in May of the same year: his post was taken over by Brezhnev himself, who at that stage, although partly incapacitated by illness, had begun looking for new titles and awards.

The lack of such an agreement does not mean that military co-operation between Moscow and independent Mozambique did not exist. Earlier, in April 1976 a delegation, mentioned above, which was headed by Chipande and included Vieira, began fruitful discussions with Marshal Grechko, Soviet Minister of Defence. Rather tragically he died the same night the talks started.[22] Nevertheless, they ended successfully, and Mozambique was granted a loan to acquire arms, in particular aircraft and anti-aircraft weapons.[23]

Moreover, later Soviet naval ships did come there, in particular soon after a South African Special Forces' attack on 30 January 1981 on Matola, a suburb of Maputo, where 15 ANC members died. Speaking at the 26th CPSU Congress the next month, Marcelino dos Santos not only surprised many delegates by conveying "proletarian greetings from communists and the working people of Mozambique", but also described "an official visit to the ports of our country by Soviet naval ships" as an expression of "genuine solidarity" with the Mozambican people; "Socialist Mozambique is not alone."[24]

Yevsyukov's memoirs contain some noteworthy observations on the work of the Soviets in Mozambique:

Some of them, for example, KGB officers, were often trying to demonstrate their special position and even independence. As a rule, all ordinary officials of the embassy and other institutions could guess who those people were, and consequently it was not difficult for the foreign intelligence to figure out who our KGB officers were. A feeling of impunity and of belonging to a high-power organisation was spoiling the people and hindered the cause they served.

In this respect representatives of the GRU of the General Staff differed for the better. They distinguished themselves by more modesty and discipline. Mildly speaking, representatives of the KGB and GRU were competing somewhat strangely and probably for this reason disliked one another. It was not causing great harm, but sometimes their information differed significantly, especially in terms of assessments, conclusions and recommendations.[25]

A group of Soviet military advisers and specialists began working in Mozambique, headed by General A.K. Cherevko.[26] However, as in a number of other countries, their work was not always efficient. One of the problems was a lack of trained personnel in the Mozambican armed forces. When Soviets "drew squares", that is, suggested structures of headquarters, formations, etc., Mozambicans as a rule would agree to them and relevant Soviet advisers would be allocated, but they would not necessarily find those whom they were supposed to advise.

I recall how in July 1984 in Maputo I had an informal discussion with a Soviet colonel. When I mentioned to him that the number of advisers and specialists was somewhat "inflated" (there were over 400 of them), he replied: "No, the Minister (of Defence) told us that if the number was to decrease, people would think we were leaving Mozambique."

Critics of the Soviet involvement in Mozambique often say that heavy arms supplied by the Soviet Union could not be used effectively in fighting RENAMO. This may be correct, but this was not their main purpose. Both Soviets and Mozambicans, at least initially, saw the main threat in racist South Africa, and I believe the very fact that the Mozambican armed forces possessed such weapons served as a restraint to Pretoria. The SADF was already deeply involved in Angola and Namibia and was hardly interested in opening a "second front". True, it was probably superior in numbers of personnel and the amount of arms, but nevertheless, the Peoples' Forces for the Liberation of Mozambique (FPLM) could inflict serious damage on them, and in case of occupation, FRELIMO's guerrilla experience would be put to good use again.

Besides, Moscow understood, though perhaps belatedly, the need for Mozambique to have special units, capable of carrying out "counter-insurgency" operations, and appropriate specialists were sent there as well.

In the first years of its independent existence Mozambique was relying on strengthening economic relations with the socialist countries. In particular, it wanted to join the Council of Mutual Economic Assistance (CMEA; in the West it was known as COMECON), initially with observer status, and then as a full member. Vieira explains:

We were realistic enough to understand that integration as full member demanded the creation of conditions to narrow the gap between advanced economies like those of most European CMEA members and ours. But we also thought that we were not far below Mongolia or Laos. We expected that an effort similar to the one undertaken by Cuba could help us to start contributing to the general framework.

Vieira correctly states that opposition to these intentions "came from Hungary, Poland and Czechoslovakia". [27] In any case, if we look at the European Union, we can see that candidates for membership have to meet many conditions, and this process sometimes takes decades.

Perhaps the FRELIMO leadership's expectations were too high, especially after signing a treaty of friendship and co-operation in 1977. Yury Andropov, having been elected CPSU General Secretary, in 1983 made a sober assessment of the situation in the Third World which was relevant to Mozambique:

It is one thing to proclaim socialism as one's aim and quite another thing to build it. For this, a certain level of productive forces, culture and social consciousness is needed. Socialist countries express solidarity with these progressive states, render assistance to them in the sphere of politics and culture, and promote the strengthening of their defence. We assist also, to the extent of our ability, in their economic development. But on the whole, their economic development, just like the entire social progress of these countries, can, of course, only be the result of the work of their people and of correct policy adopted by their leadership.[28]

Many Western academics (and some former diplomats, like George Shultz) write that after his failure to join CMEA Samora Machel was eager to leave "the Soviet camp" and shift his allegiance to the West, and this break was marked by Machel's visit to the USA in September

1983. However, in the USSR Mozambique was not regarded as a member of "the Soviet camp". In fact this militaristic terminology had not been in use in Moscow since the 1960s. Neither did Machel "shift his allegiance to the West"; he was a patriot of Mozambique and his "allegiance" was to his own motherland. One should also not forget that President Carter conferred with Machel in New York in October 1977 and Mozambique indicated then that it was amenable to American investments.[29]

Besides, through their discussions with Soviet leaders, impressions of the delegations, students, diplomats, etc., the Mozambicans sensed the deterioration of the situation in the Soviet Union, initially primarily in the sphere of the economy. If any deep reassessment of the USSR's role and capabilities took place, it happened later, during Gorbachev's time. Thus, in 1986, Machel led a delegation to the USSR, which included in particular Chissano, then Minister of Foreign Affairs, and Vieira. According to the latter, after a discussion with Gorbachev they realised that Moscow was "mainly concerned with a deal with the USA", "it was not prepared to support Mozambique", was not prepared to render it further significant economic and military support, and "did not care about the nuclear threat of South Africa" against it.[30]

This last point deserves special attention. Undoubtedly the Soviets were worried by Pretoria's nuclear programme. It was Moscow that warned the USA and other Western powers about the preparations for nuclear testing in the Kalahari in 1977. I am not aware of the top Soviet leadership having hard information about the actual production of bombs by South Africa, but certainly that possibility was always considered. In was in the same year, 1986, on 4 October that Anatoly Dobrynin raised this issue with the ANC delegation headed by Oliver Tambo. The delegation assured him that South Africa was in a position to produce such bombs.

Professor Renfrew Christie of the University of the Western Cape wrote in his paper on South Africa's nuclear history: "The most likely understanding is that President P.W. Botha successfully used the threat of a nuclear explosion, in the process of getting the Cubans to leave Angola. If this is true, apartheid's atom bomb strategy paid off."[31] This is hardly so, at least to the best of my knowledge, as the Soviet papers concerning the talks on an Angolan-Namibian settlement never referred to this as an issue of leverage.

However, it looks as if this threat did serve as leverage in relations between Maputo and Pretoria. Vieira divulges a fascinating story.

Before signing the Nkomati Accord (to be discussed later), while South Africa refused to sign the Non-Proliferation Treaty, no nuclear power was prepared to give Mozambique an umbrella. After Vieira's discussion with Dmitry Ustinov, Soviet Minister of Defence, and Yury Andropov, KGB chairman, Moscow sent a delegation to Maputo that limited itself by saying: "Everybody knows that we [Soviet Navy] have nuclear weapons in the Indian Ocean" and "never said that we could retaliate against an attack on us". So by 1983 the Mozambican leadership "dispersed the government and organised the survival of the state in case Maputo should be destroyed".[32]

Vieira underlines that having signed the Nkomati Accord, Pretoria for the first time accepted the interdiction on producing and using nuclear, chemical and bacteriological weapons.[33] Indeed, nuclear weapons were not used by the racist regime, but it did use chemical weapons in Angola, and continued production of various types of weapons of mass destruction for several years after this acceptance.

The Accord on Non-Aggression and Good Neighbourliness, signed by Machel and Botha in Nkomati on the Mozambican-South African border on 16 March 1984, remains a controversial issue even now, almost a quarter of a century later. In my book on the history of the ANC I looked at the developments that preceded and followed the agreement between Maputo and Pretoria mostly through the eyes of the ANC and its supporters in South Africa and abroad.[34] I wrote in particular that the treatment of ANC members by Mozambican officials had caused indignation among activists of the Congress. The disappointment was especially strong because the ANC was historically very close to FRELIMO; after all, John Marks and Joe Slovo gave Samora Machel a lift in a chartered plane from Francistown in Bechuanaland (Botswana) to Dar es Salaam when the future president tried to join the liberation movement in 1963.[35]

On the other hand, I noted that the Nkomati Accord provided a powerful counter to the view that decisive assistance to the liberation struggle would come from beyond South Africa's borders. I also quoted Professors Jakes Gerwel (who later became head of President Mandela's administration) and Pieter le Roux of the University of the Western Cape, who had rightly predicted that "Nkomati and similar accords might force the ANC to develop a stronger internal base".[36]

However, the view of those in Mozambique who were involved in reaching this agreement must be acknowledged as well. In Sergio Vieira's opinion, the Nkomati Accord allowed the actions of Mozambique and the liberation movement in South Africa to be put "beyond the East–West confrontation":[37] "Soon after, both in the West and in South Africa, the first signs of readiness for a political settlement in the region and in South Africa in particular appeared."[38]

Apart from the issue of nuclear weapons, mentioned above, in Vieira's opinion, the accord ensured that in spite of several attacks, the confrontation between Mozambique and South Africa never became a full-scale war, and South African "securocrats" were defeated. More to the point, Vieira practically concurs with an earlier statement by Gerwel and le Roux: "The ANC concentrated on the effort of raising the masses and looking for allies in the business community".[39]

However, Pretoria did not honour its obligations and continued supporting RENAMO. Much more effective was military assistance provided by Zimbabwe and later by Tanzania. I could feel the importance and urgency of this issue when I visited Harare for the first time in June 1985, on the way to Mozambique. A group of prominent members of the ruling Zimbabwe African National Union – Patriotic Front (ZANU-PF) party, including Vice-President Simon Muzenda, welcomed our delegation at a dinner, and the dispatch of troops to help the FRELIMO government was one of the subjects of our discussion.[40]

Another issue that is still raising controversy is the tragic death of Samora Machel, who was killed when his Tu-134, piloted by a Soviet crew, crashed on 19 October 1986 in South Africa at Mbuzini, very close to the Mozambican border. Many, including Soviet and Mozambican authorities, believed that the plane was lured off its course by a false beacon, installed in South Africa.[41] The full story of this tragedy has not yet been told. I believe that after the change of power in South Africa (and certain political changes in Mozambique as well), the opportunities to make a fair investigation are much better; all that is needed is political will. Not so long ago President Thabo Mbeki declared that a new investigation of the accident would take place. Let us hope that all the potential witnesses (and culprits?) will be found, as well as all relevant data.

Other than that, stories appear from time to time that could be called hilarious, were they not so dirty. One recent and most unfortunate example is the memoirs of Jacinto Soares Veloso, former member of the FRELIMO Politburo, who headed the Mozambican security apparatus between 1975 and 1983. He appears to be trying to put the blame not on the Soviet crew, as the regime in Pretoria had done, but on the Soviet leadership. Veloso is of the view that since Machel "betrayed the Soviet camp" in a bipolar confrontation, having made a choice in favour of "liberalisation of the economy and society", he was "doomed".[42] He even suggests that "ultra-radicals" from the apartheid regime and from "the East" had common interests and were involved "in the operation to eliminate Samora Machel".[43] He claims that an "unidentified individual" from the "East" interfered with the presidential plane in Mbala,[44] and finds it "very probable" that the South African secret services recruited him for "Operation Mbuzini".[45]

This is nonsense, and a very treacherous form of it. How could a former member of FRELIMO's leadership and Minister of Security make such statements? True, Moscow was sometimes critical of Machel's actions (though this criticism was never public), but mostly of his overly radical internal policy. However, whatever differences existed, they were differences between friends and comrades and nobody regarded Machel as a "traitor". In fact the Soviet leadership was shocked by the news of his tragic death. A high-level Soviet delegation led by Geidar Aliev, a member of the Politburo and First Deputy Prime Minister, took part in his funeral.

Later, after Chissano's visit to Moscow in 1987, Mikhail Gorbachev said at the Politburo meeting: "We shall support him ... He is a man of great erudition, and, unlike Machel, he is a realist ... Chissano asks us to understand them if they go for a compromise with imperialists in economic affairs. He says this doesn't change their principle position."[46] So Moscow, especially in the days of Gorbachev, would not have minded "liberalisation of the economy and society", though most probably it would have preferred another term, for example, "democratisation".

As for Veloso's allegations, perhaps their roots could be found in his own life story. In March 1963, Veloso, then a Portuguese airman, and another white Mozambican, Joao dos Santos Ferreira, flew from Mozambique to Tanganyika with the intention to join FRELIMO. But after some weeks there they were deported to Egypt by the Tanganyikan authorities. Marcelino dos Santos said to Maksudov: "We sent them to Cairo for security reasons, because they could be deported from Dar es Salaam back to Mozambique.[47] I trust these guys."[48] But when Maksudov met Veloso and Ferreira, he was surprised to find that their attitude to FRELIMO was rather negative: "We understood in Dar es Salaam that FRELIMO is an organisation that is unable to lead the national liberation struggle."[49]

The changes in the USSR during the period of *perestroika* affected Moscow's role in Mozambique just as in other parts of Southern

Africa. Personally I think that a radical change in Gorbachev's policy occurred in late 1988 and 1989, and initially the political relations between Moscow and Maputo were developing in a good way in this period as well. After all, the changes in both countries were going in similar directions, even if it was still disputable as to what extent they were "home-grown" and not proposed (or imposed?) from outside. However, the crisis in the Soviet Union on the threshold of the 1990s made Moscow lose its position in the area, and unlike in South-western Africa just some years earlier, it had no role to play in the talks between the FRELIMO government and RENAMO that culminated in the signing of the Complete Peace Agreement in October 1992 in Rome.

Part Three

Zimbabwe

11
ZAPU or ZANU?

Despite the similarity in the aims of the liberation movements in Southern Africa, each of them acted under different circumstances from the others. Thus Zimbabwe from 1923 had the status of self-governing colony, namely Southern Rhodesia. From 1953, together with two other British colonies, Northern Rhodesia (Zambia) and Nyasaland (Malawi), it was a part of the Federation of Rhodesia and Nyasaland, which collapsed under pressure from the growing nationalist movements in all three territories.

However, the later fate of the three countries was quite different: Malawi became independent in July 1964 and Zambia followed in October 1964, but white settlers in Zimbabwe, who voted the right-wing Rhodesian Front into power, refused to give up control. A watershed in the developments in Zimbabwe was 11 November 1965, when Ian Smith announced a Unilateral Declaration of Independence (UDI). If before that the country was, at least officially, under British jurisdiction, now the authorities in Salisbury regarded themselves as independent of London. Later in 1969 they proclaimed the Republic of Rhodesia, rejecting even symbolic ties with the UK.

Not a single country officially recognised it, and London regarded this act as tantamount to "mutiny", but did not take any practical steps to quell it. The UDI served to strengthen the rule of white settlers, who freed themselves even from minimal control of London, but on the other hand it tempted the liberation movements and independent African states to act more resolutely against the racists.

However, Moscow's support to the anti-colonial struggle began much earlier. When Morton Malianga, Vice-President of the National Democratic Party (NDP), and Jason Z. Moyo, its Secretary for Finance, visited Czechoslovakia in April 1961, information about the visit was passed to the Soviet Solidarity Committee.[1] It is worth mentioning that among other issues discussed in Prague, there was a request for "special training (security, defence)" for NDP members.[2]

Their hosts in the Czechoslovak Society for International Ties believed that theirs was the first Eastern European country that had invited delegates from Southern Rhodesia, as Zimbabwe was called in those days.[3] However, three months earlier, in January, the Soviet Committee's officials had already met another prominent NDP leader in Moscow, Tarcissius George ("TG") Silundika, future minister of communications of independent Zimbabwe.

At that time Silundika represented the liberation movement of Zimbabwe in Cairo, and took part in the session of the AAPSO Executive Committee in Beirut in November 1960 where he impressed the Soviet delegation as "a modest and purposeful man, committed to his cause. He willingly gets in contact with Soviet representatives, and appears to be sincere with them." [4]

Apart from discussing the situation in Zimbabwe, Silundika made several requests to the Soviets: funds for buying a printing shop, means of transport and financial support for leading cadres, scholarships in the Peoples' Friendship University (soon named after Lumumba) and courses for trade union, women and youth activists.[5] In the Solidarity Committee's report on his visit, sent to the CPSU, it was suggested that £5,000[6] be allocated to the NDP. It is worth mentioning the motivation for such a step: financial assistance had to be provided not only because the "National Democratic Party of Southern Rhodesia is the most progressive and mass party", but also because "this party is conducting certain work in the province of Katanga against the government of Tshombe in defence of the lawful Congolese government of P. Lumumba";[7] Moscow's preoccupation with the situation in Congo was evident.

It appears, however, that Silundika really impressed his Moscow interlocutors (often an official of the International Department would join discussions at the Solidarity Committee), and, according to archive documents, the NDP was allocated US$8,400 in 1961.[8]

Soon the Soviets received a request to receive in Moscow Joshua Nkomo, then the NDP President, and Washington Malianga, who represented that party in Cairo at the time.[9] Contact with Nkomo was established earlier. He later recalled that he had met the Committee's representatives at the AAPSO Conference in Conakry in April 1960.[10] The assessment of the NDP in a letter from the Solidarity Committee to the CPSU headquarters was rather optimistic: "Most probably, the NDP will come to power in the country and its leaders will stand at the head of the government."[11]

The reference to Nkomo, which accompanied the letter, was more restrained: "According to the data available in the archives, Nkomo is characterised by some tiredness, disbelief in victory, a certain enmity to Europeans. He regards the countries of the socialist camp with suspicion and mistrust and he is not resolved to take part in the armed struggle."[12] Most probably this assessment appeared as a result of the Soviets' contact with Malianga in Cairo, and they are largely consonant with the accusations against Nkomo put forward by the founders of ZANU in 1963.[13]

On the basis of its correspondence with the NDP and discussions with its representatives in Cairo, the Solidarity Committee expected that during their visits to Moscow the NDP leaders would "request financial assistance to the value of 100,000 pounds sterling to organise printing and create groups to conduct subversive activities (acquisition of explosives, cars, radios, etc.)".[14]

However, the request forwarded by Nkomo when he came to Moscow in July 1962,[15] was even bigger: £150,000. The sum was really huge at that time,[16] but he did not necessarily want it as a grant; he would be ready to take it as a loan as well.

The discussion with Nkomo took place in the Solidarity Committee on 14 July. Apart from the Committee's official, Yury Ivanov from the CPSU African Section and Yury Yukalov from the MFA took part in it as well.[17] He stated that the aim of ZAPU, formed after the banning of the NDP, was to achieve independence by July the next year. He said in confidence that the ZAPU leadership was working out a plan for the armed uprising. "For these purposes ZAPU needs arms, explosives, revolvers, etc ... the party also needs money to bribe persons who guard important installations, to carry out sabotage, etc."[18] Money was needed to acquire means of transport as well. He confirmed his earlier request for a printing machine and for more scholarships to study in the USSR. In case of his arrest he asked that all affairs be conducted through his representatives: Silundika in Cairo and Madlela in Dar es Salaam.[19]

On the way back from Moscow he explained to Soviet diplomats in Dar es Salaam that ZAPU was becoming convinced that it could not gain independence by only legal means.[20] Since there was no immediate reply to his request, later, in September, Nkomo again approached the Soviet embassy in (still) Tanganyika. He was visibly worried and wanted clarity on whether the money was forthcoming, and if so, how much: "... tomorrow can already be too late. We don't need a pompous funeral."[21]

It is not clear from the archives whether in 1962 any money reached Nkomo and his new party; neither the NDP nor ZAPU is mentioned in the list of allocations for that year, available in the archives. Nkomo writes in his memoirs about his calls on "friendly embassies" in Dar es Salaam: "The Soviet Union and some of the Eastern European countries were understanding, but they could give no immediate assistance."[22] However, money was definitely provided later and the amount was increasing: US$19,600 in 1963,[23] US$20,000 in 1965[24] and US$28,000 in 1966.[25] It should be mentioned, however, that this type of assistance was not necessarily related to radical positions and plans for armed struggle. Thus in 1963 an even bigger sum was provided to Kenneth Kaunda's United National Independence Party of Zambia.

Assistance in kind was provided by the Solidarity Committee as well. This included, for example, a duplicating machine, which was shipped to Dar es Salaam.[26] Besides, no later than 1961, students from Zimbabwe began coming to the USSR for academic training.[27] In July 1962, during a short spell of work at the USSR Committee of Youth Organisations before my conscription, I was dealing with arranging travel of African and other foreign students from Moscow to Finland to take part in the World Festival of Youth and Students. One of them was a young man from Southern Rhodesia, who completed his first, preparatory year in the Georgian capital Tbilisi in the Caucasus. Unlike the others, his mood was not too friendly: in Tbilisi Africans were not welcomed. In fact, he told me that none of them would stay there after the vacations.

Unfortunately he was right: although in the 1990s and later, xenophobia and even blatant racism became a feature in many cities of former Soviet republics, in those days Georgia was an exception. According to a letter from the Solidarity Committee to the CPSU CC "On the shortcomings in the work with foreign students, studying in Tbilisi",[28] African students there were "feeling enmity and antagonism from a section of the Soviet [Georgian] students".[29] The Committee suggested not sending more African students for studies there and transferring those who were there.[30]

In 1963 the ZAPU leadership requested Moscow to organise military training for its members. In particular, James Chikerema, the party's vice-president, at his meeting with Latyp Maksudov in Cairo on 24 December, asked the Solidarity Committee to convey to relevant Soviet organisations a request to train 30 persons for four months, especially "for subversive work, for military sabotage", and three persons for six months for training in the manufacturing of "simple small arms" because it was "impossible" to bring arms into the country.[31] Chikerema was going to Beijing in lieu of Nkomo and wanted to pass through Moscow in early 1964 to discuss the question of assistance.[32]

In the (northern) summer of 1964 two groups of ZAPU activists came to the Northern Training Centre. The first group included in particular Akim Ndlovu, who later became a prominent commander of ZAPU's military wing – the Zimbabwe People's Revolutionary Army (ZIPRA). A month later the second group arrived. One of its members was Phelekezela Mphoko, incumbent Zimbabwean Ambassador to Russia, who for several years headed ZIPRA logistics. ZIPRA cadres took a ten-month comprehensive course, which in particular included general military subjects and specialisation in guerrilla and conventional warfare and even field medicine.[33]

It should be emphasised, however, that the decision to begin the armed struggle and to organise military training was taken much earlier. Unfortunately, in the official historiography of Zimbabwe this fact had for a long time often been overlooked. Thus Robert Mugabe in one of his speeches attributed the decision of "the people to Zimbabwe" "to launch the armed struggle" to April 1966, when the first encounter between ZANU guerrillas and government forces took place.[34] However, much later, at the funeral of Joshua Nkomo on 5 July 1999, Mugabe said that at the beginning of 1963 at the meeting chaired by Nkomo, "It was decided ... that the way forward should be by transforming our political struggle into an armed guerrilla one."[35]

In fact the first group of cadres, consisting of 15 persons, was sent for military training in China much earlier, in 1962, but unfortunately after their return to Dar es Salaam in 1963 they split between ZAPU and the newly formed ZANU.[36] Moreover, Joshua Nkomo writes in his memoirs that he personally smuggled some arms ("24 semi-automatic assault rifles, with magazines and ammunition, and a big bag of grenades") in September 1962 and later another lot from Cairo to Dar es Salaam.[37] He even said that at that period "... the armed struggle had taken its first steps".[38]

Apart from academic and military institutions, young Zimbabweans began coming to the USSR for political training in the Institute of Social Sciences as well. However, it appears that the ZAPU leadership was sometimes in a hurry "to meet the figures", proposed by the Soviets. One of the papers I "inherited" from my predecessors in the International Department was a report from the Institute about the misbehaviour of a group of Zimbabweans who were involved in drinking at the expense of their studies. Perhaps it was caused by a "cultural shock", but more probably by lack of basic education and hence difficulties in studies. Anyhow, the phrase "We f****d your Marxism", uttered by some of the students, was not exactly balm for the ears of the Institute's lecturers and administration and the ZAPU leadership had to apologise for its members.

The Soviet Union supported joint operations of ZAPU and the South African ANC in Zimbabwe in 1967 and 1968, though its failure affected the situation in ZAPU negatively and aggravated tension there. The story of the ANC–ZAPU alliance and these joint operations in Zimbabwe in 1967 and 1968 is well known. Immediately after these events both movements maintained rather close relations. ZAPU marked Zimbabwe Day on 17 March just a few days before the anniversary of the Sharpeville massacre, 21 March, which became the International Day of Struggle against Racism and Racial Discrimination. In fact, the organisation of a joint event was the first task I received when I came to the Solidarity Committee in 1969.

The political support the USSR rendered to ZAPU included transmissions in Shona and Ndebele beamed to Zimbabwe. For the first time I met Zimbabwean radio announcers as well as students at that public meeting. Then, in June, Moscow was visited by Jason Moyo, who was regarded at that time as the Number Three in ZAPU after James Chikerema, vice-president, and George Nyandoro, secretary-general, while its president, Joshua Nkomo, and most of the other leadership members were detained or imprisoned by the Rhodesian authorities.

We instantly established good relations with Moyo, a clever, honest and modest man, and these relations we maintained until his tragic death in January 1978 – he was blown up by a bomb planted in a parcel by the Rhodesian (or South African?) government terrorists. Meetings with Nyandoro in Moscow and Chikerema in Lusaka (the former came for medical treatment) followed. These discussions helped me to understand better both the situation in Zimbabwe and the attitude of independent African countries to the anticolonial struggle there. Both of them complained about lack of support for their party in Africa; according to Nyandoro, nobody on the continent was helping his ZAPU, except Algeria. He alleged that Nyerere had several times stated to Chikerema that Tanzania supported ZAPU, but the behaviour of Tanzanian delegations abroad suggested otherwise.[39]

Then came a man who initiated ZAPU's contact with Moscow – Silundika, at that time ZAPU Secretary for Information. He took part in the conference at Alma-Ata in early October 1969, and later had a long discussion with us at the Solidarity Committee. I fully agree with the above reference to him. His distinct features were honesty, modesty and a bright mind. Somehow we immediately developed a kind and close relationship.

Silundika was also very critical of the policy of African states; he called the Lusaka Manifesto, adopted by some of them in April 1969, a "reactionary and dangerous" document.[40] As in the case of SWAPO, described below, even pocket money was a problem for freedom fighters in those days; but fortunately we managed to obtain a very modest sum for Silundika, who left Moscow for Western Europe.

Nothing in these discussions would warn us about internal problems in ZAPU. But suddenly at the beginning of 1970 a very alarming message came from the Soviet embassy in Lusaka: a split had occurred in the party leadership: Chikerema and Nyandoro, both Shona, took one side, and three others – Moyo, Silundika and Edward Ndlovu, all Ndebele – took the other, though at a lower level "Moyo's group" retained its multi-ethnic character. In any case it looked as if the split was not only on a political or personal base, but an ethnic one as well. The situation was complicated further by the fact that the "minority two" were higher in the ZAPU hierarchy than the "majority three".

Eliakim Sibanda, in his *The Zimbabwe African People's Union 1961–1967*, writes: "throughout the crisis, the ANC and the Soviet Union supported Moyo's group, mostly for its national composition."[41] In reality, however, it was hard for the Soviets to make a choice. Just as in other cases, such as problems in the MPLA in 1973 and 1974, Moscow called for unity, but to no avail. There were practical problems as well: Vladimir Lenin's centenary was celebrated in April 1970, but at the last moment the invitation to a delegation of ZAPU I had to accompany was cancelled. From time to time we used to receive information about the talks between the two groups and Moscow hoped for their reconciliation. But by the time the CPSU congress was convened in March–April 1971 the split had not yet been overcome, and though I had again been designated to accompany a ZAPU delegation, its participation had to be cancelled once more.

Psychologically, for those of us who were dealing with ZAPU and were committed to supporting it, this situation was demoralising. "My hands are falling down" (a Russian phrase, meaning he was so shocked that he was unable to move), Andrey Urnov of the CPSU Africa Section told me. "I don't want to live", I replied.

Indeed, the split in ZAPU, especially because of its ethnic flavour, dramatically aggravated the situation in the party. It was followed by a mutiny in its camps that was suppressed by the Zambian Army. The armed struggle was "forgotten" for several years; the ranks of ZIPRA dwindled; the prestige of ZAPU suffered in Zimbabwe, in Africa and on the international arena. It would not be an exaggeration to say that the split moved ZAPU back and allowed ZANU to come to the forefront of the liberation struggle.

The creation of ZANU was announced in August 1963, and hardly by accident its name resembled that of Tanganyika's ruling party – TANU, because from the very beginning they enjoyed the support of Julius Nyerere, who not long before had ordered Nkomo to leave Dar es Salaam for home.[42] Reverend Ndabangingi Sithole became its President and Robert Mugabe its General Secretary. ZANU leaders explained their decision to part from ZAPU by citing their discontent with the conduct of Joshua Nkomo who was allegedly too soft in his talks with London on the future constitutional arrangements for independent Zimbabwe.[43] However, from its inception ZANU represented first and foremost Shona, while ZAPU was genuinely multi-ethnic, although the majority of its Central Committee was always Shona-speaking.[44]

The news of a forthcoming spilt was brought to the Soviet ambassador in Dar es Salaam, Andrey Timoshchenko by Moyo, Joseph Msika and Madlela on 10 July 1963. The next day four ZAPU Executive Committee members, including Robert Mugabe and Ndabanginge Sithole, announced the deposition of Nkomo from the presidency of the party. The embassy immediately reported to Moscow that this step had been supported by the Tanganyikans who were not happy with Nkomo and prompted Mugabe, whom they regarded as "very progressive", to be the new leader. In particular they were critical of Nkomo's statement that power in Southern Rhodesia could be won by Africans only by force of arms: "This is just words."[45] At the same time the embassy stated that the British had "apparently" sought a split in ZAPU and underlined that on the eve of the events Sithole had spent two months in the USA.[46] A little later Chikerema and Msika said directly to Timoshchenko that "the split was organised by the British".[47]

Apparently ZAPU's leadership desperately needed money. They asked Timoshchenko to provide "at least 12 to 14 thousand pounds for transport means"[48] and the embassy suggested meeting their request "to some extent", underlining that "after the breakaway of

Sithole's group" ZAPU was taking "a more progressive position" and sought "support in socialist countries". In particular, for the first time its leadership requested scholarships in the Soviet Central Komsomol (YCL) School.[49]

A final breakaway of Sithole's group from ZAPU and the formation of a new party, ZANU had Moscow facing a dilemma. Having already established contact with the NDP and its successor, ZAPU, Moscow had to decide whether to enter into a relationship with ZANU as well and a negative decision was taken. I believe there were at least two reasons for this: firstly, as a rule, Moscow's approach was, as Yevsyukov put it in his memoirs, "*odnolyubstvo*".[50] "*Odnolyub*" is the Russian term for a man who loves just one woman all his life, so Moscow as a rule would also not change its political partner. The second reason was more important: ZANU from the very beginning established close contacts with China, and in view of a growing gap between Moscow and Beijing this factor played a negative role.

After the banning of both ZAPU and ZANU (the latter was banned in 1964) most of the leaders of both parties were detained. So in both cases practical control of the organisations was taken by senior leaders who were outside Zimbabwe, in the case of ZANU by its Chairman, Herbert Chitepo, and in the case of ZAPU by its vice-president, James Chikerema. It was Chikerema who in August 1967 made a joint statement with Oliver Tambo about ANC–ZAPU armed operations in Zimbabwe.[51]

When their attempts to establish control over ZAPU failed, Chikerema and Nyandoro finally dropped their claims for leadership in ZAPU, and in October 1971 they joined some ZANU members in forming the Front for Liberation of Zimbabwe (FROLIZI). "Copying" took place again; this time the new party name resembled the name of the Mozambican organisation – FRELIMO, but contrary to it, FROLIZI leaders did not succeed in bringing members of ZAPU and ZANU together, as they claimed. Instead it became a "third force" and a rather short-lived one.

For us the creation of FROLIZI was a blessing in disguise: the departure of Chikerema and Nyandoro made the situation in ZAPU clear and Moscow's relations with this organisation were fully restored. In fact, even earlier it became clear that Moyo, Silundika and Ndlovu were emerging as the true leaders of the organisation; we had a fruitful discussion with "Comrade T.G." during the AAPSO conference in Cairo in January 1972.

The first ZAPU leader who came to Moscow in August 1972, after the resumption of relations, was Edward Ndlovu (he was accompanied by Joseph Dube, then director of ZAPU Intelligence and Security).[52] Ndlovu was perhaps the most controversial figure in the leadership of ZAPU. I remember a discussion with him at the AAPSO meeting in Tripoli in early 1971 when he emphasised the role of the Ndebele in the struggle, claiming that they manned 98 per cent of ZIPRA ranks. One of my colleagues also recalls how at the meeting with the Soviets and delegates from other Southern African countries, including Yusuf Dadoo, Ndlovu, after a few drinks, began speaking like a black racist, threatening "to fix you [whites and Indians]" when his movement came to power.

In January 1972 a commission headed by Lord Pearce was sent to Zimbabwe to find out whether the population supported a draft constitution negotiated between Ian Smith's government and London, which to a large extent protected the privileges of the white minority. Contrary to the intentions of its organisers, this mission served as a catalyst for the developments in Zimbabwe. To express the opinion of Africans, a new body – the African National Council,[53] was organised. Mass rallies held all over the country convincingly proved that an absolute majority of Africans rejected the proposed constitution. According to Edward Ndlovu, the ZAPU leadership wanted to send fighters to support this "rebellion", but they had neither the means nor the funds to do so. He believed that a chance had been missed to transform it "into a war".[54]

Most of the leaders and activists of the ANC came from ZAPU, though its figurehead was Bishop Abel Muzorewa, who was recommended, according to the ZAPU external leaders, by Joshua Nkomo himself. In his discussions in Moscow Ndlovu emphasised that the external leadership was carrying out Joshua Nkomo's instructions, in particular his idea that the ANC should serve as "temporary political machinery" uniting "all points of view", including those of churches, trade unions, teacher associations and other organisations. However, Silundika, who came to the USSR in October 1972 to take part in the international conference in Tashkent, claimed that only about 5 per cent of the ANC leadership were ZANU supporters.[55]

After the creation of the Joint Military Command (JMC) of ZAPU and ZANU in 1972 at the conference in Mbeya, Tanzania, to prevent the recognition of FROLIZI by the OAU Liberation Committee and independent African countries both parties agreed to stop criticising each other in the press and to take a joint position vis-à-vis the

OAU.[56] At that time, according to Edward Ndlovu, ZAPU had over 130 fighters in the camps in Tanzania and about 300 trained fighters outside the camps. Besides, about 40 persons were in detention in Zambia.[57]

Thus ZAPU managed to overcome the crisis of the early 1970s, but the damage it caused is difficult to overestimate. The armed struggle stalled for about three years. Many cadres drifted away and the ethnic factor showed its negative significance. Moreover, it happened exactly when the movement was in a position to use a border with Mozambique to cross into Zimbabwe: FRELIMO fighters began operating in the adjacent area. Dumiso Dabengwa wrote later: "It was during this crisis that ZAPU lost its important and strategic contact with FRELIMO."[58]

Sergio Vieira recalls:

When we crossed the Zambezi in 1970 we were facing the Air Force and army of Rhodesia. We wanted to support ZAPU to open a front from Tete, we only knew ZAPU *as an authentic liberation movement*. We had no relations with ZANU. ZAPU never answered to our approach. Then we decided to infiltrate an intelligence group to understand Zimbabwe. They reported that out of the Ndebele area, in the south and neighbouring Zambia, people seldom supported ZAPU; most people spoke about ZANU. At that moment the late Chitepo and the late Tongogara come to us and requested permission and support to cross the Zambezi and start operations. So FRELIMO accepted.[59]

In fact, just a few years earlier, at the conference in Khartoum in January 1969, both FRELIMO and ZAPU, along with the ANC, SWAPO, PAIGC and the MPLA, were named among six "authentic liberation movements", but ZAPU's weakness made the FRELIMO leadership move closer to ZANU.

Initially, even when FRELIMO agreed to co-operate with ZANU in the military field, Samora Machel warned the representatives that this did not mean recognition of ZANU by FRELIMO. Nonetheless, step by step, they began strengthening their ties with this organisation at the expense of ZAPU. I believe this new choice by the FRELIMO leadership, which greatly influenced developments in Zimbabwe, was primarily pragmatic, but another factor could play its role as well: FRELIMO's rear base was in Tanzania, besides, it was receiving substantial assistance from China, and both these countries supported ZANU. In the final stage of the armed struggle the co-operation between FRELIMO and ZANU went rather far. By 1978 the government of Mozambique "authorised some 1,000 Mozambican volunteers under the command of Brigadier Ajape to join the freedom fighters in Zimbabwe".[60]

Although Moscow's attitude to ZANU was rather restrained, it does not mean that it did not have any contact with that organisation. In particular, I had an opportunity to have a lengthy discussion with Herbert Chitepo during the International Conference on Southern Africa in Oslo in April 1973.[61] Our talk over beers was quite friendly, though Chitepo did not share my enthusiasm about the JMC: while I emphasised the importance of this body and hinted at the possibility of receiving a JMC delegation to Moscow, Chitepo insisted on the establishment of direct ties between the USSR and ZANU.[62]

Incidentally, on this point his position mirrored that of Edward Ndlovu, who earlier insisted that the JMC should not have "diplomatic relations" with the USSR and other socialist countries. Earlier he told us in the Solidarity Committee that ZAPU could not "stop Soviet friends from meeting ZANU", but that this should be done after consulting ZAPU, in Dar es Salaam or Lusaka, but not in Moscow. Moreover, Ndlovu alleged that the entire force ZANU had was 45 fighters in Tanzania, but "nobody in Zambia or Zimbabwe".[63]

Jason Moyo, who came to Moscow as a guest at the celebration of the USSR's 50th anniversary in December 1972, informed us that the attitude of Zambia (which "had been disappointed with FROLIZI") to ZAPU had improved and that relations with Tanzania were improving as well. Meanwhile, the OAU Liberation Committee "was broke", because many countries were not paying their fees.[64]

The April 1974 Portuguese revolution dramatically changed the situation not only in Lisbon's colonies, but in adjacent countries as well. When independence for Mozambique and Angola became imminent, South African Prime Minister John Vorster made a dramatic statement, calling on his critics to "Give South Africa six months chance. I ask no more than this. If South Africa is given this chance, they will be amazed at where the country stands in about six or twelve months time."[65] This statement was favourably received by some African leaders, in particular by Kenneth Kaunda who spoke of "the voice of reason for which Africa and the whole world were waiting".[66]

Pretoria began speaking about "détente" in Southern Africa, but Silundika appropriately called it "misapplication of the term". The Zambian leadership first and foremost hoped for Vorster's assistance in bringing about a political settlement in Zimbabwe, and indeed Pretoria managed to bring Ian Smith to the negotiation table, though at first an informal one. However, such a settlement had to be acceptable to the Rhodesian white government and therefore required very serious concessions from their opponents.

The leaders of both ZAPU and ZANU were released from detention camps[67] and prisons, initially on a temporary basis. I recall how Silundika described to us his and his comrades' surprise when they were brought by Zambians to the place where they saw Joshua Nkomo again, after ten years!

By that time the Zimbabwean liberation movement was represented by four different organisations: ZAPU with ZIPRA, its military wing; ZANU with ZANLA (Zimbabwe African National Liberation Army); FROLIZI, which had a group of armed cadres, mostly former ZAPU members, and the ANC, which acted inside Zimbabwe as a legal entity. This chapter is not devoted to all the nuances of the relations between them, but several "milestones" should be mentioned.

The leaders of the four organisations signed a Unity Accord in December 1974.[68] The ANC delegation, which was headed by Muzorewa and included all the leaders of the Liberation Movements, met Smith in the presence of Vorster, Kaunda and the representative of the Frontline States, but the meeting was a total failure.

The ANC conference to elect new leaders took place in 1975, but by that time the four organisations were again politically very far from one another and when the congress took place, practically all those who participated in it were ZAPU supporters.

Meanwhile, on 3 February 1976, independent Mozambique imposed sanctions on Rhodesia. The issues of joining the UN and mandatory sanctions against Rhodesia were on the agenda of its government from the first days of independence. These matters were raised in particular by Kurt Waldheim, the then UN Secretary-General, as well as a representative of the Labour Cabinet in Britain. The border was closed "after very calculated preparation that took some months".[69]

Nkomo became President of the ANC, having "deposed" Abel Muzorewa from its top leadership at the congress in September 1975, and when he arrived in Moscow, at the very first meeting of the Solidarity Committee he underlined that the ANC had been "built on the basis of ZAPU".[70] I met Nkomo at the airport on 26 May together with Dmitry Dolidze, former General Secretary of the Solidarity Committee, who had taken care of him during his first trip to the Soviet Union. Nkomo was accompanied by Jason Moyo and two people from the internal leadership: Amon Jirira, Treasurer, and Clement Muchachi, Secretary for Foreign Affairs.

Plate 7   ZAPU delegation, led by Joshua Nkomo, at the Soviet Solidarity Committee, circa 1976.

Source: Vladimir Shubin archive.

This visit took place soon after Nkomo and the new ZANU leader, Robert Mugabe, signed an agreement on the formation of a united Patriotic Front. Mugabe was "nominated" to the highest level of the ZANU leadership by a group of military commanders. Earlier, having been disappointed by continuing divisions in the political leadership, the African Frontline States advanced the idea of the formation of a united military force, the Zimbabwe People's Army (ZIPA). It was officially "inaugurated" in September 1975 but was rather short-lived.

ZIPA's creation followed the assassination of Herbert Chitepo on 18 March 1973 in Lusaka and the detention of ZANU senior political and military leaders in Zambia. ZANLA supplies to camps in Tanzania and Mozambique were cut off, and Hashim Mbita, Executive Secretary of the Liberation Committee, made the formation of a joint command a condition for resuming supplies. A delegation, headed by Jason Moyo, was sent to the ZANU leadership that had been imprisoned in Zambia after the murder of Chitepo. Josiah Tongogara, then the top ZANLA commander, agreed that the fighters should be moved away from Muzorewa, who claimed to be the top leader, and supported the idea of a united force, indicating that for the time being Rex Nhongo would be the senior ZANU man in it.[71]

A slogan was put forward that "the leader should come out of the bush; he should emerge as one of those who carry a gun". Samora Machel insisted on this, having been disappointed by splits in the political leadership of the liberation movement in Zimbabwe. However, commanders of ZIPRA, though they joined a new army, insisted, in particular at their meeting with Samora Machel, that they did have a political leadership, headed by Nkomo, and one of the ZANLA commanders named Mugabe as their leader.[72]

At this stage, at the military conference held in Mozambique in 1975 and attended by both ZIPRA and ZANLA commanders, it was agreed that Soviet advisers were needed for a joint force, but this idea was not realised,[73] owing either to opposition by host countries or to ZIPA's decline.

By the time Joshua Nkomo arrived in Moscow our relations with ZAPU (even if it was called the ANC at the time) had become close and active. Silundika played a very positive role in it. As I recall it, he came to Moscow more often than his colleagues. In particular, he was our guest in January 1976 and then, together with Moyo, a guest at the CPSU congress a month later. On 19 January he and Dumiso Dabengwa had a comprehensive discussion with Ulyanovsky, and at least one piece of advice he gave deserves mentioning:

Don't seize the property of the white people now. Create a new government and a new army under your control, then you will see. You don't have cadres. Social changes, changes in property relations should come later. Of course you should improve the situation of the black population, but years will pass before the socialisation of property.[74]

Apart from Silundika and Moyo, Dumiso Dabengwa, though officially not at the very top of the leadership, was becoming its most active ZAPU member outside Zimbabwe. Officially he headed his organisation's security, but in reality his responsibilities were much wider and we realised it. Of the military commanders the most prominent was Alfred "Nikita" Mangena, and at least once these two men came to Moscow together.

Dabengwa was outstanding in his very objective assessment of the political and military situation in Zimbabwe. I recall how at one of the meetings in the Soviet General Staff he gave the number of ZIPRA fighters inside the country as just 67 or 68, although many others would definitely inflate the figure.

Apart from the Solidarity Committee, Nkomo's programme included a meeting with Ulyanovsky at the CPSU International Committee, Africa Institute, and, no less important, in the Ministry of Defence, at the *Desyatka*. Nkomo recalls in his memoirs:

Once the policy of support had been decided on [by the Soviet leadership], I was passed on to a military committee [read: Ministry of Defence], and I had to justify to it every detail of my request. If I said we had 500 men, so we wanted 500 of their basic AK rifles, they would say no, 500 men means so many rifles, so many light machine-guns, so many mortars or anti-tank rockets, and I would end up with only about 300 AKs ... Only after I had studied the way armies are run was I able to deal as an equal with the Soviet military people.[75]

True, I recall that step by step Nkomo did acquire some basic military knowledge, though hardly equal to the competence of the officers of the Soviet General Staff.

12
Patriotic Front

The international position of Nkomo's organisation improved greatly with the strengthening of its ties with Angola. However, the situation in ZANU was still confused. With a certain irony he told us how, at his meeting with ZANLA commanders, Rex Nhongo (Solomon Majuru) gave him a piece of paper with the name of Robert Mugabe on it, whom they regarded as their "spokesman".[1] Nkomo also described how he personally facilitated the approval of Mugabe by the ZANU political and military leaders who were detained in Zambia after the murder of Chitepo, and their release. Mugabe had just left Quelimane where he had to stay for several months under orders of the Mozambican government which supported the formation of ZIPA, and was not yet regarded as the undisputed leader of ZANU.

Soon after his return from Moscow, on 30 June 1976, Nkomo wrote a letter to the CPSU Central Committee, in which he informed his "dear comrades"[2] that he had discussed and agreed with the governments of Angola and Zambia the transportation of arms and other supplies for the ANC (read: ZAPU).[3]

This radically changed the situation in favour of ZAPU; it no longer depended on supplies via the port of Dar des Salaam, a route that unfortunately for ZAPU was always far from reliable. According to a former ZIPRA high commander, in the 1960s and early 1970s just a few of the arms stocked in Dar es Salaam and Mbeya (a town half-way between Dar es Salaam and Lusaka), destined for ZAPU and the ANC of South Africa, would be given to them. The rest would go to ZANU, the Panafricanist Congress of Azania (South Africa) (the PAC) and COREMO. Some arms were even sold, in particular to the Revolutionary Front for an Independent East Timor (FRETILIN) and even to Latin America. However, after the independence of Angola all supplies went through it and the Tanzanians would not know what ZAPU was receiving.[4]

Nkomo's letter, conveyed to Moscow by the new Soviet ambassador to Zambia, Professor Vassily Solodovnikov, who, until his appointment headed the Africa Institute, was accompanied by a long list of requests, signed by "A. Nikita".[5] The needs were divided into four categories: a training camp for 2,000 persons, the "Zambian Front" (of 4,000 persons), fighters inside "Southern Rhodesia" and provision of general command and co-ordination. ZAPU, in particular, requested 4,000 Kalashnikovs of different modifications, as well as 1,650 SKS Simonov self-loading carbines, 1,100 pistols, RPGs, Grad-Ps, Strelas, recoilless guns, mortars, trucks, cars, a launch, rubber boats, etc.[6]

Nkomo's request was favourably received by the CPSU top leadership, who ordered the Ministry of Defence and other relevant government bodies to study the list of requests and to submit their proposals in a month's time.[7]

No doubt, Moscow's favourable attitude to Nkomo's requests was to a large extent the result of the close relations he had established with Solodovnikov. Nkomo writes in his memoirs:

The former Soviet ambassador in Lusaka, Mr Solodovnikov, was reputed to be associated with the KGB. He was a very nice fellow and we got on very well on a personal level. Moreover, he was entirely professional about his work, and if you discussed a request with him you could be sure that it would soon get onto the agenda of the right committee in Moscow, and the decision would come back without too much delay.[8]

The story about "KGB General Solodovnikov", just like the story about "General Konstantin Shaganovitch", continues from one publication to another. After his appointment the "liberal" *Rand Daily Mail*, in an article titled "Reds send 'KGB man' to Lusaka", wrote: "Dr Solodovnikov has been named by Western intelligence sources as a senior officer in the Soviet secret police, KGB ... ."[9]

These "experts" apparently just could not believe that a Soviet official could be influential and successful if he was not an officer of the State Security Committee. However, Solodovnikov's strength lay in something different: his experience as a senior diplomat at the UN headquarters was greatly enhanced by his excellent knowledge of Africa and, last but not least, by his friendly and honest nature.

By the time he arrived in Lusaka, in July 1976, Moscow's relations with Zambia were at their lowest ebb. Kenneth Kaunda did his best to bring Savimbi to power in Angola. The records of the US National Security Council show that he suggested to President Ford to "get Savimbi in" and to conduct elections in Angola only later:

The President: At dinner he [Kaunda] was very forceful on this. He said that it was important to get his man in first, and then he will win the election. I asked him if there were not going to be elections, and he said yes, and that was why it was important to put Savimbi in first and then he would win.

Secretary Kissinger: Kaunda was giving the President a lesson in political science [Laughter].[10]

In his policy towards Angola, Kaunda found himself on the same side as Pretoria, not even mentioning Washington and Beijing. Indeed, he "distinguished" himself by a thinly veiled insult of Moscow and Havana, when soon after the MPLA's victory he spoke about "the plundering tiger with its deadly cubs".[11]

However, Solodovnikov managed not only to restore Moscow's ties with Lusaka, but also to enhance and diversify them greatly. Soon these ties included even such "sensitive" issues as a supply of arms and sending Soviet military specialists to Zambia. The US ambassador informed Washington prior to Solodovnikov's return to Moscow:

Solodovnikov, a long favourite of the American and Western European media which touted him as Moscow's Southern African wizard, leaves behind an impressive record in Zambia ... Solodovnikov can take considerable personal credit for Soviet successes in Zambia. His patient, unaggressive style coupled with an impressive understanding of Africa put him in good stead with Kaunda and the Zambian leadership.[12]

It was not by accident that Solodovnikov's activities became an issue of deep concern to all the enemies of the liberation struggle in Southern Africa. Thus there are dozens of papers on his stay in Lusaka in the archive documents of the US State Department. As for South Africa, Louis le Grange, Minister of Police, stated: "The Russian ambassador in Lusaka, Dr Solodovnikov, played an important role in the planning of ANC and communist strategy and he was assisted by a South African refugee woman, Frene Ginwala."[13]

A rebuff of these accusations came from Oliver Tambo: "One must pity the South African government for they are going to be misled into suicidal positions. These actions are done by blacks within the country ... No one outside South Africa – not even the Soviet ambassador – has got a way of reaching into South Africa and telling the people exactly what to do."[14] Anyhow, be it an exploit of a Western, South African or South Rhodesian "special service" (all of them were active in Zambia), somebody managed to install a bugging device in his residence; it was promptly detected but left intact to confuse his "adversaries".

A new request was forwarded by Nkomo after the failure of the Geneva Conference on the political settlement in Zimbabwe, which began on 28 October 1976 and was interrupted on 14 December "for the Christmas holidays". It was to be reconvened on 17 January 1977, but this was never done because of the intransigence of Ian Smith's regime. It is worth mentioning that at Nkomo's request the International Department sent two Soviet experts, Dr Venyamin Chirkin and Ambassador Vladimir Snegirev, to Geneva to advise the ZAPU delegation on legal and especially constitutional matters.[15]

On the eve of the conference on 9 October 1976, Nkomo and Mugabe announced the formation of a joint Patriotic Front of ZAPU and ZANU. It was created on an equal basis, but quite probably Nkomo thought that he would be able to play a leading role.

It was also clear from Nkomo's explanations that the new front was, at least at this stage, virtually a marriage of convenience, and its formation was an exclusively political, even ostentatious step. Although the co-presidents of the PF agreed to attend any conference as a joint delegation under joint leaders, in reality both organisations worked separately, whether in their offices abroad or in military units, though Moscow tried its best to get them to co-operate better. Thus I was glad to hear later from Silundika on this matter: "On the ZAPU–ZANU front some progress has been made – at least on paper – regarding closer links on a unitary basis – both army and political. The programme and ideology are being worked out this week … ." However, "Comrade T.G." was worried by "the Far East [read: Beijing] influence" on ZANU and "the Far East misdirection".[16]

When we met Nkomo again in Moscow in early January 1977, he informed us that when the Patriotic Front (PF) advanced its proposals for settlement in Geneva, the British and Americans replied: "Your scheme is difficult for the white population to accept. Give us a chance to make up our plan and to see how your plan goes with our plan" and requested an interval in the talks. Then Ivor Richard, British ambassador to the UN, who chaired the conference, finally put it on paper; Nkomo was critical of it, but in any case Smith rejected it and the Geneva conference was never resumed. "Nobody told us what has happened with it," commented Nkomo, "but we want a new conference with transfer of power on its agenda. We don't want a new concert. There will never be a political solution in Zimbabwe until the regime and the British understand that we are a fighting force. Until we push them by military means."[17]

Nkomo had a chance to discuss military matters with the Soviet military on 4 January 1977, immediately after the conference breakdown.[18] A written request followed, mostly on training matters. In his letter Nkomo informed the Soviet leadership that the number of ZIPRA combat personnel had increased fivefold, that 600 cadres were expecting departure for Zimbabwe, 1,200 were undergoing training, 1,000 were starting training in a new camp and 3,000 recruits were in transit camps in Zambia and Botswana.[19] Agreement had been reached with the authorities of Angola and Zambia on the opening of a training camp in Angola, and the Cubans took responsibility for supplies and maintenance in the initial stage, for three or four months.[20]

However, Nkomo wanted the Soviets to take over as far as these matters are concerned, as well as to send a group of Soviet military instructors to Angola.[21] Other requests included the provision of a Soviet transport plane for bringing Zimbabwean personnel and goods from Angola to Zambia, and receiving 200 activists in the USSR for military training, including 20 pilots. He also wanted 20 persons to be trained in "party security".[22]

In a *zapiska* to the CPSU CC, signed by Ulyanovsky, Nkomo's new request for assistance was connected with "the breakdown of the Geneva conference on peaceful settlement which was done by the racist regime".[23]

Again the relevant state bodies were urgently ordered, within two weeks, to consider Nkomo's request.[24] Since the archive materials are only partly accessible, it is not clear whether all these requests were met. However, most of them undoubtedly were. Nkomo expressed his satisfaction with Soviet support when he visited Moscow again soon after the assassination of Jason Moyo.[25]

His death on 22 January 1977 showed once again that in spite of previous tragedies, leaders of the liberation movements hardly observed rules of security. While in Maputo together with Silundika and Msika, he telephoned his people in Lusaka and asked them not to open a parcel he expected from his friend (or, rather, girlfriend) in Botswana. He opened it himself and was killed when it exploded. Either the parcel was "contaminated" from the very beginning or intercepted on the way; the telephone conversation could have been intercepted as well.[26]

In July 1977 the first group of twelve Soviet officers arrived at the ZAPU camp, situated 18 kilometres from Luena, a town in Eastern Angola (formerly Vila Luso), not too far from the Zambian border.

Its head was Lieutenant Colonel Vladimir Pekin. The young Captain Anatoly Burenko was his deputy for political affairs.[27] Then this first group was replaced by another one, commanded by Lieutenant Colonel Zverev.[28]

The Soviet group had a mission to train ZAPU fighters and commanders and spent exactly a year there, till July 1978. Up to 2,000 ZAPU members would come to Angola for training in two-month shifts. The syllabus included the tactics of a group, a platoon and a company. Each course would be completed by staging a field exercise, which included crossing "a water obstacle", that is, a river or a lake.[29] The Soviet military specialists stayed in the camp together with ZAPU combatants and shared all the hardships with them. They lived in brick buildings without any amenities; some of them lacked windowpanes and even window frames. In spite of all hardships they performed their duties in an exemplary way.[30]

Cubans stayed there as well and provided everything necessary for combat training, including food and water, for ZAPU fighters and for the Soviets. They were also responsible for guarding the camp, and during training they acted as platoon and company commanders. Burenko recalls them with a feeling of gratitude, and writes about their efficiency, professionalism, honesty, jovial character and friendly attitude to the Soviets.[31]

Since ZAPU was preparing for taking power by force, the movement urgently needed a big number of fighters, trained in using small arms and able to act efficiently as combat units. Therefore the main task of the Soviets was to train them in the tactics of regular units. However, particular attention was also paid to guerrilla tactics, "which would be needed in case of temporary setbacks of the regular forces".[32] Thus by mid 1977 the ZAPU leadership and ZIPRA command, apart from broadening guerrilla activities, had already been planning an offensive in Zimbabwe with the use of regular forces.

The syllabus, organisation and conduct of studies, as well as all managerial issues, were co-ordinated by the Soviets with "Ban", the camp commissar. In 1978 Joshua Nkomo visited the camp, and this visit raised the morale of fighters. Nkomo was fully satisfied with the training and this heightened the prestige of the instructors further.

The group was subordinate to the GVS in Angola, at that time to Lieutenant General Vassily Shakhnovich.[33] Once a month, one of the officers would go to the Soviet military mission in Angola, usually by Soviet An-12, receive a monthly allowance for the whole group there and purchase foodstuffs. A Soviet-made UAZ truck was at their disposal in Luena.[34]

The attitude of the Angolan central and local authorities towards ZAPU was very friendly. Every two months, up to 2,000 Zimbabweans would cross the Angolan-Zambian border each way. In a year the Soviet officers trained over 10,000 fighters and commanders up to company level.

ZIPRA fighters in Angola mostly had small arms though there were several recoilless guns to fight armoured targets. The danger of a surprise attack by the Rhodesian troops was always taken into account, be it in the camp, during field exercises, marches or rest. Deep trenches were dug out around the camp and aim was laid on all terrain within one kilometre of the camp.[35]

A serious problem was the lack of proper air defence of the camp, because of the absence of anti-aircraft weapons. Air observation was organised, trenches and shelters dug out. However, it did not prevent heavy losses when, on 26 February 1979 at 08:10, the Rhodesian Air Force attacked with seven bombers (earlier supplied by London); 192 fighters lost their lives and about 1,000 were wounded.[36] These included six Cuban instructors who were killed and 13 who were wounded.[37] A Soviet warrant officer, Grigory Skakun, who was a specialist on fire-range equipment, was hit by a cluster bomb containing ball bearings and died after some days.[38]

In the same period ZAPU began training its cadres in the USSR for heavy equipment.[39] Moreover, at Nkomo's request three Soviet military specialists were sent to Lusaka as advisers to render practical support to the ZAPU political leadership and ZIPRA command in planning and organising combat action in Zimbabwe. The group of three officers, headed by Colonel Lev Kononov, arrived in Lusaka on 13 July 1978.[40] Solodovnikov writes:

Outwardly, for the public, the group was assigned to Zambia's Ministry of Defence, but it didn't work even a single day there. In reality, the military specialists worked as councillors to the Chief Commander of the People's Revolutionary Army, Joshua Nkomo. These people were first-class specialists in guerrilla warfare.[41]

Nkomo claims in his memoirs: "... there was never any question of sending combat troops, or even advisors, from the Soviet Union or any other country to help us fight our war".[42] He is right on the first point, but wrong on the second: in one of his letters to the CPSU, Nkomo especially expressed appreciation for the work of Kononov's advisory group. Moreover, Nkomo claims that apart from a few Ghanaian instructors who served in the camps in Tanzania and two Cuban security officers, all the people at ZAPU bases were Zimbabweans,[43] "having forgotten" dozens of Soviets and Cubans who risked their lives in Boma camp.[44]

Anyhow, the fact that Soviet military personnel appeared in the ZIPRA headquarters soon became known to the Rhodesians and their friends, and their role remained a controversial issue for many years.

To what extent did the Soviet military advisers initiate a plan for conducting an offensive of the regular ZIPRA forces from the territory of Zambia across the Zambezi?[45] Jakkie Cilliers, now Director of the Institute for Security Studies in Pretoria, believes that it was sponsored and crafted by the Soviet Union.[46] However, Dumiso Dabengwa says that, on the contrary, the Soviet military advisers expressed serious reservations about the strategy drafted by the Zimbabweans themselves.[47] Besides, as stated above, training of mostly regular troops began before the Soviet group came to Zambia. However, some influence of Moscow cannot be excluded. I recall how at one of Nkomo's meetings at the Soviet Ministry of Defence, most probably in early 1978, Colonel General Georgy Skorikov, the chief of *Desyatka*, advised Nkomo not to disperse his forces but to concentrate them for decisive blows against the enemy.

However, it should be emphasised that ZIPRA cadres were trained by the Soviets in both regular and guerrilla warfare. When Nkomo led a ZAPU delegation to the USSR in March 1978, we organised his trip to the Crimea to meet ZIPRA fighters who were undergoing training in Perevalnoye. We watched how they were braving a snow-covered field, running and even crawling with AKs or RPGs in their hands, and somebody joked: "If Ian Smith were to see this he would immediately surrender." Besides, the Soviet military organised a radio link between a group of Zimbabweans who studied in Perevalnoye and another group in Moscow or near it, one that specialised in armed underground and guerrilla warfare. To listen to their radio exchange was a revelation for Nkomo himself and for those in his delegation, who were essentially civilians.

One more detail, a human one. We stayed in an ordinary Soviet hotel in Simferopol and had our dinner at a restaurant there. To the surprise of Zimbabweans many visitors were dancing there, as always happened in restaurants in the USSR those days. Then one of them, in a warrant officer's uniform, began dancing in a typically Russian (or Ukrainian, for that matter) way – making a wheel with his body. Nkomo commented to his colleagues: "These people are really free. Can you imagine somebody dancing this way, with all his feelings, in London?"

13
Lancaster House

The mood of the Zimbabweans during their trips to the USSR varied depending on the situation "at home" and in neighbouring countries. I recall that in June 1978, Dumiso Dabengwa, who was a frequent visitor to Moscow, was rather gloomy. He spoke of the pressure of the independent African states on the Patriotic Front and was worried that even Zambia, which was closest to ZAPU, could forbid the use of its territory for the armed struggle. "Then not to become permanent exiles, we shall all have to move inside the country."[1]

He was worried that the liberation movement could be forced into agreement on unfavourable terms. It did not happen. The racist regime reached a compromise, but with those forces which had discredited themselves. A so-called "internal settlement" and "election" held in April 1979 brought Abel Muzorewa to the post of (figurehead) Prime Minister of "Zimbabwe-Rhodesia", but the real control remained in the hands of Smith and his "securocrats". Chikerema and Nyandoro became cabinet ministers, thus vindicating Moscow's earlier decision to support their rivals in the ZAPU leadership.

During the next visit of the ZAPU delegation, in early 1979, the mood was different. ZIPRA was getting stronger in spite of numerous bombings and acts of sabotage by Rhodesians in Zambia and, to a lesser extent, in Botswana. The issues Nkomo raised on that occasion included a top priority for him: to ensure the success of the offensive into Zimbabwe, he wanted to acquire Soviet-made airplanes. By that time ZAPU cadres were already being trained in the Air Force Centre in Frunze, the capital of the Soviet Republic of Kirgizia, but as a stopgap solution Nkomo hoped to receive pilots from "friendly countries", though not from the Soviet Union.[2]

The story of "Soviet MiGs for ZAPU" is rather controversial. To set the record straight, this idea was immediately met with scepticism in Moscow.[3] The Cuban leadership was not enthusiastic either: Cuban Communist Party CC member Raul Valdes Vivo, who visited several African countries under orders from Fidel Castro, informed Nkomo and Mugabe that Cuba was "unable to satisfy their request to send pilots for the repulsion of air attacks on the training camps for the Patriotic Front armed forces".[4]

However, information on Nkomo's intentions apparently reached Smith's regime, and in late 1980, when Zimbabwean aviators came home after the completion of their training in the USSR, former Rhodesian white officers asked them: "Where are your MiGs?"[5] It appears that the prospect of facing them with outdated planes really worried the command of the Rhodesian Air Force and this, just like the concentration of ZIPRA hardware in Zambia, did make the regime more compliant.

Western and African academics also write on this issue, again in a controversial way. For example, some believe that MiGs arrived in Zambia, but were not "uncrated". On the other hand, Eliakim Sibanda claims that the "Russian and East German governments sabotaged the offensive by keeping ZIPRA pilots who were supposed to form a large part of the air service men".[6] Moreover, Sibanda, referring to an interview with Joshua Nkomo he conducted in August 1990, alleges that this took place after the ZAPU president had refused to allow "Russians, East Germans and Cubans to fly planes for ZIPRA".[7] In truth, on the contrary, it was Nkomo who told us that he hoped to involve pilots from the GDR or Cuba (he did not mention the Soviets). Sibanda continues: "Nkomo went further to say he detected some racism from the Russians who did not want to see their own Caucasian group defeated by blacks."[8] I just cannot believe that the ZAPU president could say this; at least in his memoirs he spoke of his experience in the Soviet Union with distinct sympathy and appreciation. I felt his sympathy again when in 1991 Nkomo visited Moscow as Vice-President of independent Zimbabwe. Besides, I never heard him substituting "Caucasians" for whites; this term is common in the USA or Canada, where Sibanda lives, but not in Africa.

In any case the story Nkomo told in his book is quite different from that of Sibanda, though it contradicts the truth as well. He writes: "... we have been assured [by the Soviets] that the training of our aircrews could be completed a year in advance, in time for the end of 1979".[9] He even claims that "by the end of the war" ZIPRA had "the complete flying and maintenance staff for a squadron of combat aircraft, who had passed out of the Soviet training schools".[10]

It is hard to believe that the Soviets would agree to let students of Air Force Training Centre graduate a year earlier than needed, and neither in Moscow nor in Harare could I find any proof of Nkomo's words.

Plate 8   Fifteen years later: Joshua Nkomo and Vladimir Shubin, 1991.

Source: Vladimir Shubin archive.

Several times I was present at Nkomo's discussions with the Soviet military and could sense how happy he usually was to hear from them that ZAPU requests were being satisfied. One of these occasions was rather peculiar: having been informed about forthcoming supplies of uniforms (20,000 pieces, if my memory serves me well), Nkomo asked for one set to be made "extra large", and indeed, soon his picture in uniform appeared on the pages of a ZAPU magazine.

The volume and diversity of Soviet supplies in late 1970s was really impressive. Once, in early 1978, at a meeting in the *Desyatka* after receiving information on the value of allocated hardware and other goods, he remained silent for a couple of minutes and then said: "This is 73 times more than we received from the OAU Liberation Committee."

True, the equipment was often not the most modern, but as a rule it was superior to armament available in Rhodesia. Besides, intensive training of ZIPRA cadres, both in Africa and in the Soviet Union (as well as in the GDR, Cuba and some other socialist countries) made them staunch fighters. One of the British diplomats who took part in the "Witness seminar: Britain and Rhodesian Question: The Road to Settlement 1979–1980" (in the UK National Archives), organised by the London School of Economics (LSE) Cold War Studies Centre and Centre for Contemporary British History on 5 July 2005, recalled:

During the Lancaster House discussions when I was sent for in Salisbury, I remember a Rhodesian senior general commenting to me that some of the troops had just had a nasty shock. They were used to be being flown in by helicopter, landing and disembarking, and the guerrillas would fade away.

However, a week before when Rhodesians got out of the helicopter to engage "a group of ZIPRA forces, newly trained by the Russians ... 'The devils didn't run away. They stopped and fought.' So perhaps that did influence matters in Rhodesia."[11]

It would not be an exaggeration to say that by mid 1979 the forces of the Patriotic Front – ZIPRA and ZANLA – were winning the liberation war, even though unfortunately they were not united. The discussion on the efficiency of their actions continues even now, almost three decades later. Perhaps it would be fair to say that ZANU managed to "penetrate" deeper into the areas populated by Africans, while ZAPU conducted the most serious armed operations against the racist regime.

Sibanda writes that the Selous Scouts [Rhodesian special forces] commander confessed that by the beginning of 1987 the RSFs [Rhodesian Security Forces] had lost control of the military situation partly because of a shortage of planes. Most of the war planes had possibly been shot down by the ZIPRA forces, since it was they who at the time had [Soviet-made] anti-aircraft missiles, and their camps were attacked first and more often by the RSFs.[12]

As important as Soviet assistance in the military field was, it would be quite wrong to reduce the relationship between Moscow and ZAPU to this. Apart from political support, the supply of civilian goods, providing air tickets to international conferences and training of various types, co-operation with ZAPU included the assistance of highly skilled Soviet lawyers and diplomats to its delegations at the talks in Geneva, mentioned above, and at the infamous Lancaster House conference from September to December 1979.

Margaret Thatcher came to power in Britain after her election victory in May 1979, and in her first statements she hinted at the possibility of recognition of the Muzorewa government, but soon had to abandon this idea. Instead she used the Commonwealth Conference, held in Lusaka, to advance a new initiative: talks that would include "the government of Zimbabwe-Rhodesia", practically involving Muzorewa and Smith, both wings of the Patriotic Front and other less significant groupings. According to a former ZIPRA high commander, by that time the British were worried by ZAPU's stockpiles of weapons and training of cadres for heavy equipment. They were in a hurry "to avoid another Vietnam", and they thought that if ZAPU had six months more of fighting, Rhodesian forces would suffer a military defeat, and this would threaten stability in South Africa.[13] The South African factor was apparently very important, although it is often overlooked: both London and Pretoria knew of close relations between ZAPU and the ANC and, in particular, of the presence of its military personnel in the ranks of ZIPRA.

At the witness seminar, mentioned above, former British diplomats underlined the fact that their government prevented representatives from any country except the UK and Zimbabwe from taking part in the conference at Lancaster House. However, I had to remind them that although this is correct, London could not prevent "aliens" from coming to the British capital at the time of the conference.

Dr Chirkin was again helping the ZAPU delegation in connection with Nkomo's request, this time together with V. Fedorinov of the Soviet MFA. In his reminiscences he writes in detail about discussions with Nkomo and the requests that the ZAPU leader forwarded to Moscow through him and his colleague:

Most of all Nkomo was interested in a supply of Soviet heavy armament, thinking that if he received such weapons, his role would be more important and his chances to become the leader of the state would grow. In this regard he referred to the mentality and perception of the African population, which had not seen such weapons before.[14]

Chirkin writes: "We conveyed to Moscow many of Nkomo's requests on various kinds of support, and the replies from Moscow ... were always positive."[15]

The very convening of the conference on Zimbabwe in London was a diplomatic success of the new British government. On the surface it looked like a return to an era of constitutional conferences held at the end of British rule in a number of African countries, but in essence the situation was quite different: London had to deal with the growing forces of liberation, which had strong supporters, including Moscow and Beijing.

African countries, especially Frontline Sates, were of course in principle on their side as well, but in practice some of them exerted enormous pressure on ZAPU and ZANU urging them to make concessions. Strange as it may seem, there was a certain convergence of interests between African countries, adjacent to Zimbabwe, on the one hand, and Pretoria and its Tory friends in Britain, on the other: they wanted to solve the "Rhodesian problem" as soon as possible and almost at any cost.

Both before the conference and during it, Rhodesian forces conducted numerous bombings and acts of sabotage in Zambian territory, even including a ground attack on Nkomo's house in Lusaka on 15 April 1979 with the aim of assassinating him.[16] According to a summary drafted by Lev Kononov from 17 February to 9 December 1979, Rhodesian forces carried out about 50 air and ground raids against ZAPU political, military and security installations.[17]

These steps, especially the blowing up of bridges, were partly intended to prevent an expected ZIPRA offensive, but at the same time they were to put pressure on the government of Zambia. Similar action was taken against ZANLA camps in the territory of Mozambique.

I heard many times from Zimbabwean friends that the governments of African countries that served as a rear base for ZAPU and ZANU virtually put an ultimatum to their leaders: if they did not reach an agreement at Lancaster House, they would not be in a position to return from London. When, at a difficult time in the conference, Tekere of ZANU and Chinamano of ZAPU were sent to the Frontline States to look for support, instead their leaders "whipped" the representatives of Zimbabwe.[18]

The results of the conference are well known. On 21 December the agreement on a cease-fire was signed. Transitional arrangements stipulated a temporary return of control over Zimbabwe to a British Governor General, the concentration of ZIPRA and ZANLA fighters in assembly points under control of Commonwealth forces, elections from 27 to 29 February 1980, and independence in two months' time. The approved constitution contained obvious concessions to the white minority: for seven years, 20 of the 100 seats in Parliament were reserved for them, and for ten years, land ownership could not be changed. According to Chirkin, he was very surprised to find out that "in spite of all the assurances, the [Patriotic] Front unequivocally agreed to the formula which provided a fifth of seats in parliament to the whites (while their share [of the population] was about 1/23)".[19]

Nevertheless, the agreement provided liberation movements with a good chance to obtain the majority of seats and to form a government of independent Zimbabwe, especially if they went to the election as a united front.

Unfortunately, it did not happen. According to Nkomo, Mugabe refrained from discussing a common approach and left London immediately after the conference was over.[20] Then, at the meeting of the Frontline States in Beira, Mugabe, who was accompanied by Simon Muzenda and Edgar Tekere, announced that ZANU would fight the election separately, saying that some ZANU members had accused him of giving up the leadership to ZAPU. Nyerere nodded in reaction to his words and Machel applauded, while Kaunda looked unhappy, as did Quett Masire, President of Botswana.[21]

Because of legal problems (the name ZANU was "monopolised" by its former leader, Sithole), Mugabe's party decided to use the name ZANU-PF, and after that ZAPU changed itself into PF-ZAPU.

At the witness seminar all the UK diplomats insisted that their hope was in Muzorewa's (relative?) success in predominantly Shona areas and a possible coalition of his party (the so-called United African National Council) with Nkomo. However, ZAPU leaders and their supporters strongly believed that Britain, South Africa, Mozambique and Tanzania were united in their preference of ZANU over ZAPU, of Mugabe over Nkomo. According to them, London was ready to support any force, save ZAPU, because the British were worried by the growth of the Soviet influence in Southern Africa and at the same time by the possibility of the use of Zimbabwean territory by the ANC of South Africa.[22]

As for Samora Machel, he maintained contact with ZAPU, in particular, through its office in Maputo, and even rendered material support to this party on the eve of the election, providing it with US$300,000,[23] but undoubtedly his choice was ZANU, and support to it included sending Mozambican military personnel inside Zimbabwe. I even heard from a former prominent member of ZAPU that on the eve of the Lancaster House Conference Machel had told him that "Russian tanks" would never come into Zimbabwe. Machel was determined to prevent ZIPRA's offensive and this was an important reason for his support of the forthcoming conference.

Indeed, the Soviet-made tanks and other heavy arms supplied to ZAPU were not put in action owing to the Lancaster House Conference, but the very threat of these undoubtedly made the Rhodesian regime feel vulnerable and more ready to compromise.

The results of the election, an absolute majority for ZANU-PF, were a severe blow to Nkomo and his closest lieutenants. As "patriarch" of the liberation struggle in Zimbabwe, he definitely expected to win. The outcome, 57 seats won by ZANU-PF and just 20 by PF-ZAPU, was not one that Nkomo had anticipated.

Most of the observers explain this by the "ethnic factor", by the reflection of the Shona majority among the African population. But is this explanation adequate? Why is it that now, when Zimbabwe is suffering from a serious crisis, opposition to Mugabe enjoys overwhelming support in both major cities – Harare and Bulawayo – though the ethic composition of the population there is quite different? Besides, strictly speaking, Nkomo himself was not Ndebele, but belonged to the Kalanga, a group that was historically closer to the Shona, but later came under strong Ndebele influence.

On the surface a political settlement in Zimbabwe looked quite successful, at least in the beginning, when Mugabe proclaimed the much-praised policy of national reconciliation. In particular, on the advice of Mozambique and Tanzania, he accepted "the principle of keeping the Rhodesian civil servants, but with deputies appointed by the new government that should replace the former ones, as they would be retired progressively".[24]

However, as one of the former ZIPRA commanders put it: "The aim of Lancaster House was to disarm us and not to look into substantial issues."[25] The most crucial of these was the issue of land, and when this "time-fuse bomb" exploded two decades later, it shattered both economic and political stability in Zimbabwe. The leaders of the Frontline States (FLS) advised the Patriotic Front delegation to accept that instead of putting the obligations on the funding of the purchase of land from white owners in the agreement "it would be in the official speech of the British Secretary of State on behalf of Her Majesty".[26]

14
Moscow and Independent Zimbabwe

However, initially, when trouble began, it happened within the government, between former allies in the Patriotic Front. These internal contradictions are, of course, beyond the theme of this book. However, the "discovery" of caches of Soviet-made weapons in properties belonging to PF-ZAPU in February 1982, as well as a copy of Dabengwa's letter to Yury Andropov, then the KGB chairman, with a request to continue the support of his party, introduced the "Soviet factor" once again.

The story of these caches is also rather controversial. I heard from a former ZIPRA commander that when the Lancaster House conference came to an end, General Peter Walls, the commander of the Rhodesian Defence Force, declared that the Patriotic Front had capitulated. At the meeting of ZIPRA and ZANLA commanders they considered it to be a trap and decided not to surrender weapons until the situation become clear. To be on the safe side the top military commanders did not go to assembly points either. My interlocutor claimed that ZIPRA's arms caches discovered in 1982 were made on the basis of his agreement.[1]

With hindsight it is clear that Moscow's refusal to establish proper contact with ZANU even when that party became rather influential was a mistake. Some Soviet representatives, especially in countries whose governments supported ZANU, tried to rectify it. Petr Yevsyukov, then Soviet ambassador to Mozambique, wrote:

From Maputo the balance of forces in Rhodesia ... was seen better. It was clear that Mugabe enjoyed the support of the majority of the African population as well as of Mozambique, especially President Samora Machel ... The necessity of amending our policy with regard to support of the forces of national liberation in Zimbabwe, taking into account the likelihood of Mugabe becoming the leader of the independent country, became evident for the Soviet embassy in Mozambique.

To begin with, I invited Mugabe for a meeting. The discussion took place in my residence, which was almost next to the mansion where Mugabe lived. I communicated the content of our talk and the embassy's proposal to Moscow.

Soon after the meeting with Mugabe I flew to Moscow, when I received support on this issue from a number of influential people and institutions, including L.F. Ilyichev, Deputy Minister of Foreign Affairs, and Petr Ivanovich Ivashutin, Chief of the GRU of the General Staff. But at the discussion in the CC International Department, I faced resolute opposition from R.A. Ulyanovsky ... Having got angry, he said: "Why have you met Mugabe? Nobody instructed you to do so." Such a position resulted in me feeling awkward, when Zimbabwe became independent and Mugabe became its first Prime Minister.[2]

This example shows once again that Moscow was not something "monolithic", that different opinions were expressed on various crucial issues, but at the same time, it shows that at least as far as the issue of the liberation struggle was concerned, the International Department played a decisive role.

Chirkin was "on the same wavelength" as Yevsyukov. He recalls:

According to the instructions received by both of us in Geneva and later in 1979 in London we could only have contact with Nkomo's party. In our messages to the CPSU CC we twice suggested establishing contact with Mugabe, but both times we received in reply a categorical instruction not to interfere in somebody else's business.[3]

Such a policy even brought about a violation of the formal protocol. Thus, when Mugabe requested a visa to spend some time in Moscow on the way from Vietnam, it was refused – though to be on the safe side we in the Solidarity Committee sent an official to Sheremetyevo to meet Mugabe if he should be there just in passing.

However, by the time of the Zimbabwean election Moscow's assessment of the situation was quite sober. The Soviets deplored the fact that the two wings of the Patriotic Front went into the election as separate entities, and I recall how, at the meeting of the Solidarity Committee on the eve of the election, Andrey Urnov did not exclude a ZANU victory.

On 6 March 1980 Leonid Brezhnev sent a message of congratulations "To the leaders of the Patriotic Front Comrade Robert Mugabe and Comrade Joshua Nkomo". However, inter-state relations between the USSR and Zimbabwe went wrong from the very beginning. The reception of the Soviet delegation at the celebration of Zimbabwean independence, proclaimed on 18 April, was rather cool. The delegation was headed by Sharaf Rashidov, the CPSU leader in Uzbekistan, who was somewhat of a specialist in the Politburo on the Third World, but a planned meeting with Mugabe did not take place; in fact, they only met him almost accidentally at the airport when the delegation was leaving. I heard that Mugabe suggested that they delay their departure, but they did not do so, probably feeling offended enough. Anyhow, this episode created further tension in bilateral relations. In fact, official diplomatic relations between the two countries were established only ten months later.

Solodovnikov describes in detail all the problems encountered in this respect.[4] Draft documents on the establishment of diplomatic relations were left in the Zimbabwean capital by the delegation, but no reply was received. In fact, a selective approach to international relations was expressed even earlier: at least Moscow was invited to the independence celebration, but among the other 95 invited countries, its close allies – the GDR, Poland, Czechoslovakia, Hungary – were missing. At the same time, as Solodovnikov puts it, "allies and partners of Ian Smith's regime – the US, Britain, France, FRG [Federal Republic of Germany]" – were there.[5] He continues:

The government of R. Mugabe ... was in a hurry to establish diplomatic relations with those countries that in the period of the struggle for independence of the people of Zimbabwe were openly calling ZANU leaders and its rank and file fighters terrorists, who were allies of Ian Smith's regime and who were clandestinely supplying him with oil and weapons, used to shoot Zimbabwean refugees in the camps in Mozambique and Zambia and fighters of the PFZ [Patriotic Front of Zimbabwe], including those from ZANU.[6]

Indeed, unlike the USSR, all Western countries were welcome to establish diplomatic relations without any delay!

Solodovnikov himself came to Zimbabwe in November 1980 to discuss the issue. His efforts were in vain: while PF-ZAPU was a partner of ZANU-PF in government, Zimbabwean diplomats insisted on Moscow ending its "historic relations" with the former and limiting its inter-party contacts to the latter only.[7] (As for material support to ZAPU, both the Soviet government and Soviet NGOs stopped it immediately after the political settlement was reached.[8])

Finally, the agreement on establishing diplomatic relations was reached in February 1981, after talks, conducted in the Zimbabwean capital by another Soviet Ambassador, Valentin Vdovin, who replaced Yevsyukov in Maputo on rather unprecedented, even humiliating conditions: Moscow had to agree to cease all contact with the PF-ZAPU.[9]

Fortunately, the choice of the first Soviet ambassador to Zimbabwe was perfect: Georgy Ter-Gazariants, a brilliant and charismatic person, a war veteran and a former party leader in Armenia. He was transferred there from Dakar; and step by step he managed to develop bilateral relations in various fields.

As for inter-party contact with ZANU-PF, the first concrete step was taken when, in mid November 1982, Sidney Sekeremayi, then Minister of State for Defence, visited Moscow. His main interlocutors were government officials dealing with military supplies, but a meeting at the CPSU International Department took place as well.

As could be expected, Sekeremayi used this opportunity to complain about Moscow's earlier attitude to ZANU and it became clear to us that certain forces were supplying Zimbabwean authorities with false information.[10] For example, he claimed that Moscow was "hiding" a prominent ZIPRA commander, Akim Ndlovu, while in reality, to avoid arrest after the "disclosure of caches", he had left for a Scandinavian country.

However, Ulyanovsky, who conducted the discussion on our side, stated the Soviet position in a friendly but firm way: having expressed his regret that Moscow's relations with ZANU had not been developed during the years of armed struggle, he suggested sharing responsibility. "Let's do it in God's way: fifty-fifty", he said, reminding Sekeremayi how ZANU in the past, following Beijing, accused Moscow of "social imperialism".[11]

Then a real breakthrough followed, when Nathan Shamuyarira, a prominent Zimbabwean intellectual, then Minister of Information and ZANU-PF Secretary, came to Moscow in December 1982 for the celebration of the Soviet Union's 60th anniversary. We immediately established a good rapport, which I still cherish now, 25 years later.

Conditions for the development of political ties with Zimbabwe became more favourable when, at its congress in 1984, attended by the CPSU delegation, ZANU-PF dropped "Mao Zedong thought" from its basic documents. Then Robert Mugabe, who for the first seven years of independent Zimbabwe was Prime Minister (he was elected President after a change in the constitution), paid an official visit to Moscow in December 1985 and had talks with Gorbachev and Nikolay Ryzhkov, the Soviet Prime Minister.

Moscow's relations with Zimbabwe were allocated additional importance when it became clear that after the conference of the Non-Aligned Movement (NAM) in Harare in 1987 the country would chair it. At that time the Soviet top leadership paid constant attention to the activities of NAM; a special department was created in the Ministry of Foreign Affairs, headed by Sergey Sinitsyn, himself a leading expert on Africa and a senior diplomat. Vladimir Sokolov was sent to Zimbabwe specifically to deal with that movement.[12]

Naturally, Moscow followed the internal developments in Zimbabwe as well, and was worried by the conflict between ZANU-PF and PF-ZAPU, which was one of the reasons for the so-called "rebellion" in Matabeleland, in the western part of the country. The dismissal of PF-ZAPU ministers, Nkomo's flight to Botswana and then to London,[13] the trial of Dumiso Dabengwa and former ZIPRA commander "Lookout" Masuku[14] – all these developments were of concern to us, although we were not in a position to influence them. We were especially worried that Pretoria would try to exploit the grievances of the population there for its own purposes, arming and instigating some of the so-called "dissidents". One fact, as a rule overlooked, drew our attention: in this very period the South African government tried (but failed) to speed up the creation of a pseudo-independent KwaNdebele Bantustan near the border with Zimbabwe.

Therefore we were glad to hear about the return of Nkomo to Zimbabwe and his talks with Mugabe, which resulted in the unity agreement in 1987. A final merger of the two parties (or, to put it straight, a final "swallowing" of Nkomo's party by ZANU-PF) took place at the congress on Christmas Eve 1989. Attending it as a member of the CPSU delegation, I could only be glad that our old friends had become active again in Zimbabwean politics. For me, personally, a chance to hug Dumiso Dabengwa, newly elected member of the Central Committee (soon he would be appointed Deputy Minister and then Minister of Home Affairs) was very precious.

If the bilateral relations in the political field developed well, the situation was rather different in other spheres. By the mid 1980s a number of the Soviet government structures established their offices in Zimbabwe (perhaps the country's excellent climate played its role too). However, their work was often hardly efficient. On the eve of Mugabe's visit we requested relevant information from them and found, for example, that trade turnover between the Soviet Union and Zimbabwe was less than the local expenditure of the offices of the MVT (Ministry of Foreign Trade) and the GKES (State Committee for Economic Ties with Foreign Countries; this body was responsible for development co-operation).

Co-operation in the military field hardly fared better. A large delegation of Soviet experts, representing the Ministry of Defence and the GIU GKES (Main Engineering Department, which was directly responsible for supplies of defence equipment) came to Zimbabwe at the request of its authorities, and drafted proposals for the reorganisation and strengthening of the armed forces. However, they were too grandiose to be realistic. When I asked an officer of the GIU how their proposals correlated with the defence budget of Zimbabwe, I discovered that even he did not know its volume.

The only important project that initially seemed to be a success was the purchase of the Soviet MiG-29 fighters Zimbabwe wanted to counter the threat from Pretoria. They were totally superior to any aircraft available in the South African Air Force. In fact, as stated above, even their predecessors, the MiG-23s, were a cut above the Mirages and their local analogues. Moreover, I heard that even rumours about supplies of MiG-29s to Angola made Pretoria extremely worried.

The attention Zimbabwe's leadership paid to this project was evident from the fact that the negotiation team sent to Moscow in 1987 not only included airmen, in particular Air Force Commander Josiah Tungamirayi, but was moreover headed by Morris Nyagumbo, ZANU Politburo member and minister. Initially, however, the delegation and representatives of the GIU and other Soviet state bodies could not find a common language. Once, on a Saturday, a telephone rang in my apartment. Andrey Urnov, then Deputy Head of the International Department, asked me to go to the guest house on the Lenin Hills where the Zimbabweans were staying and find out from Nyagumbo (I had met him earlier in Moscow and Harare) what the problem was.

It became clear from our conversation that, just as in many other cases, the differences were caused by misunderstanding, probably even by inadequate translation. The discussion continued on a higher level, with Georgy Kornienko then First Deputy Head of the International Department, and after this "interference of the party in state affairs" the agreement was soon reached. It was mutually advantageous. The Soviet credit was rather soft, but, nevertheless, Moscow could receive payment in hard currency, which it badly needed in those days. Besides, the arrival of MiG-29s could positively (and radically) change the balance of forces in the region.

The Zimbabwean leaders were quite serious about this purchase, and Mugabe confirmed their intentions to Gorbachev when they met in 1987 in Moscow. (That time he accompanied his wife, Sally, who had come to attend the World Women's Congress.)

However, this project was a failure as well. On 21 March 1991 I was present at the reception held by President Sam Nujoma in Windhoek on the occasion of the first anniversary of Namibia's independence. Robert Mugabe was the chief guest at the celebration. Nathan Shamuyarira, then Minister of Foreign Affairs, who came with him, approached me: "So what, Shubin, has Gorbachev sold the Soviet Union to the US?" I regret that I began telling him that this was not so. Nevertheless, Shamuyarira had good reason for saying that. He told me how some weeks earlier the second or first secretary of the US embassy in Harare had told Zimbabweans: "Don't expect MiGs. We were always against this deal and we told Moscow it should be cancelled."[15] And only later Yury Ukalov, newly appointed ambassador, informed Zimbabwean authorities that the bilateral agreement could not be carried out: Moscow then requested payment in cash at once instead of granting credit.

So on the surface the issue was financial, rather understandable in view of the deterioration of the state of the Soviet economy as a result of Gorbachev's "reforms". But since the matter had been discussed and settled initially between the two leaders – Gorbachev and Mugabe – Zimbabweans would expect at least some message from the former to the latter explaining the situation. Instead they heard appalling news from an American "diplomat".

Part Four

Namibia

15
SWANU or SWAPO?

The early history of Moscow's relations with the South-West Africa People's Organisation (SWAPO) differed considerably from that of its ties with other liberation movements in Southern Africa. Initially these relations lagged behind. The fact is that in the beginning in the USSR, just as in Africa and in the West, supporters of the liberation struggle gave rather more priority to another organisation – the South West Africa National Union (SWANU). In particular, SWANU was a member of AAPSO, and its headquarters in Cairo as well as various conferences were an important gateway for the establishment of Moscow's contacts with African freedom fighters.

Most probably, two factors led to this approach. Firstly, from the moment of its inception SWANU portrayed itself as a national organisation, while SWAPO was initially founded in 1959 as the Ovamboland People's Organisation, thus it claimed to represent the interests of one ethnic group in Namibia, even though this was a major group. Besides, according to one of its founding members, Ben Amathila, its initial goal was to defend the economic rights of Ovambo workers.[1]

Secondly, the forces whose opinion Moscow took into account in those days, especially the ANC and SACP, were initially closer to SWANU. This is clear, in particular, from the fact that SWANU, together with the ANC and Panafricanist Congress (PAC), became a member of the South African United Front, formed in June 1960. Ruth First, a prominent South African journalist and writer, who at that time was a member of the SACP CC, in a book published in Britain in 1963 and later translated into Russian, wrote about both organisations, but expressed more sympathy for SWANU.[2] Andrey Urnov, who was later the first Soviet Ambassador to Windhoek, put it in the following way: "There was nobody around to introduce SWAPO to us."[3]

Moreover, in very early 1960s, perhaps because of good relations between SWANU and the ANC, the SWAPO leaders saw their organisation as closer to the PAC. At that stage it was even regarded as part of a so-called "Congo alliance", with PAC, FNLA and ZANU, because some SWAPO members were sent to Kinkuzu camp in Zaire (now the DRC) for training.[4]

However, even though SWAPO was slightly outside the informal group of "recognised" movements, some contact did exist between SWAPO officials and Soviet representatives abroad. The first SWAPO document available in the Solidarity Committee's archive is a translation of a letter from Ismail Fortune, its General Secretary and "representative in North Africa and the Middle East", sent to the Committee's representative in Cairo in August 1961 via a representative of Rwanda-Urundi.[5] This very fact attests to the lack of direct contact between SWAPO and Moscow at that stage. However, Fortune's letter was addressed to nobody but "His Excellence Minister of Defence of the USSR" and expressed his wish to visit the Soviet Union to discuss training "in military arts" because "in due time we shall have to begin armed actions". Furthermore, he expressed the hope that "Mr [Luis] Nelengani [SWAPO's vice-president] and others" would be received for such training.[6]

The letter was dispatched from the Solidarity Committee to its addressee the next day, 24 August 1961. In fact, later both of them, Fortune and Nelengani, came to Moscow for training, although not in a military establishment, but in the Central Komsomol (YCL) School.[7] Their career in SWAPO was rather short: Fortune returned to Namibia and was accused of betrayal,[8] Nelengani was dropped from the leadership after he stabbed Fortune's successor, Jacob Kahangua, and also returned home, was detained and became a state witness.

The Solidarity Committee's plan of exchanges for 1963 envisaged a visit of a three-man SWAPO delegation to the USSR for two weeks.[9] Its leadership wanted SWAPO President Sam Nujoma to lead it, but in August that year he informed them that he could not come but was ready to send either Kahangua or Nelengani. However, the Committee's representative in AAPSO, Latyp Maksudov, advised Moscow that it would be better to receive Sam Nujoma even if it was only to happen later.[10]

Then the Committee received a letter dated 2 December 1963 from the SWAPO Executive Committee, signed by "Ismail van Fortune", which contained requests for material support, including not only food and clothes, but arms and ammunition. Moreover, Fortune divulged plans to begin armed action in 1965 and emphasised that SWAPO needed £100,000 for that purpose.[11]

In its covering letter the Soviet embassy in Dar es Salaam was not particularly enthusiastic. It suggested receiving SWAPO members "to Central Komsomol school and analogous courses", but not to consider requests for material support, especially because the organisation had just received £2,000 from the Committee of Nine (OAU Liberation Committee).[12]

Indeed, at that stage some of SWAPO's plans were hardly realistic. Ben Amathila recalls: "Once I received a task from Peter Nanyemba [then SWAPO representative in Dar es Salaam] to look for sites on the [Atlantic] coast, where 500 young Namibians could be taken aboard a ship to bring them abroad for military training."[13]

However, Moscow's approach began changing when in late 1963 the SWANU leaders took an openly "pro-Chinese" stand. The Solidarity Committee officials felt it when a SWANU delegation, led by Jariretundu Kozonguizi, was in Moscow in transit from Beijing in early November 1963. Kozonguizi, future Ombudsman of the Republic of Namibia, even "distinguished" himself by physically mishandling a Committee official at the Sheremetyevo airport. Nevertheless, at his request the Committee invited another SWANU delegation to the USSR, although "judging by his behaviour and pronouncements during a stopover in Moscow the Chinese managed to impose on him moods hostile to Soviet representatives".[14]

All in all, at that stage Moscow's attitude can be seen from the fact that in 1963 the allocation of five scholarships for SWAPO and four for SWANU was planned.[15]

Though SWAPO representatives regularly visited Beijing as well, they were more cautious and were not following every twist of the Chinese policy. Nevertheless, even after SWAPO replaced SWANU as a member of AAPSO, its relations with Moscow did not develop rapidly. Material assistance to SWAPO was provided, its cadres were invited to Moscow for training, both academic and military; but, on the other hand, political ties were limited almost exclusively to contact with the Soviet Afro-Asian Solidarity Committee and other NGOs.

Such an attitude to SWAPO reflected its low level of activity (though long distances between Namibia and independent African countries were serious obstacles; the only exception was the Caprivi Strip bordering on Zambia.) Besides, SWAPO's leadership was considered somewhat "immature". I heard a story of a discussion between Nujoma and Ulyanovsky around 1966 or 1967, when the SWAPO leader suggested sending Soviet fishing vessels to Namibian territorial waters to provoke a negative reaction from Pretoria, and thus an international crisis. The Soviets believed that this idea, which appeared to be provocation, had been suggested to the SWAPO leadership by their "friends" in the West. In any case, after this meeting Nujoma was not given a chance to visit the International Department for several years.

However, with the rise in SWAPO activities, both military and political, its image improved and the need for stronger support became evident. The first members of the SWAPO leadership whom I met were Peter Nanyemba and his colleagues, Joseph Ithana, then editor of *Namibia Today*, and Peter Katjavivi, the SWAPO representative in London. The three of them came to Moscow from Berlin, where they had taken part in the World Assembly for Peace. At the meeting at the Solidarity Committee premises on 2 July 1969 they expressed their satisfaction with particularly the results of the Khartoum conference held in January 1969, which helped "to mobilise all progressive and peace-loving forces in support of the liberation struggle".[16] However, I could sense that some misunderstanding, if not tension, still existed between Moscow and SWAPO. Nikolay Bazanov, who was the author's predecessor as the Committee's Secretary for African affairs, reiterated political support to SWAPO as "the only organisation fighting for the freedom of Namibia" and underlined that supplies of both military and civilian goods from the USSR continued. Nevertheless, he reminded the delegation that while SWAPO representative in Cairo Andreas Shipanga had complained to the AAPSO Soviet Secretary that Moscow had allegedly weakened its attention to SWAPO, but Moscow had, on the contrary, for two years been suggesting in vain that SWAPO should send a new group of cadres for military training. Moreover, for two years Sam Nujoma had been expected to visit the USSR as well.[17]

SWAPO representatives explained the delay of Nujoma's visit by his presence in the south-western part of Zambia, where he was "meeting the people", that is, refugees from Namibia. Peter Katjavivi, who had recently returned via Zambia and Tanzania from a visit to his home country, said that attacks against the enemy were taking place in the Caprivi Strip and in the Okavango region. The South African authorities were intensifying their repression of the civilian population, burning fields and villages, and up to 3,000 Namibian refugees had left for Zambia and some for Botswana, where the government's attitude to SWAPO was "not too good". SWAPO created a Recruitment Commission to bring young refugees into its combat units, but had to be careful to avoid the penetration of Pretoria's agents into its ranks. It was those young Namibians that SWAPO was going to send to the USSR for training, because "they knew how the enemy was operating against SWAPO and could tell Soviet representatives about it".[18] SWAPO delegates spoke highly of the fighters who had studied in the Soviet Union earlier, especially in military intelligence and operational planning.

By that time Moscow had agreed, with the consent of the government of Zambia, to send food and other supplies to the Namibian refugees there. Nanyemba, on his part, promised to submit a request for goods for SWAPO and informed us that SWAPO urgently needed £10,000 to ensure military operations inside the country and administrative matters.

As for supplies of arms, Nanyemba (who would soon be appointed SWAPO Secretary for Defence) was glad that the governments of Tanzania and Zambia had agreed that SWAPO would receive arms directly from Moscow and not through the OAU Liberation Committee. "I don't want to denounce the Committee," said Nanyemba, "but it takes a lot of time. Besides, it co-operates not only with progressive organisations, but with others as well."

SWAPO hoped to return more trained cadres to Namibia by the next year. "We have regions under our control, but they are depopulated; only fighters are there. To bring back the population we need more arms and more cadres, they must feel that they depend on SWAPO and not on the enemy."[19]

At that time SWAPO was not satisfied with the work of the UN Commissioner for Refugees, who was spending "just some pennies" on each one.

SWAPO regards those Namibians who left the country not as refugees, but as fighters. We want them to trust less in the UN and more in the party of SWAPO, in themselves, in our true friends. We have already become victims of some international organisations.[20]

The lack of proper organisation of bilateral co-operation is clear from the fact that the delegation had a message for the Namibian students who were studying in the USSR, but could not find their addresses at the SWAPO headquarters.

An interesting detail: two of the delegation members were intended to proceed from Moscow to Mongolia, and this was hardly accidental. At that time, prominent members and activists of the African liberation movements (including Thabo Mbeki, by the way) regularly visited Ulan-Bator. Moreover, Mongolia provided them with material assistance, such as well-made and strong shoes and, at least in the case of SWAPO, even a substantial sum of hard currency.

We had more discussions with SWAPO representatives when we visited Lusaka and Dar es Salaam a month later. In particular, in the capital of Zambia we could feel that no love was lost in relations between SWAPO and the MPLA. At the meeting with our delegation, Afonso van Dunem, in particular, accused SWAPO of transferring arms destined for that organisation to UNITA. Because at that stage UNITA was not allowed to operate in Zambia, after training its members were allegedly sent to Angola disguised as SWAPO combatants.[21]

16
Co-operation Broadens

The discussion on the situation in Namibia and bilateral co-operation continued when SWAPO President Sam Nujoma led a delegation to the USSR in early October 1969. They took part in the international conference in Alma-Ata, mentioned earlier, and then had discussions in Moscow.

The threshold of the 1970s was an extremely difficult period for SWAPO. Apart from the northern part of Namibia, where first clashes took place in August 1966, its fighters attacked targets in the Caprivi Strip, but Pretoria managed to rebuff these attacks and increase its military presence in the area. The SWAPO leadership looked for strategic targets – industrial enterprises, railways, roads, bridges – but, quite realistically, it did not try to create permanent guerrilla bases in Namibian territory at that stage but preferred its fighters "to be always on the move", and at the same time assigned them the very difficult task of bringing war materials to the central part of the country.[1]

Like many other leaders of the liberation movements earlier and later, Nujoma was critical of the Liberation Committee, which had not provided SWAPO with any goods for ten months. He asked the Soviets to send whatever was available directly to his organisation, avoiding the OAU structure. "We can't rely on African countries", he said bluntly.[2]

Among other questions raised by the SWAPO president was the organisation's attitude to the liberation struggle in Angola. He believed that Holden Roberto's GRAE was "finished" and no more active, that the MPLA was "the most active and progressive", while UNITA "operated in some areas close to the border of Zambia". Nujoma was visibly worried about the MPLA's attitude to his organisation and complained that it had launched a campaign against SWAPO.

The MPLA suspects that SWAPO assists UNITA. We told them we have no capacity to assist, and this is a problem of the Angolans themselves. In Namibia SWAPO won the support of the people and the world knows that SWAPO, and not SWANU, is a serious organisation. We have nothing against the MPLA, we are ready to co-operate with them.[3]

The archive documents of the 1960s that are accessible to researchers contain no reference to regular allocation of financial assistance to SWAPO, as distinct from liberation movements in other Southern African countries. Quite probably it was provided from time to time, but in minimal amounts. I recall how in 1969 all we could provide to the SWAPO delegation from the small chest of the Solidarity Committee was US$60. However, even this sum was valuable: they were leaving Moscow for the West where they could rely, as a rule, only on themselves. Soon after this visit Alexander Dzassokhov sent a strictly confidential hand-written letter to the CP Central Committee on this issue, and if my memory serves me well, US$15,000 was allocated to SWAPO.

Nujoma also described plans to convene a consultative conference of SWAPO and asked for help, in particular, with the transportation of its delegates. This conference, convened in the Tanzanian town of Tanga in the last days of 1969 and first days of 1970, was an important milestone in SWAPO's international as well as internal activities. The assistance was provided and four students came from the USSR: Ngarikutuke (better known as Ernest) Tjiriange, who later became SWAPO General Secretary, Helmut Angula, now Minister of Works and Transport, Phillip Indongo (who later became President Sam Nujoma's personal doctor) and a fourth one who soon left SWAPO and settled somewhere in the West.

The Tanga conference, attended by about 30 delegates, discussed the crisis caused by the difficult conditions of the struggle and especially by the betrayal of Leonard Philemon Nangolo, known in SWAPO as "Castro", who, after the death in action of Tobias Hanyeko, had been the senior military commander. Having been detained, "Castro" agreed to co-operate with the South African authorities and was released. It resulted in the failure of a number of SWAPO operations in Namibia and even after the traitor had been exposed and detained, some fighters were still reluctant to go on missions.[4]

These events influenced the delegates, who expressed criticism of the leadership, but all in all the conference's results were quite positive. Sam Nujoma remained President of the organisation, and almost all delegates were elected to the posts of SWAPO Secretaries or Deputy Secretaries. However, most of them had the word "Acting" in front of their position, because relevant posts were occupied by other persons inside Namibia, where officially SWAPO had never been banned.

One of the conference decisions was an announcement of the creation of the PLAN – the People's Liberation Army of Namibia. Sam Nujoma became the Commander-in Chief, assisted by Peter Nanyemba, Secretary for Defence, and Dimo Amaambo, PLAN Commander.

But even in April 1970, when Moscow celebrated Lenin's centenary, SWAPO was once again not invited. Nevertheless, Nujoma sent a cable of congratulation to the Solidarity Committee from Bucharest, where he was on a visit; Romania – just like Yugoslavia and North Korea, both countries somewhat distant from Moscow – was quite friendly with SWAPO.

It would be no exaggeration to say that a massive strike of Namibian workers in 1971 was extremely important, not only for the rise of the liberation struggle in Namibia but also for developments in Southern Africa as a whole. Some 48,000 workers, mostly migrants from the northern part of the country, employed in the mining and processing industry, took part in it, demanding the end of the recruitment system and a pay rise. The SWAPO leadership noted that this strike, in particular, caused a split in the white community; German settlers were calling for a compromise and the West German authorities supported them.[5]

The political situation in the country changed, the African population "awakened": workers, students, and religious circles. To a large extent this was an after-effect of the decision of the International Court of Justice, which in 1971 at last rejected Pretoria's claim for Namibia. This created hopes for rapid transition to independence and supporters of change began acting more openly.

The SWAPO leadership abroad reconnected with the internal leadership, in particular with the party's Chairman, David Meroro. However, most of the tribal chiefs co-operated with the colonial regime. The election to Bantustan "assemblies", held in April 1973, confirmed this.

The increased activity of the popular movement in Namibia created favourable conditions for convening the international conference on Namibia in Brussels from 26 to 28 May 1972. The Soviets, in particular the Solidarity Committee, supported it, though a little cautiously. As in other initiatives in the international field, SWAPO was supported by a broader coalition of forces than other liberation movements. The West obviously considered SWAPO more malleable;

in particular, social-democratic organisations such as the Friedrich Ebert Foundation tried to influence SWAPO "through individuals" in its ranks.[6]

In Britain, the "Friends of Namibia" organisation was politically to the right of the Anti-Apartheid Movement; moreover, it was government officials who advised SWAPO to deal with that organisation. The Foreign and Commonwealth Office (FCO) in its internal papers emphasised that SWAPO was a special case, although the FCO position on Namibia was rather shaky, and its documents prove once again Pretoria's influence on London. When, in December 1971, Nujoma requested a meeting with a British minister, initially Lord Lothian agreed to see him: "While the South African government may resent Nujoma being seen by a minister, in view of the special character of the territory of South West Africa and to avoid seeming negative about its problems ... ." Internal FCO correspondence noted: "It is not our normal practice to recommend that Ministers should see leaders of African Liberation movements ... [But]: Because of the particular status of South West Africa Mr Nujoma is in a different category from the leaders of any other African independence movement."

However, Sir Arthur Snelling, British Ambassador to Pretoria, was worried:

Presumably the principal aim of Nujoma in seeking an interview is that of obtaining publicity ... It would be helpful if I could have material to use defensively with South African Ministers who may be surprised that we have decided, on this particular point, to pay official attention to SWAPO. Information from [sanitised] shows that SWAPO in general and Nujoma in particular have been involved in the past in armed raids on South West Africa.

So Lord Lothian backtracked: "... we should have another look ... It seemed to me when I decided to see SWAPO that it was particularly important at this delicate moment over Rhodesia that we should avoid upsetting Black Africa... ... I shall plead illness." Yet another excuse was found; Foreign Secretary Douglas Home informed the embassy in Pretoria: "Lord Lothian has reconsidered his decision in the light of your telephone call ... and it has now been decided that he should not meet the SWAPO delegation. SWAPO have been told that Lord Lothian has had to leave London unexpectedly ... ."[7]

The conference in Brussels was chaired by Sam Nujoma and Lord Caradon, former Minister of State for Foreign Affairs and British Ambassador to the United Nations. The SWAPO leadership wanted to create a follow-up committee to be run by its representatives, the Belgian Socialist Party and Caradon, but in practice it hardly functioned.[8]

The armed struggle in Namibia continued, especially in the rainy seasons, in spite of all the difficulties; cross-border attacks by South Africans on Zambian territory from the Caprivi Strip, and extremely long distances to cover for fighters sent to Northern Namibia via Angola.

This very route went through the areas of Angola where UNITA was present and it gave an excuse (or a reason?) to suspect SWAPO of being in co-operation with that organisation. Such accusations were regularly presented, in particular by some MPLA representatives.[9]

A leitmotiv of SWAPO leaders' analysis of the war situation was complaints about lack of assistance from the OAU Liberation Committee, which "practically did not supply SWAPO with arms". In this period, apart from the USSR, assistance to SWAPO was provided mostly by the GDR, other East European countries and North Korea.[10]

Step by step, with the growth of SWAPO activities in Namibia and its international prestige, demonstrated at the conference in Brussels, Moscow's attitude to this organisation was becoming more positive. These changes were reflected in the invitation to Sam Nujoma to attend the celebration of the 50th anniversary of the USSR in December 1972.

Optimism and self-control were striking features of the SWAPO President, who would not show his temper even under the most difficult circumstances. However, especially by the end of 1972, such a mood was common and largely justified. In Moscow, Nujoma not only spoke about SWAPO success in the struggle and confidence in victory, but also sought to show his Soviet interlocutors the future role of Namibia in the Southern African region. He believed that Namibia was "a gate to independent South Africa", that liberation of his country would allow Botswana to use Namibian ports for export and import and therefore to be free of dependence on South African ports, and, moreover, that it would prevent further assistance from Pretoria to Portugal in Angola and thus stop the war there.[11]

This scenario was not too far from what really happened in the region. Although the ANC did not use independent Namibia as "a gate" for military operations, a successful political settlement in South Africa's "fifth province" increased the chances of a similar solution in South Africa. It greatly affected the psychological climate: if SWAPO, portrayed by Pretoria's propaganda for many years as "communist terrorists", came to power in Namibia, the same could happen with the ANC in South Africa. Finally, though the liberation struggle in Angola ended much earlier than in Namibia, Namibian independence greatly obstructed Pretoria's conduct in support of its ally, UNITA.

The discussion with Nujoma demonstrated that SWAPO was trying to create a united front of all "strata of population" in Namibia. For this purpose it sent a message to the internal cadres asking them to take part in the formation of the National Convention to present common demands to the UN Secretary-General. SWAPO's work inside Namibia was getting more sophisticated. It established good contact with religious organisations; their associates were not requested to become party members, but they supported SWAPO and served as a channel for financial support to its structures inside Namibia. (When a church newspaper in Ovamboland became more political and began criticising the authorities, its premises were blown up.) Nujoma himself had a productive meeting with Bishop Auala, who earlier openly supported the strike, calling the contract system imposed on workers unchristian and inhumane.

Nujoma was satisfied that the conference in Brussels reiterated the UN's responsibility to Namibia. He praised the role of Peter Mueshihange, SWAPO International Secretary, who represented the organisation in New York. It was clear, however, that the SWAPO leadership was losing its early illusions about the role of the UN. "The United Nations will not help us without our armed struggle", said Nujoma.[12] The armed struggle was inspiring people to wage a political struggle. On the other hand, the enemy was afraid of human losses among white personnel and began mobilising blacks, coloureds and Asians: "There is no racial discrimination in this respect." Pretoria was facing two alternatives: either to leave Namibia or to begin making concessions there.[13] (In fact, it chose the second way, but failed in that too.)

Nujoma proudly said that in spite of the intensification of the struggle, PLAN had suffered no human losses during the previous three years, but Pretoria avenged this by new repression against the civilian population.

Contrary to the early period, our discussions with Nujoma showed no signs of discontent on either side. Supplies were coming from the USSR via Tanzania and Zambia, SWAPO members underwent training in increasing numbers and Soviet embassies were helpful. According to the decision taken in Tanga, the leading SWAPO members were due to undertake military training as well.[14]

If my memory serves me well, during that very visit the SWAPO President for the first time called upon the USSR Ministry of Defence. I accompanied him to the office of Major General Galkin, one of the top officers in *Desyatka*, whom I knew from the time when I myself served in this Department. Nujoma was visibly delighted with the meeting; his mood was quite optimistic. Thus, he spoke of prospects of co-operation between the future independent Namibia and the USSR in the military field.

Repression against the Namibian population increased in 1973. Some 400–600 persons were reported missing. These actions by Pretoria, as well as certain successes by PLAN, such as mortar attacks against three bases in Caprivi, ambushes and mining of roads, convinced more and more people to join SWAPO.[15] Meanwhile, Pretoria continued its policy of "Bantustanisation"; the dialogue between the UN Secretary-General and Pretoria did not bring results.

There were plans to hold a legal SWAPO conference inside Namibia. The party's external leadership was not opposed to the idea, being sure that it would manage to control it, but believed that Pretoria would hardly allow the conference, "unless it had enough agents there".[16] This conference did take place, but later.

The paradox of the situation in Namibia was evident: SWAPO waged an armed struggle against the South African colonial authorities, but officially it had never been banned, and from time to time Pretoria would allocate "internal SWAPO" the political space to operate. Apart from the specific international status of Namibia, it is quite probable that the South African regime continued to hope it would be able to split "internal" SWAPO from the "external" part and to "co-opt" the former into schemes of the so-called "internal settlement".[17]

SWAPO and its military wing, PLAN, faced tremendous logistical problems. The distance from the main port of supply, Dar es Salaam, to the nearest area of military operations in Namibia, the Caprivi Strip, was far enough, and it was much further (via Angola) to other areas of operation, namely Okavango and Ovamboland in the north of Namibia. PLAN fighters had to move on foot and cross several rivers.[18] (Angolan freedom fighters faced similar problems and the OAU Liberation Committee was even planning to bring donkeys to Zambia from Sudan.)

The SWAPO representatives were thankful to the Soviets for supplying three ZIL trucks, which performed better on muddy

African roads than Mercedes models. (The fact that the roads were far from perfect in the Soviet Union forced us, the Soviets, to make strong cross-country vehicles both for military and civilian purposes.) However, they were short-lived: soon one of them crashed into a tree, one hit a mine and exploded, and the last one got stuck in Tanzania, while spare parts had been sent to Zambia.[19]

Arms and ammunition were supplied as well, but problems arose for various reasons. For example, SWAPO did not have ammunition depots, and therefore supplies had to be brought regularly and not in advance. The growing use of helicopters by Pretoria's forces also demanded more anti-aircraft weapons.

It should be emphasised that civilian (or double-purpose) goods were supplied to SWAPO as well, both through government sources and by Soviet NGOs, primarily the Solidarity Committee. I recall how once SWAPO representatives thanked us for supplying animal fat in barrels; PLAN fighters would add it to game meat, sometimes even to elephant meat, to make it tender.

After strikes and the student revolt, more youth began leaving Namibia, often via Botswana. However, this country, though independent from September 1966, could not "stop the Boers from doing all they wanted there"[20] and its authorities did not allow Namibians to be brought out of that country to Zambia via ferry in Kazangula until a new road, more distant from the border with Namibia, had been built. On top of this, sometimes large groups of Namibians (150, 200 or even 300 persons) assembled there, and if SWAPO did not have enough money for their transportation further away, they would return home.[21] Foreign assistance, both in cash and in kind, was essential for SWAPO, especially since the number of its members abroad rose from about 500 in 1971 to 900 or even 1,000 in 1973. Money was needed to buy clothes and food, for transportation of goods from Dar es Salaam and sometimes even for bribing local officials to speed up deliveries.[22]

Apart from the socialist countries, assistance was provided by SIDA and the World Council of Churches, which allocated SWAPO US$20,000 in 1972 and US$25,000 in 1973. Some African countries, such as Zambia, Tanzania, Zaire (after the resignation of the notorious Minister of Foreign Affairs, Bomboko), Egypt, Nigeria, Senegal and Morocco were helpful too. The work of the Liberation Committee improved as well, when Hashim Mbita replaced George Magombe as its Executive Secretary in 1972, but some African countries still preferred to render assistance directly.[23]

In their discussions in Moscow the SWAPO executive members also indicated that China, having been disappointed with SWANU (in spite of its "Pro-Chinese" rhetoric) had started to become closer to SWAPO. This was demonstrated vividly during a visit of the delegation headed by Sam Nujoma to China in July 1973.

The delegation spent a week in China (and two weeks in North Korea) and on the way back its members shared their experience with us. They said that SWAPO wanted to find out what Beijing's attitude to their organisation really was, because "for the last four years the relations were cool and Chinese assistance was insignificant".[24] The delegation members regarded their discussions in China as "sincere".

The Chinese believe that we are pro-Soviet, we don't know why. We told them that we want to have friendly relations with both China and the USSR, the two most important countries. "We don't understand why your attitude to SWAPO is cool. We have good relations with the Soviet Union and we hope that the relations between Moscow and Beijing will improve." The Chinese did not say much in reply, but we are grown-up people and even some slips of the tongue could show their spirit: they still regard us as pro-Soviet.[25]

The delegation members – Moses Garoeb, Administrative Secretary; Dimo Amaambo, PLAN's Commander; Richard Kapelwa, Deputy Secretary for Defence, and Peter Tsheehama – briefed us on developments in Namibia. Taking into account the composition of the delegation, it is not surprising that they paid most attention to military affairs.

According to them, the struggle was mostly developing in three areas: Caprivi, Okavango and Ovamboland. SWAPO fighters defended villages there from enemy raids. At that stage Caprivi was of special significance. From early 1973 intensive action was taking place there: SWAPO combatants attacked enemy strongholds and over 20 vehicles were hit by mines. Our interlocutors proudly said that their organisation was able to exhibit captured arms and communication equipment in Addis-Ababa. "We proved SWAPO have better arms, better discipline, better training."

The delegation members underlined that these successes were achieved thanks to Soviet assistance in terms of supplies and training. In contrast to the case of the MPLA, discussed above, they praised especially Vladimir Bezukladnikov of the Soviet embassy in Lusaka.[26]

The second direction of the struggle was political. The mass strike of migrant workers was followed by other strikes in various industries, which damaged the infrastructure of the country. Many schools were closed, because students stood against the colonial regime. Churches, teachers' associations and other groups were joining the political struggle. Protests during the visit of Alfred Escher proved a high degree of political mobilisation, and in his report this UN high official admitted that Namibia's population rejected Pretoria's rule.

A new development in UN activities on the Namibian issue was Secretary-General Kurt Waldheim's visit to South Africa and Namibia. In one of his reports Waldheim mentioned Pretoria's promise to grant independence to Namibia within ten years. According to SWAPO leaders, Western countries – the USA, Britain and France, supported this. They were trying to convince SWAPO representatives that ten years is not a long time, that the door to Namibia's independence had been opened and should not be shut.

However, both SWAPO and the OAU rejected this idea. Moreover, they suggested bringing to an end the UN dialogue with Pretoria. The SWAPO leadership was also worried about the status of the UN Council on Namibia, which according to UN decisions had legal power in that country, while SWAPO claimed to represent the Namibian people. However, in 1973 at its session in Lusaka the Council officially supported SWAPO's claim.[27]

SWAPO displayed a great interest in the forthcoming appointment of the UN Commissioner for Namibia, especially since substantial financial resources would be at his disposal. They hoped to influence the process of allocation from this fund and were worried about "UN bureaucracy".[28]

The delegation was also given a chance to discuss relevant matters, in particular the training of SWAPO fighters, including leading figures (all of them were to spend at least a month annually in the PLAN camps) at the USSR Ministry of Defence.

Sam Nujoma was not well those days, but he flew to Simferopol to meet PLAN fighters who had undergone training in Perevalnoe. A Soviet officer who accompanied him was quite impressed by Nujoma's stand in his discussions with the Centre Command and especially by the content of his speech to the PLAN cadres.

On our part, the Solidarity Committee officials did our best to make relations with SWAPO more cordial. It should be mentioned in this regard that though the Committee operated under strict control of the CPSU International Department (Ulyanovsky in his discussion with Africans once called the Committee "an extension of our apparatus"), the space for our own initiative was left open, especially in the cases when the Department was not dealing directly with a specific organisation, as in the case of SWAPO in the 1960s and 1970s. So when Nujoma was leaving Moscow for Bucharest, I, in the presence of a Romanian ambassador, called him "Comrade President of Namibia" (almost 17 years before he finally took this post) and, as I could sense, he appreciated it.

17
Armed Struggle Intensifies

Just like other liberation movements, SWAPO developed entirely different perspectives after the April 1974 revolution in Portugal. Even before the independence of Angola SWAPO was in a position to increase its presence in Angolan territory, and, what was especially important, young Namibians began crossing the border in large numbers seeking to join SWAPO in the struggle for independence. As a rule they had to go from Angola to Zaire, and then to Zambia. Afterwards, as hundreds and then thousands of young Namibians joined PLAN, their training had to be organised.

This problem was discussed when the first high-level SWAPO delegation came to Moscow in December 1974 after radical changes had taken place in the situation owing to the Portuguese revolution. It had a certain "militarist" flavour: Sam Nujoma was not only President, but also Commander-in-Chief; Peter Nanyemba was Secretary for Defence and Solomon Hawala a senior PLAN commander. This composition truly reflected the situation in and around Namibia at that time.

This time Sam Nujoma spoke about the concentration of South African troops close to the Angolan-Namibian border (he counted 30,000 soldiers, though that figure was perhaps an exaggeration), about the failure of the election of Bantustan authorities in Namibia in 1973, which were boycotted by many Africans and about Pretoria's plans to create a puppet state in the north of Namibia, which would be used as a reservoir of cheap labour and to annex the remaining three-quarters of the territory.

Nujoma believed that while Pretoria was strengthening the occupation regime after the collapse of Portuguese colonialism, the imperialist forces wanted "to put a black face, a puppet government in Namibia, as in Zaire". In his opinion, it was the USA, Britain, France and West Germany that controlled Angola, Namibia and South Africa itself, and the West proposed a so-called "dialogue" on Zimbabwe to Vorster. They were planning the same approach for Namibia – to arrange "a dialogue on the conditions put forward by racists". However, Nujoma believed that in the circumstances a peaceful solution for Namibia was impossible. "We can defeat Vorster", he insisted.[1] He was somewhat worried that if power in Namibia was transferred to the UN and not to Namibians themselves, the world organisation could be used as a cover for imperialist forces. Naturally he wanted to discuss these issues at the Soviet Ministry of Foreign Affairs.[2]

By that time SWAPO had to take care of about 5,000 Namibians, including women and children. Fortunately Western social democrats, especially ones from Sweden, and even some organisations in the USA, began providing humanitarian assistance to SWAPO. However, a lot was urgently needed for PLAN, which absorbed many newcomers: arms, training facilities, food and clothes. SWAPO was planning to broaden the area of armed operations, first to the Atlantic coast and then to the centre of the country.

Nujoma said that SWAPO's programme was being prepared: "We believe in socialism, we want to create a socialist state, but we don't want to announce it."[3]

At an earlier discussion Peter Nanyemba and Solomon Hawala underlined that PLAN received 75 per cent of its arms from the Soviet Union and these proved to be superior to arms used by the SADF. They were interested not only in military, but also in political training of new cadres. The "exodus" of people from Namibia was so intensive that SWAPO wanted to stop it for two or three months to create favourable conditions for their training.[4]

Nanyemba told us that they had brought a draft list of their needs for training and supplies and wanted to discuss it in a preliminary way, before submitting it officially. So Anatoly Shirshikov, a retired colonel who dealt with supplies in the Solidarity Committee, and I went to see him in the evening in the Rossiya Hotel and discovered that the request for training showed a lack of training by the Secretary of Defence himself. The list consisted largely of equal numbers of places for infantry, artillery, the communications service, etc., without any correlation to the existing or future structure of PLAN. Fortunately, however, Peter was always ready to listen to constructive criticism and advice from friends. An amended request was submitted and many Namibians were accepted for training in the Crimea, at the Vystrel and in the Northern Training Centre.

The SWAPO commanders naturally hoped to use the territory of independent Angola as their rear base, but at the end of 1974 the situation there was quite confusing. The forthcoming independence of Angola was marred by conflicts between major nationalist organisations.

As was mentioned above, SWAPO initially had good relations with the FNLA but later it was in the same group of "genuine" movements with the MPLA, and at the same time had at least "working relations" with UNITA. Moreover, Fred Bridgland and other authors who supported Savimbi claimed that SWAPO provided vital assistance to UNITA in its inception stage and even provided it with the very first weapon.[5] On the other hand, Sam Nujoma in his memoirs sought to downgrade SWAPO relations with UNITA: "Those who spread false stories that SWAPO and UNITA were allies, did not know of the connection between SWAPO and MPLA – and especially the relationship between me personally and President Neto – which had begun long before in Dar es Salaam."[6]

In December 1974 our Namibian interlocutors were worried that Angola was moving towards "a horrible civil war". Mobutu was openly supporting the FNLA; the MPLA, which had been "strong enough" earlier, suffered "a split", and Chipenda had his armed people in Angola. On the other hand, UNITA, whose very existence earlier had not been recognised ("though we had said earlier that it was operating in the south-eastern part of Angola", added Nanyemba), became an equal partner in negotiations.[7]

The SWAPO leaders were also satisfied that "at least the UN began spending money on Namibians", in particular for the creation of the Namibia Institute in Lusaka in 1975. They praised the newly appointed UN Commissioner for Namibia, Sean McBride, a prominent diplomat and politician from Ireland. Decree no. 1, adopted by the UN Council for Namibia on his initiative, threatened those in the West who were exploiting the national resources of the country. They compared McBride's activity with "psychological warfare"; the whites in Namibia began believing his words after the changes in Angola. "Not all whites are bad," said Nanyemba. "SWAPO should think about their future in Namibia, should find a formula for these people."[8]

For SWAPO 1975 was a year of great promise and great danger. When in late April we met Hifikepunye (in those days he was better known as Lucas) Pohamba, then the CC member and representative in Dar es Salaam, he spoke about new problems SWAPO faced: "We feel pressure from a number of African states, although we don't say it publicly." Officially Zambia and some other countries had talks with Pretoria on the Rhodesian problem, but the SWAPO leadership believed that they discussed the problem of Namibia with

Vorster as well. Moreover, because of manoeuvres of Pretoria and the government of Liberia, SWAPO happened to be drawn into these talks when President Walter Tolbert invited Sam Nujoma to visit Monrovia urgently "to brief him about the situation in Namibia", but did not tell him that Vorster would come there three days later. Pohamba was satisfied with the decisioins of the meeting of the OAU Council of Ministers in Dar es Salaam in April, but added: "As usual, they will not implement them."[9]

The further deterioration of the situation in Angola and its effect on SWAPO's activities was an important theme of the discussions between the delegation headed by Nujoma and the Soviets in October 1975. This time, apart from business, Nujoma came for a medical check-up ("I am tired", complained the SWAPO President).[10]

He was worried by increasing support given to South Africa by "imperialist countries" – the USA, France, West Germany and the UK. Referring to the failure of negotiations on Zimbabwe, Nujoma rejected the possibility of similar talks on Namibia. "The enemy is not sincere", he insisted.

He informed us that PLAN would have about 8,000–9,000 trained fighters by mid 1976 and wanted to send more cadres for military studies in the USSR, at least 200 before the New Year. "The only solution for SWAPO is armed struggle, accompanied by political work inside the country."[11] The list of requests the SWAPO leader submitted to Moscow was quite impressive.

SWAPO hoped for support from independent Angola. Peter Nanyemba spent several weeks there in May and June 1975[12] and Nujoma was visibly worried by the developments in Angola, especially by the South African intervention in southern Angola, deeper than Pretoria admitted.

Another of his worries was the "power struggle" that was taking place in Angola. "The MPLA is a progressive movement, UNITA also can be called progressive; as far as we know, the FNLA is utterly reactionary." The Soviet interlocutors maintained that the MPLA was a mass organisation, the first to launch an armed struggle. In reply Nujoma spoke about the desirability of an alliance between the MPLA and UNITA "in our interest, in the interest of the people of Angola". "We have contact with both UNITA and the MPLA. We deplore clashes between them, but perhaps the situation will change before November."[13]

Other leading SWAPO members admitted that in some regions of Angola their organisation could not operate "without co-operation with UNITA", though relations were getting strained, because Savimbi's supporters were taking arms from SWAPO. PLAN soldiers suspected that UNITA was co-operating "with the Boers" and therefore they "were almost fighting it".[14]

I do not know to what extent Nujoma was influenced by the open Soviet preference for the MPLA and by rather candid information about the Cuban instructors in Angola, which Petr Manchkha shared with him at a farewell dinner some weeks later. No doubt the main reason SWAPO's leadership moved to the side of the MPLA was UNITA's collaboration with Pretoria. It became quite clear that Pretoria would be against any government in Angola that supported SWAPO. Anyhow, at the time of Angola's independence the SWAPO leadership definitely supported the MPLA government, and then Nujoma personally headed the SWAPO delegation to the international solidarity conference in Luanda in early February 1976.

Moreover, PLAN fighters themselves had to battle South Africans and their new allies from Chipenda's wing of the FNLA (former MPLA members) in eastern Angola from 9 to 14 November 1975.[15] Later Sam Nujoma claimed that through its actions SWAPO "contained thousands of South African troops" during the 1975–76 war in Angola.[16]

This created a basis for closer co-operation between the MPLA and the Namibian liberation movement. Soon SWAPO was in a position to establish not only refugee camps, but also a network of PLAN structures on Angolan territory. During his next visit to Moscow, in August 1976, Sam Nujoma specially thanked the CPSU for its "bold stand in support of Angola. In response to the victory of the MPLA we intensified our struggle."[17]

However, Jonas Savimbi initially still hoped that he could use his old contacts with SWAPO to his benefit. Moses Garoeb, then its Executive Committee member and Administrative Secretary, described to me how the UNITA leader had invited him to his suite in the Addis Ababa hotel during the OAU meeting there in January 1976 and tried to convince him that not only UNITA, but "everybody in Africa" was dealing with Pretoria.[18] Yet by that time the position of SWAPO was clear enough; that was demonstrated by the fact that a Nanyemba-led SWAPO delegation took part in the congress of the Cuban Communist Party in December 1975, during the days of fierce fighting in Angola.

In late 1976 Savimbi declared "Nujoma and his exiled followers" UNITA's "fourth enemy" after "the Soviet Union, the Cuban forces in Angola and the so-called Faplas of the MPLA".[19] He even called SWAPO "the most savage" in comparison with Cuban and Angolan governmental forces.[20]

As for SWAPO's official bilateral relations with the CPSU, these began when the former was invited for the first time to the congress of the Soviet ruling party in late February 1976 and was represented there by Moses Garoeb.[21] The following year Nujoma himself represented SWAPO at the celebration of the 60th anniversary of the 1917 revolution.[22] A month earlier he was had been received by Boris Ponomarev in the CC headquarters.[23]

So, after the withdrawal of the South African troops from Angola, new prospects for the struggle for Namibian independence emerged and SWAPO's international prestige grew a great deal. At the next CPSU congress in 1981 Nujoma himself led the SWAPO delegation.[24]

However, the swelling of SWAPO's ranks abroad created new problems as well. As the experience of other movements, such as the MPLA, showed, prospects of speedy success activated power-hungry elements.

SWAPO faced a serious crisis in 1976 due to both objective and subjective reasons. When hundreds and then thousands of young Namibians went abroad, the leadership faced the difficult task of accommodating them, organising military, academic or vocational training. Dissatisfaction with the conditions of life in the camps in Zambia resulted in a type of mutiny against the leadership. One of the excuses for this was a demand to convene a new SWAPO conference. Indeed, it was decided in Tanga that the next one would take place in five years, but the delay was quite understandable in the circumstances of war in Angola and the exodus from Namibia.

These disturbances coincided with differences (if not a split) in the SWAPO top leadership. Among those who opposed the leadership and Sam Nujoma in particular were Andreas Shipanga and Solomon Mifima. They used a decision to hold the next conference in five years' time as a pretext for opposition, probably hoping that with the arrival of many Namibians from home they would receive their support and come to the very top of the leadership.

Recently the critics of SWAPO have claimed that Shipanga and Mifima had nothing to do with the "genuine" discontent of some members. However, Shipanga later definitely tried to associate himself with them: having returned to Namibia with the "blessing" of Pretoria, he claimed in 1979 that 1,800 of his "supporters" had been detained in Zambia.[25]

Shipanga was one of the prominent SWAPO members. He represented it in a number of countries, working as Secretary for Information. I remember him not only as a capable person, but also as a person who would easily spend somebody else's money. I heard, for example, that when he represented SWAPO at a conference in Madagascar, he left a large bill from the bar for its organisers to pay. Personally I also felt it. During the international conference on Southern Africa in Oslo in 1973 he suddenly phoned me and requested a meeting. I thought he wanted to discuss some important matter and rushed from a small modest hotel, where we stayed, to the centre of town. However, all he wanted was money, since the conference organisers, as was announced in advance, were ready to pay only half his expenses. I had to remind him that we were not in the Soviet Union where we always paid for our guests' accommodation, and advised him to discuss his problems with his Norwegian friends.

Having been detained and then sent from Lusaka to Dar es Salaam, Shipanga and his supporters later found their way to Sweden where they founded their own organisation, the so-called SWAPO-Democrats. Whatever their differences with Nujoma were, they proved to be selfish opportunists when after several years they returned to Namibia and took part in attempts to form "internal" political structures opposing SWAPO.[26] Shipanga got a ministerial post in the so-called "transitional government" in 1985 and even chaired it twice.

Unfortunately, some prominent members of the SWAPO Youth League who had recently arrived from Namibia also took part in this "rebellion" against the leadership, in particular its president, Nathaniel Keshii, and Sheeli Shangula. For us it was rather unpleasant news, since Keshii had spent several months in Moscow studying in the Komsomol School, while Shangula came there in January 1975 to take part in the conference of the SWAPO youth abroad, organised with the assistance of the USSR Committee of Youth Organisations (read: Komsomol's International Department) and the Solidarity Committee.

From 28 July to 1 August 1976 an enlarged meeting of the SWAPO CC took place, which practically replaced the envisaged conference. It adopted a new programme for the organisation, which spoke particularly of the creation of a classless society on the basis of "scientific socialism". As far as I can judge this was the only SWAPO document of that nature. Besides, the CC confirmed the decisions of the "internal" SWAPO congress that took place the previous May in Walvis Bay. Thus the unity between "external" and "internal" SWAPO was underlined, as well as the supremacy of its top leadership, headed by Sam Nujoma.

When Nujoma visited Moscow soon after this meeting, he emphasised that there was no "split in SWAPO", but "imperialists, especially West Germany, spent money in Lusaka to destroy" his organisation. According to him, those who stood against the leadership included agents sent from Namibia ("It was not easy to check them when thousands of Namibians came out") who "met the reactionaries inside SWAPO" in Zambia.[27]

The changes in Angola made Western governments and political forces pay more attention to Namibia. Most of them supported anti-SWAPO forces there. In particular, the USA collaborated with Pretoria; thus a group of "internal leaders", selected and dispatched by the South African authorities, was received in Washington as guests of the Department of State.[28]

By that time the SWAPO leadership faced the prospect of the creation of a puppet regime in Namibia, and regarded it as even more dangerous than the bantustan scheme. Therefore Sam Nujoma asked Moscow to apply, if necessary, a veto in the Security Council to prevent it. "We shall not allow a puppet government in Namibia, we shall create a socialist government, like in Angola and Mozambique."[29]

By mid 1976 the prestige of SWAPO in Moscow was high enough for Nujoma to meet the head of *Desyatka*, three-star Air Force General Georgy Skorikov,[30] in the General Staff Headquarters and I had to accompany him and his five colleagues there. Nujoma described Namibia as an "imperialist base" in Southern Africa, where, apart from the 50,000 South African troops, there were about 10,000 UNITA and FNLA cadres. According to him, Henry Kissinger at his meeting with South African Prime Minister Vorster promised that Washington would not allow the creation of progressive governments in Namibia and Zimbabwe, hence the need for the intensification of the armed struggle and new requests to the USSR.

Indeed, Washington for many years encouraged Pretoria's intransigence. George Schultz, Reagan's Secretary of State, in his preface to Crocker's book later confessed: "We were not ready to see a new nation created only to become enrolled in a Soviet camp."[31] Firstly, nobody was going to "enrol" Namibia into any camp; besides, this terminology ceased to be used in Moscow in the 1960s. More important, however, is Schultz's admission that, in spite of all the talk about democracy and human rights, the US administration was not ready to allow the Namibian people to make their own choices and preferred to keep the country under South African occupation at the cost of many thousands of lives.

At his meeting with Skorikov, Nujoma spoke about such heavy weapons as tanks and APCs, as well as anti-aircraft guns and Strela rocket launchers. He also raised the issue of sending Soviet instructors to train the PLAN in Angola. Skorikov's reply was by and large favourable, but cautious:

We shall consider all your requests when the Central Committee instructs us to do so and put forward our proposals. We shall train cadres for you but, frankly speaking, hardly for tanks or aircraft. The experience of struggle of the MPLA, FRELIMO, PAIGC shows that successful action was taken by well-trained light mobile units.

Nujoma, in his turn, did his best to explain that SWAPO had to have trained cadres for a regular army by the time it came to power. Skorikov was equally cautious on the question of Soviet instructors. "This is a big political question. Personally I would refrain from sending them, but you should discuss it with the Central Committee. Angola must have enough time to strengthen itself."[32]

At the same time he informed Nujoma that a new lot of supplies, which in particular included twelve Grad-P launchers, were ready to be sent to Angola, as soon as SWAPO secured an agreement with the Angolan government. Nujoma assured him that it would not be a problem. Nujoma also emphasised that SWAPO generally used its own instructors, but there were not enough of them, especially to train cadres in the use of new equipment.[33]

The next year the discussion with Nujoma on military matters was led from the Soviet side by Lieutenant General Postnikov, the second man in *Desyatka*. Nujoma described the developments rather optimistically, in particular a successful attack by PLAN against a South African base in Caprivi, where Grad-P and mortars managed to set fuel tanks on fire. "You liberated us", Zambian officials told SWAPO, because this base was previously used for attacks on Zambian territory.[34]

By that time, despite the initial hesitation of General Skorikov, the first group of 16 Soviet instructors headed by "Comrade Yury" (Colonel Zapurdyaev) had already started training Namibians in Lubango, and Nujoma wanted to receive at least seven more in 1978. He also insisted that SWAPO urgently needed arms and ammunition for newly trained units of PLAN.[35] During that visit Sam Nujoma for the first time expressed his wish to buy a (medium-sized) plane for urgent transportation of goods and personnel.[36] As for the activities of the Western "contact group", Nujoma called it a "rescue operation" for Pretoria. "If the political solution fails we shall act and take over the country."[37]

This group was formed in 1977 by Western members of the UN Security Council including Canada, France, the West Germany, the United Kingdom, and the United States. The next year, their joint diplomatic effort led to the Security Council Resolution 435 for settling the Namibian problem. It called for the holding of elections in Namibia under UN supervision and control, a cease-fire and UN-supervised elections. From the very beginning Moscow was sceptical; it did not use its veto, because African states (and SWAPO) agreed to it, but abstained.

Indeed, although Pretoria agreed to cooperate in achieving the implementation of Resolution 435, it sabotaged it for a decade, trying to transform the territory into a quasi-independent buffer. Its strategy was based on the co-option of Bantustan chiefs and other "black elite" (Nujoma called them "black Boers") as an alternative to SWAPO, while leaving control of Namibia in its hands.

However, soon a somewhat restrained attitude towards SWAPO was expressed again, this time not by the Soviets, but by the Cubans, who were extremely active in Angola. Although, as was mentioned above, most of the Soviet archive documents, especially on military matters, are still sealed, some became accessible, often almost accidentally. When the Russian Constitutional Court considered the legality of the banning of the CPSU by Boris Yeltsin's decree, his supporters (as distinct from his opponents) had an opportunity to browse the archives in their efforts to prove the "fusion" of the party and state apparatus. In this way a huge number of documents were collected and declassified. One of these was the minutes of the discussion at the Politburo on 18 October 1979, where the situation in SWAPO was mentioned.

Mikhail Suslov, who chaired the meeting in the absence of Brezhnev, referred to "telegrams from Havana Spec. no 741 and 744". Apart from the issues of replacement of the Cuban troops in Ethiopia and maintenance of the Cuban troops in Angola, Raul Castro, in his discussion with the Soviet ambassador, gave a rather negative assessment of SWAPO's activities:

The next question concerned assisting SWAPO with arms. He [Raul Castro] remarked, that Soviet comrades assisted SWAPO with arms but the SWAPO men definitely did not fight and did not want to fight. One then wonders why we should help them with weapons. Briefly, there are a number of very important principal questions, which we should consider. I think that we should order the Ministry of Defence and the International Department of the CC to consider the questions advanced in these telegrams, taking into account the exchange of opinions that took place at the meeting of the Politburo; the proposals will be forwarded to the CC.

His opinion was supported by all participants in the meeting.[38]

Raul Castro's accusations look very strange to me, even if, in Andrey Urnov's words, "Cubans never particularly loved SWAPO".[39] Late 1979 was exactly the time when PLAN was active in its incursions from Angola into Namibia. Though the results of the investigation carried out by the Soviet military and the International Department are not available, I can say with certainty that they were not negative. That year, 1979, the composition of the Soviet team maintaining contact with SWAPO was broadened, and Colonel (later Major General and Commander of the "Northern Training Centre") Nikolay Kurushkin became its head.

Kurushkin was undoubtedly a very popular Soviet officer, who was highly respected by the SWAPO political leaders and PLAN commanders. He established very close, brotherly relations with Peter Nanyemba, sharing with him trestle beds in dug-outs during operations against UNITA in Southern Angola. The mission of the Soviet specialists and advisers was primarily training of PLAN personnel. However, it appears as if in the field their duties sometimes went far beyond this. I recall how in March 1991, on the first anniversary of Namibian independence, we went to the north of the country, close to the Angolan border, together with Colonel Nikolay, accompanied by General Namoloh,[40] then Army Chief of Staff (and now Minister of Defence). When we reached Oshakati, Namoloh said to Nikolay: "You see, it is such a nice place. And you always told me: 'Attack Oshakati, attack Oshakati.'"[41]

Colonel Nikolay's trail can be found not only in the archive documents and verbal history, but in fiction as well. A well-known (though highly controversial) Russian writer, Alexander Prokhanov, based the main character of his novel *Afrikanist* on Colonel Nikolay,[42] having only slightly changed his family name – from Kurushkin to Kadashkin. This book is a kind of thriller, full of love, sex and

Plate 9   Peter Nanyemba and "Colonel Nikolay", Lubango, early 1980s.

Source: Nikolay Kurushkin archive.

suspense, but not much truth, though the author was Colonel Nikolay's guest during his trip to Angola in 1981.

The exception is a scene in the bath built by the Soviet military in Lubango, where Kadashkin, in true Russian tradition, was lashing this "Africanist" with a besom, though made not of birch twigs as in Russia, but of eucalyptus. It was a really nice place, visited not only by myself, but also by such prominent Soviet persons as Yegor Ligachev, a future Politburo member, and Valentina Tereshkova, the first woman cosmonaut.

However, Prokhanov fails when he writes about armed action and political issues. Thus he claims that under the command of Kadashkin, Soviet marines landed near Porto-Alexandre to prevent the attack of South Africa's "Buffalo" Battalion, though in reality they never took part in actions in Angola, and that battalion was manned mostly not by Boers, as the author claims, but by black Africans.

In any case, for one reason or another Prokhanov in his novel puts strong criticism of the SWAPO leadership in the mouth of Aurelio, a Cuban intelligence officer, who tells his Soviet counterpart:

He [Sam Nujoma] is cunning, haughty, and perfidious. I don't trust him, his talks about friendship, Marxism, how he sings Soviet songs … when he wins and comes into Windhoek, he'll forget about Marxism, Cuba and the Soviet Union. Only the British will be in his palace.[43]

This is utterly unfair. To begin with, Nujoma sent all three of his sons to do military training in the USSR. Besides, I do not remember Nujoma singing Soviet songs or talking much about Marxism, but, what is more important, after the victory, after Namibia became independent, Sam Nujoma as President valued and appreciated the friendship with Moscow and Havana. I could sense it myself when several times I met the President of Namibia in his home country. Incidentally I never met the British in his "palace", that is, in the State House.

By the 1980s most of the SWAPO cadres were concentrated on Angolan territory, but some structures and some members of the leadership remained in Zambia, headed by Mishake Muyongo. Muyongo, the second man in the Caprivi National Union (CANU), joined SWAPO in 1966, when his organisation merged with SWAPO. CANU's leader, Brendan Simbaye, who was made SWAPO's Vice-President, had been by that time been detained by South African authorities, so Muyongo became its Acting Vice-President.

When SWAPO's top leadership moved to Angola, Muyongo distanced himself somewhat from its core. He preferred to stay in

Zambia; apparently he felt himself more confident next door to his native Caprivi.

Muyongo was in close contact with SWAPO supporters and other people in the West who in one way or another dealt with Namibian problems. At that time I had good relations with Sean McBride, UN Commissioner on Namibia, and I recall how he expressed criticism of "SWAPO generals" in Angola, obviously preferring "civilian" Muyongo to them. A group of Western supporters once even sent a letter in defence of Muyongo to the SWAPO leadership.

I met Muyongo for the first time in April 1970, when, although accidentally, he happened to be in Moscow during the days of Lenin's centenary and was therefore even awarded a jubilee medal. I do not know why, but he always looked somewhat strange to me; he was undoubtedly a capable person, but too ambitious. Besides, for a Russian it looked odd that this man would never drink alcohol. I discovered this when I once visited him at the Ukraina Hotel, as often, with a bottle in my briefcase and had to finish it off alone, which was not easy even for a young man.

Over 30 years later, at a friendly party in Windhoek, held by one of the Namibian ministers, the host reminded me in his toast that I had once asked him whether he trusted the then SWAPO Vice-President. Honestly, I do not remember this, but further developments, Muyongo's breakup with SWAPO in late 1980, him joining the so-called Democratic Turnhalle Alliance, notorious for its co-operation with Pretoria, his running against Sam Nujoma in the presidential election, and finally the organisation of an abortive separatist mutiny in Caprivi and his flight to Denmark, show that I was right in my doubts. In fact I did not have palpable reason to suspect Muyongo, but my intuition did not betray me.

SWAPO's position in Angola was by and large ensured. In the success of SWAPO's struggle the Angolan leadership saw a guarantee of the security of its southern borders, which allowed it to establish a whole network of political and military headquarters, training facilities and refugee centres there. Nevertheless, from time to time some limitations to its activities were introduced, especially when Luanda conducted talks with Pretoria. Thus SWAPO never received all the tanks and APCs sent to PLAN from the Soviet Union, though, as always, the Angolan government agreed on the list of supplies in advance.

Trying to contain the PLAN activities in Namibia, on 4 May 1978 the SADF carried out an operation that became known as the "Cassinga massacre". Using paratroopers and transport planes, acquired earlier in the West, Pretoria destroyed a major SWAPO camp in that area, claiming that it was a training centre for "terrorists". However, most of the victims of this raid were civilians, women and children. Nevertheless, while its military victory was dubious, Pretoria tried to get a propaganda one, claiming that "Cassinga was the end of SWAPO". On the contrary, this massacre raised sympathy for SWAPO, both inside Namibia and in the international arena.

The Soviet mission in Angola highly appreciated the combat readiness and high morale of PLAN units, especially of its two regular brigades.[44] As was mentioned above, "General Konstantin" initially resisted plans to use SWAPO units in fighting UNITA on a regular basis, regarding them as a basis of the future army of independent Namibia.[45]

The Cubans did not share this high opinion; indeed, their command in Angola had apparently had some prejudice towards SWAPO for many years. For example, in July 1983, when Kurochkin proposed transferring 20 tanks and 30 APCs to the SWAPO brigade, to be used as a reserve if the situation worsened and new South African aggression had to be dealt with, "Polo" objected to it. He alleged that SWAPO operations showed a big danger of losing this hardware owing to the weak combat efficiency and low morale of SWAPO fighters.[46] Why the Cuban command underestimated PLAN is still a mystery to me.

Finally, however, when the situation became really threatening, Kurochkin himself advised dos Santos to deploy a Namibian brigade in a crucial area of Angola in mid 1983.[47] This brigade played an important role in a counter-offensive against UNITA. More than once Sam Nujoma urged its return to southern Angola, but the FAPLA command resisted it, apparently not only because of its role in fighting, but also because its presence near the border would annoy Pretoria.

In their efforts to reach an agreement with Pretoria in early 1984, the Angolans hoped not only to ensure the SADF's withdrawal from their territory, but also that it would open prospects for a political settlement in Namibia. These talks and their results – the Lusaka Agreements of 16 February 1984 – were quite different from the Nkomati Accord on Non-Agression and Good Neighbourliness between Mozambique and South Africa concluded a month later. However, the very talks made the SWAPO leadership worried. It felt (and, as was shown above, rightly so), that the agreement would mean a serious limitation of SWAPO's freedom of action in Southern Angola.

This growing tension between SWAPO and the Angolan government was the main reason for a working visit by Andrey Urnov, who succeeded Manchkha as Head of the African Section of the International Department, and me in January 1984 to meet both sides. In Luanda we had a comprehensive discussion with Afonso van Dunem "Mbinda", MPLA International Secretary (and future Minister of Foreign Affairs), who confirmed that Luanda would reject any idea of a non-aggression pact with Pretoria.[48] We also had a detailed discussion with the GVS and his superior, General Varennikov, who as was mentioned above, at that time was inspecting the Soviet military mission in Angola.

Then, since Sam Nujoma happened to be in Lubango, where PLAN headquarters and the main training base were situated, we flew there by An-12, a workhorse of the Soviet VTA (Military Transport Aviation). For me, personally, this flight was a return to my youth, to the years when, in the early 1960s, we maintained an air bridge between Cairo and Sanaa, assisting Nasser's troops in North Yemen.

Our discussions with Nujoma once again demonstrated his cool determination to face all possible obstacles on the way to independence. A striking feature was his ability to remain calm and unruffled under the most difficult circumstances, when the developments were negative for him and his organisation. This time he also behaved as if nothing had happened, and only when he and Urnov had a tête-à-tête in a dug-out in a PLAN camp was he frank in telling the Soviet representative how complex the situation was.

We did our best to encourage both sides – Angolans and Namibians – to strengthen strategic bilateral relations in spite of current tactical disagreements. In addition to discussions, we were invited to the parade of the new "graduates" of Tobias Hanyeko Training Centre, named after the first top commander of SWAPO. When we listened to Nujoma's speech to hundreds of young fighters, one point in it drew our attention: he emphasised Pretoria's subversive activity: "There are spies among you … ."

This was hardly accidental: in this very period a number of SWAPO members were arrested by its security structures and accused of working for South Africa. The need to prevent and to neutralise the penetration of Pretoria's agents into its ranks created a growing mood of suspicion and mistrust within SWAPO. I can hardly judge whether the actions of SWAPO security were always justified or not: the whole

Plate 10   Sam Nujoma, Andrey Urnov, Vladimir Shubin and others, Lubango, 1984.
Source: Vladimir Shubin archive.

truth could be established only if the archives of the South African security services are opened for researchers, though many believe that the most "sensitive" documents have been shredded.

Anyhow, we were worried about the scale of detentions. Alexander Maksyuta, a Soviet diplomat, who at that stage was the main liaison between the embassy in Luanda and the SWAPO leadership, was instructed by Moscow to express our concern. He had a long discussion with Nujoma, referring specifically to tragic pages of Soviet history, when security bodies accumulated too much power and abused it.[49]

I also recall my discussion with Homateni Kaluenja who accompanied Nujoma to Yury Andropov's funeral in March 1984. In particular, I reminded him that of the five First Marshals of the Soviet Union, we lost three before the war against Hitler's Germany began.[50]

The story of "SWAPO pits" and "missing persons" is still a subject of hot debate in Namibia, often fuelled from abroad. I have no right or wish to be involved in it, but I want to underline my objections to authors who publish articles under titles such as "Lubango and after".[51] I cannot agree when Lubango is reduced to cases of detention, when it is regarded as a symbol of "human rights violations". For me Lubango is first and foremost a symbol of resistance to the colonial regime, the venue of the PLAN headquarters and its training centres and other facilities.

From time to time one can also hear calls for the creation of a Truth and Reconciliation Commission in Namibia along the lines of the South African TRC. Naturally, this is an entirely domestic Namibian matter, but as researchers have proved, the TRC was hardly more productive for national reconciliation than its absence would have been.[52]

The February 1984 visit by Nujoma to Moscow took place at a rather crucial time, just before the Lusaka agreement between Luanda and Pretoria and some months before another conference in Lusaka, held in May, attended by both SWAPO and so-called "internal parties". It demanded great effort from Kenneth Kaunda to organise this conference. Raul Castro told Kurochkin on 12 February in Havana: "Kaunda, like Selestino, prepares SWAPO for talks with South Africa".[53]

Though some conditions SWAPO put forward were met, such as permission for SWAPO leading members "from home" to attend, the organisation was not happy with the modalities of the conference, especially its co-chairmanship (along with Kaunda) with Pretoria's "Administrator-General of SWA", van Niekerk. I heard that Kaunda physically took Nujoma by the hand and brought him to the conference hall.

However, the conference proved that Kaunda's (and Luanda's for that matter) hopes of a speedy beginning to the political settlement in Namibia according to the "UN plan", that is, Security Council Resolution 435, were not realistic. Pretoria was not ready for it, trying to win time to promote a so-called "transitional government of national unity". Van Niekerk admitted to Sam Nujoma that he was in Luanda "just to accompany these people"[54] (participants in the so-called Multi-party Conference organised by Pretoria to counterpose SWAPO).

I also heard from SWAPO representatives that these people, who were regarded as "puppets", indeed depended fully on Pretoria: after the failure of the conference they apologised to Kaunda and told him that van Niekerk had ordered them not to come to any agreement.[55] Theo-Ben Gurirab, then SWAPO International Secretary, had a valid reason to tell us once that Kaunda had an inexhaustible capacity for patience and understanding. "Smith, Vorster, Botha – all deceived him."[56]

On the eve of the meeting in Lusaka, in March 1984, Pretoria, in its attempts to split SWAPO by provoking the power struggle and to promote a so-called "Multi-party Conference", made a blunder: the South African authorities released Andimba Toivo ya Toivo, detained after the first encounters in northern Namibia and sentenced in 1968 to 20 years' imprisonment. Soon Toivo, elected SWAPO Secretary-General, visited Moscow. Apart from political meetings, he had a chance to visit one of the sites we jokingly used to call "terrorist hide-outs" in the environs of Moscow. Officers of the Northern Training Centre were happy to show him all the classrooms full of various arms and equipment, and Toivo, whom I accompanied, repeated many times: "*Jes* [Jesus] ... *Jes* ... ." He was surprised to find out that the whole camp was reserved for PLAN fighters.

Apart from the PLAN cadres, hundreds of Namibians came to Soviet universities and dozens underwent training in the Institute of Social Sciences, on its campus in Nagornoe outside Moscow. Hifikepunye Pohamba, who succeeded Sam Nujoma as President of Namibia in 2006, was among them.

The last visit of a Nujoma-led delegation to Moscow before independence took place from 16 to 20 April 1988. This time he was invited officially "by the Soviet leadership".[57] The very procedure was to show that the bilateral relations went beyond pure inter-party contact. In fact, the Politburo entrusted his reception to Gorbachev, but he, who by that time was visibly losing interest in the Third World, sabotaged the collective decision of the top CPSU body and shifted this duty to Andrey Gromyko and Anatoly Dobrynin, who had replaced Ponomarev as the CPSU International Secretary. Moreover, though we had informed the embassy in Luanda in advance, Nujoma was not made aware of this change. So we had the unpleasant obligation to inform the SWAPO President about the modalities of the visit.

Nevertheless, the visit was quite successful and this success was underlined in the official TASS report under the title "SWAPO leadership in the Kremlin".[58] Indeed, apart from Nujoma, the delegation included other leaders – Theo-Ben Gurirab, International Secretary; Hidipo Hamutenya, Secretary for Information; and Peter Mueshihange, who succeeded Nanyemba as Secretary for Defence.[59] The growing prospects of a political settlement and continued Soviet assistance to PLAN were discussed. "Now we shall really hit the enemy", Nujoma expressed his mood when we parted at the airport.[60]

Nujoma, in particular, took part in the official opening of the SWAPO Mission in Moscow.[61] It was headed by Fillemon Malima, former Commissar of PLAN and future Minister of Defence. This issue was discussed earlier, in April 1987, when Theo-Ben Gurirab visited Moscow.[62] Although, just like the ANC mission, which opened at about the same time, the SWAPO mission was accredited to the Solidarity Committee, it had all the attributes of diplomatic representation, from immunity to the right to hoist the SWAPO flag on the premises and use it on the official car.[63]

By that time Nujoma was at the head of a sophisticated structure, which to some extent performed governmental duties towards many thousands of Namibians, and had an army better armed and better trained than most African ones. The days when he would sometimes come to Moscow on his own, not even accompanied by an aide, were over. In fact, at the airport we had to negotiate a temporary surrender of arms by a couple of his bodyguards, assuring them that in Moscow they could have a bit of rest.

18
SWAPO's Victory

SWAPO welcomed the December 1988 New York agreements mentioned earlier, though its leadership was hardly satisfied with the limited role the organisation had in their drafting. True, it had been consulted both by Angolans and Cubans, as well by Soviet "unofficial observers", but some of the provisions, such as the concentration of PLAN on Angolan territory, were a deviation from the original UN plan.

Besides, the beginning of its implementation was marred by differences between the Soviets and SWAPO, which in this case was supported by African countries and other members of the Non-Aligned Movement. Soviet diplomats, just as representatives of other permanent members of the Security Council – China, the UK and France – agreed to the American proposal to cut down the number of UN troops to be deployed in Namibia in the pre-election period for a financial reason: the USSR, Ukraine and Belarus (these two Soviet republics were also UN members) were making a large contribution to the budget of the United Nations Transition Assistance Group (UNTAG).

The agreement was reached in a wrong way, behind the backs of Havana and SWAPO. Cuban delegates, for example, were first informed of the arrangements by the Americans and not by the Soviets. This decision, which caused political complications for the USSR, was taken by the Minister of Foreign Affairs, Eduard Shevardnadze, acting practically single-handedly. Unfortunately, this practice of substituting the collective leadership with the decisions of one person, or at best by an agreement between Shevardnadze and Gorbachev soon became routine. Only later, to be on the safe side, did Shevardnadze seek and receive the approval of the CC. However, when the wave of criticism grew, the "Silver Fox", as Shevardnadze became known, sent another memorandum, suggesting concessions. This in turn became obsolete when quite soon a compromise was reached in the UN.

Subsequent events showed the reduced strength of the UNTAG units did not harm its functioning, especially since the number of UN police officers was increased, but the delay caused by lengthy discussions on the issue prevented their deployment on time. So, on 1 April, the day when the implementation of the UN plan began, only one UNTAG officer was available in northern Namibia.

Instead of a cessation of hostilities on 1 April, that day witnessed bloodshed in the areas adjacent to the Angolan border. South African authorities claimed that PLAN fighters were sent across the border, while the SWAPO leadership insisted that they were in Namibia earlier, and had just undergone redeployment, looking for assembly points run by UNTAG.

Hardly accidentally, Sam Nujoma underlined the presence of SWAPO forces in Namibia when I met him in Lisbon some weeks earlier.[1] I went there to attend the International Emergency Meeting for the Genuine Independence of Namibia, but the discussion with the SWAPO President was at the top of my agenda. Indeed, PLAN fighters in larger or smaller numbers were present in Northern Namibia from at least mid 1970, though more of them crossed from the Angolan side of the border that day. In any case their intentions were absolutely peaceful – to report to the UNTAG representatives, but the UN machinery, headed by Marti Ahtisaari, Special Representative of its Secretary-General, was not yet in place. A *Pravda* correspondent reported from Windhoek about 1,000 UNTAG troops who had already come to Namibia, but no monitors had been dispatched to the north of the country.[2] The South African *Weekly Mail* published a very similar story: "On a 300 km front, there was just one UN officer."[3] "UN to blame. Bloodshed could have been avoided if Ahtisaari had acted", is how *The Namibian*[4] summarised the developments. Moreover, Ahtisaari allowed South African units, confined to base in terms of Resolution 435 passed by the UN Security Council, which set out proposals for a cease-fire and UN-supervised elections, to be unleashed to attack PLAN soldiers.[5]

To a certain extent this tragedy was a consequence of the fact that SWAPO was not part of the talks on the political settlement; and the confinement of PLAN units to the north of the 16th parallel in Angola was not required by the original UN plan. In any case it is clear that the PLAN combatants had no aggressive intentions whatsoever. They were going to surrender their arms to the UN. The process of settlement was finally resumed, primarily because the

SWAPO leadership agreed to a compromise and ordered its fighters to move to Angola.

The November 1989 general elections provided an opportunity for me to visit Namibia for the first time. I was part of the delegation of Soviet NGOs, which was broad enough – ranging from the Chairman of the Solidarity Committee from Kazakhstan to an Orthodox priest from Ukraine. Hundreds of foreign observers were coming to Namibia in those days, but "special treatment" was prepared for us. Even though entry for all of us had been negotiated in advance and guaranteed by the South African missions in New York and in Windhoek, the immigration authorities refused entry to most of us, and our luggage was taken back to the Zambian Airways plane that had brought us from Lusaka. A low-ranking coloured policeman and a black Zambian airline representative tried to force us to board the plane again, but we flatly refused. Only after vigorous efforts on the part of Pavel Pavlov, my university friend, then the Head of the Soviet Liaison Mission in Windhoek, were we allowed in. Just then a top-ranking white officer appeared on the scene for the first time.

The stay in Namibia was amazing and revealing. We went to the town of Gobabis where the last election rally of SWAPO took place, met representatives of several parties, observed the election procedures, saw mile-long queues at the polling stations in Katatura, and, of course, had a comprehensive discussion with Nujoma on 7 November in his home in his African township just after he had voted himself.

The situation on the eve of the election was alarming: Roelof ("Pik") Botha, referring to "intercepted messages", stated that PLAN units were going to cross into Namibia again from Angola. That was entirely untrue, and, as Nujoma told us, Botha had indicated that his source of information was the same as on 1 April. "It means the previous information was also wrong", concluded Nujoma.[6]

If for us the stay in Namibia was astonishing, the presence of Soviets in Windhoek was equally amazing for locals and South Africans. I remember vivid conversations with Afrikaners in a bar of a fully booked hotel (they paid for our drinks behind my back), and an even more odd chat with a couple of blacks who admitted that they were serving in Pretoria's security service. They were visibly in disarray: "What should we do now?" one of them asked me. "Make peace with your people", was the only thing I could tell them.

Our way back home from Windhoek was, strangely enough, via Johannesburg and Maputo. No politics were involved. In those days our routes were as a rule determined by Aeroflot flights, and to join one in the capital of Mozambique we had to pass through South Africa. We did not ask for visas, but had a chance to spend a night in a neat and very reasonable hotel at (still) Jan Smuts airport – they charged just US$10 per night. However, even though we were "confined" it was very special for us to celebrate the 72nd anniversary of the October 1917 Russian revolution right in the "den of racists"!

Having won the general election, SWAPO pursued a policy of national reconciliation, which resulted in unanimous adoption of the constitution and unanimous election of Sam Nujoma to the post of president. On 21 March 1990, the flag of the independent Republic of Namibia was hoisted in Windhoek.

Part Five

Last But Not Least: South Africa

19
ANC: Co-operation Begins

Whatever country of Southern Africa we touch upon, we always see the involvement of the Pretoria regime, be it in the occupation of Namibia, full-scale aggression in Angola, terrorist action in Mozambique or assistance to the racist government in Rhodesia. If, unfortunately, co-operation between the liberation movements was hardly adequate, their adversaries fared better in this respect. Therefore the developments inside South Africa had crucial significance.

However, the history of the ANC and its relations with Moscow in the period under review was discussed in detail in my previous book[1] and in the relevant chapter of the volume on international solidarity published by the South African Democracy Education Trust (SADET).[2] I shall therefore pay attention only to the most important developments here.

Moscow's relations with the ANC have a history of over 80 years: its president, Josiah Gumede, came to the USSR in November 1927, when the 10th anniversary of the Bolshevik revolution was celebrated, and contact with the SACP was established even earlier. When the Soviet Consulate was opened in 1942 in Pretoria, as well as its branch in Cape Town, some contact with the anti-racist forces in South Africa was resumed, but in 1956 these offices were closed at the request of the National Party government. Occasionally South Africans, including Walter Sisulu, then ANC Secretary-General, and such prominent communists as Brian Bunting and Ruth First, would visit the USSR in the 1950s, but these trips did not constitute the resumption of regular bilateral ties.

This happened much later, in July 1960, soon after the Sharpeville massacre and the banning of the ANC (the Communist Party had been banned ten years earlier), when SACP Chairman Dr Yusuf Dadoo, who was also a prominent leader of the South African Indian Congress and the Congress Alliance,[3] and Vella Pillay, SACP representative in Western Europe, came to Moscow and had meetings at the CPSU headquarters. As Yusuf Dadoo later described: "We have open honest discussions as between Communists, and the Soviet comrades have never insisted on this or that line."[4]

Among the issues Dadoo discussed in Moscow were "forms of fraternal assistance from the CPSU and workers' parties of the Socialist Countries",[5] and by the end of 1960 the SACP had been allocated US$30,000 from the so-called "International Trade Union Fund".[6] This money was not only used for CP activities, but also helped the ANC underground. In fact, Yusuf Dadoo underlined that the SACP was assisting the ANC Emergency Committee in this respect. The same applies to the growing allocations in 1961 (US$50,000)[7] and 1962 (US$112,445).[8]

The developments in South Africa, in particular the intransigence of the racist regime, made both the SACP and ANC decide that "non-violent" methods of struggle could not be the only ones employed. Yusuf Dadoo again went to Moscow in October 1961, this time together with Moses Kotane, SACP General Secretary and a prominent leader of the ANC. They were guests of the 22nd CPSU congress, and in their discussions at the CPSU headquarters – and in particular with the newly elected CPSU International Secretary, Boris Ponomarev – Kotane and Dadoo raised the question of "using violence". They specifically mentioned that their party had already established a special sub-committee whose task was to decide on the practical steps in training cadres preparing for sabotage.[9]

However, the language of a document titled *Notes on Some Aspects of the Political Situation in the Republic of South Africa*, signed and forwarded by Moses Kotane, as well as his oral statement, was rather guarded: he mentioned "some elements of violence" during struggle, "such as picketing and breaking of communications".[10]

In response, their Soviet interlocutors underlined "the Marxist-Leninist doctrine on the combination of all forms of struggle". Since the SACP leaders asked for help in training military instructors, they were informed that Moscow "would possibly be able to render the SACP assistance, using for this in particular the facilities of some friendly African countries, for example Guinea and Ghana".[11]

The discussions were followed by an official reply from the Soviet leadership, which read:

Taking into account the situation we agree with the opinion expressed by comrades Kotane and Dadoo. At the same time the intention of the SACP to take a course of armed forms of struggle places great responsibility on the Party. It is necessary not to counterpoise one form of struggle against the others but to combine all these forms skilfully. The armed struggle is a struggle of the broad people's masses.[12]

It is worth recording that this reply reached Kotane after 16 December 1961, that is, after the formation of the armed organisation Umkhonto we Sizwe (MK) was made public and its sabotage actions had begun.[13]

So the archive documents clearly show that the decision to use "violence" was taken by South Africans themselves, while Moscow respected it but emphasised the priority of political work.

As for practical co-operation in the military field, it apparently began with the visit of the SACP representatives Arthur Goldreich (he was also a prominent figure in MK) and Vella Pillay[14] in early 1963. This visit is covered in a number of books, but as a rule in a faulty way. Thus, Tom Lodge claims that Goldreich "visited Eastern Europe to arrange military assistance from the Soviet bloc ... at about the same time as Mandela's trip abroad",[15] while it happened a year later; moreover, some of the points Goldreich raised in Moscow were influenced by Mandela's mission. In Goldreich's words, "The scope and scale of specific needs discussed in Moscow were of a very limited nature though [they] covered issues of wider significance and touched upon possibilities for continued assistance."[16] Consultations on military matters were organised for him in Moscow and the request to receive South Africans for training, initially in small numbers, was favourably received.

The first groups of MK personnel, which included such persons as Chris Hani, future Chief of Staff of Umkhonto; Archibald Sibeko (Zola Zembe), a prominent commander; and Lambert Moloi, future Lieutenant General of the new South African National Defence Force, came to Moscow in mid 1963 to study in the military establishment known to the liberation movements as the Northern Training Centre. Hani, who spent almost a year "in the environs of Moscow", said later: "How can the working class forget the Soviet Union? I went to Moscow when I was 21 for military training. I was accepted there and treated wonderfully."[17]

Thus the first contact with the forces of liberation in South Africa was established, or, rather, re-established, through the SACP. However, Moscow was ready to have direct contact with the ANC as well, and a delay in this regard was not its fault. Oliver Tambo, then ANC Deputy President and Head of the External Mission, trying to avoid accusations of taking sides in the East–West conflict, did not hide the fact that he was in no hurry to visit Moscow. However, the reality of the situation made him change his mind. No substantial support was coming from the West and the capacity of the African countries was rather limited: during his trip across the continent in 1962 Nelson Mandela received in cash or in pledges just about £25,000. "Money collecting is a job which requires a lot of time. You must be prepared to wait. A visit to socialist countries has become imperative",[18] he wrote in his report, later captured in Rivonia.

The opening of the Soviet embassy in Dar es Salaam, capital of newly independent Tanganyika, which became the main "rear base" for the ANC, also helped, and the decision of the CPSU CC Secretariat to extend an invitation to Tambo "to come to the USSR at any time convenient to him" was conveyed by the ambassador there.[19]

The first visit by Oliver Tambo to the Soviet Union took place in April 1963. Moses Kotane accompanied him in his talks in Moscow. On 5 April 1963, at the meeting with Boris Ponomarev, Tambo informed the Soviets that the ANC urgently needed £250,000 for its activities. The ANC External Mission had tried to collect it from various sources, but he indicated that his main hope was Moscow.

This hope was not futile, because US$300,000, that is, over 40 per cent of the ANC's needs, was provided to it later in the same year.[20] It meant that the ANC, along with, but separate from the SACP, began receiving direct regular financial assistance. It is worth mentioning that the SACP's allocation was reduced to US$56,000 in 1963,[21] and this confirms that to a large extent the ANC and MK were the final recipients of a substantial part of previously huge allocations to the SACP.

However, limited, almost symbolic assistance was provided to ANC earlier as well. In February 1962, Mziwandile Piliso, then its representative in Cairo, requested modest help of £50 for the ANC delegation that attended the conference of writers of Asian and African countries: a writers' meeting again, just as in the case of Angola and Mozambique. However, in this case nobody among the South Africans could really be called a writer: according to the message received in the Solidarity Committee, the delegation was composed of Oliver Tambo, "Nelson Mandella [sic]" and "Robert Resh [sic]". With the party headquarters' permission, 100 roubles in foreign currency (equivalent to US$111 those days) was allocated "from the limited fund of the Committee".[22]

Assistance from the International Fund helped the ANC to overcome the problems caused by the sharp decline in support from China. Initially, Beijing was very active in Africa, and the ANC delegation, headed by Oliver Tambo, was warmly received in China in September–October 1963, but the relationship soured when the ANC (and SACP) failed to side with China in the growing Sino-Soviet dispute.

The ANC leadership and Oliver Tambo in particular were increasingly critical of Beijing's policy, especially during the "Great Proletarian Cultural Revolution". In particular, this was because, according to Tambo, Beijing established contact with Pretoria, and its influence on the governments of Tanzania and Zambia created difficulties for the ANC. However, the ANC remained patient and did not publicly react to attacks from China, in particular from the Xinhua news agency.[23]

Another important issue discussed by Tambo in Moscow in 1963 was immediate preparation for guerrilla warfare: first of all, military training. Only a small number of fighters could be trained "at home", in South Africa, as control at the borders was becoming increasingly strict. Besides, African countries could either receive only limited numbers for training or imposed conditions unacceptable to the ANC.

"The Northern Training Centre", a highly sophisticated establishment, was perfectly suited for this purpose. However, when Tambo requested hundreds of fighters to be admitted, special arrangements were needed. So, in approximately six months' time, one of the military colleges in Odessa, commanded by General Checherin,[24] was prepared to receive the first MK group, and by the time Tambo came to Moscow again in October 1963 in transit from Beijing (he was invited there for the 14th anniversary celebrations of the People's Republic of China) the relevant CPSU CC's decision had already been taken. The next month, in November 1963, Umkhonto members began arriving there,[25] and in February they were joined by a team of MK leaders. Joe Modise, who was known in those days as Thabo More, became commander of the group, and Moses Mabhida its commissar.[26] All in all, 328 Umkhonto fighters were trained in Odessa from 1963 to 1965 in two groups.

The story of Soviet involvement in the training of MK cadres is still to be told. Terry Bell claims in his *Unfinished Business. South Africa, Apartheid and Truth*, written with Dumisa Buhle Ntebeza, that "there were also reportedly agreements in place between the US and USSR. These restricted any military aid provided to the ANC to conventional training involving artillery and tanks – not much use in the conditions of the time",[27] because Moscow held the ANC and SACP "in reserve as surrogates in the global game of superpowers".[28]

This is sheer nonsense. Archibald Sibeko recalls in his memoirs:

We were taught military strategy and tactics, topography, drilling, use of firearms and guerrilla warfare. We also covered politics, with heavy emphasis on skills needed [for] the construction and use of explosives, vehicle maintenance, feeding a mobile army and first aid in the field: everything necessary for survival under guerrilla conditions.[29]

True, unlike Moscow and its environs, training in Odessa was organised in a "normal" military college. However, the Soviets did their best to adapt it to the conditions of guerrilla warfare. When a group of officials, led by Petr Manchkha, arrived in Odessa in June 1964, on the whole they were content with the level of training of the MK cadres, but insisted on higher specialisation in guerrilla training. So, apart from the Northern Training Centre, another special centre, mentioned above, was established in Perevalnoye in the Crimea.

For the next two decades these two institutions were the main training bases for the MK members in the USSR, but later, at the request of the ANC leadership, in anticipation of radical changes in South Africa and in particular in its armed forces, training of officers for a regular army, navy and air force began as well in a number of Soviet cities, from Minsk in Belarus to Frunze in Central Asia,

During his first visit to Moscow Tambo underlined the necessity of supplying small arms and explosives, to be followed by heavier weapons: machine-guns, and anti-tank, recoilless and anti-aircraft guns. The question of arms delivery had already been touched upon by Goldreich, and the extracts from his diary, captured by South African police, show that the Soviet military were quite sensible. They rejected his idea of "transfer of armaments on high seas" from Soviet ships to a ship to be acquired by the ANC, and suggested as the "safest and surest way, transfer of arms through a country where they [the Soviets] have normal relations with the agreement of its government". Goldreich wrote in his diary: "Willingness of this government to us [the liberation movement]. Govt. gives us their armaments and Soviet compensates."[30] Practically, this was the very way supplies to the ANC were organised, first via Dar es Salaam, and later via Maputo and especially via Luanda, although as a rule no compensation mechanism was needed, because with the consent of independent African states Soviet supplies intended for the ANC were sent to their defence forces. Whether all of these actually reached MK is another matter.

Having trained hundreds of fighters in the USSR and elsewhere, the ANC leadership faced fundamental obstacles in getting them back to South Africa. The failure of attempts to do so via Mozambique in 1967 and via Zimbabwe, in co-operation with ZAPU, in 1967–68,[31] created tension in ANC ranks and MK in particular.

This tension was eased as a result of the ANC Consultative Conference, held in Morogoro in April–May 1969. However, the ANC soon faced another problem. "In July 1969 our headquarters received a notice requiring that the ANC vacate its military cadres from the Kongwa Camp [in Tanzania] within a period of 14 days. The reason given for this unprecedented notice was that our cadres in Kongwa had stayed so long that they had now become a security risk to the country", says the report presented to the ANC National Executive Committee session two years later, in 1971. "In other words this meant the liquidation of Umkhonto we Sizwe." According to the report, fighters were sent on "refresher courses" and, after these were completed, "we were able to obtain permission for their return to Kongwa".[32]

Later, at the ANC Conference in Kabwe in 1985, Oliver Tambo was more straightforward: "In 1969 as a result of complications that our movement faced in this region, we had to evacuate [most of] our army to the Soviet Union at very short notice."[33] Indeed, they had to go to the USSR, because unfortunately not a single African country was ready to replace Tanzania as a home for the MK fighters. Soviet assistance rendered to the ANC at this crucial moment, when the whole military machinery of the congress faced "liquidation", compellingly shows its value to the liberation struggle. Moreover, Moscow not only agreed to accept ANC cadres for a year at very short notice, but when it became obvious that the return of MK fighters to Africa would be delayed for more than a year, Moscow satisfied the ANC leadership's request to extend the course of "retraining" them.[34]

This conduct corresponded to the spirit of the discussion between the SACP delegation, led by its chairman John Marks and Alexey Kosygin in June 1969, during an international communist meeting. The delegation reported:

A meeting was held with the Prime Minister, A. Kosygin. He was especially interested in the conditions of the mineworkers in South Africa. He was given a verbal report on the subject.

He informed our delegation that the Soviet people are very interested in South Africa. He also said that they recognise that the South African struggle is probably the most difficult one in the world. He assured us of their total support for our struggle and invited us to ask for any support we may require whenever we need this.[35]

20
Helping to Return Home

A desperate situation the MK cadres faced abroad forced the ANC and SACP leadership to return to the idea of using a sea route to transfer a group of MK cadres to South Africa. As cautious as the Soviets were, following continual requests, Moscow agreed to support the plan,[1] which included training of personnel to reconnoitre suitable sites for landing, assisting in acquiring a vessel,[2] supplying the necessary equipment and training the landing party.

Alas, "Operation J", as Tambo called this project, actually in honour of its initiator Joe Slovo, failed completely, just like "Operation Chelsea", an attempt to save at least some preparation efforts.[3] A different story was that of Chris Hani, a military and political leader of the ANC and Assistant General Secretary at the SACP Central Committee who managed to "penetrate" into South Africa successfully and then into Lesotho in 1974. Although Moscow was not directly involved in this operation, Hani's second round of studies in the Northern Training Centre somewhat earlier was crucial. He recalled:

We had undergone a course in the Soviet Union on the principles of forming an underground movement. That was our training: the formation of the underground movement, then the building of guerrilla detachments. The Soviets put a lot of emphasis on the building of these underground structures, comprising in the beginning very few people.[4]

The April 1974 Portuguese revolution that prompted the independence of Mozambique and Angola and the Soweto uprising on 16 June 1976 radically changed the situation in South Africa and in the region. After many years of virtual isolation, the ANC re-established close ties with "home".

However, this change resulted in the ANC facing new problems. Hundreds and then thousands of South Africans, mostly youths, left home to join liberation movements. Their accommodation, maintenance and training became serious challenges to the organisation, and again Moscow was there to help. Even before the events in Soweto, in February 1976, Alfred Nzo, ANC Secretary-General, and Thomas Nkobi, its Treasurer-General, requested the Solidarity Committee urgently to send to Angola all that was necessary for 400 newcomers – from binoculars to socks and shoes.[5] Apart from new supplies to Angola, they also wanted Moscow's help in transferring to Luanda some supplies from the USSR, previously sent at the ANC's request to Tanzania and newly independent Mozambique.

In this crucial period Moscow again increased the number of MK cadres who could come to the USSR for training. All in all, it received 140 of them from 1976 to 1978.[6] However, training was not limited to military institutions; in total about 200 South Africans graduated in the USSR, mostly with Masters degrees, and 200 more studied for a shorter time at the Institute of Social Sciences or the Komsomol School.

One should also not forget Moscow's consistent political and diplomatic support of the liberation struggle in South Africa, be it at the UN, other international organisations or during bilateral contacts. It would be apt to compare it with the stance of the major Western powers at that period. One example of this is well known, the so-called Memorandum 39, prepared in 1969 under Henry Kissinger, then the US National Security Adviser[7]. Another document is less famous, but no less interesting. A circular sent from the UK Foreign and Commonwealth Office to a number of British embassies in Africa stated: "… you are at liberty to maintain overt but reasonably discreet contact with the political leaders [of various freedom movements from Southern Africa], though you should not offer assistance to them". Moreover, the definition of this "reasonably discreet contact" was rigid enough:

– You may speak to leaders of freedom movements if you happen to meet each other on neutral ground;
– You may receive them if they come on legitimate business to your office (though you may think it better to depute a member of your staff to do this in most cases);
– You should not be seen to take the initiative in seeking a meeting;
– You should under no circumstances invite them to your own residence and members of your staff should refer to you before inviting them.

The FCO warned British diplomats: "Greater circumspection needs to be observed in regard to South African and Portuguese Africa groups, than in the case of South West African and Rhodesian ones, which are opposed to Governments of more or less dubious legitimacy."[8]

Solodovnikov[9] recalls that when he came to Lusaka as the Soviet ambassador in 1976, his colleagues, Western ambassadors, used to say: "Why are you dealing with the ANC? ... The ANC does not have any support inside the country." In his opinion, "the Western countries maintained their unfriendly attitude towards the ANC almost until the end of the 1980s, and only when they saw that the ANC was rapidly advancing to victory they hurried to make 'friends' with it".[10]

On the contrary, the late 1970s witnessed a new stage in the development of Moscow's relations with the ANC. During his visit to Moscow in October 1978, Tambo asked for Soviet assistance with the training of MK cadres in Angola,[11] and a written request followed.[12] Thus, 17 years after this issue of Soviet instructors had been discussed for the first time, the situation became favourable.

The first group of Soviet officers, still small, was headed by Navy Captain Vyacheslav Shiryaev, who became a rather legendary figure in ANC circles, though under his *nom de guerre*, "Comrade Ivan".[13] Soon the group's size began to grow and finally, by the late 1980s, it reached about 30 persons; altogether, in 1979–91 more than 200 Soviet advisers, specialists and interpreters (not counting their families) shared the hardships of life and service in Angola with their ANC comrades.[14]

Shiryaev recalls: "The ANC faced a huge well-adjusted [war] machine, able through its strategy, tactics and technical capacities to counter practically the whole African continent." Besides, according to him, "there was an opinion among the high military command of the former USSR" that "no force in Africa was able to shake the foundations of apartheid in South Africa".[15]

Whether such a mood was present or not, at the ANC leadership's request Moscow sent specialists in various fields: tactics, engineering, MCW ("military-combat work", that is, building of an armed underground network), hand-to-hand fighting, automobiles, communications and communications equipment repair, medicine, etc., to Angola. Arms and ammunition were coming in increased volume (to the Angolan Ministry of Defence, but earmarked for the ANC) and by mid 1982 its stocks would allow MK units to conduct large-scale armed action for a protracted period of time.[16]

All in all, from 1963 to 1990 the total value of Soviet military supplies to the ANC was about 36 million roubles. However, it would be wrong to calculate this sum in any foreign currency, because prices were very low in the USSR, and the list of equipment is more clear-cut: several

Plate 11 Mziwandile Piliso, ANC Executive member and "Comrade Ivan", Angola, circa 1984.

Source: Vyacheslav Shiryaev archive.

thousand AK-47s of various modifications, 3,362 Simonov self-loading carbines (SKS), 6,000 pistols, 275 grenade launchers, 90 Grad-P missile launchers, over 40 Strela 2M anti-aircraft missile launchers, 20 Malyutka anti-tank rocket launchers, over 60 mortars, etc.[17]

"Comrade Ivan" co-operated closely with the ANC representatives in Angola, in particular with Timothy Makoena, the commander of the main camp situated in Malange province.[18] He also underlines that, in spite of all difficulties,

... the attitude of the Angolan government and people to South African patriots was more than friendly. Under the state of civil war and practically full economic dislocation, Angola was nevertheless looking for opportunities to do what it could to help the ANC. The goodwill of the Angolans extended to the Soviet military specialists attached to the ANC.[19]

One more sentence from Shiryaev's account is worth quoting: "The USSR embassy in Angola also paid attention to the training of ANC patriots, although it preferred not to look into details of the attuned process of studies, considering it a prerogative of the International Department of the CPSU CC."

The ANC leadership put the Soviet group to the "task to lay the basis for the formation of regular armed units in the framework of 'Umkhonto we Sizwe'".[20] Its members, and especially Joe Modise, future Minister of Defence, believed that knowledge of conventional warfare was needed for the future, when the new armed forces of South Africa would be created. However, training for guerrilla warfare was carried out as well, although the balance between the two changed now and again.

When Andrey Urnov and I visited Angola in early 1984 (the purpose of the trip was explained above) we were a bit surprised when "Comrade George" (German Pimenov, a specialist in MCW, who had succeeded "Comrade Ivan" as head of the group) told us that the Umkhonto command had set itself the task of forming and training at least five infantry battalions, and that the first of these was to be combat-ready soon.[21] We believed that at that time the emphasis on regular units was excessive; anyhow, later the approach was changed, and in the late 1980s, apart from the formation of two battalions to fight UNITA, training was conducted mostly for guerrilla operations and underground activities within South Africa.[22]

Moscow's support to the ANC and especially to MK increased in the early 1980s, which saw several stunning operations by Umkhonto, which helped to develop a mood of defiance among the African population, especially in the townships. In the middle of that decade they began to "explode" one by one, and even the state of emergency declared by Pretoria could not effectively suppress the mass movement.

The intake in Umkhonto increased and so did the number of cadres to be trained in Angola. It resulted in the strengthening of the Soviet group. As for training in the USSR in the second half of the 1980s, it was organised in two major fields in the specialities determined by the ANC, naturally after consultation with the Soviet military in Angola and/or Moscow.

The first was the preparation of cadres to enable them to form and maintain armed underground structures. After my discussion with Oliver Tambo in the GDR in August 1986 (he was there for medical treatment), the annual intake of ANC members for training in the Northern Training Centre in the MCW was increased to 60. Taking into account the changing situation in South Africa and the rise of repression, Joe Modise, the MK commander, and Ronnie Kasrils, then head of Military Intelligence, specifically requested the inclusion of the methods of transition from legal activities to underground ones in the programme of training.

Skills acquired by fighters of Umkhonto we Sizwe in the Soviet Union or with Soviet instructors and advisers in Angola no doubt greatly helped them in the underground struggle. However, prescribed rules were not easy to follow. Our South African friends used to say: "Don't worry that MK members do not always work according to the rules, the enemy also know them." (Sometimes we had to violate the rules too. When our delegation was leaving Lesotho in 1984, at the last moment, at the airport, a counsellor of the newly established Soviet embassy passed me an envelope that ANC comrades asked me to deliver to their colleagues in Mozambique. Moreover, the name of the recipient, Jacob Zuma,[23] was marked on it. True, I carried a diplomatic passport, but on the way to Maputo the plane was to land at Matsapa airport in Swaziland, practically controlled by Pretoria's security. "But, on the other hand," I thought, "perhaps this letter can save somebody's life, so I have to take the risk.")

Secondly, the MK command and especially Joe Modise felt that it was time to train cadres in handling heavy arms, including aircraft and naval ships. However, as a rule, foreigners would be trained to handle equipment to be supplied from the Soviet Union or equipment that was already available. But by 1986, the International Department and those in the Ministry of Defence who were dealing with the ANC managed to convince the top military to begin such training. It was clear to us that the end of the apartheid regime was imminent and the ANC should prepare highly skilled officers for all branches of the armed forces.

So in 1986 the first group of MK cadres arrived in Perevalnoye for a three-year course for motorised infantry officers, and, from 1987, full-course training (up to five years) of South Africans began in several fields, including helicopter and then jet pilots, aircraft engineers and naval officers. Besides, in November 1986, after his discussion with Mikhail Gorbachev, Oliver Tambo, accompanied by Joe Modise and Chris Hani, met Soviet security experts and requested them to organise training in the relevant specialties in the USSR.

All these activities were in contrast to the policy of "constructive engagement" with Pretoria, carried out by Washington. It was expressed in unambiguous terms by President Reagan himself: "Can we abandon a country [South Africa] that has stood behind us in every war we have fought, a country that strategically is essential to the free world in its production of minerals we all must have?"[24]

He was rebuffed by Tambo in an interview with an American magazine: "We stood together with the Soviet Union and the allied forces in fighting Nazism during the Second World War. True to this position the Soviet Union and other socialist countries stand with us to this day fighting the apartheid system itself and its leaders ... of Nazi ideology and practice."[25]

Parallel to increased support for the ANC's military and underground activities, Moscow began looking for contact with the emerging legal opposition in South Africa. A CPSU CC decision taken in 1981 envisaged the establishment of contact with such forces inside South Africa. Moreover, some communication between Moscow and Pretoria was anticipated, though in a very limited form, just permitting the Soviets "not to shun" protocol contact with South African government representatives. Although correct in principle, I believe this decision was premature: in the early 1980s the legal opposition was still weak. Any contact with Moscow could make it vulnerable and be detrimental to its lawful status, while the intensification of South African aggression against Angola and other Frontline States in the early 1980s was not conducive even to protocol contact with Pretoria.

Exceptions were very rare. Most of the contacts were required because of the capture of Soviet citizens either by the SADF (as in the case of Warrant Officer Nikolay Pestretsov, seized in August 1981 during "Operation Protea", a large-scale SADF invasion into Angola) or by its "clients" – UNITA and RENAMO.

Besides, several times Moscow sent Pretoria warning messages, usually to the South African mission in New York. For example, one of them, conveyed in November 1983, was very clear and strict: if South Africa continued its aggression against Angola, Soviet assistance to

Luanda would increase. Pik Botha was unhappy that it "boiled down" to a warning that the USSR viewed the issue of Namibia in a more serious light than ever, and that the occupation of Angolan territory by South African troops, coupled with Pretoria's support for UNITA, was "unacceptable".[26] Chester Crocker quoted that message exactly in his memoirs, and this is one more proof of close relations between the USA and South Africa at that time. However, he completely misread it, alleging that Moscow was trying to open a channel with the USA on Africa "without having to ask" or trying "to bluff Pretoria out of Angola".[27]

To the best of my knowledge, the only bilateral contact with particular substance was a meeting between Soviet and South African officials in August 1984 in Vienna. It took place soon after the Nkomati Accord, which, although assessed critically in Moscow, provided an argument for those in the Soviet governmental structures who were somewhat soft on Pretoria. Sergey Sinitsyn, who led the Soviet delegation, writes in an article published many years later:

In the summer of 1984, through contact with "close neighbours" (KGB)[28] who were dealing with the issue of setting our people free, South African officials informed Moscow about their wish to organise a confidential meeting at working level on the problems of the situation in Southern Africa ... After comprehensive interdepartmental discussion and getting the consent of the Old Square[29] (though without participation of its representative in the [forthcoming] meeting), it was decided to agree to their proposal.[30]

Sinitsyn at that time was a deputy head of the MFA Third African Department, which was dealing with Southern Africa, but the South African delegation was led by (Da)Niel Barnard, head of the National Intelligence Service, and this very fact demonstrates that Pretoria was much more eager to establish contact.[31]

According to Sinitsyn, Niel Barnard emphasised in Vienna that Pretoria was conducting independent foreign policy and did not want to be closely connected with any superpower. At the same time Pretoria wanted Moscow to influence countries and forces close to it to stop their "hostile actions towards South Africa" and so assist the process of "peace and dialogue".[32] In particular, it was against the rise to power of "the radical forces" in Namibia, namely SWAPO.[33]

A "carrot" was prepared for the Soviets as well: the South Africans emphasised the possibility of co-operation between the two countries in several fields, especially in control over a number of strategic mineral resources,[34] but the Soviets rejected the idea of exchanging Moscow's support for its friends for a dubious chance of Pretoria's distancing itself from Washington. So later, during less formal contact, National Intelligence Services representatives could not hide their disappointment.

21

"Rebuilding" or Destroying?

The subsequent years, especially 1986–87 and maybe 1988, could be regarded as the peak of Moscow's relations with the ANC. Those were the first years of so-called *perestroika*, that is, "rebuilding" or "restructuring", proclaimed by Mikhail Gorbachev soon after his election as General Secretary of the CPSU CC. Before long, the term became well known and even fashionable all over the world.

Later, owing to the ultimate failure of Gorbachev's policy, which resulted in the dismembering of the USSR and restoration of capitalism in its "wildest" form, this term acquired a very negative meaning in our part of the world. Nevertheless, the *perestroika* era can be divided into two periods. In the course of the first, socialism in the USSR was still viable, but the second, beginning in late 1988 or early 1989, in the words of Yegor Ligachev, then the second man in the CPSU leadership, meant "disorganisation of economy … destruction of the Party and the USSR".[1]

This division can be applied to the state of Moscow's relations with the ANC as well. The positive and dynamic development culminated in the meeting between Tambo and Gorbachev, which took place in the Kremlin on 4 November 1986. An atmosphere of friendship prevailed at the meeting and the only issue they "disagreed" on was Gorbachev's reluctance to schedule his visit to Southern Africa, which in Tambo's opinion could "transform the situation in the region".

At the time Gorbachev was still honest in his dealings with the ANC: informing Tambo about attempts of P.W. Botha to contact Moscow "through a third, even a fourth, party"; he assured him that any step in this direction would be taken in consultation with the Congress.[2]

The official press release, agreed upon by both sides, stated that three major conditions had to be met to achieve the political settlement in Southern Africa: an end to Pretoria's acts of aggression against independent African states, the granting of independence to Namibia in accordance with UN resolutions and the removal of the apartheid regime in South Africa as "the primary cause of the conflict situation in the region",[3] and this is exactly what happened later.

Stephen Ellis and his renegade co-author claimed that at the Soviet-American summit in Reykjavik with Reagan in October 1986, Moscow "committed itself to withdraw its forces or to refrain from seeking the overthrow of the existing order [in South Africa], leaving the field to the USA and its allies on the ground". South Africa was allegedly included "in the category of countries where the USSR would henceforth refrain from aggression" and Moscow promised no longer to "throw its weight behind the effort by the ANC and the SACP to ferment a revolution in South Africa". [4] They gave no reference, but if they had read the published minutes of the summit they would see that South Africa had not been mentioned in the Gorbachev–Reagan discussions at all.[5] Moreover, in reality at that very time Soviet support for "a revolution in South Africa" was unwavering and strengthening.

Apart from Gorbachev, this was reiterated to the ANC delegation in November 1986 at the meeting at the Ministry of Defence with Army General Varennikov, and then with Anatoly Dobrynin, successor to Ponomarev as the CPSU International Secretary, who assured the delegation of "100 per cent support for the ANC – and, if you want it, 120 per cent support".[6]

One of the issues discussed with Dobrynin was the ANC's suggestion to explore the possibility of joint Soviet-American action against apartheid, or at least a joint statement. By that time Washington was in a hurry to establish official contact with the ANC, but although "technically" the proclaimed aims of the USA and USSR in South Africa were identical – the eradication of apartheid – the American administration declined the relevant Soviet proposals in this respect. Roughly speaking, the approach of Washington was "What's mine is mine, and what's yours – let's discuss how to divide it." Indeed, while the USA was ready to discuss Angola, where the Soviet position was strong enough, it felt that South Africa was its "domain".

One of the results of Tambo's visit to Moscow in November 1986 was the opening of the official ANC mission in the USSR. It enjoyed all diplomatic privileges, even though it was accredited to a non-governmental organisation, the Soviet Afro-Asian Solidarity Committee, and was financed by the non-governmental Soviet Peace Fund.[7] As in the case of SWAPO, the privileges included diplomatic immunity, the right to hoist the ANC flag on the premises and on its official car, and even to have a radio station for confidential communications.[8] Unfortunately, however, the ANC did not use its mission to its full capacity, though the developments in the USSR on the eve of the 1990s demanded it.

Beginning from 1985, under the guidance of the International Department and in consultation with the ANC, Soviet NGOs, publishing houses and academic bodies began establishing contact with legal anti-apartheid bodies and personalities in South Africa, and the stream of visitors to the USSR from that country became increasingly broad.

The rise of the liberation struggle in South Africa and the growing recognition of the role of the ANC as its leader created an atmosphere where negotiations on a political settlement, on the eradication of apartheid by peaceful means, were becoming feasible. Multi-faceted support for the ANC from the USSR facilitated it, as well as a general relaxation of international tension, which made it difficult for Pretoria to use the bogey of a "total communist onslaught".

The approach to the political settlement was discussed in detail at the confidential tripartite consultations involving the USSR, the ANC and Cuba representatives in Moscow in September 1987. Dobrynin, Tambo and Risquet led their delegations accordingly and a common position on all major issues was confirmed.

The Soviet position vis-à-vis the struggle for national liberation and the countries of the Third World was confirmed in a confidential message the CPSU CC sent to friendly organisations, including the ANC and SACP, following the third Gorbachev–Reagan summit in December 1987:

While discussing the problems of regional conflicts and other issues with the Americans we stressed the point that our aspiration for a dialogue with the USA should by no means be construed in such a way that we give up solidarity with the liberation struggle of the people or ignore the interests of developing countries. Never and under no circumstances shall we deviate from the course of supporting the right of nations to independent development, never shall we go for any accord with the Americans at the expense of or to the prejudice of the people of developing countries. For us, solidarity with those who struggle for national liberation, against imperialism and neo-colonialism, remains a permanent factor that is not influenced by temporary changes.[9]

The tripartite meeting for me was also the beginning of Soviet involvement in Operation Vula, aimed at the creation of an armed underground network inside South Africa. It signified mutual trust between the ANC top leadership and us in this sensitive sphere and went into the post-February 1990 period.[10] Oliver Tambo told me in confidence that Mac Maharaj, Ronnie Kasrils (both future ministers) and Siphiwe Nyanda (future chief of the SANDF) had been chosen to go into South Africa to lead the armed underground forces there. Moscow's assistance was needed, first of all to support their "legends". Nyanda later commented:

The Moscow visit of 1988 was the final leg of my preparation to infiltrate South Africa. It afforded me the opportunity to brush up on my disguises and gain more confidence on these. More identities were added to existing ones, enabling me to shed some of them as I advanced from Moscow to Schipol (Holland) to Nairobi (Kenya) and to Matsapa (Swaziland), thus breaking the trail and preparing for safe infiltration into South Africa ... From an operational point of view, the Moscow leg was probably the most important for my cover story.

Without exception, those who were not privy to the information believed I was in the Soviet Union for [military] studies. The enemy therefore never expected me to be right on its doorstep"[11]

Meanwhile, a "pilgrimage" to Moscow by prominent (and sometimes not so prominent) anti-racist figures from South Africa continued. Bishop Tutu came in June 1988 for the celebration of the Millennium of the Russian Orthodox Church, followed by Alex and Jenny Boraine from the Institute for a Democratic Alternative for South Africa (IDASA), the Reverend Alan Boesak, prominent journalist Alistair Sparks, Frederick van Zyl Slabbert, and many others.

Discussions in Moscow as a rule helped them to dispel the rumours that the Soviets were "selling out", that is, changing their stance in favour of Pretoria. Such rumours originated after the Second Soviet-African Conference held in Moscow in June 1986 by the Africa Institute. Its Deputy Director, Gleb Starushenko, speaking there, called for "comprehensive guarantees for the white population" in South Africa.[12] In principle, such personal initiative was acceptable in the spirit of *perestroika*, even if it contained some weird proposals, such as the creation of a chamber in a future South African parliament "possessing the right of veto, on the basis of equal representation of four communities".[13] However, in the West and in South Africa his presentation was regarded as a virtually official position. The "Soviet-ologists" believed that Gorbachev was using Starushenko and another former Deputy Director of the Africa Institute, Victor Goncharov, "as vehicles to introduce new ideas".[14]

A statement by the IDASA delegation, headed by Frederick van Zyl Slabbert, which visited Moscow in April 1989, said:

It would be a dangerous distortion of reality to seize upon the personal view of any single academic or official to determine what the official policy of the USSR is or how it has possibly changed with regard to South and Southern Africa ... We found no evidence at all that the USSR is putting pressure on the ANC to abandon the armed struggle before the conditions for a negotiated settlement had been created by those in power in South Africa, or that the USSR is considering abandoning support for the ANC in favour of closer contact and relations with those who are in power in South Africa at present.[15]

Both phrases were quite correct for the moment, and, indeed we in the International Department and the Solidarity Committee sometimes joked: "The role of academics is to confuse the enemy about our real intentions", but, taking into account later developments, perhaps we were too optimistic ...

The last official visit by Oliver Tambo to the Kremlin took place in March 1989. However, this time Tambo's top interlocutor was not Gorbachev, but Anatoly Lukyanov, his first deputy in the state structures, because it became increasingly difficult to "mobilise" the Soviet leader to meet Africans. His attention had evidently shifted to the West. However, the situation in South Africa, which was rapidly changing, necessitated a meeting at the highest possible level, with or without Gorbachev.

Having analysed the developments in Southern Africa, the ANC President said that Moscow should "be part of the solution of the problem; the South African situation should not remain only the concern of the US, UK and other Western states".

Lukyanov in turn emphasised that "the settlement of regional conflicts" (this phrase was very fashionable in Moscow in those days) did not mean the sacrifice of the struggle for national and social liberation for the eradication of apartheid. He confirmed that, in its contacts with the legal opposition in South Africa, Moscow was acting on the recommendations of the ANC and the Congress would be the first Moscow would seek advice from on matters regarding bilateral relations with South Africa.[16]

The essence of this meeting flatly negates insinuations typical of some Western academics, including former diplomats. Thus, Professor Herman Cohen, Crocker's successor in the State Department, writes: "When the ANC leadership travelled to Moscow for guidance, they could not believe their ears. Gorbachev and his colleagues bluntly told the South Africans not to make the same mistakes they had made ... Nelson Mandela and his team decided to follow Gorbachev's advice to take the capitalist road."[17] Poor Department of State! If a former

Assistant Secretary thought so, what about other diplomats? First of all, it is insulting to the ANC to affirm that its ANC leaders were coming to Moscow for guidance. Secondly, Gorbachev had only one meeting with the ANC leaders, described above, and nothing of the sort happened either there or at any other high-level meetings. They were comradely discussions and I attended all of them, beginning from 1982.

As to advice to avoid our mistakes, that has been a refrain in our conversation with foreign comrades from various parts of the world for many years. As Professor Ulyanovsky used to tell them: "You have the full right to make your own mistakes, but you don't have the right to repeat our mistakes."

However, on the threshold of the 1990s the Soviet Union underwent serious political and institutional changes. Its foreign policy, directed by Gorbachev and Shevardnadze, was rapidly changing as well, and not in favour of the liberation struggle. In a speech to the UN General Assembly in September 1989, Shevardnadze pledged "to oppose ... resolutely all kinds of violence, no matter what had caused or motivated it",[18] and this could be read, in particular, as opposing any resolute action again the racist regime in South Africa.[19]

Nevertheless, Shevardnadze, a clever and canny politician, could easily change his language depending on the circumstances. Thus, when he met the ANC leaders, including Alfred Nzo, Joe Slovo, and Thabo Mbeki in Lusaka on 20 March 1990 (he was there on the way to Windhoek), his words were quite different: "We would be ready to work with you on all of this ... We are ready to work with you in your revolutionary work."[20] Yet he hardly managed to convince the South Africans that he was genuine. Mbeki underlined this: "The USSR should continue to be seen not to begin establishing links with a system on its way out ... We wouldn't want a negative perception of the USSR among our people."[21]

This meeting took place soon after de Klerk announced on 2 February 1990 the unbanning of the ANC, the SACP, and a number of other organisations, as well as the imminent release of Nelson Mandela. Radical changes in the situation in South Africa, and in particular the transfer of the ANC headquarters from Lusaka to Johannesburg, necessitated the opening of a Soviet liaison mission in Pretoria. This was done on a bilateral basis with the consent of the ANC and SACP's leadership. Both the Soviet (in Pretoria) and South African (in Moscow) missions were attached to the embassies of Austria as sections of interest, and, according to the agreement

262 The Hot "Cold War"

reached on 26 February 1991, they were deprived of the right to use the national flag, emblem and other state symbols,[22] meaning that the status of the South African mission in Moscow was lower than that of the ANC office. To avoid any speculation the Soviet press statement specifically stated: "The creation of the sections of interest does not mean the establishment of diplomatic or consular relations."[23] It was somewhat symbolic that the Soviet mission was headed by Dr Alexey Makarov, known to many leaders and activists of the liberation movements from 1963 in Odessa, and especially after 1970, when he became an official of the Solidarity Committee and later of the CPSU International Department.

However, further "erosion" of the Soviet position on South Africa worried the leadership of the liberation movement: "It is a pity that there are some forces in the Soviet Union [that] are in a hurry to have all kinds of links with South Africa ... For the moment, given the support that we have received from the Soviet Union, for all these years, it would be a tragedy if it should be soured by hurried moves."[24]

The release of Nelson Mandela made it possible for him to visit the USSR for the first time. However, rather unexpectedly his visit became a problem in Moscow's relations with the ANC. True, an invitation "on behalf of the USSR leadership" was sent to Mandela in the name of Gorbachev, but up to the end of his administration nothing came of it.

On the surface, the reasons for this were purely technical, but beneath the surface these delays reflected far-reaching changes in Gorbachev's policy. Anatoly Chernyaev, then his assistant for international affairs (and a CC member!), who proved to be another turncoat, wrote in his memoirs:

Gorbachev had a rather good nose for people who had no prospects and were "useless to us" ... He "froze" his meeting with Mandela, though both academics and Ministry of Foreign Affairs officials (true, with some resistance on my part) more than once argued wordily that it had to be done: that one [Mandela] travelled all over the world, everywhere – at the highest level – and yet could not come to Moscow! Gorbachev did not believe that by supporting the ANC and supplying it with arms we were assisting the correct process in South Africa. He did not stop it "automatically"; he had no time to do it. And he realised that it was one thing to receive Mandela in Washington and another thing to do the same in "red" Moscow, suspected of the expansion of communism.[25]

To say that Gorbachev was "expanding communism" in the last years of his administration is nothing but a poor joke, but it was he who warmly received Tambo in 1986, when Moscow really still remained "red", and it was he who voted for all the decisions of the CPSU Politburo and Secretariat on assistance to the ANC, be it political or military.

Mandela raised the question of his visit with my colleagues and me on 3 July 1991 in Durban during the ANC National Conference. He told us that he had heard about one more postponement of the trip when he was already in Nigeria on his way to Moscow. "Gorbachev must have had a good reason to do it", Mandela commented. Otherwise his attitude to the USSR was very clear: "Without your support we would not be where we are now."[26]

The delegates to the conference welcomed the Soviet representatives warmly. During my address, they applauded when I spoke about future relations between "democratic South Africa and the renovated Soviet Union".

Whatever my expectations were, hope of this was lost during stormy events in Moscow the next month, August 1991, when a "very strange coup",[27] organised by a group of people from Gorbachev's retinue, was followed by a "counter-coup" led by Boris Yeltsin, the banning of the CPSU and then the "dissolution" of the USSR in December.

The political renegades and sell-outs who controlled the country and its foreign affairs during that period did their best to distance themselves from the ANC (just as from other old friends of Moscow) and embrace Pretoria. While the Umkhonto cadres were sent away, Pik Botha, visiting Moscow, signed a protocol in November 1991 restoring consular relations between the two countries, then in February 1992 Yeltsin's notorious Minister of Foreign Affairs, Andrey Kozyrev, signed an agreement on the establishment of diplomatic relations between Russia and South Africa in Pretoria. Finally, instead of receiving Mandela, Yeltsin welcomed de Klerk in the Kremlin in late May 1992. He even told him that "Mandela would not be received as the ANC President in Moscow but would be visiting the Russian capital as an international figure, a fighter for human rights",[28] and such assurances made Pretoria more intransigent at the talks with the ANC.

The further developments are beyond the scope of this book. However, to end the chapter on a more optimistic note, I can say that the prospects for the development of Moscow's relations with the ANC-led South Africa improved in the late 1990s, after the defeat of the overtly pro-Western political forces in Russia.

Postscript

At one of the conferences I attended in Moscow, a prominent scholar stated: "The division into East and West was the main source of the conflicts after World War Two." The man in question was Russian, but this opinion is popular in other parts of the world as well. On the contrary, I believe that most of the conflicts in the world during that period were caused not by the struggle between the "two blocs", but by the internal dynamics of one region or another. In particular, in Southern Africa the conflicts were the result of people's desire to get rid of colonialism and apartheid, on the one hand; and the resistance of Pretoria, Salisbury and Lisbon and their benefactors in the West to inevitable decolonisation, on the other. I always remember the words of Oliver Tambo, that the ANC had been founded five years before the 1917 Revolution in Russia!

This does not mean, of course, that the involvement of the "superpowers" did not affect the situation; on the contrary, as we could see, it often made the conflicts harsher, yet in some cases, though rather seldom, interaction between them helped to extinguish the fire.

In my opinion, the internal dynamics of countries and regions play a great role nowadays as well. However, a new cause of conflicts has appeared, namely an attempt, as futile as it may be, of one country to dominate the world.

For many years the Western media, as well as many academics, did their best to prove that the subversive "hand of Moscow" was responsible for all kinds of trouble in the world. It was seen everywhere, be it in South Africa or in North Korea. But has the world become more secure and stable now? Do the people in most parts of it live happier lives?

The end of the "Cold War", the disappearance of the supposedly main threat to world stability – the "communist superpower" – signalled the beginning of a series of very "hot" wars. Why is this so? Is it just because when two superpowers confronted each other the overall balance was preserved? Or is it because there was something essentially positive in the policy, in the stance of one of those superpowers, and this very factor was forcing the other one to uplift itself, to play better and more fairly than it wished to play at that time, and that it is playing now, after this factor disappeared?

Undoubtedly, after the collapse of the Soviet Union Washington could not resist the temptation to establish its domination all over the world. However, a prominent African academic, Samir Amin, warned right away, in 1992: "The United States is not 'invincible' and the resistance of the Third World people is the Achilles' heel of its hegemonic project."[1]That is exactly what we see now, be it in Iraq or Afghanistan. This resistance sometimes takes unacceptable forms, but it is a policy of domination that encourages the new confrontation. New proof of the refusal to accept US domination is the growing opposition to US military activity in Africa, in particular to the creation of AFRICOM, a special American command on the African continent.

A few final points. The natural resistance to the diktat of external forces is often branded as "international terrorism", but one should not forget that during the years of liberation of Southern Africa, freedom fighters were branded as "terrorists" as well. Besides, one can hear sometimes not only in the West but in Russia as well that during the "Cold War", terrorists could find support from one of the warring sides. This is quite wrong, because Moscow's ties with the liberation movements, especially its involvement in training fighters both in the USSR and in Africa, helped to prevent them from using terrorist methods. Refusal to use such methods was, as a rule, a striking feature of all the liberation movements supported by the Soviet Union.

Besides, I am convinced that whatever importance practical support by Moscow had, especially at the crucial moments of the liberation struggle, its greatest contribution to the elimination of colonialism and apartheid in Southern Africa was not material assistance or the provision of training facilities, but the encouragement of non-racialism through fraternal relations, which developed between "white" Soviets and "black" members of the liberation movements.

Moscow, 2000–08

Notes

PREFACE

1. See, for example, O.A. Westad, *The Global Cold War. Third World Intervention and the Making of Our Times* (New York: Cambridge University Press, 2005).

INTRODUCTION

1. 44 years later in an interview Kulikov recalled fascinating details: "There was an instance in my life when the chief took a dislike to me … Due to the enmity he decided to send me to serve in Africa – in Ghana – to deal with formation of the armed forces there. In January, while having a terrible cold, I travelled to Paris, then to London and further through other European countries. This was a secret mission and to make sure that we were not exposed I had to go in circles. According to my documents during the trip I was a specialist in land-reclamation." Kulikov continues: "I went to the African continent three times. I was helping to restore Sekou Toure's regime" (http://www.pobeda-60.ru/main.php?trid=6022, consulted on 25 December 2007). However, here either Kulikov or his interviewer made a mistake: Kulikov's other mission (or two) was connected with an attempt to restore Kwame Nkruma's regime in 1966: of course, "this is another story".
2. Constitution (Fundamental Law) of the Union of Soviet Socialist Republics Adopted at the Seventh (Special) Session of the Supreme Soviet of the USSR Ninth Convocation on October 7, 1977, Article 28.
3. Memoirs of P. Yevsyukov (in Russian, unpublished), pp. 2–3. From early 1961 to late 1975 Yevsyukov, known to his African friends as "Camarada Pedro", was a desk officer of the African Section of the CPSU International Department.
4. Quoted in G. Wright, *The Destruction of a Nation. United States' Policy Towards Angola Since 1945* (London and Chicago: Pluto Press, 1997), p. 43.

CHAPTER 1

1. Memoirs of P. Yevsyukov, 1993, p. 3.
2. L. Lara, *Um amplo movimento. Itinerário do MPLA através de documentos e anatacões de Lucio Lara*. Vol. I, (Luanda: Lucio e Ruth Lara, 1998), p. 206. (Letter of Mario de Andrade to Lucio Lara, Paris, 9 December 1959.)
3. State Archive of the Russian Federation (hereafter – SARF), collection 9540, inventory 1, file 689, pp. 1–3.

4. Ibid. p. 104. De Andrade came from Conakry, using a passport in the name of Maurice Keita.
5. Ibid. p. 105.
6. Memoirs of P. Yevsyukov, p. 24.
7. Although some researchers question the MPLA's role in the attacks against prisons in Luanda on that day, it should be remembered that this organisation on 6 December 1960 "declared that direct action was the only means by which the people of Angola could attain independence" (Communiqué of the People's Movement for Liberation of Angola, SARF, collection 9540, inventory 1, file 689, p. 117).
8. Memoirs of P. Yevsyukov, p. 24. Some Russian military historians claim that the USSR "assisted the MPLA armed formations" from 1958 (*Nezavisimoe voennoe obozrenie* [Independent Military Review], Moscow, no. 24, 1998). However they do not substantiate their claim; in any case in 1958 such "formations" simply did not exist.
9. SARF, collection 9540 gs, inventory 2 s, file 40, p.141.
10. Russian State Archive of Modern History (hereafter RSAMH), collection 89, inventory 38, file 4, p. 4. The report of the Head of the CPSU CC International Department B.N. Ponomarev on expenditures of the International Trade Union Fund for Assistance to Left Workers' Organisations.
11. Ibid. file 22, p. 1. Extract from the Minutes of the Politburo of the AUCP (b) Central Committee, N 76/12, 19 July 1950.
12. Ibid.
13. RSAMH, collection 89, inventory 38, file 55, p.1. The memorandum of the Head of the CPSU CC International Department V. M. Falin, 17 December 1988.
14. *Pravda*, 16 June 1961. De Andrade sent it on behalf of the MAC.
15. SARF, collection 9540 gs, inventory 2 s, file 53, pp. 113–16. De Andrade was accompanied by the MPLA representative in Mali "Viano" (probably Gentile Viana). Yevsyukov took part in this discussion. It is worth mentioning that he and Yury Yukalov, a Ministry of Foreign Affairs official, were introduced to the MPLA representatives just as members of the Solidarity Committee.
16. Ibid. p. 113.
17. Ibid. p. 118.
18. Memoirs of P. Yevsyukov, p. 25. Anatoly Khazanov, a Russian historian, states in his biography of Neto that his first visit to Moscow was in 1964 (A. Khazanov, *Agostinho Neto* (in Russian) (Moscow: Nauka, 1985), p. 107), but though Yevsyukov writes "I don't remember the exact date", most probably it happened earlier.
19. SARF, collection 9540 gs, inventory 2c, file 69, p.32.
20. Paul Nitze was US Assistant Secretary of Defense for International Security Affairs.
21. The National Archive, FO 371/155454. Portuguese Africa. 1961.
22. Department of State. Confidential. From AmEmbassy Lisbon to SecState Washington. August 10, 1962. The irony is that a quarter of a century later the Comoros were indeed used as a base for Pretoria's supplies to the Mozambican National Resistance (RENAMO).

23. Memoirs of P. Yevsyukov, p. 25.
24. Ibid.
25. J. Marcum, *The Angolan Revolution. Volume II. Exile Politics and Guerrilla Warfare (1962–1976)* (Cambridge and London: MIT Press, 1978), p. 92.

CHAPTER 2

1. *Pravda*, 7 July 1970.
2. Memoirs of P. Yevsyukov, p. 19.
3. Ibid., p. 20.
4. T. Sellstrom, *Sweden and National Liberation in Southern Africa. Volume I: Formation of a Popular Opinion 1950–1970* (Uppsala: Nordiska Afrika-institutet, 1999), p. 428.
5. A. Kabral's speech at the Rome conference (the author's notes).
6. F. Bridgland, *Jonas Savimbi: A Key to Africa* (Johannesburg: Macmillan South Africa, 1986), p. 66.
7. The late Oleg Nazhestkin first published his article under the title "Angola. In a fire ring of the blockade (reminiscences of an intelligence officer)" (*Azia i Afrika segodnya* [Asia and Africa Today], Moscow, 1996, no. 1, pp. 69–76, no. 2, pp. 32–7), under the pen-name "Oleg Negin"; then an extended version of it appeared under his own name in a collection of memoirs of Soviet intelligence officers V.N. Karpov (ed.), *Vneshyaya Razvedka* [External Intelligence] (Moscow: XXI vek – soglasie, 2000). Finally a more "academic" version was published under the title "Superpowers and events in Angola (1960s–1970s)" in *Novaya I noveishaya istoriya* [New and Newest History]. (Moscow, no. 4, 2005).
8. Professor Rostislav Ulyanovsky was a consultant and later deputy head of the Department, but not the first one.
9. *Novaya i noveishaya istoriya*, no. 4, 2005, p. 31.
10. Yevsyukov in one of his papers characterises the Committee as "a kind of cover-up for initial acquaintance with various nationalists" (Autobiography of P. Yevsyukov, unpublished, p. 7); I would prefer to call it a "purgatory".
11. Memoirs of P. Yevsyukov, pp. 24–5.
12. Ibid. p. 25.
13. Autobiography of P. Yevsyukov, p. 7.
14. Memoirs of P. Yevsyukov, p. 4. F.A. Guimaraes claims that Moscow "provided only relatively minor levels of assistance to the MPLA ... to avoid any potential conflict with Lisbon" (*The Origins of the Angolan Civil War. Foreign Intervention and Domestic Political Conflict* (Basingstoke and London: Macmillan, 2001), p. 162). But the USSR did not even have formal diplomatic relations with Portugal!
15. RSAMH, collection 89, inventory 38, file 4, p. 4; ibid. file 9, p. 4; ibid. file 40, p. 4.
16. Discussion with R. Monteiro "Ngongo", Moscow, 13 January 2003.
17. Memoirs of P. Yevsyukov, p. 17.
18. Ibid.

19. V. Kirpichenko, *Razvedka: litsa i lichnosti* [Intelligence: Faces and Personalities] (Moscow: Gea, 1998), pp. 205–6.
20. K. Brutents, K. *Tridtsat let na Staroi ploshchadi* [Thirty Years on the Old Square] (Moscow: Mezhdunarodnye otnoshenia, 1998), p. 204. Staraya Ploshchad – the Old Square – was a site of the CPSU headquarters in Moscow.
21. Ibid. p. 205.
22. I heard a similar story from Manchkha as well (discussion with P. Manchkha, Oslo, 13 April 1973).
23. National Archives, FCO 371/161626. Portuguese Africa. 1962. British Consulate-General, Luanda, April 16 1962 (J.C. Wardrop to A. Rose. British Embassy, Lisbon, copy – to Roger Stevens).
24. Memoirs of P. Yevsyukov, p. 26.
25. Ibid. Apparently Yevsyukov refers to Midtsev's article published in *Pravda* on 17 March 1964 under the title "Angola: for the unity of patriots".
26. Ibid.
27. Marcum, *The Angolan Revolution, Volume II*, p. 97; SARF, collection 9540, inventory 1, file 692, p. 55.
28. SARF, collection 9540 gs, inventory 2s, file 64, pp. 282–4.
29. Ibid. pp. 282–3.
30. Ibid. p. 283.
31. Ibid. pp. 283–4.
32. Ibid. p. 284.
33. Memoirs of P. Yevsyukov, p. 29.
34. Marcum, *The Angolan Revolution, Volume II*, pp. 171, 187.
35. Discussion with the SAASC delegation to Congo-Brazzaville, Moscow, 4 September 1972.
36. Three of his children later studied at the famous International Boarding School in Ivanovo.
37. Discussion with P. Luvualu, Moscow, 29 September 1972.
38. By 1968 the OAU Liberation Committee stopped providing assistance to the FNLA and in 1971 the OAU withdrew its recognition of GRAE. But as soon as "reconciliation" between Neto and Roberto was achieved, the FNLA's international position improved, thus in July 1972 Roberto was invited to Algeria to take part in a celebration of that country's ten years of independence (Marcum, *The Angolan Revolution, Volume II*, p. 227; Guimaraes, *The Origins of the Angolan Civil War*, p. 115).
39. Discussion with P. Luvualu, Moscow, 29 September 1972.
40. Ibid.
41. Dzassokhov, who practically headed the Solidarity Committee for 20 years as its General Secretary and then the First Vice-President, was well known to the leaders of the liberation movements. In 1990–91 he was a member of the CPSU Politburo and is now a member of the Council of Federation (upper house of the Russian Parliament), where he represents his native Republic of Northern Ossetia – Alania in the Caucasus.
42. Discussion with P. Luvualu, Moscow, 29 September 1972.
43. Ibid.

44. Discussion with S. Monimambo, Moscow, 20 December 1972.
45. Discussion with R. Monteiro"Ngongo", Moscow, 17 July 2002.
46. According to Ulyanovsky, Moscow had raised the issue of creating a liberated area on the coast to facilitate supplies with Neto, but the MPLA could not make it (author's notes on the discussion of R. Ulyanovsky with T.G. Silundika and D. Dabengwa, Moscow, 19 January 1976).
47. Discussion with S. Monimambo, Moscow, 20 December 1972.
48. Discussions with R. Monteiro "Ngongo", Moscow, 13 January 2003 and 15 December 2004.
49. Discussion with S. Monimambo, Moscow, 20 December 1972.
50. Ibid.
51. Author's notes made at a meeting with an MPLA delegation headed by A. Neto, Moscow, 21 January 1973. The delegation included, in particular, Lucio Lara, "Spartacus" Monimambo, Pascoal Luvualu, who was responsible for foreign affairs, and Ruth Neto, a leader of the MPLA's women's organisation.
52. Ibid.
53. Ibid.
54. Ibid.
55. Both Neto and Lara married local women when they were studying in Western Europe.
56. Discussion with R. Monteiro "Ngongo", Moscow, 13 January 2003.
57. Marcum, *The Angolan Revolution. Volume II*, pp. 203–4. Nazhestkin wrongly attributes Chipenda's "split" to the beginning of 1974 (p. 33).
58. Khazanov, *Agostinho Neto*, pp. 128–9. Some "intellectuals" who joined this *revolta* came to Brazzaville from Europe. Monimambo was the only leading commander who joined it and he soon returned to the mainstream MPLA, occupied important posts in the People's Armed Forces for Liberation of Angola (FAPLA), and was later ambassador.
59. Discussion with R. Monteiro "Ngongo", Moscow, 13 January 2003.
60. T. Sellstrom, (ed.), *Liberation in Southern Africa – Regional and Swedish Voices. Interviews from Angola, Mozambique, Namibia, South Africa, Zimbabwe, the Frontline and Sweden* (Uppsala: Nordiska Afrikainstitutet, 1999), p. 17.
61. Discussion with D. Chipenda, Lusaka, 4 August 1969.
62. P. Yevsyukov, O. Ignatyev, P. Mikhalev and A. Nikanorov, *Password "Anguimo". Reports from Angola, Guinea-Bissau and Mozambique* (Moscow: Novosti Press Agency, 1974), pp. 88–9.
63. A typical mistake by the Russian translators; read: the Republic of South Africa.
64. One more mistake: in Russian Britain is usually called "Anglia", that is, England.
65. Yevsyukov et al. *Password "Anguimo"*, pp. 90–1.
66. Ibid. p. 91.
67. *Azia I Afrika segodnya*, no. 1, 1996, p. 72.
68. Memoirs of P. Yevsyukov, p. 64.
69. A.J. Freitas, *Angola. O longo caminho da liberdade* (Lisboa: 1975), p. 163. Quoted in Khazanov, *Agostinho Neto*, p. 128.

70. *Azia I Afrika segodnya*, no. 1, 1996, p. 72.
71. I recall how, soon after the Portuguese revolution, Neto said to a correspondent; "Je ne suis pas un Marxist doctrinaire, je suis un socialist militant."
72. Memoirs of P. Yevsyukov, p. 17.
73. Ibid.
74. Discussion with R. Monteiro "Ngongo", Moscow, 17 July 2002.
75. Ibid.
76. RSAMH, collection 89, inventory 46, file 104, pp. 4–6. This letter and other relevant documents were regarded as highly confidential; they were classified both as "Top secret" and "Special file'. Besides, it should be explained that after the International Department, it was the Defence Ministry and General Staff that played, at least from the mid 1960s, the most important role in Moscow's relations with the national liberation movements. As for the evident difference between the stances of Nazhestkin and Kulikov, one gets the impression that Moscow's attitude towards the crisis in the MPLA, just as in some other cases (Afghanistan in particular), reflected an "age-long competition" between the KGB and the Ministry of Defence.
77. Ibid. pp. 1–3.
78. Ibid. p. 2. However, nothing was said there about contact with the FNLA.
79. Marcum, *The Angolan Revolution. Volume II*, p. 201.
80. Discussions with R. Monteiro "Ngongo". Moscow, 17 July 2002 and 13 January 2003.
81. Ibid.
82. Discussion with R. Monteiro "Ngongo", Moscow, 13 January 2003.
83. Ibid. At that stage Tanzania was somewhat neutral towards warring groups in MPLA, while Zambia was much closer to Chipenda: Kaunda regarded Neto and his supporters as "communists".
84. Ibid.
85. Sellstrom, *Liberation in Southern Africa – Regional and Swedish Voices*, p. 17.
86. Discussion with R. Monteiro "Ngongo". Moscow, 15 December 2004. However, according to "Camarada Pedro", these supplies began after successful visits to the liberated areas of Guinea-Bissau in 1972 and Mozambique in 1973 by the Soviet teams, which included Major General Ivan Plakhin and Yevsyukov. These trips were undertaken on Yevsyukov's initiative and resulted in the CPSU CC's decision on new supplies (Autobiography of P.N.Yevsyukov, p. 6). Meanwhile nothing similar could be done in Angola at that time owing to the MPLA's internal problems.
87. RSAMH, Collection 89, inventory 38, file 40, p. 4. This sum was much higher than allocations for the PAIGC (US$150,000) and FRELIMO (US$85,000).
88. Ibid. p.33.
89. RSAMH, collection 89, inventory 46, file 104, p. 2.
90. Memoirs of P. Yevsyukov, p. 33.

91. Later, Pedro van Dunem, until his untimely death in 1997 served as a member of the Angolan government.
92. *Novaya i noveishaya istoriya*, no. 4, 2005, p. 34. Unfortunately a reader has to bear in mind that Nazhestkin's article contains a number of mistakes. For example, he writes about a conflict between the MPLA, FNLA and CNA (instead of UNITA); CNA is a Russian version of UPA, the FNLA's predecessor.
93. Yevsyukov et al., *Password "Anguimo"*.
94. SARF, collection 9540, inventory 1, file 703, p. 7.

CHAPTER 3

1. J. Ciment, *Angola and Mozambique: Postcolonial Wars in Southern Africa* (New York: Facts on File, 1997), p. 46.
2. Declaration of the Executive and delegates of the MPLA to the congress, Lusaka 22 August 1974. SARF, collection 9540, inventory 1, file 703, pp. 30–2.
3. Statement of the MPLA Inter-regional Conference of Militants, Angola, 18/9/1974. pp. Ibid. 38–9.
4. *Azia I Afrika segodnya*, no. 1, 1996, p. 72.
5. Record of discussion [of the SAASC delegation] with the head of the African Section of the SUPG [Socialist Unity Party of Germany] CC International Department [Berlin, 30 May 1974]. SARF, collection 9540, inventory 1, file 703, p. 48.
6. Ibid. p. 49.
7. Vladimir Bezukladnikov, a World War Two veteran, was dealing with liberation movements as a counsellor of the Soviet embassy in Lusaka.
8. Their trip was funded by Soviet NGOs with the blessing of the CPSU International Department; this is an example of continuing support to the MPLA in 1974.
9. Discussion with Angolan students, Moscow, 9 September 1974.
10. Discussion with G. Bires, Moscow, 21 October 1974.
11. Discussion with B. Putilin, Moscow, 10 and 17 November 2004. Putilin, now a leading researcher of the Moscow Institute of Military History and a retired colonel of military intelligence, in that period was the First Secretary of the Soviet embassy in Brazzaville and then in Luanda.
12. It is worth remembering that two years earlier the same Chipenda had criticised Neto for his alliance with Roberto.
13. For me personally Chipenda became "no more" when I saw his picture in a paper in Windhoek; he came there for discussions with South African authorities in July and reportedly had a meeting with General van den Berg, the head of the notorious Bureau for State Security (O. Ignatyev, *Secret Weapon in Africa* (Moscow: Progress, 1977), p. 137). However, in the 1980s Chipenda rejoined the MPLA and was appointed as ambassador to Egypt, before creating his own minor political party.

14. Discussion with the MPLA delegation headed by H. Carreira, Moscow, 30 December 1974. According to Yevsyukov, when Moscow enquired about Julius Nyerere's opinion of Neto, "he told the Soviet ambassador that Neto was not a politician, it would be better if he stuck to his [medical] profession" (Memoirs of P. Yevsyukov, p. 28).

15. The author's notes of the discussion with the MPLA delegation headed by H. Carreira, Moscow, 30 December 1974.

16. Ibid.

17. SARF, collection 9540, inventory 1, file 703, p. 12. Record of discussion with the delegation of the MPLA, 30 December 1974.

18. The author's notes of the discussion with the MPLA delegation headed by H. Carreira, Moscow, 30 December 1974.

19. SARF, collection 9540, inventory 1, file 703, p. 12. Record of the discussion with the delegation of the MPLA, 30 December 1974.

20. Ibid.

21. Ignatyev, *Secret Weapon in Africa*, p. 93.

22. Ibid. pp. 97–8.

23. I met Igor Uvarov for the first time as a fellow student of the Institute of International Relations. He was three years older than me but both of us were specialising in Afghanistan and studied Pashto and Farsi. We could not imagine that later both of us would come to Northern Yemen, though in different periods of a civil war there, and finally meet again as Africanists. The farewell to Colonel Uvarov took place in Moscow with all military honours on 8 December 2006.

24. Discussion with I. Uvarov, Moscow, 23 October 2003.

25. Rosa Coutinho, in particular, helped Neto's supporters to come to the MPLA "Congress" (M. Venancio and S. Chan, *Portuguese Diplomacy in Southern Africa. 1974–1994* (Johannesburg: South African Institute of International Relations, 1996), p. 25).

26. This hotel became a "home" for dozens of foreigners claiming to be journalists, though according to Uvarov, "half of them did not even know how to operate telex" (Discussion with I. Uvarov, Moscow, 23 October, 2003).

27. Yevsyukov writes in his unpublished memoirs: "This man was always an enigma for me in all respects ... On the whole his attitude to us was restrained and critical ..." (p. 18).

28. Such a government was envisaged in the agreement signed in Alvor on 15 January 1975 between the MPLA, the FNLA, UNITA and Portugal.

29. J. Stockwell, *In Search of Enemies. A CIA Story* (London: Andre Deutsch, 1978), p. 67. In fact, according to Stockwell, the CIA began funding Roberto in July 1974 without the 40 Committee's approval, though "small amounts at first" (ibid.).

30. Ibid.

31. Discussion with I. Uvarov, Moscow, 23 October 2003. Rather consonant is Stockwell's revelation that the CIA had "disappointing" information about its allies – UNITA and the FNLA – and its "knowledge of MPLA was nil" (Stockwell, *In Search of Enemies*, p. 181).

32. Discussion with I. Uvarov, Moscow, 23 October 2003.

33. A. Dzassokhov, *Formula politicheskogo dolgoletiya* [A Formula of Political Longevity] (Moscow: Sovershenno Sekretno, 2004), p. 271. The name of this publishing house in Russian means "Top Secret".
34. Ibid. pp. 271, 273.
35. Ibid. p. 272.
36. Ibid.
37. The author's notes at the meeting of the African Commission of the SAASC, Moscow, 14 February 1975.
38. I asked Dubenko, whom I had known since 1960, in the days when he was assistant military attaché in Egypt, how he could get a visa. He said that he went to Angola ostensibly "to study the local educational system". Dubenko soon received the rank of rear admiral and became the first Soviet military attaché in Angola. The decision to open this office was taken on 19 April 1976. Requesting this step and explaining why the office should be manned by six persons, the Ministry of Defence referred not only to developing military ties with Angola, but also to "the volume of tasks facing the Main Intelligence Department of the General Staff in the southern part of the African continent" (RSAMH, collection 89, inventory 27, file 1, pp. 1–6).
39. According to Ignatyev (*Secret Weapon in Africa*, p. 114), Holden Roberto accompanied Mobutu on his Asian tour.
40. Stockwell, *In Search of Enemies*, p. 67.
41. A. Tokarev, *FNLA v antikolonialnoi borbe i grazhdanskoi voine v Angola* [FNLA in anticolonial struggle and civil war in Angola] (Moscow: Institut Afriki, 2006), p. 111.
42. Ignatyev, *Secret Weapon in Africa*, p. 118.
43. Presentation by Roberto Leal Ramos Monteiro "Ngongo", Angola's ambassador to the Russian Federation at the meeting with the Soviet veterans at the Angolan embassy in Moscow on the occasion of the 25th anniversary of independence, 13 November 2000.
44. Yanaev was elected the USSR vice-president in December 1990 and took over from Mikhail Gorbachev as acting president for three days during a so-called "coup" in Moscow in August 1991.
45. Eduard Kapsky, who wrote a PhD thesis on the anti-colonial struggle in Guinea-Bissau and personally knew many leaders of the liberation movements in late 1975, replaced Yevsyukov as an official of the International Department.
46. The author's notes on the meeting in the SAASC with the delegation leaving for Angola, 24 April 1975. Piero Gleijeses writes that a trip to Tanzania, Zambia and Angola was undertaken by Major Alfonso Pérez Morales "Pina" and Carlos Cadelo, "who was a Central Committee staffer on Angola" (P. Gleijeses, *Conflicting Missions. Havana, Washington, and Africa, 1959–1976* (Chapel Hill and London: University of North Carolina Press, 2002), p. 245).
47. Report of the delegation of the Soviet Afro-Asian Solidarity Committee on their stay in Angola. SARF, collection 9540, inventory 1, file 704, p. 6.
48. Memoirs of P. Yevsyukov, p. 30.
49. Ibid. pp. 30–1.

50. Ibid. p. 31.
51. Ibid. p. 32.
52. Report of the delegation of the Soviet Afro-Asian Solidarity Committee on their stay in Angola. SARF, collection 9540, inventory 1, file 704, pp. 6–20.
53. SARF, collection 9540, inventory 1, file 704, p. 6.
54. Ibid. p. 10.
55. Ibid. p. 9.
56. Ibid. p. 14.
57. Ibid. p. 15.
58. The author's notes at the meeting in the CPSU International Committee with the delegation that came back from Angola, 13 May 1975.
59. Ibid.
60. Ibid.
61. Stockwell, *In Search of Enemies*, p. 52.
62. The author's notes at the meeting in the CPSU International Department, 13 May 1975.
63. Ibid.
64. Discussion with B. Putilin and A. Tokarev, Moscow, 17 November 2004. Putilin says that soon after the independence he saw two hangars full of Soviet-made small arms, mortars and ammunition.
65. SARF, collection 9540, inventory 1, file 704, p. 18.
66. Ibid. p. 19.
67. Ibid.
68. The author's notes at the meeting in the CPSU International Department with the delegation that came back from Angola, 13 May 1975.
69. Record of conversation between E. Afanasenko and A. Neto, Brazzaville, 4 July 1975. RSAMH, collection 5, inventory 68, file 1962, pp. 157–9. (Washington: Cold War International History Project (CWIHP), Bulletin 8–9).
70. Stockwell, *In Search of Enemies*, p. 66.
71. Ibid. p. 68.
72. Discussions with B. Putilin, Moscow, 10 and 17 November 2004.
73. Discussion with R. Monteiro "Ngongo", Moscow, 17 July 2002.
74. Stockwell, *In Search of Enemies*, pp. 52–3.
75. Ibid. p. 55.
76. Ibid. pp. 63–4. Much earlier a similar assessment was made by the British Consulate in Luanda: "Of the three Angolan nationalist organizations opposing the Portuguese in Angola, the MPLA would seem to be the most effective both in the present terms and in future potential" (National Archives, FCO 25/266. Portuguese colonies. 1968. MPLA Brit. C-te –Gen. Luanda, 9 July 1968).
77. Piero Gleijeses's interview with Robert W. Hultslander, former CIA Station Chief in Luanda, Angola, http://www.gwu.edu/~nsarchiv/NSAEBB/NSAEBB67/transcript.html, consulted on 22 September 2007.
78. Marcum, *The Angolan Revolution. Volume II*, p. 16.
79. Piero Gleijeses's interview with Robert W. Hultslander.
80. Ibid.

81. Record of conversation between E. Afanasenko and A. Neto, Brazzaville, 4 July 1975. F.A. Guimaraes in his *The Origins of the Angolan Civil War*, referring to the book by W.R. Duncan, writes about "the decidedly "chilly reception" of Neto on his visit to Moscow in June, which was aimed at "securing deeper Soviet involvement" (p. 145). I have never heard about such a visit.

82. Record of the discussion with the MPLA delegation (Moscow, 19 August 1975). SARF, collection 9540, inventory 1, file 704, pp. 51–62; Record of discussion with the MPLA delegation (Moscow, 21 August 1975). Ibid. pp. 1–5.

83. The author's notes on the discussion with the MPLA delegation headed by E. Carreira, Moscow, 19 August 1975. John Marcum, referring to a newspaper article, writes that the MPLA sent Carreira to Moscow in July 1975 to ask for help, "only to have the Soviets suggest that he try the Cubans". (Marcum, *The Angolan Revolution, Volume II*, p. 443). My notes say the opposite.

84. Apparently an important role was played in the MPLA's success by a couple of Soviet-made BTR-60PB APCs supplied according to "Ngongo" by Yugoslavia, although Putilin believes they came from Algeria.

85. Discussion with the MPLA delegation headed by E. Carreira, Moscow, 19 August 1975.

86. According to Stockwell, the CIA chart, prepared for the Committee of 40, on the contrary indicated that the MPLA had about 20,000 soldiers and the FNLA 15,000. He writes: "Roberto had repeatedly claimed to have 30 000 troops, but we had arbitrarily halved that figure because none of us believed him." (Stockwell, *In Search of Enemies*, p. 91). So it looks as if the CIA grossly overestimated FAPLA's strength.

87. Ibid.

88. Ibid.

89. Discussion with the MPLA delegation (G. Bires and M. Neto), Moscow, 25 September 1975.

90. Ibid.

91. Stockwell *In Search of Enemies*, p. 185.

92. Admiral Lionel Cardoso replaced his namesake on 5 September 1975.

93. Discussion with I. Uvarov, Moscow, 23 October 2003.

94. G. Kornienko *Holodnaya voina. Svidetelstvo eyo uchastnika* (Cold War: Testimony of a Participant) (Moscow, Mezhdunarodnye otnosheniya, 1995), p. 166.

95. Ibid.

96. Discussion with Vladillen Vasev, Moscow, 15 January 2001.

97. Tokarev, *FNLA*, p. 110.

98. Bridgland writes that in 1971 UNITA donated two tons of maize to Zambia, but if this happened, it was really nothing but "a small publicity coup" (*Jonas Savimbi*, p. 95).

99. In fact, it closely watched the developments in Angola from the beginning of the armed liberation struggle there; the fact that the future chief of the South African Defence Force (SADF), General Jannie Geldenhuys, was Pretoria's Vice-Consul in Luanda from 1965 to 1970 speaks for itself.

100. Discussion with the MPLA delegation, Moscow, 15 May 1975.
101. Kornienko, *Holodnaya voina*, p. 166.
102. Ibid.
103. A. Dobrynin *In Confidence: Moscow's Ambassador to America's Six Cold War Presidents 1962–1986* (New York: Times Books, 1995), p. 362.
104. *Azia i Africa segodnya*, no. 2, 1996, pp. 33–4. Nazhestkin writes: "Then [before November 1975] the Soviet external [political] intelligence had no intelligence capacities directly in Angola itself" (*Novaya i noveishaya istoriya*, no. 4, 2005, p. 38). It is correct, but he forgot other Soviets who were present there.
105. Ibid. p. 34.
106. Ibid.
107. C. Andrew and V. Mitrokhin, *The Mitrokhin Archive II. The KGB and the World* (London: Penguin, 2005), p. 452.
108. Ibid. *Azia i Africa segodnya*, no. 2, 1996, p. 35.
109. Discussions with B. Putilin and A. Tokarev, Moscow, 10 and 17 November 2004.
110. Ciment, *Angola and Mozambique*, p. 163 (as usual, no reference is given). Several other authors write about this fictitious "American-Soviet agreement"; for example, Marcum, *The Angolan Revolution. Volume II*, p. 229.
111. Ciment *Angola and Mozambique*, p. 163.
112. Interview with Gerald Ford. Transcripts of CNN *Cold War* series, http://www.gwu.edu/~nsarchiv/coldwar/interviews/episode-16/ford2.html. Episode 16. Détente.
113. Ciment, *Angola and Mozambique*, p. 167.
114. The author's notes at the meeting with S. Nujoma (the end of October 1976). By that time a considerable part of the contingent had already arrived in Angola.
115. *Novaya i noveishaya istoriya*, no. 4, 2005, p. 37.
116. Ibid.
117. Discussions with B. Putilin and A. Tokarev, Moscow, 10 and 17 November 2004.
118. Ibid.
119. O.A. Westad, *Moscow and the Angolan Crisis, 1974–1976: A New Pattern of Intervention* (Washington: Cold War International History Project, Bulletin 8–9, p. 21).
120. Stockwell, *In Search of Enemies*, p. 215. He mistakenly mentioned 11 November as the date of this combat.
121. The BM-21 is the "heir" of the famous Katyusha ["Stalin organ"], widely used during World War Two.
122. Stockwell, *In Search of Enemies*, pp. 214–15.
123. According to R. Monteiro "Ngongo", Grad-P, then moved on bicycles, were used for the first time by the MPLA on the Eastern Front in 1974, after the Portuguese revolution, on the eve of a cease-fire.
124. Discussion with R. Monteiro "Ngongo", Quifangondo, 21 November 2004. He trained as a Grad operator in Simferopol in 1972–73 and then as an artillery commander in Solnechnogorsk near Moscow in

March–July 1975 and for five years served as Angolan ambassador to Russia, and in 2006 was appointed Minister of the Interior.

125. Gleijeses, *Conflicting Missions*, p. 311.
126. Discussion with R. Monteiro "Ngongo", Moscow, 10 October 2002.
127. Ibid. Moscow, 15 December 2004.
128. These actions are covered in Piero Gleijeses's book *Conflicting Missions*. Tragically enough, Chipenda's forces, partly integrated later in the SADF's notorious 32nd ("Buffalo") battalion, included some persons who were trained earlier in the USSR as MPLA members.
129. Discussion with I. Uvarov, Moscow, 23 October 2003. In his *Another Day of Life*, Ryszard Kapuscinski, a well-known Polish journalist, claims that in September 1975 "there was one person from Eastern Europe – me [in Angola]" (R. Kapuscinski, *Another Day of Life* (San Diego, New York, London: Helen and Kurt Wolff Book, Harcourt Brace Jovanovich Publishers, 1987), p. 7); for some reason he forgot about Uvarov, though they stayed next door to each other.
130. Ignatyev, *Secret Weapon in Africa*, p. 122.
131. Discussion with I. Uvarov, Moscow, 23 October 2003. Apparently Nazhestkin left Luanda before 11 November to report back to his superiors.
132. Ibid.
133. I remember, though it happened far away from Angola, how Soviet An-12 technicians were complaining when they had to paint the Aeroflot red flag over the Air Force's red star, and then paint the insignia of the local Air Force over the flag, and the whole way back again.
134. Discussions with B. Putilin and A. Tokarev, Moscow, 10 and 17 November 2004.
135. According to Putilin, it was Jose Eduardo dos Santos, a Soviet graduate, who translated the ambassador's speech into Portuguese.
136. Discussions with B. Putilin, Moscow, 10 and 17 November 2004.
137. The name of this "republic" was hardly accidental; as in the case of GRAE, it followed the Algerian model.

CHAPTER 4

1. The detailed story of this mission was described in [Colonel] A. Tokarev, *Komandirovka v Angolu* (Mission to Angola), *Aziya i Afrika segodnya*, no. 2, 2001, pp. 36–41.
2. Interview with A. Grigorovich, Moscow, 15 March 2005, conducted by G. Shubin.
3. Tokarev, *Komandirovka v Angolu*, pp. 38–9.
4. Ibid. p. 41. Willem Steenkamp, in *South Africa's Border War. 1966–1989* (Gibraltar: Ashanti Publishing, 1989, p. 54), claims that in December 1975 South African forces at Cariango "were attacked by jet fighters"; however, this is just one of many "inaccuracies" in his propagandistic book.
5. Stockwell, *In Search of Enemies*, p. 177. Klinghoffer, referring to American journalists, wrongly alleges that "Soviet advisors were present in Angola

as early as August." He claims Igor Uvarov "was actually a member of a Soviet military intelligence (GRU) and the director of the Soviet arms program in Angola" (A. Klinghoffer, *The Angolan War: A Study in Soviet Policy in the Third World* (Boulder: Westview Press, 1980, p. 23). It was not difficult to link up Uvarov with the Soviet military because earlier he had served at the Soviet military attaché office in Morocco, but the second allegation is utterly wrong.

6. Discussion with B. Putilin, 10 and 17 November 2004. It is worth noting that the relevant Cuban structure was called "Décima [the Tenth] Dirección de las Fuerzas Armadas Revolucionarias".

7. Gleijeses, *Conflicting Missions*. p. 305.

8. Ibid. p. 308. Ignatyev claims (*Secret Weapon in Africa*, p. 170) that Raoul told him on 12 November "in strict confidence" that "regular Cuban army elements ... were already en route and would arrive shortly after 11 November". One can only guess whether a Cuban commander did not want to disclose the fact that they began arriving before that date, or Ignatyev had changed dates deliberately.

9. Discussions with B. Putilin, Moscow, 10 and 17 November 2004.

10. Gleijeses, *Conflicting Missions*, p. 308.

11. Ibid.

12. Record of conference with president of MPLA Agostinho Neto, 4 July 1975. RSAMH, collection 5, inventory 68, file 1962, pp. 157–9. I have to refer to the English translation of this record published in Bulletin 8–9 of the Cold War International History Project, because even the archive documents passed on earlier to the USA are still inaccessible to Russian historians.

13. National Archives, Department of State Record, Policy Planning Staff Director's Files, 1969–77, box 373, President Ford Trip to China. Memorandum of conversation, 2 December 1975.

14. National Security Archive, China and United States, Doc # 00398, pp. 19–22.

15. Sergio Vieira to the author, 19 July 2007.

16. National Security Archive, China and United States, Doc # 00398, pp. 19–22.

17. Ignatyev, *Secret Weapon in Africa*, p. 122.

18. http://www.gwu.edu/~nsarchiv/nsa/publications/DOC_readers/kissinger/item10.htm. Consulted on 22 September 2007.

19. *Pravda*, 1 February 1976.

20. Discussion with A. Lukoki and A. van Dunem, Moscow, 14 January 1976.

21. Quoted in R. Wilmont, *Ideology and National Consciousness* (Ibadan: Lantern Books, 1980), p. 183.

22. Ibid. pp. 183–4. Murtala Muhammed paid the ultimate price for his bold stand: he was killed a month later in an attempted *coup d'état*.

23. Ibid. Such a "gap" between protocol arrangements for foreign state officials and representatives of liberation movements was typical of the Soviet governmental bureaucracy.

24. The author's notes at the discussion with J.E. dos Santos, Moscow, 23 January 1976.

25. Ibid.
26. Ibid.
27. The author's notes at the discussion with J.E. dos Santos, Moscow, 23 January 1976.
28. T. Sellstrom, *Sweden and National Liberation in Southern Africa. Volume II: Solidarity and Assistance* (Uppsala: Nordiska Afrikainstitutet, 2002), pp. 136–7. Earlier, in November 1975, during his visit to the USA, Palme stated that "American emphasis on Soviet support for the movement [MPLA] overlooked the fact that Sweden and other nations had supported [it] before the Soviet Union did" (ibid. p. 135). In fact Stockholm's direct support to MPLA began in 1971, that is, not before Moscow, but a decade later.
29. The author's notes about the discussion with J.E. dos Santos, Moscow, 23 January 1976.
30. Ibid.
31. The author's notes about the report by A. Dzassokhov, head of the Soviet delegation, Moscow, 16 February 1976.
32. Ibid.
33. Hadzhi Mamsurov, a three-star general, ethnically an Osetian like Dzassokhov, was for many years Number Two in the Soviet Military Intelligence.
34. Dzassokhov, *Formula politicheskogo dolgoletiya*, p. 181. Plakhin, well known to the freedom fighters as "General Ivan" was responsible in the Ministry of Defence for contacts with the liberation movement. Earlier he went with "Camarada Pedro" to Guinea-Bissau and Mozambique during the liberation wars there, but that was his first visit to Angola.
35. Record of discussion with the MPLA delegation (Moscow, 2 March 1976). SARF, collection 9540, inventory 1, file 705, p. 59.
36. The author's notes made at the meeting with the MPLA delegation headed by Nito Alves, Moscow, 2 March 1976.
37. *Pravda*, 28 February 1976.

CHAPTER 5

1. B. Petruk's notes at the meeting with B. Ponomarev, June 1976.
2. Ibid.
3. B. Petruk's notes at the discussion with Lucio Lara, Luanda, 12 July 1976. This approach was supported by the Soviets, but the final decision of the Angolan leadership was different.
4. Ibid.
5. Ibid.
6. B. Petruk's notes at the discussion with Lucio Lara, Luanda, 6 August 1976.
7. B. Petruk's notes at the discussion with Nito Alves, Luanda, 26 July 1976.
8. Discussion with R. Monteiro "Ngongo", Moscow, 15 December 2004. Jose van Dunem, who earlier accompanied Alves to Moscow, was involved as well.

9.   Discussion with R. Monteiro "Ngongo", Moscow, 17 July 2002.
10. Ciment, *Angola and Mozambique*, p. 127.
11. See, for example, ibid. p. 135.
12. In the opinion of Andrey Urnov, a veteran of the CPSU African Section, Moscow's involvement in Alves's coup is "absolutely ruled out". (Discussion with A. Urnov, Istanbul, 4 November 2006).
13. Brutents, *Tridtsat let*, p. 494.
14. Ibid.
15. Ibid., p. 296.
16. This attempted *coup d'état* had one more consequence: the formation by Agostinho Neto's decision of the Presidential Regiment, a special unit, better manned and equipped than other FAPLA units. It was directly subordinate to the Commander-in-Chief (president) and commanded by the Chief of Staff and MPLA Politburo member "Ndalu" who was advised by both Cuban and Soviet officers.
17. Bridgland, *Jonas Savimbi*, p. 282.
18. Discussion with A. Urnov, Istanbul, 4 November 2006.

CHAPTER 6

1.   Conference proceedings, *40 let vmeste. 1961–2001. Materialy naucho-prakticheskoi konferentsii* [40 years together. 1961–2001, Materials of scientific-practical conference] (Moscow: Lean, 2002), p. 62.
2.   Ibid.
3.   *Krasnaya zvesda* [Red Star], 9 September 2000. However, all these facilities were not regarded as Soviet military bases, after all Angola's constitution (article 16) expressly prohibited "the installation of foreign military bases".
4.   Ibid.
5.   Discussion with K. Kurochkin, Moscow, 18 September 2001.
6.   CWIHP, Bulletin 8–9, Washington, pp. 18–19. Fidel Castro's 1977 Southern Africa Tour: A Report to Honecker.
7.   F. Bridgland, *The War for Africa. Twelve Months that Transformed a Continent* (Gibraltar: Ashanti Publishing House, 1990), p. 62. For many years Bridgland had been "lionising" Savimbi, but finally he had to face reality and began to catalogue the murders Savimbi committed inside UNITA. It resulted in such serious death threats against him that "De Klerk's people had given him security minders" (J. Harding, "The Late Jonas Savimbi", *London Review of Books*, vol. 24, no. 6, 21 March 2002).
8.   Ibid. p. 17.
9.   Mikhail Petrov did exist, and did serve in Southern Africa, but as first Soviet resident ambassador to Botswana.
10. M. Radu and A. Klinghoffer, *The Dynamics of Soviet Policy in Sub-Saharan Africa* (New York and London: Holmes and Meir, 1991), p. 62.
11. General Vassily Petrov was in Ethiopia during the war with Somalia, but not as "an overall commander".

12. Radu and Klinghoffer, *The Dynamics of Soviet Policy in Sub-Saharan Africa*, p. 98.
13. R. Labuschagne, *On South Africa's Secret Service* (Alberton: Galago, 2002), pp. 112–13. The book is really silly: Labuschagne claims that he recruited the Soviet military attaché in Botswana (p. 13), but such a post has never existed; he writes about ten Su-23 aircraft being supplied to Angola (p. 111), but such a plane has never been sent there; Sverdolvsk is not a family name, as he claims (p. 158), but a Soviet city. These are but a few of the numerous examples of factual errors.
14. Steenkamp, *South Africa's Border War*, pp. 148–50.
15. Assessment of the probable results of activities of the Truth and Reconciliation Commission (TRC) as perceived by former Chiefs of the SADF (http://www.rhodesia.nl/trurec1.htm, consulted on 22 September 2007). There is a reference to "General Mikhail Petrov, first deputy on the Soviet Politburo" in this submission as well.
16. In his outstanding *Prologue, Post-Prologue and Continuation of the Book by Professor Gleijeses* (Havana, unpublished, p. 16) Jorge Risquet calls Ponomarenko "Soviet Marshal", while Odd Arne Westad in his *Moscow and the Angolan Crisis* calls him "Vice-minister". Both are mistaken, before coming to Angola Major General Ponomarenko was Chief of Staff of the 8th Guards Army, a formation consisting of several divisions.
17. It was not his first assignment to Africa; in the late 1960s and early 1970s he headed the Soviet military mission in Somalia. His former subordinates admired his activities in Angola, including assistance in the creation of the ANC camps there. He was heavily wounded during World War Two and, though the Angolan President and Minister of Defence wanted him to prolong his mission in Angola, he replied: "My wounds demand rest, I can't stay longer in hot Angola, I would like to go home" (interview with V. Kostrachenkov, Moscow, 22 February 2002, by G. Shubin). Shakhnovich died not long after this.
18. Academician Ambartsumian was a real person, a prominent astronomer and president of the Armenian Academy of Sciences.
19. Bridgland, *The War for Africa*, p. 17.
20. *40 let vmeste*, p. 22; Discussions with K. Kurochkin, Moscow, 10 February and 25 September 2001.
21. Bridgland, *The War for Africa*, p.17.
22. *Osnovnye napravlenia i resultaty deyatelnosti sovetskogo voennogo apparata v NRA v 1982–1985 gg* (in Russian) [Main Directions and Results of the Activities of the Soviet Military Apparatus in the PRA in 1982–1985]. Presentation by Colonel General K. Ya. Kurochkin at the conference "40 years of the Armed struggle of the Angolan People for National Independence and Soviet-Angolan Military Co-operation", Moscow, 29 March 2001, p. 2.
23. S. Ellis and T. Sechaba *Comrades against Apartheid: The ANC and the South African Communist Party in exile*. (Bloomington: J. Currey; Indianapolis: Indiana University Press, 1992), p. 183.
24. Discussion with V. Kazimirov, former Soviet ambassador to Angola, Moscow, 14 November 2006.

25. "The role of the Soviet Union, Cuba and East Germany in fomenting terrorism in Southern Africa", US Government Printer, Washington, vol. 2, Addendum, p. 801. I explained the case of "Konstantin Shaganovitch" in my book *ANC: A View from Moscow*, (Belville: Mayibuye Books 1999), but he was reported alive again and again.
26. *CAMCO message to all active, inactive and retired members of FAR by General de Brigada (FAR) Rafael del Pino, CAMCO Vice-Chairman*, January 31 2003 (http://www.camcocuba.org/news/EN-RAF.html, consulted on 16 February 2006). CAMCO is the so-called "Cuban-American Military Council", a subversive organisation aimed at the Cuban military.
27. K. Kurochkin's notebook 3, p. 69.
28. K. Kurochkin's notebook 1, p. 7. One detail: while using the Soviet naval ships for strengthening Angola's position vis-à-vis Pretoria, Luanda was cautious. Thus, when the Soviets suggested holding a press conference, "Pedale" objected to it: "We are trying not to advertise the matters which concern the armed forces" (ibid. p. 16).
29. Ibid. p. 49.
30. Ibid. pp. 2, 5.
31. Ibid. pp. 3–4.
32. Ibid. p. 29.
33. In 1982, Cubans had 136 instructors in each light brigade and 100 more were to be added (ibid. p. 43).
34. Discussion with R. Monteiro "Ngongo", 10 October 2002.
35. K. Kurochkin's notebook 1, p. 7.
36. Ibid. pp. 9–13.
37. Ibid. p. 12.
38. Ibid. p. 47.
39. Ibid. p. 15.
40. Ibid. p. 14.
41. Ibid. pp. 25–6.
42. Ibid. p. 34.
43. Ibid.
44. Ibid. p. 37.
45. Ibid.
46. Ibid. p. 40.
47. *CAMCO message*.
48. K. Kurochkin's notebook 1, p. 43.
49. Ibid. p. 44.
50. Ibid. p. 48.
51. Ibid. p. 45.
52. Ibid.
53. Ibid. pp. 46–7.
54. Ibid. p. 48.
55. Ibid.
56. Ibid. pp. 51–2.
57. Ibid. p. 52.
58. Ibid. p. 53.
59. Ibid. p. 55.
60. Ibid. p. 78.

61. Ibid. p. 81.
62. As in Algeria, colonel was the highest rank in the Angolan armed forces at that time.
63. K. Kurochkin's notebook 1, p. 63.
64. K. Kurochkin's notebook 2, p. 34; notebook 3, p. 51.
65. K. Kurochkin's notebook 1, p. 68.
66. Ibid. p. 74.
67. K. Kurochkin's notebook 2, p. 12.
68. K. Kurochkin's notebook 3, p. 51.
69. Ibid. p. 92.
70. Ibid. pp. 86–7.
71. Ibid. p. 87.
72. K. Kurochkin's notebook 2, pp. 11–12.
73. Ibid. pp. 3–4.
74. Ibid.
75. Ibid. p. 9.
76. Ibid. p. 15.
77. Ibid. p. 32.
78. K. Kurochkin's notebook 3, p. 78.
79. Discussion with R. Monteiro "Ngongo", 10 October 2002; K. Kurochkin's notebook 3, p. 79.
80. K. Kurochkin's notebook 2, pp. 13–14. Much later an air raid on Savimbi's headquarters had the same purpose. Kurochkin recalls: "Once after our [read: Angolan] air raid information was even received about J. Savimbi's death. But it was found that he had only been heavily wounded and had recuperated in Britain" (*Krasnaya zvesda*, Moscow, 29 March 2001).
81. K. Kurochkin's notebook 2, p. 15.
82. Ibid. p. 29.
83. Ibid. p. 38.
84. Ibid. p. 37.
85. Ibid. p. 40.
86. Ibid. p. 47.
87. Ibid. p. 43.
88. Ibid. p. 50.
89. Ibid. pp. 43–4.
90. Ibid. p. 52.
91. Press conference of R. Monteiro "Ngongo", Deputy Chief of General Staff, 24 August 1983, *Angola Information Bulletin*, London, 23 September 1983.
92. K. Kurochkin's notebook 2, p. 50.
93. *Angola Information Bulletin*, London, 23 September 1983.
94. K. Kurochkin's notebook 2, p. 50.
95. K. Kurochkin's notebook 2, p. 18.
96. Ibid. p. 50.
97. Ibid. p. 51.
98. Interview with V.N. Belyaev, *Krasnaya zvesda*, 9 September 2000.

99. Interview with V. Sagachko, Moscow, 21 April 2004, by G. Shubin. Colonel (Rtd) Vadim Sagachko is the chairperson of the Union of Angola Veterans, founded in 2004.
100. Ibid.
101. K. Kurochkin's notebook 2, pp. 54, 60.
102. Ibid. p. 54.
103. Ibid. p. 55.
104. Discussion with R. Monteiro "Ngongo", 10 October 2002.
105. Ibid.
106. K. Kurochkin's notebook 2 p. 56.
107. Ibid. pp. 56, 58, 60, 64, 65.
108. Ibid. pp. 58–9.
109. Risquet, *Prologue*, p. 22.
110. K. Kurochkin's notebook 2, pp. 46, 59.
111. Ibid. p. 60.
112. Ibid. pp. 60–1.
113. Ibid. p. 59.
114. Ibid. p. 76.
115. Ibid. p. 61.
116. Ibid. pp. 62–3.
117. Ibid. p. 64.
118. Ibid. p. 66.
119. Ibid. p. 94.
120. Ibid.
121. Ibid. p. 68.
122. Discussion with R. Monteiro "Ngongo" 10 October 2002.
123. K. Kurochkin's notebook 2, p. 70.
124. Ibid. p. 74.
125. Ibid. p. 74. Kurockhin made a reservation: the responsibility for the success of operations should have remained with the Angolan leadership.
126. Ibid. pp. 72–3.
127. Ibid. p. 75.
128. K. Kurochkin's notebook 3, p. 15.
129. Ibid. pp. 91–2.
130. K. Kurochkin's notebook 2, p. 88.
131. Ibid. p. 91.
132. Ibid. pp. 95–6.
133. K. Kurochkin's notebook 3, p. 14.
134. Ibid, p. 3.
135. Ibid. pp. 9. 11, 12.
136. Ibid. p. 25.
137. Ibid. p. 26. It was found that the acting brigade commander gave an order to retreat as soon as communication had been cut off; as Kurochkin said to dos Santos, "the brigade ran away not during the combat, but after it. If the brigade had stayed in its positions, South African troops would have retreated" (ibid. p. 33).
138. Ibid. p. 27.

139. W. Minter, *Apartheid's Contras. An Inquiry into the Roots of War in Angola and Mozambique* (Johannesburg: Witwatersrand University Press; London and New Jersey: Zed Books, 1994), p. 44.
140. K. Kurochkin's notebook 3, p. 27.
141. Ibid. p. 28.
142. Ibid. p. 29.
143. Ibid.
144. Ibid.
145. Ibid.
146. Ibid.
147. Most probably, the Cubans did it at a tripartite meeting in Moscow on 7–8 January 1984.
148. Discussion with K. Kurochkin, Moscow, 18 September 2001; K. Kurochkin's notebook 3, p. 34. Varennikov again visited Angola in August 1984 (K. Kurochkin's notebook 3, p. 66).
149. V. Varennikov, *Nepovtorimoye* [Unrepeatable], Part 6 (Moscow: Sovetsky pisatel, 2001), pp. 264–88.
150. Ibid. pp. 286–7.
151. Ibid. p. 288. As valuable as Varennikov's eyewitness report is, he made a number of mistakes when he wrote about what was not his personal experience. For example, he claims that "UNITA split from the Neto-led MPLA", that Savimbi "at one time" was Neto's "companion in the party", that the "FNLA also split" from the MPLA (p. 226) and that Savimbi leaned for support on "troops of South Africa and Southern Rhodesia" (p. 227).
152. Discussion with K. Kurochkin, Moscow, 18 September 2001.
153. Ibid.
154. K. Kurochkin's notebook 3, p. 36.
155. Ibid. pp. 38–40.
156. Ibid. p. 39. This meeting took place on 12 February 1984, when it had already become clear that Mozambique was going to sign an agreement with Pretoria.
157. Ibid. p. 40.
158. Ibid. p. 52.
159. Ibid. p. 57.
160. Discussion with K. Kurochkin, Moscow, 18 September 2001.
161. K. Kurochkin's notebook 3, p. 40. Cubans' expectations were strengthened by the fact that UNITA began moving its troops towards Zaire which had to become its rear base in case South Africa withdrew from Namibia.
162. Ibid. p. 36.
163. Ibid.
164. Discussion with K. Kurochkin, Moscow, 18 September 2001.
165. K. Kurochkin's notebook 3, pp. 40, 44–5.
166. Ibid. pp. 45–6.
167. Ibid. p. 46.
168. Ibid. p. 50.
169. Ibid. p. 52.
170. Ibid.

171. Ibid. p. 53.
172. Ibid. p. 53.
173. Ibid. p. 54.
174. Ibid.
175. Ibid. p. 63. The Cubans believed that the infantry brigades should have few (if any) heavy arms, and should therefore be light enough to manoeuvre better.
176. Ibid. p. 60.
177. Ibid. p. 61.
178. Ibid.
179. Ibid. p. 68.
180. Ibid. p. 65.
181. Ibid. pp. 70–1.
182. Ibid. pp. 72–3, 76.
183. Ibid. p. 76.
184. Ibid. p. 80
185. *Pravda*, 12 January 1985.
186. *Time* magazine, 10 June 1985.
187. *Krasnaya zvesda*, 29 March 2001.
188. K. Kurochkin's notebook 1, p. 15.
189. *Krasnaya zvesda*, 29 March 2001.

CHAPTER 7

1. Discussion with K. Kurochkin, Moscow, 19 September 2001. One of the Soviet specialists recalls: "They [Soviet military authorities] understood thus and began inviting *GVSs* from the *VDV*, because the tactics of the airborne troops are more suitable for guerrilla warfare, while officers from ground troops were adopting linear tactics" (interview with V. Mityaev, Moscow, 11 April 2005, by G. Shubin).
2. After his return from Angola, Belyaev from 1991 till 1998 served as the Chief of Staff of the Russian Airborne Troops and was promoted to the rank of colonel general. However, he could apparently not adapt to civilian life after his retirement, and in July 2003 he shot himself (*Moskovsky Komsomolets*, 19 July 2003).
3. Discussion with R. Monteiro "Ngongo", 15 December, 2004. A South African medical officer was captured there, which proved that SADF personnel acted deep into Angolan territory.
4. Ibid.
5. E. Windrich, *The Cold War Guerrilla: Jonas Savimbi, the US Media, and the Angolan War* (New York: Greenwood Press, 1992), p. 43.
6. Discussion with R. Monteiro "Ngongo", 10 October, 2001.
7. *Izvestia*, Moscow, 9 June 1986.
8. J. Hanlon, *Beggar Your Neighbours. Apartheid Power in Southern Africa* (London: Catholic Institute for International Relations, 1986), p. 165. For a detailed history of the escalation of Washington's intervention in Angola also see G. Wright, *The Destruction of a Nation*.
9. Quoted in Hanlon, *Beggar Your Neighbours*, p. 170.

10. There are many mistakes in academic publications on this issue. Thus Stephen Chan in his *Kaunda and Southern Africa. Image and Reality in Foreign Policy* (London and New York: British Academic Press, 1992), claims that "As 1987 closed and 1988 began, the Soviet-equipped MPLA and its Cuban allies prepared for their annual offensive" (p. 58), though it began a half a year earlier. Besides, his claim that "the Soviets has dispatched a squadron of latest generation MiG fighters – almost certainly piloted by Soviet officers" (p. 59) is wrong on two points: MiG-23s arrived in Angola almost four years earlier, and Soviet pilots did not take part in combat action there.

11. J.A. Geldenhuys, *A General's Story. From An Era of War and Peace* (Johannesburg: Jonathan Ball, 1995), p. 225.

12. Quoted in Steenkamp *South Africa's Border War*, p. 163. Cuito Cuanavale probably had symbolic value for Pretoria; from the 1960s its airport was used by the South African Air Force and a Portuguese-South African command centre was established there for operations against Angolan and Namibian fighters (Bridgland, *Jonas Savimbi*, p. 82).

13. Discussion with R. Monteiro "Ngongo", Moscow, 10 *October 2002*.

14. Diary of Igor Zhdarkin, in Russian, unpublished, 10 October, 1987. A Cuban doctor was sent by helicopter to evacuate Snitko, but he did not survive (interview with O. Mityaev, Moscow, 11 April 2005, by G. Shubin).

15. Diary of Igor Zhdarkin, 27 and 28 November, 1987. Mityaev recalls: "Gorb was sitting under a shed near our bath. We all hid in a refuge and called him as well. He replied: 'I will instruct the sentries and come.' Then we heard an explosion of Valkiria's shell. We get out of the shelter. I saw a man lying near a GAZ-66 truck. I ran to him. Colonel Gorb was absolutely intact, but one ball had hit his carotid artery and killed him. We drew him into the shelter, a doctor began helping him right away. But he died at once, I closed his eyes" (interview with O. Mityaev, 11 April 2005, by G. Shubin).

16. Diary of Igor Zhdarkin, 15 March 1988.

17. Ibid. 29 October 1987.

18. Quoted in H. Campbell, *The Siege of Cuito Cuanavale* (Uppsala: Scandinavian Institute of African Studies, 1990), p. 21.

19. Speech by Dr Fidel Castro Ruz, President of the Republic of Cuba, at the ceremony commemorating the 30th anniversary of the Cuban Military Mission in Angola and the 49th anniversary of the landing of the "Granma", Revolutionary Armed Forces Day, 2 December 2005.

20. According to Soviet archives, from 1976 to February 1989 these supplies amounted to 3.7 billion roubles, and arms for 600 million roubles were to be delivered in 1989 and 1990 (RSAMH, collection 89, inventory 10, file 20, p. 2).

21. Speech by Dr Fidel Castro Ruz.

22. Colonel Jan Breytenbach, former Commander of 32nd Battalion, admits that South African forces in Northern Namibia were "suddenly faced with a major threat ... The SADF's preoccupation with saving Savimbi had left its Owamboland flank wide open" (J. Breytenbach, *The Buffalo Soldiers. The Story of South Africa's 32-Battalion 1975–1993* (Alberton: Galago, 2002), pp. 316–17.

23. Speech by Dr. Fidel Castro Ruz. The figure of 55,000 was much higher than Washington estimated.
24. F. Castro, Speech in Mandela Park, Kingston, Jamaica, 30 July 1998. *Granma*, Havana, 7 August 1998.
25. F. Castro, *Vindicación de Cuba* [Cuba's Vindication], (Havana: Editora Política Publishers, 1989), p. 404. According to Soviet archives the Cuban command in Angola in February 1989 had at its disposal over 1,000 tanks, 200 APCs, over 500 pieces of artillery and rocket launchers, 70 anti-aircraft missile installations and 44 combat aircraft (RSAMH, Collection 89, inventory 10, file 20, p. 2)
26. Risquet, *Prologue*, p. 28.
27. A. Adamishin, *The White Sun of Angola* (Moscow: Vagrius, 2001), p. 117.
28. J. Risquet, *Prologue*, p.35.
29. Adamishin, *The White Sun of Angola*, p. 110. Anatoly Adamishin in his memoirs describing his meeting with Fidel in Havana on 28 March 1988, quotes Fidel's words: "[South Africans are] Such fools, they attacked us [at Cuito Cuanavale] on 23 March, while from 18 March we were advancing south, getting into their rear" (ibid. p. 98).
30. R. Bloomfield, (ed.), *Regional Conflicts and US Policy: Angola and Mozambique*. Algonac: Reference Publications, 1988, p. 220.
31. RSAMH, Collection 89, inventory 10, file 20, p. 2.
32. Quoted in Wright, *The Destruction of a Nation*, p. 193.
33. Quoted in ibid. p. 90.
34. C. Crocker, *High Noon in Southern Africa: Making Peace in a Rough Neighbourhood* (New York and London: W.W. Norton, 1993).
35. Adamishin, *Beloye solntse Angoly*, p. 194.
36. Ibid. pp. 196–7.
37. Quoted in Risquet, *Prologue*, p. 19.
38. K. Brutents, *Nesbyvsheesya. Neravnodushnye zametki o perestroike* [Dampened expectations. Partial notes on *perestroika*] (Moscow: Mesh-dunarodnye otnosheniya, 2006), p. 453.
39. V. Kazimirov, *Moi MGIMO* [My Moscow State Institute of International Relations], www.vn.kazimirov.ru.d002.htm, consulted on 5 January 2008.
40. *Izvestia*, 13 December 1990.
41. Savimbi was killed in action in February 2002.
42. Kazimirov, *Moi MGIMO*.
43. Brutents, *Nesbyvsheesya*, p. 453.
44. Wright, *The Destruction of a Nation*, p. 158. According to Wright (pp. 166, 171) and other sources in both Washington and Pretoria, they continued their covert assistance to UNITA.
45. *Krasnaya Zvezda*, 9 September, 2000.
46. Discussion with R. Monteiro "Ngongo", Moscow, 13 January 2003.

CHAPTER 8

1. P. Yevsyukov, *Iz vospomonanii o rabote v Mozambike* [From reminiscences of the work in Mozambique], in *Afrika v vospomonaniyah veteranov dip-*

lomaticheskoi sluzhby [Africa in reminiscences of veterans of diplomatic service] (Moscow: XXI Vek-Soglasie, 2000), p. 243.

2. Ibid. p. 37.
3. SARF, collection 9540gs, inventory 2s, file 36, p. 35.
4. Ibid.
5. SARF, collection 9540, inventory 1, file 102, p. 119 (translation of the letter in Russian). The Soviet Embassy in Dar es Salaam had not yet been established.
6. Ibid. pp. 121–4. Marcelino dos Santos signed it as UDENAMO representative in Morocco.
7. Yevsyukov, *Iz vospomonanii o rabote v Mozambike*, p. 243.
8. Ibid. p. 38.
9. RSAMH, collection 89, inventory 38, file 4, p. 4. In the list of the receiving parties the Mozambican organisation is named Demokraticheskaya partiya Mozambika, that is, Mozambique Democratic Party, but most probably this is just a mistake. Some loose contacts existed also between the Solidarity Committee and MANU (SARF, collection 9540gs, inventory 2s, file 53, pp. 120–1.)
10. I could not trace it in the archive papers.
11. Memoirs of P. Yevsyukov, p. 38.
12. SARF, collection 9540gs, inventory 2s, file 58, p. 19.
13. RSAMH, collection 89, inventory 38, file 8, p. 4.
14. Memoirs of P. Yevsyukov, p.38.
15. Ibid. p. 39.
16. SARF, collection 9540gs, inventory 2s, file 53, pp. 129–30.
17. Ibid. file 58, p. 118; also pp. 128–30, 121–32.
18. Ibid. p. 141.
19. Ibid. file 68, p. 48.
20. Ibid. p. 64. Maksudov attended the conference as a member of the AAPSO delegation.
21. Ibid. file 69, p. 116.
22. Ibid.
23. Ibid. file 70, pp. 53–65.
24. Ustinov later became Ambassador to Tanzania, Head of 3rd African Department of the Soviet MFA, UN Deputy Secretary General and finally a Soviet representative in the Commission on South-western Africa, formed after the 1988 New York agreements.
25. SARF, collection 9540gs, inventory 2s, file 70, p. 59.
26. Ibid.
27. Ibid.
28. Ibid. pp. 63–4.
29. Ibid. p. 65.
30. Ibid. file 69, p. 38.
31. Ibid. file 70, p. 146.
32. Ibid. p. 147.
33. Memoirs of P. Yevsyukov, p. 39.
34. CWIHP, Bulletin 8–9, p. 18. Fidel Castro's 1977 Southern Africa Tour: A Report to Honecker.
35. Discussion with V. Zhikharev, Moscow, 22 March 1969.

36. Memoirs of P. Yevsyukov, p. 9.
37. Discussion with A. Glukhov, Moscow, 13 May 2003.
38. Discussion with O. Shcherbak, Harare, 19 February 2006.
39. The author's notes at the discussion with U. Simango and J. Chissano, Moscow, 11 August 1969.
40. The author's notes at the discussion with M. dos Santos and M. Khan, Moscow, 4 March 1970.
41. Discussion with S. Vieira and A. Panguene, Moscow, 25 May 1970. Initially both of them were regarded as acting office bearers.
42. Yevsyukov, *Iz vospomonanii o rabote v Mozambike*, p. 231.
43. The role of the International Department can be seen from the fact that the visit of the Soviet military was made on the initiative of "Camarada Pedro". (ibid. p. 239). Arkady Glukhov in his memoirs claims that the visit took place in 1971 (A. Glukhov, *Nashi pervye shagi v Mozambike* [Our first steps in Mozambique], in *Afrika v vospomonaniyah veteranov diplomaticheskoi sluzhby* [Africa in reminiscences of veterans of diplomatic service], 2 (5) (Moscow: Institut Afriki RAN, Sovet veteranov MID RF. 2001), p. 122).
44. Ibid. p. 231.
45. Discussion with A. Guebuza, Moscow, 27 April 1970.
46. S. Vieira to the author, 1 February 2007.
47. Ibid. 19 July 2007.
48. Ibid.
49. Discussion with J. Chissano, Moscow, 28 December 1970.
50. RSAMH, collection 89, inventory 38, file 40, p. 4.
51. S. Vieira to the author, 1 February 2007.
52. Discussion with S. Vieira, Moscow, 31 December 1970.
53. In those days such activities were called "propaganda", but this term has acquired too negative a meaning nowadays.
54. Discussion with J. Chissano, Moscow, 20 December 1972.
55. Ibid.
56. Discussions with S. Vieira, Robben Island, 13 and 14 February 1999; S. Vieira to the author, 1 February 2007.
57. S. Vieira to the author, 1 February 2007.
58. Ibid.
59. *Notes: Some Negative Factors in the Contemporary Southern African Situation*, Mayibuye Centre Historical Papers, Yusuf Dadoo Collection. Unfortunately for Machel, the ANC delegation included a member of the SACP Central Committee. I am not sure that these very words of Machel reached Moscow then, but quite probably Machel's critical attitude to the SACP and the CPSU was a subject of bilateral discussions between the two parties.
60. Radu and Klinghoffer, *The Dynamics of Soviet Policy in Sub-Saharan Africa*, p. 138.
61. Yevsyukov, *Iz vospomonanii o rabote v Mozambike*, pp. 231–2.
62. K. Virmani, (ed.), *Angola and the Super Powers* (Delhi: University of Delhi, 1989), p. 75.

CHAPTER 9

1. Sergio Vieira to the author, 1 February 2007.
2. Discussions with S. Vieira, Robben Island, 13 and 14 February 1999.
3. S. Vieira to the author, 1 February 2007, 14 February 2007.
4. Ibid.
5. Discussion with A. Urnov, Istanbul, 2 November 2006.
6. Discussion with S. Kokin, 15 January 2007.
7. Ibid.
8. S. Vieira to the author, Moscow, 29 July 2007.
9. Ibid.
10. Quoted in P. Janke, "Southern Africa: End of Empire", *Conflict Studies*, no. 52, December 1974, p. 116.
11. Perhaps the author should explain that in those days the Soviets, as well as our friends who studied in the USSR would usually refer to the country just as "the Union" (and not as "Russia").
12. Discussion with F. Umbero, Muruppa, 4 May 1975.
13. Discussion with J. Chissano, Lourenco Marques, 1 May 1975.
14. Discussions with A. Guebuza, Lourenco Marques/Nampula, 3 May 1975, and Lourenco Marques, 7 May 1975.
15. Glukhov, *Nashi pervye shagi v Mozambike*, pp. 114–15.

CHAPTER 10

1. Ilyichev, a former editor-in-chief of *Pravda* and secretary of the CPSU Central Committee, was an influential figure in Moscow, in spite of his advanced age. From 1974 he regularly visited Africa and played a very important role in strengthening Moscow's relations with African countries.
2. Glukhov, *Nashi pervye shagi v Mozambike*, p. 122.
3. Yevsyukov, *Iz vospomonanii o rabote v Mozambike*, pp. 223–4.
4. The capital of Mozambique was renamed soon after independence.
5. Yevsyukov, *Iz vospomonanii o rabote v Mozambike*, p. 224.
6. Ibid. p. 235.
7. Ibid. p. 236.
8. Ibid.
9. S. Vieira to the author, 19 July 2007.
10. Ibid.
11. L. Shinkarev, *Gorky dym savanny* [Bitter Smoke of Savannah] (Moscow: Sovetskaya Rossiya, 1989), pp. 103–16, 183–204.
12. Yevsyukov, *Iz vospomonanii o rabote v Mozambike*, p. 232.
13. Ibid.
14. Ibid. p. 233.
15. Ibid. p. 237.
16. The delegation was composed of about 150 persons who came to Mozambique in three aircraft.
17. Yevsyukov, *Iz vospomonanii o rabote v Mozambike*, p. 237.
18. Discussion with S. Vieira, Robben Island, 13 February 1999; S. Vieira to the author, 14 February 2007.

19. Yevsyukov, *Iz vospomonanii o rabote v Mozambike*, p. 238.
20. Ibid. p. 237.
21. Discussion with S. Vieira, 13 February 1999.
22. S. Vieira to the author, 19 July 2007.
23. CWIHP Woodrow Wilson International Center for Scholars. Fidel Castro's 1977 Southern African Tour. Castro mentioned a figure of 100 million roubles.
24. *Pravda*, 1 March 1981.
25. Yevsyukov, *Iz vospomonanii o rabote v Mozambike*, p. 238.
26. Glukhov, *Nashi pervye shagi v Mozambike*, p. 125.
27. Ibid.
28. *Pravda*, 16 June 1983.
29. Radu and Klinghoffer, *The Dynamics of Soviet Policy in Sub-Saharan Africa*, p. 141.
30. S. Vieira to the author, 19 July 2007.
31. R. Christie, "South Africa's Nuclear History". Paper presented at the Nuclear History Program Fourth International Conference, Sofia-Antipolis, Nice, France, 23–27 June 1993, pp. 55–7.
32. S. Vieira to the author, 19 July 2007.
33. Ibid. 20 July 2007.
34. Shubin, *ANC: A View from Moscow*, pp. 248–63.
35. *African Communist*, 1983, N 95, p.81.
36. *Rand Daily Mail*, 18 April 1984.
37. Discussion with S. Vieira, Robben Island, 14 February 1999.
38. Ibid.
39. Ibid.
40. Discussion with S. Muzenda and other prominent members of ZANU-PF, Harare, 12 June 1985.
41. On a Soviet version of these events see Shubin, *ANC: A View from Moscow*, p. 304.
42. J. Veloso, *Memórias em Voo Rasante* (Maputo, 2006), p. 205.
43. Ibid. p. 206.
44. Ibid. p. 207.
45. Ibid. p. 204.
46. *V Politburo TsK KPSS* [In the Politburo of the CPSU CC] (Moscow: Alpina, 2006), p. 217.
47. At that time there was still a Portuguese consulate in Dar es Salaam.
48. SARF, collection 9540gs, inventory 2s, file 68, p. 62.
49. Ibid. p. 51. Veloso writes in his memoirs: "Maksudov was certainly a representative of the USSR secret services for work with liberation movements" (p. 51). Nonsense again: before his appointment to Cairo, Maksudov was head of the department in the Central Asian University in Tashkent; later he became ambassador.

CHAPTER 11

1. Information on the stay of the delegation of the National Democratic Party of Southern Rhodesia in the Czechoslovak Socialist Republic (in Russian). SARF, collection 9540, inventory 1, file 102, pp. 98–101.

2. Ibid. p. 100.
3. Ibid. p. 98.
4. SARF, collection 9540 gs, inventory 2s, file 25, p. 98.
5. Ibid. file 40, pp. 26–27.
6. Ibid. p. 27.
7. Ibid.
8. RSAMH, collection 89, inventory 89, file 4, p. 4.
9. SARF, collection 9540gs, inventory 2s, file 36, p. 103.
10. Discussion with J. Nkomo, Moscow, 27 May 1976.
11. SARF, collection 9540gs, inventory 2s, file 36, p. 103. The NDP was banned in December 1961 but "resurrected" in early 1962 as ZAPU, only to be banned again in September that year.
12. Ibid. p. 104.
13. Joshua Nkomo in his memoirs writes that Washington Malianga had been one of the "main promoters of tribal propaganda against me" (J. Nkomo, *The Story of My Life* (London: Methuen, 1984), p. 117).
14. SARF, collection 9540 gs, inventory 2s, file 36, p. 106.
15. SARF, collection 9540 gs, inventory 2s, file 48, p. 3. Nkomo writes in *The Story of My Life* that he visited Moscow in 1961, but this is a mistake, unless he was there in transit to China.
16. Kenneth Kaunda was more reasonable. He requested through the Soviet ambassadors in Addis Ababa in February 1962 and then in Dar es Salaam in August "at least 30 thousand pounds" (SARF, collection 9540 gs, inventory 2s, file 58, p. 85), and received £10,000 in 1962 and £30,000 in 1963 (RSAMH, Head of the CPSU Central Committee International Department, B.N. Pomonarev's report, 3 January 1963, ibid. 29 December 1963).
17. SARF, collection 9540 gs, inventory 2s, file 53, p. 67. Much later, in 1991, Yury Yukalov became the Soviet Ambassador to Zimbabwe.
18. Ibid.
19. Ibid. p. 68.
20. Ibid. file 58, p. 94.
21. Ibid. p. 96.
22. Nkomo, *The Story of My Life*, p. 103.
23. RSAMH, Head of the CPSU Central Committee International Department, B.N. Pomonarev's report, 29 December 1963. According to ZAPU Vice-President James Chikerema, Nkomo requested financial support in a letter to Nikita Khrushchev in March 1963 (SARF, collection 9540gs, inventory 2s, file 70, p. 102).
24. RSAMH, collection 89, inventory 38, file 8, p. 4.
25. Ibid. file 9, p. 4.
26. SARF, collection 9540 gs, inventory 2s, file 47, p. 3.; ibid. file 69, p. 105.
27. According to the official data, in four decades 599 Zimbabweans received Masters degrees and 17 PhD degrees in the USSR/Russia.
28. There were about 80 of them, 60 at the Preparatory Faculty of the Tbilisi Polytechnic Institute and the rest at the Medical Institute.
29. SARF, collection 9540 gs, inventory 2s, file 48, p. 3.
30. Ibid. p. 5.

31. Ibid. file 68, p. 188.
32. Ibid. p. 189. According to Chikerema, several ZAPU members were undergoing military training in China, though the hosts "stuffed them with politics instead of serious training" (ibid. p. 188).
33. Discussion with P. Mphoko, Moscow, 21 March 2007. However, Nkomo writes in his book that Bobylock Manyonga, arrested (in late 1992 or early 1963) by Rhodesian police while transporting the arms Nkomo earlier brought from Egypt, "never revealed ... that his weapons training had been acquired on a short course in the Soviet Union, as the first of many who were to go there" (*The Story of My Life*, p. 103).
34. R. Mugabe, *Our War of Liberation* (Gweru: Mamba Press, 1983), p. 9.
35. Address delivered by His Excellency Cde President R.G. Mugabe at the funeral of Vice-President Dr Joshua Mqabuko Nkomo at the National Heroes Acre, Monday 5 July, 1999, p. 17.
36. Discussion with a former ZIPRA commander.
37. Nkomo, *The Story of My Life*, pp. 102–3.
38. Ibid. p. 103.
39. Discussion with G. Nyandoro, Moscow, 17 July 1969; discussion with J. Chikerema, Lusaka, 4 August 1969.
40. Discussion with T.G. Silundika, Moscow, 16 October 1969. The Lusaka Manifesto on South Africa was approved by the conference of the Eastern and Central African states in Lusaka in April 1969. The signatories confirmed that the liberation of Southern Africa was their aim, while stating their readiness to normalise relations with colonial and racist regimes. They would urge the liberation movements "to desist from their armed struggle" if those regimes recognised "the principle of human equality" and the right to self-determination. The moderate tone of the Manifesto was used by collaborationists such as President Banda of Malawi to justify their policy of a so-called "dialogue" with South Africa.
41. E. Sibanda, *The Zimbabwe African People's Union 1961–1967. A Political History of Insurgency in Southern Rhodesia* (Asmara: Africa World Press, 2005), p. 145.
42. Nkomo, *The Story of My Life*, p. 115. Some ZAPU veterans claim that "ZANU was created by the West", but this is an exaggeration, although the UK and its allies hardly regretted the split in the liberation movement.
43. Much later Mugabe said: "It was our different perceptions of the proposed armed liberation struggle which, plus the fact that we lacked the opportunity for a get-together to discuss them, that caused the serious division which saw ZANU being formed" (Address delivered by His Excellency Cde President R.G. Mugabe at the funeral of Vice-President Dr Joshua Mqabuko Nkomo at the National Heroes Acre, Monday 5 July 1999, p. 18).
44. Ibid. p. 114.
45. SARF, collection 9540 gs, inventory 2s, file 69, p. 159.
46. Ibid. p. 160.
47. Ibid. file 70, p. 48.
48. Ibid. p. 92.

49. Ibid. p. 96.
50. Memoirs of P. Yevsyukov, p. 24.
51. Declaration by Oliver Tambo, Deputy President of the African National Congress of South Africa and J.R.D. Chikerema, Vice-President of the Zimbabwe African People's Union, August 1967, http://www.anc.org.za/ancdocs/history/or/or67–6.html, consulted 12 September 2007.
52. Discussion with E. Ndlovu, Moscow, 4 August 1972.
53. Its English abbreviation was ANC, just like the ANC in South Africa, and we used to joke about the ANC–ANC alliance.
54. Discussion with E. Ndlovu, Moscow, 4 August 1972.
55. Discussion with T.G. Silundika, Moscow, 16 October 1972.
56. Discussion with E. Ndlovu, Moscow, 4 August 1972.
57. Ibid.
58. N. Bhebhe and T. Ranger *Soldiers in Zimbabwe's Liberation War* (London: James Curry; Portsmouth: Heinemann; Harare: University of Zimbabwe Publications, 1995), p. 31.
59. S. Vieira to the author, 19 July 2007.
60. S. Vieira to the author, 20 July 2007.
61. Its official title was UN-OAU International Conference of Experts in Support of Victims of Colonialism and Apartheid. However, the representatives of the liberation movements refused to regard themselves as victims, while most of the participants were unhappy to be reduced to the level of "experts". In any case this title reflected the lack of enthusiasm in some UN quarters for the anti-colonial and anti-racist struggle.
62. Discussion with H. Chitepo, Oslo, 14 April 1973.
63. Discussion with E. Ndlovu, Moscow, 4 August 1972.
64. Discussion with J. Moyo, Moscow, 29 December 1972.
65. Quoted in *African Affairs*, Oxford, vol. 39, no. 316, p. 430.
66. *Sechaba*, no. 5, 1975, p. 16.
67. As hard as conditions in Ian Smith's camps were, sometimes for us complaints about them look strange. Thus ZAPU complained that Joshua Nkomo had to eat starchy food, which affected his health negatively, while for us who lived through World War Two, camps were always a symbol of starvation.
68. Sithole signed it on behalf of ZANU, although he had been "deposed" by his fellow leaders in prison, and his status became rather controversial.
69. S. Vieira to the author, 20 July 2007.
70. Discussion with J. Nkomo, Moscow, 27 May 1976.
71. Discussion with a former ZIPRA commander. Rex Nhongo (Solomon Majuru), who soon after independence became Commander of the Zimbabwe Defence Force was one of the ZAPU cadres who crossed over to ZANU during the crisis in ZAPU in the early 1970s.
72. Ibid.
73. Discussion with a former ZIPRA commander.
74. Author's notes made at the discussion of R. Ulyanovsky with T. G. Silundika and D. Dabengwa, Moscow, 19 January 1976.
75. Nkomo, *The Story of My Life*, pp. 174–5.

CHAPTER 12

1. Discussion with J. Nkomo, Moscow, 27 May 1976; see also Nkomo, *The Story of My Life*, p. 160.
2. This term was still not quite familiar to Nkomo. I recall how more than once Nkomo would address somebody in Moscow as "Mister So and So" and then would hurriedly correct it to "Comrade So and So."
3. RSAMH, collection 89, inventory 27, file 21, p. 19.
4. Discussion with a former ZIPRA commander.
5. RSAMH, collection 89, inventory 27, file 21, p. 30.
6. Ibid. pp. 20–30.
7. Ibid. p. 1.
8. Nkomo, *The Story of My Life*, pp. 175–6.
9. *Rand Daily Mail*, Johannesburg, 12 August 1976.
10. The National Security Council (2999), Minutes National Security Council Meeting, Friday 27 June 1975.
11. Quoted in Klinghoffer, *The Angolan War*, p. 51.
12. Report sent to Solodovnikov, AmEmbassy Lusaka to SecState WashDC. Subj: Soviet-Zambian relations; the end of Solodovnikov era. Doc_nbr: 1981Lusaka0149.
13. *Rand Daily Mail*, 3 June 1980.
14. *Guardian*, London, 4 June 1980. Solodovnikov hardly met Ginwala, who was staying in the UK at that time.
15. Chirkin described his missions to Geneva and later to London in *S tainoi missiei v Genevu i London* [With a Secret Mission to Geneva and London], in *Afrika v vospominantiyah veteranov diplomaticheskoi sluzhby* [Africa in Reminiscences of Veterans of Diplomatic Service] (Moscow: XXI vek-Soglasie, 2000), pp. 124–33.
16. T.G. Silundika to the author, 19 September 1977.
17. Discussion with J. Nkomo, Moscow, early January 1977. Unfortunately the exact date of the meeting is missing from my notes.
18. Author's notes at Nkomo's discussion at the USSR Ministry of Defence, 4 January 1977.
19. RSAMH, collection 89, inventory 27, file 34, p. 7.
20. Ibid. pp. 7–8.
21. Ibid. p. 8. Nkomo reiterated his requests during his visit to Moscow.
22. RSAMH, collection 89, inventory 27, file 34, pp. 8–9.
23. Ibid. p. 5.
24. Ibid. p. 1.
25. Discussion with J. Nkomo, Moscow, early 1977.
26. Discussion with a former ZIPRA commander.
27. A. Burenko, *A Hard but Exclusively Important Period of Life* (sent to the author on 13 December 2006), p. 1. Publication of this and other memoirs of the Soviet officers who served in Angola is expected in 2008. Now Professor Burenko has the rank of major general.
28. Ibid. p. 4.
29. To come to Zimbabwe from Zambia, ZIPRA fighters had to cross the Zambezi.
30. Burenko, *A Hard but Exclusively Important Period of Life*, p. 4

31. Ibid. p. 1.
32. Ibid. pp. 1–2.
33. Ibid. p. 3.
34. Ibid.
35. Ibid.
36. Ambassador Solodovnikov's hand-written note on the paper *Udary rodeziislkih voisk po ob'ektam ZIPRA v Zambii* (Attacks of Rhodesian troops against ZIPRA installations in Zambia). I am indebted to Ambassador Solodovnikov for this paper. Its last line contained the words "Sincerely yours. SIBANDA", and a small picture of a handshake. Apparently "SIBANDA" was Colonel Kononov's *nom de guerre*.
37. Risquet, *Prologue*, p. 14.
38. Burenko, *A Hard but Exclusively Important Period of Life*, p. 5.
39. Discussion with a former ZIPRA commander.
40. Discussion with V. Solodovnikov, Moscow, 17 January 2003. By that time in March and May 1978, two inter-governmental agreements had been signed on the purchase of Soviet arms, including MiGs, and the sending of Soviet military specialists to Zambia.
41. V. Solodovnikov, "The Cold War in the Southern Africa: 1976–81" *IAS Newsletter*, no. 4, 1998, p. 2.
42. Nkomo, *The Story of My Life*, p. 175.
43. Ibid.
44. The author of the most comprehensive book so far on the history of ZAPU fares a bit better: he does mention training of ZIPRA cadres "under Cubans" in Angola (Sibanda, *The Zimbabwe African People's Union 1961–1967*, p. 175), but fails to mention Soviet instructors.
45. It was called the Zero Hour Plan (ZHP).
46. Quoted in Sibanda, *The Zimbabwe African People's Union 1961–1967*, p. 206.
47. Ibid.

CHAPTER 13

1. Discussion with D. Dabengwa, Moscow, 21 June 1978.
2. Discussion with J. Nkomo, Moscow, early 1979.
3. The author's personal recollection and discussion with A. Urnov, Istanbul, 4 November 2006.
4. RSAMH, collection 5, inventory 76, file 834, pp. 82–4.
5. Discussion with a Zimbabwe Air Force high commander, Harare, 18 February 2006.
6. Sibanda, *The Zimbabwe African People's Union 1961–1967*, p. 203.
7. Ibid. p. 232.
8. Ibid.
9. Nkomo, *The Story of My Life*, p. 197.
10. Ibid. p. 175.
11. UK National Archives, CWSC-CCBH Conference Proceedings (5 July 2005), Witness Seminar: Britain and Rhodesian Question: The Road to Settlement 1979–1980", p. 77.

12. Sibanda, *The Zimbabwe African People's Union 1961–1987*, p. 304.
13. Discussion with a former ZIPRA commander.
14. Chirkin, *S tainoi missiei*, p. 132.
15. Ibid. p. 133.
16. This attack coincided with an international conference in support of Zimbabwe's liberation struggle, held by AAPSO in Lusaka.
17. *Udary rodeziislkih voisk po ob'ektam ZIPRA v Zambii.*
18. Discussion with a former ZIPRA commander.
19. Chirkin, *S tainoi missiei*, p. 133.
20. Nkomo, *The Story of My Life*, pp. 198–9.
21. Discussion with a former ZIPRA commander.
22. Ibid. Curiously enough, others believed the opposite: they were sure that the UK, South Africa and the USA were rendering support to Joshua Nkomo (S. Vieira to the author, 20 July 2007).
23. Ibid.
24. S. Vieira to the author, 19 July 2007.
25. Discussion with a former ZIPRA Commander.
26. S. Vieira to the author, 20 July 2007.

CHAPTER 14

1. Discussion with a former ZIPRA commander.
2. Memoirs of P. Yevsyukov, pp. 13–14.
3. Chirkin, *S tainoi missiei*, p. 127.
4. V. Solodovnikov, *K istorii ustanovleniya diplomaticheskih otnoshenii mezhdu SSSR i Zimbabwe* [On the history of the establishment of the diplomatic relations between the USSR and Zimbabwe], in *Afrika v vospominaniyah veteranov diplomaticheskoi sluzhby*, pp. 134–74.
5. Ibid. pp. 137–8.
6. Ibid. p. 139.
7. Ibid. pp. 150–61.
8. Ibid. p. 165.
9. Ibid. p. 173. Apart from Moscow "humbly" accepting this condition, another factor could play a role: in the eyes of ZANU's leaders, Solodovnikov personified Soviet relations with ZAPU, while Vdovin was accredited to Mozambique, a former rear base of ZANU.
10. We should remember that the government of independent Zimbabwe "inherited" the intelligence apparatus of the old regime.
11. The author's notes at R. Ulyanovsky's discussion with S. Sekeremayi, Moscow, 15 November 1982.
12. Sokolov published very interesting memoirs, devoted not only to NAM, but also to the situation in Zimbabwe from 1986 to 1989 (*Hararskie dnevniki* [Hahare Diaries], in *Afrika v vospominaniyah veteranov diplomaticheskoi sluzhby*, pp. 202–22). Some of his observations are very revealing. For example, he writes about a "weird combination of the 'infantile leftism' of the national liberation movement and Westminster's arrogance about the 'African audience with Anglo-Saxon traditions' in Zimbabwe" (p. 219).

13. He sent a copy of his memoirs, published in London, to the CPSU CC.
14. They were acquitted in court but had to spend about five more years in detention under the emergency law, "inherited" by Zimbabwe from Ian Smith's days.
15. Discussion with N. Shamuyarira, Windhoek, 21 March 1991.

CHAPTER 15

1. Discussion with B. Amathila, Moscow, 15 September 2003.
2. R. First, *South-West Africa* (Baltimore: Penguin Books, 1963).
3. Discussion with A. Urnov, Istanbul, 2 November 2006.
4. Sellstrom, *Sweden and the National Liberation in Southern Africa. Volume 1*, p. 271.
5. SARF, collection 9540, inventory 1, file 102, pp. 52–3.
6. Ibid. p. 52.
7. SARF, collection 9540 gs, inventory 2s, file 47, p. 61.
8. Nelengani became popular with the first generation of the Soviet Solidarity Committee's staff, maybe because his name sounded almost like the Russian word *nelegalni*, meaning "illegal" or "underground". As for Fortune, about 25 years later he visited a Soviet embassy in one of the Southern African countries and claimed innocence. When I raised this matter with Sam Nujoma, the SWAPO president's reply was definite: "He is a traitor."
9. SARF, collection 9540 gs, inventory 2s, p. 76.
10. Ibid. file 68, p. 125.
11. Ibid. file 70, p. 161.
12. Ibid. p. 152.
13. Discussion with B. Amathila, Moscow, 15 September 2003.
14. SARF, collection 9540 gs, inventory 2s, file 60, p. 90.
15. Ibid, file 65, p. 40.
16. Discussion with the SWAPO delegation headed by P. Nanyemba, Moscow, 2 July 1969.
17. Ibid.
18. Ibid.
19. Ibid.
20. Ibid.
21. Discussion with A. van Dunem, Lusaka, 4 August 1969.

CHAPTER 16

1. Discussion with S. Nujoma, Moscow, 12 October 1969. At the next day's discussion in the Africa Institute Nujoma was more optimistic (and less overt) than at the Solidarity Committee: he did not hesitate to show on the map areas close to Windhoek, where SWAPO fighters were allegedly operating.
2. Ibid.
3. Ibid.

4. Discussion with B. Amathila, Windhoek, 3 April 2004.
5. Discussion with H. Kaluenja, Moscow, 11 October 1972.
6. Ibid.
7. National Archives. FCO 45/1016. South West African People's Organisation. 1971. Documents 4, 5, 6, 7.
8. Discussion with H. Kaluenja, Moscow, 15 November 1972.
9. Ibid.
10. Ibid.
11. Discussion with S. Nujoma, Moscow, 23 December 1972.
12. Ibid.
13. Ibid.
14. Ibid. This decision, which was at least partly carried out later, caused controversy in that period, since some of the leading members preferred academic studies in the West.
15. Discussion with S. Shikomba, Moscow, 12 July 1973.
16. Ibid.
17. Discussion with S. Mifima, Moscow, 16 May 1973. The prestige of SWAPO inside Namibia was so high that a splinter group (to be discussed later) named their organisation "SWAPO-Democrats". Moreover, Solomon Mifima occupied a leading position in this body, which took part in the puppet structures.
18. Discussion with S. Mifima, Moscow, 16 May 1973.
19. Ibid.
20. Ibid.
21. Ibid.
22. Ibid.
23. Ibid.
24. Discussion with the SWAPO delegation, Moscow, 23 July 1973.
25. Ibid.
26. Ibid.
27. Ibid.
28. Ibid.

CHAPTER 17

1. Discussion with S. Nujoma, Moscow, 10 December 1974.
2. Ibid.
3. Ibid.
4. Discussion with P. Nanyemba and S. Hawala, Moscow, 8 December 1974.
5. Bridgland, *Jonas Savimbi*, pp. 69, 79, 84, 94, 95, 388–9.
6. S. Nujoma, *Where Others Wavered. The Autobiography of Sam Nujoma* (London: Panaf Books, 2001), p. 236.
7. Discussion with P. Nanyemba and S. Hawala, Moscow, 8 December 1974.
8. Ibid.
9. Discussion with H. Pohamba, Dar es Salaam, 29 April 1975.
10. Discussion with S. Nujoma, Moscow, 9 October 1975.

11. Ibid.
12. Discussion with P. Nanyemba, Moscow, 29 December 1975.
13. Discussion with S. Nujoma, Moscow, 9 October 1975.
14. Discussion with S. Shikomba, Moscow, 25 September 1975.
15. Discussion with P. Nanyemba, Moscow, 29 December 1975.
16. Discussion with S. Nujoma, Moscow, 6 August 1976.
17. Discussion with S. Nujoma, Moscow, 6 August 1976.
18. Discussion with M. Garoeb, Moscow, 25 February 1976.
19. Bridgland, *Jonas Savimbi*, p. 250.
20. Ibid. p. 137.
21. *Pravda*, 2 March 1976.
22. *Pravda*, 5 November 1976.
23. *Pravda*, 10 October 1976.
24. *Pravda*, 5 March 1981.
25. Discussion with K. Shangula (head of Namibian students' association in the USSR), 13 April 1979.
26. The SWAPO-Democrats were routed at the national election in November 1989. The last I heard about Shipanga was that he was employed as a guard somewhere in northern Namibia.
27. Discussion with S. Nujoma, Moscow, 6 August 1976.
28. Ibid.
29. Ibid.
30. Later Skorikov was appointed Chief of the Soviet Air Staff and promoted to the rank of Marshal of Aviation.
31. Crocker, *High Noon in Southern Africa*, p. 12.
32. The author's notes at the discussion of S. Nujoma with G. Skorikov, Moscow, 10 August 1976
33. Ibid.
34. The author's notes at the discussion of S. Nujoma with Postnikov, Moscow, 6 October 1977.
35. Ibid.
36. Discussion with S. Nujoma, Moscow, 7 October 1977.
37. Ibid.
38. RSAMH, collection 89, inventory 25, file 6, p. 1.
39. Discussion with A. Urnov, Istanbul, 2 November 2006.
40. His *nom de guerre* was Ho Chi Minh.
41. However, the degree of the involvement of Soviet military personnel should not be exaggerated. Thus the author could not find any proof of General Varennikov's claim that Soviet "intelligence officers who were acting in SWAPO units on the territory of Namibia and in south Angola had direct contact with troops of UNITA [Savimbi] and supporters of South Africa, hired by the latter for small pay, but capable [also for payment] of giving exclusively valuable information on South African groupings". He even claimed: "Our intelligence officers, beside personal observations, used also the paid services of pygmies" (Varennikov, *Nepovtorimoye*, Part 6, p. 229).
42. A. Prokhanov, *Afrikanist* (Moscow: Armada-press, 2002).
43. Ibid. p. 139.
44. Discussion with K. Kurochkin, Moscow, 21 September 2001.

45. K. Kurochkin's notebook 2, p. 50.
46. Ibid. pp. 42, 45.
47. Discussion with K. Kurochkin, Moscow, 21 September 2001.
48. Discussion with A. van Dunem, Luanda, 24 January 1984.
49. Discussion with A. Maksyuta, Moscow, 30 October 2005.
50. Discussion with H. Kaluenja, Moscow, 15 February 1984.
51. J. Saul and C. Leys "Lubango and After: 'Forgotten Histories' as Politics in Contemporary Namibia", in *Journal of Southern African Studies*, vol. 29, no. 2, June 2003, pp. 333–53.
52. Relevant conclusions were made, for example, by Ian Liebenberg of the University of South Africa in his PhD thesis.
53. K. Kurochkin's notebook 3, p. 40.
54. Nujoma, *Where Others Wavered*, p. 342.
55. Discussion with a SWAPO delegation, Moscow, 25 May 1984.
56. Discussion with T.-B. Gurirab, Moscow, 16 April 1987.
57. *Izvestia*, 17 April 1988.
58. *Pravda*, 21 April 1988.
59. Peter Nanyemba was killed in a car accident in Angola in 1983.
60. Discussion with S. Nujoma, Moscow, 20 April 1989. This time he was leaving Moscow for Atlanta in the USA, and that very fact attested to the growing prestige of SWAPO and its leadership.
61. *Pravda*, 20 April 1988.
62. Discussion with T.-B. Gurirab, Moscow, 15 April 1987.
63. Mayibuye Centre Historical Papers, ANC Lusaka Collection, Rules, governing the privileges and immunities granted to the Mission of the African National Congress (ANC) of South Africa.

CHAPTER 18

1. Discussion with S. Nujoma, Lisbon, 19 March 1989.
2. *Pravda*, 7 April 1989.
3. *Weekly Mail*, Johannesburg, 7–13 April 1989.
4. *The Namibian*, Windhoek, 5 April 1989.
5. Ahtisaari's role in the Namibian settlement was highlighted in his native Finland and helped him to become its president. After the retirement he again got involved in conflict settlement, and again in a controversial way; he drafted a plan of Kosovo independence, which contradicted the UN Security Council resolution.
6. Discussion with S. Nujoma, Windhoek, 7 November 1988.

CHAPTER 19

1. Shubin, *ANC: A View from Moscow* (Bellville: Mayibuye Books, 1999).
2. V. Shubin with M. Traikova, "There is no threat from the Eastern Block", in *The Road to Democracy. Volume 3. International Solidarity* (Pretoria: SADET/Unisa Press, 2008).
3. The Congress Alliance consisted of the African National Congress, the South African Indian Congress, the South African Coloured People's

Congress, the Congress of [white] Democrats and the South African Congress of Trade Unions.

4. Mayibuye Centre Historical Papers, Yusuf Dadoo Collection (hereafter MCHP, YDC), E. Pahad "Yusuf Dadoo. A Political Biography" (unpublished manuscript), p. 211.

5. Ibid. p. 6.

6. RSAMH, collection 89, inventory 38, file 3, p. 6.

7. Ibid. file 4, pp. 3–5.

8. Ibid. file 5, pp. 5–6.

9. Kotane did not mention in Moscow that the first operations of Umkhonto would start on 16 December 1961, in two months' time; most probably such a decision was taken after his departure from South Africa.

10. M. Kotane, *Notes on Some Aspects of the Political Situation in the Republic of South Africa* (Moscow, 9 November 1961), p. 12.

11. RSAMH, Decisions taken by the instruction of the Secretaries of the CPSU Central Committee without recording in the minutes, N 478, 28 November 1961.

12. Ibid.

13. Ibid.

14. RSAMH, Minutes of the Secretariat, N 50, item 46g, 11 December 1962.

15. T. Lodge, *Black Politics in South Africa since 1945*, (London and New York: Longman, 1983), pp. 234–5.

16. Arthur Goldreich to the author, 24 August 1993.

17. *Star*, Johannesburg, 11 December 1991.

18. Quoted in L. Strydom, *Rivonia Unmasked!* (Johannesburg: Voortrek-kerpers, 1965), p. 108.

19. RSAMH, Minutes of the Secretariat, N 52, item 10g, 22 December 1962. Tambo's visit was arranged with certain precautions: he was formally invited by the Soviet Afro-Asian Solidarity Committee "for rest", although the party machinery took care of him and the International Department's official, Vladimir Shemyatenkov, accompanied him (discussion with V. Shemyatenkov, Moscow, 6 January 1997).

20. RSAMH, collection 89, inventory 38, file 6, pp. 11–12.

21. Ibid.

22. SARF, collection 9540gs, inventory 2s, file 47, p. 20; RSAMH, Decisions of the Secretariat, N 17, item 37g, 10 March 1962.

23. Discussion with O. Tambo, Lusaka, 4 August 1969.

24. Discussion with H. Loots (J. Stuart), Johannesburg, 30 April 2005.

25. Discussion with A. Makarov, Pretoria, 21 November 1993.

26. Ronnie Kasrils described his and his comrades' experience in Odessa in his *Armed and Dangerous. From Undercover Struggle to Freedom* (Johannesburg and Cape Town. Jonathan Ball Publishers, 2003) pp. 65–72. See also Shubin, *ANC: A View from Moscow*.

27. T. Bell with D.B. Ntebeza, *Unfinished Business. South Africa, Apartheid and Truth* (London and New York: Verso, 2003), p. 119.

28. Ibid. p. 274.

29. A. Sibeko (Zola Zembe) with J. Leeson, *Freedom in our Lifetime* http://www.anc.org.za/ancdocs/history/congress/sactu/zz1.htm, consulted 15 September 2007.
30. Quoted in Strydom, *Rivonia Unmasked!*, p. 113.
31. On these attempts see *The Road to Democracy in South Africa. Volume I: 1960–1970* (Pretoria: SADET, 2005), pp. 487–528.
32. MCHP, ANC Lusaka Collection. The report of the Secretariat covering the last two years (1971), p. 5.
33. MCHP, ANC Lusaka Collection. African National Congress National Consultative Conference. President's Statement, p. 19.
34. Decision of the Politburo of the CPSU Central Committee P 135/19, 1 September 1969, referred to in RSAMH, Minutes of the Secretariat, N 103, item 24g, 20 July 1970.
35. MCHP, ANC London Collection, Report of the work of the delegation of the SACP to the International Conference of Communist and Workers' Parties. Moscow/1969, p. 2.

CHAPTER 20

1. Decision of the Politburo of the CPSU Central Committee P 58/52 of 18 October 1967, item 1, referred to in RSAMH, Minutes of the Secretariat, N 103, item 24g, 20 July 1970; Decision of the Politburo of the CPSU Central Committee P 183/13 of 20 October 1970 and Order of the USSR Council of Ministers 2217s of 20 October 1970, referred to in RSAMH, Minutes of the Secretariat, N 103, item 24g, 20 July 1970 as proof of fulfilment of the last-mentioned.
2. £75,000 were allocated for the purchase of the ship (SACP to CPSU, 6 September 1970, referred to in E. Maloka, *The South African Communist Party in Exile 1963–1969* (Pretoria: Africa Institute of South Africa, 2002), p. 29).
3. See *The Road to Democracy in South Africa. Volume 2: 1970–1980*, (Pretoria: SADET/Unisa Press, 2006), pp. 457–9.
4. *Echo*, 21 February 1990. Hani's comments utterly contradict the nonsense of Bell and Ntebeza's fallacies.
5. Discussion with A. Nzo and T. Nkobi, Moscow, 3 February 1976.
6. ANC internal document, *Brief Report of the Revolutionary Council*, p. 6.
7. *The Kissinger Study of Southern Africa. National Security Study Memorandum 39* (Westport: Lawrence Hill & Company, 1976).
8. National Archives. FCO 45/1016. Circular 0 229/69. London, 16 September 1969. African Freedom Movements.
9. Solodovnikov was the first Russian citizen awarded the South African Order of Companions of O.R. Tambo.
10. *Sovietskaya Rossiya* [Soviet Russia], Moscow, 23 September 2004. This is correct not only with reference to diplomats. Thus the ANC was not even included in the index of J. Seiler's (ed.) book *Southern Africa Since the Portuguese Coup* (Boulder: Westview Press, 1980).
11. According to an ANC document, the initiative to involve the Soviets came originally from Jorge Risquet who at that stage headed the Cuban

contingent in Angola (*Brief Report of the Revolutionary Council*, April 1979, pp. 5–6).

12. Discussion with S. Kokin, a former official of the Soviet embassy in Angola, Moscow, 14 January 2007.
13. V.F. Shiryaev, *Menya zvali tovarishch Ivan* [They called me Comrade Ivan], in *VVITKU VMF. Vospominaniya vypusknikov 1961 goda* [Red Banner Higher Naval Engineering and Technical College. Reminiscences of graduates of 1961] (Moscow, 2005), pp. 88–92.
14. *Segodnya*, no 5, Moscow, 1993.
15. V. Shiryaev ("Comrade Ivan") to the author, 2 April 2003.
16. Ibid.
17. *Nezavisimaya Gazeta*, Moscow, 8 August 1992.
18. V. Shiryaev ("Comrade Ivan") to the author, 2 April 2003. Timothy Makoena was a *nom de guerre* of Godfrey Ngwenya, who is now Chief of the SANDF.
19. Ibid.
20. Ibid.
21. Discussion with G. Pimenov ("Comrade George"), Luanda, 30 January 1984.
22. Discussion with M. Konovalenko ("Comrade Michael"), Moscow, 10 September 2003.
23. At that time Jacob Zuma headed the ANC machinery in Mozambique.
24. Quoted in Crocker *High Noon in Southern Africa*, p. 81.
25. *Sechaba*, December 1982, p. 20.
26. *Times*, 6 January 1984.
27. Crocker, *High Noon in Southern Africa*, p. 180.
28. The term "close neighbours" originated from the fact that, before moving to the Smolenskaya Square in the mid 1950s, the Soviet People's Commissariat (later Ministry) of Foreign Affairs for several decades occupied a building close to the Security and Intelligence headquarters, while the Department of Military Intelligence, situated further away, became known as "distant neighbours".
29. The CPSU Central Committee machinery was located at the Old Square, not far from the Kremlin.
30. S. Sinitsyn, *Vensky "vals" s burami* [Vienna waltz with the Boers], *Afrika v vospominaniyah veteranov diplomaticheskoi sluzhby*, p. 184.
31. Ibid. p. 185. Each delegation also included two diplomats and two intelligence officers.
32. Ibid. pp. 187–8.
33. Ibid. pp. 192–3.
34. Ibid. p. 197.

CHAPTER 21

1. *Sovetskaya Rossiya*, Moscow, 20 March 2006.
2. The author's notes at the discussion of O. Tambo with M. Gorbachev, Moscow, 4 November 1986.

3. *Pravda*, 5 November 1986.
4. Ellis and Sechaba, *Comrades against Apartheid*, p.182.
5. *Mirovaya ekonomika i mezhdunarodnye otnosheniya* [World Economy and International Relations], nos 4, pp. 79–86; 5, pp. 81–90; 7, pp. 88–91; 8, pp. 69–78; Moscow, 1993.
6. The author's notes at the discussion of A. Dobrynin with the ANC delegation, led by O. Tambo, 5 November 1986.
7. Anatoly Karpov, former world chess champion, who headed the Soviet Peace Fund, disclosed recently that about 60 per cent of the money coming to the Fund at that time came from the Russian Orthodox Church (*Literaturnaya Gazeta*, Moscow, 12–18 April 2006).
8. MCHP, ANC Lusaka Collection. Rules governing the privileges and immunities granted to the Mission of the African National Congress (ANC) of South Africa.
9. MCHP, ANC Lusaka Connection. Our assessment of the outcome of the Washington summit between General Secretary of the CPSU Central Committee Comrade M.S. Gorbachev and US President R. Reagan.
10. This operation is described in the third edition of Ronnie Kasrils's *Armed and Dangerous: From Undercover Struggle to Freedom* (Johannesburg and Cape Town: Jonathan Ball, 2004), and Timothy Jenkin's *Talking to Vula. The Story of the Secret Underground Communications Network of Operation Vula*, http://www.anc.org.za/ancdocs/history/vula.html.
11. Siphiwe Nyanda to Vladimir Shubin, 10 December 2002. For more on the Soviet role see Shubin, *ANC: A View from Moscow*, pp. 332–8, 360, 381. One episode is worth mentioning here: on 11 and 12 July 1989, at a time when Pretoria and Western propaganda were claiming that the USSR had "dropped" the ANC, Moscow was still the safest place for Oliver Tambo and other ANC leaders to meet Mac Maharaj, the head of their underground machinery.
12. G. Starushenko, *Problems of Struggle against Racism, Apartheid and Colonialism in South Africa* (Moscow: Africa Institute, 1986), p. 12.
13. Ibid.
14. *Soviet Review*, Stellenbosch, N 4, 1987, p. 30. Goncharov gave an interview in 1987 in Harare to *Work in Progress* magazine; just like Starushenko's presentation, it contained factual mistakes and wrong judgements.
15. Statement by IDASA delegation on their visit to the USSR.
16. The author's notes at the discussion of O. Tambo with A. Lukyanov, Moscow, 11 March 1989.
17. H. Cohen, *The United States and Africa. Non-vital Interests Also Require Attention*, http://www.americandiplomacy.org, consulted 25 December 2007.
18. *Izvestia*, 27 September 1989.
19. A bitter irony is that two years later, in early 1992, Shevardnadze was installed as the leader of his native Georgia by the insurgents, many of them with a criminal record, who had won a short civil war.
20. MCHP, ANC Lusaka Collection, Report on the ANC Meeting with the Soviet Foreign Minister. 20.3.90 at 9.00 hrs. p. 6.
21. Ibid. p. 4.

22. *Pravda*, 28 February 1991.
23. Ibid.
24. E. Pahad to the author, 2 January 1991.
25. A. Chernyaev, *Shest Let s Gorbachevym* [Six Years with Gorbachev], (Moscow: Progress – Kultura, 1993), p. 195.
26. Discussion with N. Mandela, Durban, 3 July 1991.
27. I used this expression in the article published under the pen name "Mkhulu" in *the African Communist*, no. 128, 1st quarter 1992.
28. *Rossiyskaya Gazeta*, Moscow, 2 June 1992.

POSTCRIPT

1. S. Amin, "US militarism and the new world order", *Southern African Political and Economic Monthly*, Harare, November, 1992, p. 17.

Soviet Personalities

Adamishin, Anatoly – Deputy Foreign Minister of Affairs
Afanasenko, Yevgeny – ambassador to Congo-Brazzaville
Andropov, Yury – General Secretary of the CPSU Central Committee, Chairman of the Presidium of the USSR Supreme Soviet
Arkadaksky, Alexander – official of the CPSU International Department
Belokolos, Dmitry – ambassador to Zambia
Belyaev, Valery – Lieutenant General, adviser of the Chief of General Staff of FAPLA
Brezhnev, Leonid – General Secretary of the CPSU Central Committee, Chairman of the Presidium of the USSR Supreme Soviet
Brutents, Karen – Deputy Head of CPSU International Department
Checherin – Major General, Commander of the Military College of Odessa
Cherevko, A. – General, Chief Military Adviser in Mozambique
Chernyaev, Anatoly – assistant to CPSU General Secretary and to USSR President
Chirkin, Venyamin – Professor of Law
Dobrynin, Anatoly – Secretary of the CPSU Central Committee
Dolidze, Dmitry – General Secretary of the Soviet Afro-Asian Solidarity Committee
Dubenko, Alexey – Rear Admiral, Soviet military attaché in Angola
Dzassokhov, Alexander – General Secretary, and after that First Vice-President of the Soviet Afro-Asian Solidarity Committee, later member of the Politburo and Secretary of the CPSU Central Committee, incumbent member of the Council of Federation (upper house of the Russian Parliament)
Fasylov, Malik – Minister of Foreign Affairs of Kazakhstan, later Soviet ambassador
Fedorenko, Fyodor – Colonel, Commander of the Training Centre, later Major General
Fedorinov, Vitaly – Soviet diplomat
Fomin, Gennady – Head of the Third African Department, the USSR Ministry of Foreign Affairs
Galkin – Major General
Gavrilov, Yury – geologist
Glukhov, Arkady – diplomat, later ambassador
Goncharov, Victor – Deputy Director of the Africa Institute
Gorb, Andrey – Colonel, military adviser in Angola.
Gorbachev, Mikhail – General Secretary of the CPSU Central Committee, President of the USSR
Grechko, Andrey – Marshal of the Soviet Union, Minister of Defence
Gromov, Valentin – Major General, adviser to the Chief of Staff of FAPLA
Gusev, Petr – Lieutenant General, Chief Military Adviser – adviser to the Minister of Defence of Angola

Ignatyev, Oleg – *Pravda* correspondent
Ilyichev, Leonid – Deputy Minister of Foreign Affairs
Istomin, Victor – geologist in Mozambique
Ivanov, Yury – Official of the CPSU International Department
Kapsky, Eduard – Associate Professor of the Institute of Social Sciences, later official of the PSU International Department
Kharazov, Valery – Second Secretary of the Communist Party of Lithuania
Khrushchev, Nikita – First Secretary of the Central Committee, CPSU, Chairman of the USSR Council of Ministers
Kirpichenko, Vadim – Head of the African Division in the KGB, later Lieutenant General and First Deputy Chief of the PGU
Kokin, Stanislav – Soviet diplomat
Konovalenko, Mikhail ("Comrade Michael") – Colonel, Chief Military Adviser to ANC
Kornienko, Georgy – First Deputy Minister of Foreign Affairs, later First Deputy Head of the CPSU International Department
Kozyrev, Andrey – Minister of Foreign Affairs of the Russian Federation
Kulikov, Victor – Marshal of the Soviet Union, Chief of General Staff, USSR Armed Forces, later Commander-in-Chief of the United Armed Forces of the Warsaw Pact Organisation
Kurochkin, Konstantin – Lieutenant General, later Colonel General, Chief Military Adviser – adviser to the Minister of Defence in Angola
Kurushkin, Nikolay – Colonel, Chief Military Adviser to SWAPO, later Major General
Kuzmenko, Leonid – Lieutenant General, Chief Military Adviser – Adviser to the Minister of Defence
Lipatov, Yury – diplomat in Angola
Loginov, Vadim – ambassador to Angola
Lukyanov, Anatoly – First Deputy Chairman of the Presidium of the USSR Supreme Soviet
Lyashenko, Evgeny – Captain, Soviet military specialist
Makarov, Alexey – Military interpreter, after that official of the Soviet Afro-Asian Solidarity Committee and CPSU International Department, later diplomat
Maksudov, Latyp – Soviet representative in AAPSO, later ambassador
Maksyuta, Alexander – diplomat in Angola
Mamsurov, Hadzhi – Colonel General, Deputy Chief of GRU
Manchkha, Petr – Head of the African Section, the CPSU International Department
Midtsev, Veniamen – Official of the CPSU International Department
Mitin, Yury – Colonel, military adviser
Muhitdinov, Nuretdin – Member of Presidium and Secretary of the CPSU Central Committee
Nazhestkin, Oleg – KGB officer
Nikanorov, Anatoly – *Izvestia* correspondent
Ogarkov, Nikolay – Marshal of the Soviet Union, Chief of General Staff, USSR Armed Forces
Pavlov, Pavel – Head of the Soviet Liaison Mission in Namibia, later ambassador

Pestretsov, Nikolay – Warrant Officer, military Soviet specialist

Petrov, Mikhail – Soviet ambassador to Botswana

Petrov, Vassily – Marshal of the Soviet Union, Commander-in-Chief of the Soviet Ground Forces, later First Deputy Defence Minister

Petrovsky, Georgy – Lieutenant General, Chief Military Adviser – adviser to the Minister of Defence

Petruk, Boris – Official of the CPSU International Department

Pimenov, German ("Comrade George") – Colonel, Chief Military Adviser to ANC

Podgorny, Nikolay – Chairman of the Presidium of the USSR Supreme Soviet

Ponomarenko, Ilya – Major General, Chief Military Adviser – Adviser to the Minister of Defence in Angola

Ponomarev, Boris – Candidate Member of Politburo and Secretary of the CPSU Central Committee

Potekhin, Ivan – Professor, founding Director of the Africa Institute, Chairman, Soviet Association of Friendship with African Peoples

Predvechnyi, German – diplomat

Prokhanov, Alexander – writer

Putilin, Boris – diplomat (and officer of Military Intelligence)

Ryzhkov, Nikolay – Chairman of the USSR Council of Ministers

Sagachko, Vadim – Colonel, military adviser in Angola, incumbent Chair of the Union of Veterans of Angola

Shakhnovich, Vassily – Lieutenant General, Chief Military Adviser – Adviser to the Minister of Defence

Shemyatenkov, Vladimir – official of CPSU International Department, later Ambassador

Shevlyagin, Dmitry – Deputy Head of the International Department

Shirshikov, Anatoly – Retired colonel, official of the Soviet Solidarity Committee

Shiryaev, Vyacheslav ("Comrade Ivan") – Navy Captain, Chief Military Adviser to ANC

Sinitsyn, Sergey – Soviet ambassador

Skakun, Grigory – warrant officer, military specialist in Angola

Slipchenko, Sergey – ambassador to Tanzania

Snegirev, Vladimir – ambassador

Snitko, Oleg – Lieutenant, Soviet interpreter in Angola

Sokolov, Vladimir – Soviet diplomat

Solodovnikov, Vassily – Director of the Africa Institute, later ambassador to Zambia

Stalin, Joseph – General Secretary of the Central Committee, CPSU and Chairman of the Council of Ministers, USSR

Starushenko, Gleb – Deputy Director of the Africa Institute

Ter-Gazariants, Georgy – ambassador to Zimbabwe

Timishchenko, Andrey – ambassador to Tanzania

Tokarev, Andrey – student of the Military Institute of Foreign Languages, interpreter in Angola, later Colonel

Trofimenko, Vassily – Colonel, head of the group of Soviet military advisers in Angola

Ulyanovsky, Rostislav – Deputy Head of the CPSU International Department, Vice-President of the Soviet Afro-Asian Solidarity Committee

Urnov, Andrey – Deputy Head of the CPSU International Department, later ambassador

Ustinov, Dmitry – Marshal of the Soviet Union, Minister of Defence

Uvarov, Igor – TASS correspondent (and Soviet officer)

Varennikov, Valentin – Army General, Deputy Chief of the General Staff, later Commander-in-Chief of the Soviet Ground Forces and Deputy Minister of Defence

Vasev, Vladillen – Ambassador, Head of the 3rd African Department, Ministry of Foreign Affairs

Vdovin, Valentin – Soviet ambassador to Mozambique

Vydrin, Sergey – official of the Soviet Afro-Asian Solidarity Committee

Yanaev, Gennady – Chairman of the Committee of Youth Organisations of the USSR, later member of the Politburo and Secretary of the CPSU Central Committee, Vice-President of the USSR

Yeltsin, Boris – President of the Russian Federation

Yevsyukov, Petr ("Camarada Pedro") – Official of the CPSU International Department, later ambassador

Zapurdyaev, Yury – Colonel, Chief Military Adviser to SWAPO

Zhdarkin, Igor – student of the Military Institute, later Lieutenant Colonel.

Index

Compiled by Sue Carlton

Page numbers in **bold** refer to photographs

Lusaka Agreements (Feb 1984) 226–7, 229
Luvualu, Pascoal 20–1, 31
Luzzatto, Lucio 13
Lyashenko, Evgeny 57

Mabhida, Moses 39, 243
Mabote, Sebastio 132
Mabunda, David 123
McBride, Sean 214, 225
Machel, Samora 125, 126, 128, 129, 130, 131, 132, 161, 165, 182, 183
    death of 137–47
Madlela, Agrippa 153, 158
Magombe, George 208
Maharaj, Mac 259
Makarov, Dr Alexey 262
Makoena, Timothy 250
Maksudov, Latyp 146, 154, 196
Maksyuta, Alexander 228
Malan, Magnus 74, 104, 109
Malange 24, 92, 93, 250
Malianga, Morton 151
Malianga, Washington 152, 153
Malima, Fillemon 231
Manchkha, Petr 16, 43, 52, 63, 67, 244
Mandela, Nelson 241, 242, 260, 261, 262–3
Mangena, Alfred ("Nikita") 165
MANU (Mozambican African National Union) 119, 121
Mao Zedong 60
Marcum, John 28
Marks, John 144, 245
Masire, Quett 182
Masuku, "Lookout" 189
Matveev, Vikenty 65
Mbeki, Thabo 145, 199, 261
Mbita, Hashim 164, 208
Memorandum 39 (1969) 248
Meroro, David 203
MFA (Movement of Armed Forces-Portugal) 34 35, 131
Midtsev, Veniamin 18
Mifima, Solomon 217
Mitin, Yury 57
MK (Umkhonto we Sizwe) 241, 242, 243, 245, 247, 249, 251–3, 263
Mobutu Sese Seko 20–1, 23, 28, 33, 34–5, 39–40, 49, 53–4, 113, 214
Modise, Joe 243, 251, 252, 253
Moises, Antonio dos Santos ("Ndalu") 82, 85, 86–7, 90, 93, 101

Moises, David ("Ndozi") 54
Moloi, Lambert 241
Mondlane, Candido 125
Mondlane, Eduardo 120–5, 136
Monimambo, Floribert ("Spartacus") 21–3
Monteiro, Roberto Leal Ramos ("Ngongo") 28, 29, 44, 53–4, 57, 90, 93–4, 105, 115
Moyo, Jason Z. 151, 156, 157, 162, 163, 164, 165, 171
Mozambique 2, 52, 82, 119–47
    after independence 137–47
    support for MPLA 35, 60–1
    transitional period 130–6
    see also FRELIMO
MPLA (Popular Movement for the Liberation of Angola) 3, 13–55, 58–62, 64–71, 113
    alliance with FNLA 18–21, 22–4, 27–8
    and battle of Cuito Cuanavale 105, 112
    Congress (1977) 16, 43, 69
    "Congress of MPLA" (1974) 32–3
    delegations to Moscow 8–9, 34–5, 46–7, 61–2, 63, 65–6
    internal divisions 10–11, 20, 24, 26, 28, 29–30, 34, 35, 40
    Soviet support 7, 9, 15–16, 17, 29–30, 43–4, 46, 58, 64
    and SWAPO 200, 201–2, 214, 215–16
    see also Neto, Agostinho
Msika, Joseph 158, 171
Muchachi, Clement 163
Mueshihange, Peter 206, 230
Mugabe, Robert 155, 158, 164, 165, 167, 170, 176, 182–3, 185–9, 190–1
Muhammed, Murtala 62–3
Muhitdinov, Nuretdin 8
Muyongo, Mishake 224–5
Muzenda, Simon 182
Muzorewa, Abel 160, 163, 164–5, 176, 180

Namibia 2, 82, 195–235, 256
    1989 general elections 234–5
    International Conference (Brussels) (1972) 203–6
    and South African troops 48, 73, 80, 81, 94, 97–8, 212, 217
    see also SWANU; SWAPO

Printed and bound by CPI Group (UK) Ltd, Croydon, CR0 4YY

09/06/2025

14685865-0004